THE
DATA
WRANGLING
WORKSHOP

SECOND EDITION

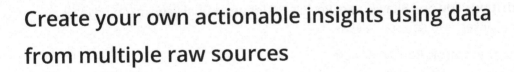

Create your own actionable insights using data
from multiple raw sources

Brian Lipp, Shubhadeep Roychowdhury, and Dr. Tirthajyoti Sarkar

THE DATA WRANGLING WORKSHOP
SECOND EDITION

Authors: Brian Lipp, Shubhadeep Roychowdhury, and Dr. Tirthajyoti Sarkar

Reviewers: John Wesley Doyle, Harshil Jain, Robert Thas John, Akshay Khare, Nagendra Nagaraj, Bhargav Reddy JM, Samik Sen, Dr. Vlad Sebastian Ionescu, and Ratan Singh

Managing Editor: Ranu Kundu

Acquisitions Editors: Bhavya Rao, Royluis Rodrigues, Kunal Sawant, Anindya Sil, Archie Vankar, and Karan Wadekar

Production Editor: Roshan Kawale

Editorial Board: Megan Carlisle, Samuel Christa, Mahesh Dhyani, Heather Gopsill, Manasa Kumar, Alex Mazonowicz, Monesh Mirpuri, Bridget Neale, Dominic Pereira, Shiny Poojary, Abhishek Rane, Brendan Rodrigues, Erol Staveley, Ankita Thakur, Nitesh Thakur, and Jonathan Wray

First published: February 2019
Second edition: July 2020
Production reference: 2230221
ISBN: 978-1-83921-500-1
Published by Packt Publishing Ltd.
Livery Place, 35 Livery Street
Birmingham B3 2PB, UK

WHY LEARN WITH A PACKT WORKSHOP?

LEARN BY DOING

Packt Workshops are built around the idea that the best way to learn something new is by getting hands-on experience. We know that learning a language or technology isn't just an academic pursuit. It's a journey towards the effective use of a new tool—whether that's to kickstart your career, automate repetitive tasks, or just build some cool stuff.

That's why Workshops are designed to get you writing code from the very beginning. You'll start fairly small—learning how to implement some basic functionality—but once you've completed that, you'll have the confidence and understanding to move onto something slightly more advanced.

As you work through each chapter, you'll build your understanding in a coherent, logical way, adding new skills to your toolkit and working on increasingly complex and challenging problems.

CONTEXT IS KEY

All new concepts are introduced in the context of realistic use-cases, and then demonstrated practically with guided exercises. At the end of each chapter, you'll find an activity that challenges you to draw together what you've learned and apply your new skills to solve a problem or build something new.

We believe this is the most effective way of building your understanding and confidence. Experiencing real applications of the code will help you get used to the syntax and see how the tools and techniques are applied in real projects.

BUILD REAL-WORLD UNDERSTANDING

Of course, you do need some theory. But unlike many tutorials, which force you to wade through pages and pages of dry technical explanations and assume too much prior knowledge, Workshops only tell you what you actually need to know to be able to get started making things. Explanations are clear, simple, and to-the-point. So you don't need to worry about how everything works under the hood; you can just get on and use it.

Written by industry professionals, you'll see how concepts are relevant to real-world work, helping to get you beyond "Hello, world!" and build relevant, productive skills. Whether you're studying web development, data science, or a core programming language, you'll start to think like a problem solver and build your understanding and confidence through contextual, targeted practice.

ENJOY THE JOURNEY

Learning something new is a journey from where you are now to where you want to be, and this Workshop is just a vehicle to get you there. We hope that you find it to be a productive and enjoyable learning experience.

Packt has a wide range of different Workshops available, covering the following topic areas:

- Programming languages

- Web development

- Data science, machine learning, and artificial intelligence

- Containers

Once you've worked your way through this Workshop, why not continue your journey with another? You can find the full range online at http://packt.live/2MNkuyl.

If you could leave us a review while you're there, that would be great. We value all feedback. It helps us to continually improve and make better books for our readers, and also helps prospective customers make an informed decision about their purchase.

Thank you,
The Packt Workshop Team

Table of Contents

Chapter 2: Advanced Operations on Built-In Data Structures   49

Chapter 5: Getting Comfortable with Different Kinds of Data Sources | 237

Chapter 6: Learning the Hidden Secrets of Data Wrangling

Chapter 7: Advanced Web Scraping and Data Gathering

PREFACE

ABOUT THE BOOK

While a huge amount of data is readily available to us, it is not useful in its raw form. For data to be meaningful, it must be curated and refined.

If you're a beginner, then *The Data Wrangling Workshop, Second Edition* will help to break down the process for you. You'll start with the basics and build your knowledge, progressing from the core aspects behind data wrangling, to using the most popular tools and techniques.

This book starts by showing you how to work with data structures using Python. Through examples and activities, you'll understand why you should stay away from traditional methods of data cleaning used in other languages and take advantage of the specialized pre-built routines in Python. Later, you'll learn how to use the same Python backend to extract and transform data from an array of sources, including the internet, large database vaults, and Excel financial tables. To help you prepare for more challenging scenarios, the book teaches you how to handle missing or incorrect data, and reformat it based on the requirements from your downstream analytics tool.

By the end of this book, you will have developed a solid understanding of how to perform data wrangling with Python, and learned several techniques and best practices to extract, clean, transform, and format your data efficiently, from a diverse array of sources.

AUDIENCE

The Data Wrangling Workshop, Second Edition is designed for developers, data analysts, and business analysts who are looking to pursue a career as a full-fledged data scientist or analytics expert. Although this book is for beginners who want to start data wrangling, prior working knowledge of the Python programming language is necessary to easily grasp the concepts covered here. It will also help to have rudimentary knowledge of relational databases and SQL.

ABOUT THE CHAPTERS

Chapter 1, Introduction to Data Wrangling with Python, describes the importance of data wrangling in data science and introduces the basic building blocks that are used in data wrangling.

Chapter 2, Advanced Operations on Built-in Data Structures, discusses advanced built-in data structures that can be used for complex data wrangling problems faced by data scientists. The chapter will also talk about working with files using standard Python libraries.

Chapter 3, Introduction to NumPy, Pandas, and Matplotlib, will introduce you to the fundamentals of the NumPy, Pandas, and Matplotlib libraries. These are fundamental libraries for when you are performing data wrangling. This chapter will teach you how to calculate descriptive statistics of a one-dimensional/multi-dimensional DataFrame.

Chapter 4, A Deep Dive into Data Wrangling with Python, will introduce working with pandas DataFrames, including coverage of advanced concepts such as subsetting, filtering, grouping, and much more.

Chapter 5, Getting Comfortable with Different Kinds of Data Sources, introduces you to the several diverse data sources you might encounter as a data wrangler. This chapter will provide you with the knowledge to read CSV, Excel, and JSON files into pandas DataFrames.

Chapter 6, Learning the Hidden Secrets of Data Wrangling, discusses data problems that arise in business use cases and how to resolve them. This chapter will give you the knowledge needed to be able to clean and handle real-life messy data.

Chapter 7, Advanced Web Scraping and Data Gathering, introduces you to the concepts of advanced web scraping and data gathering. It will enable you to use Python libraries such as requests and BeautifulSoup to read various web pages and gather data from them.

Chapter 8, RDBMS and SQL, will introduce you to the basics of using RDBMSes to query databases using Python and convert data from SQL and store it into a pandas DataFrame. A large part of the world's data is stored in RDBMSes, so it is necessary to master this topic if you want to become a successful data-wrangling expert.

Chapter 9, Applications in Business Use Cases and Conclusion of the Course, will enable you to utilize the skills you have learned through the course of the previous chapters. By the end of this chapter, you will be able to easily handle data wrangling tasks for business use cases.

CONVENTIONS

Code words in text, database table names, folder names, filenames, file extensions, pathnames, dummy URLs, user input, and Twitter handles are shown as follows: "This will return the value associated with it – **["list_element1", 34]**".

A block of code is set as follows:

```
list_1 = []
    for x in range(0, 10):
    list_1.append(x)
list_1
```

Words that you see on the screen, for example, in menus or dialog boxes, appear in the text like this: "Click **New** and choose **Python 3**."

CODE PRESENTATION

Lines of code that span multiple lines are split using a backslash (\ ). When the code is executed, Python will ignore the backslash, and treat the code on the next line as a direct continuation of the current line.

For example:

```
history = model.fit(X, y, epochs=100, batch_size=5, verbose=1, \
                    validation_split=0.2, shuffle=False)
```

Comments are added into code to help explain specific bits of logic. Single-line comments are denoted using the **#** symbol, as follows:

```
# Print the sizes of the dataset
print("Number of Examples in the Dataset = ", X.shape[0])
print("Number of Features for each example = ", X.shape[1])
```

Multi-line comments are enclosed by triple quotes, as shown below:

```
"""
Define a seed for the random number generator to ensure the
result will be reproducible
"""

seed = 1
np.random.seed(seed)
random.set_seed(seed)
```

SETTING UP YOUR ENVIRONMENT

Before we explore the book in detail, we need to set up specific software and tools. In the following section, we shall see how to do that.

INSTALLING PYTHON

INSTALLING PYTHON ON WINDOWS

To install Python on Windows, do the following:

1. Find your desired version of Python on the official installation page at https://www.anaconda.com/distribution/#windows.

2. Ensure that you select Python 3.7 on the download page.

3. Ensure that you install the correct architecture for your computer system, that is, either 32-bit or 64-bit. You can find out this information in the **System Properties** window of your OS.

4. After you have downloaded the installer, simply double-click the file and follow the user-friendly prompts onscreen.

INSTALLING PYTHON ON LINUX

To install Python on Linux, you have a couple of options. Here is one option:

1. Open the command line and verify that **Python 3** is not already installed by running **python3 --version**.

2. To install Python 3, run this:

```
sudo apt-get update
sudo apt-get install python3.7
```

3. If you encounter problems, there are numerous sources online that can help you troubleshoot the issue.

Alternatively, install Anaconda Linux by downloading the installer from https://www.anaconda.com/distribution/#linux and following the instructions.

INSTALLING PYTHON ON MACOS

Similar to the case with Linux, you have a couple of methods for installing Python on a Mac. To install Python on macOS X, do the following:

1. Open the Terminal for Mac by pressing *CMD + Spacebar*, type **terminal** in the open search box, and hit *Enter*.

2. Install Xcode through the command line by running **xcode-select -install**.

3. The easiest way to install Python 3 is using Homebrew, which is installed through the command line by running **ruby -e "$(curl -fsSL https://raw. githubusercontent.com/Homebrew/install/master/install)"**.

4. Add Homebrew to your **$PATH** environment variable. Open your profile in the command line by running **sudo nano ~/.profile** and inserting **export PATH="/usr/local/opt/python/libexec/bin:$PATH"** at the bottom.

5. The final step is to install Python. In the command line, run **brew install python**.

6. You can also install Python via the Anaconda installer available from https://www.anaconda.com/distribution/#macos.

INSTALLING LIBRARIES

pip comes pre-installed with Anaconda. Once Anaconda is installed on your machine, all the required libraries can be installed using **pip**, for example, **pip install numpy**. Alternatively, you can install all the required libraries using **pip install -r requirements.txt**. You can find the **requirements.txt** file at https://packt.live/30UUshh.

The exercises and activities will be executed in Jupyter Notebooks. Jupyter is a Python library and can be installed in the same way as the other Python libraries – that is, with **pip install jupyter**, but fortunately, it comes pre-installed with Anaconda. To open a notebook, simply run the command **jupyter notebook** in the Terminal or Command Prompt.

PROJECT JUPYTER

Project Jupyter is open source, free software that gives you the ability to run code written in Python and some other languages interactively from a special notebook, similar to a browser interface. It was born in 2014 from the IPython project and has since become the default choice for the entire data science workforce.

Once you are running the Jupyter server, click **New** and choose **Python 3**. A new browser tab will open with a new and empty notebook. Rename the Jupyter file:

Figure 0.1: Jupyter server interface

The main building blocks of Jupyter notebooks are cells. There are two types of cells: **In** (short for input) and **Out** (short for output). You can write code, normal text, and Markdown in **In** cells, press *Shift + Enter* (or *Shift + Return*), and the code written in that particular **In** cell will be executed. The result will be shown in an **Out** cell, and you will land in a new **In** cell, ready for the next block of code. Once you get used to this interface, you will slowly discover the power and flexibility it offers.

When you start a new cell, by default, it is assumed that you will write code in it. However, if you want to write text, then you have to change the type. You can do that using the following sequence of keys: *Escape -> m -> Enter*:

```
In [1]:   import numpy as np
          import pandas as pd

In [2]:   a = np.random.randn(5, 3)

In [3]:   a

Out[3]:   array([[ 8.37235095e-01, -5.37907860e-01,  9.10259320e-01],
                 [ 3.25343803e+00, -1.36313039e+00,  1.66336086e-01],
                 [ 2.08849405e-01,  1.44449165e+00,  1.28198815e-01],
                 [ 4.31214651e-01,  3.24061116e-01, -2.80120534e-03],
                 [-2.52064176e-01,  3.17086224e-01,  7.28020973e-02]])
```

Hey There! I am a Markdown cell

```
In [ ]:
```

Figure 0.2: Jupyter notebook

When you are done with writing the text, execute it using *Shift + Enter*. Unlike the code cells, the result of the compiled Markdown will be shown in the same place as the **In** cell.

To have a *cheat sheet* of all the handy key shortcuts in Jupyter Notebook, you can bookmark this Gist: https://gist.github.com/kidpixo/f4318f8c8143adee5b40. With this basic introduction and the image ready to be used, we are ready to embark on the exciting and enlightening journey.

ACCESSING THE CODE FILES

You can find the complete code files of this book at https://packt.live/2YenXcb. You can also run many activities and exercises directly in your web browser by using the interactive lab environment at https://packt.live/2YKlrJQ.

We've tried to support interactive versions of all activities and exercises, but we recommend a local installation as well for instances where this support isn't available.

If you have any issues or questions about installation, please email us at workshops@packt.com.

1

INTRODUCTION TO DATA WRANGLING WITH PYTHON

OVERVIEW

This chapter will help you understand the importance of data wrangling in data science. You will gain practical knowledge of how to manipulate the data structures that are available in Python by comparing the different implementations of the built-in Python data structures. Overall, this chapter describes the importance of data wrangling, identifies the important tasks to be performed in data wrangling, and introduces basic Python data structures. By the end of this chapter, you will be adept at working with lists, sets, and dictionaries, which are the key building blocks of data structures in Python.

INTRODUCTION

Since data science and analytics have become key parts of our lives, the role of a data scientist has become even more important. Finding the source of data is an essential part of data science; however, it is the *science* part that makes you – the practitioner – truly valuable.

To practice high-quality science with data, you need to make sure it is properly sourced, cleaned, formatted, and pre-processed. This book will teach you the most essential basics of this invaluable component of the data science pipeline: data wrangling. In short, data wrangling is the process that ensures that the data is being presented in a way that is clean, accurate, formatted, and ready to be used for data analysis.

A prominent example of data wrangling with a large amount of data is the analysis conducted at the Supercomputer Center of the **University of California San Diego (UCSD)** every year. Wildfires are very common in California and are caused mainly by the dry weather and extreme heat, especially during the summers. Data scientists at the UCSD Supercomputer Center run an analysis every year and gather data to predict the nature and spread direction of wildfires in California. The data comes from diverse sources, such as weather stations, sensors in the forest, fire stations, satellite imagery, and Twitter feeds. However, this data might be incomplete or missing.

After collecting the data from various sources, if it is not cleaned and formatted using ways including scaling numbers and removing unwanted characters in strings, it could result in erroneous data. In cases where we might get a flawed analysis, we might need to reformat the data from **JavaScript Object Notation (JSON)** into **Comma Separated Value (CSV)**; we may also need the numbers to be normalized, that is, centered and scaled with relation to themselves. Processing data in such a way might be required when we feed data to certain machine learning models.

This is an example of how data wrangling and data science can prove to be helpful and relevant. This chapter will discuss the fundamentals of data wrangling. Let's get started.

IMPORTANCE OF DATA WRANGLING

A common mantra of the modern age is *Data is the New Oil*, meaning data is now a resource that's more valuable than oil. But just as crude oil does not come out of the rig as gasoline and must be processed to get gasoline and other products, data must be curated, massaged, or cleaned and refined to be used in data science and products based on data science. This is known as wrangling. Most data scientists spend the majority of their time data wrangling.

Data wrangling is generally done at the very first stage of a data science/analytics pipeline. After the data scientists have identified any useful data sources for solving the business problem at hand (for instance, in-house database storage, the internet, or streaming sensor data such as an underwater seismic sensor), they then proceed to extract, clean, and format the necessary data from those sources.

Generally, the task of data wrangling involves the following steps:

1. Scraping raw data from multiple sources (including web and database tables)

2. Imputing (replacing missing data using various techniques), formatting, and transforming – basically making it ready to be used in the modeling process (such as advanced machine learning)

3. Handling read/write errors

4. Detecting outliers

5. Performing quick visualizations (plotting) and basic statistical analysis to judge the quality of formatted data

The following is an illustrative representation of the positioning and the essential functional role of data wrangling in a typical data science pipeline:

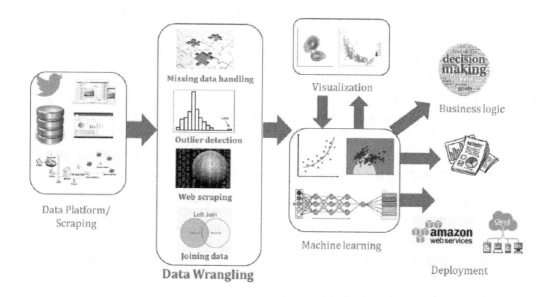

Figure 1.1: Process of data wrangling

The process of data wrangling includes finding the appropriate data that's necessary for the analysis. Often, analysis is exploratory, so there is not enough scope. You often need to do data wrangling for this type of analysis to be able to understand your data better. This could lead to more analysis or machine learning.

This data can be from one or multiple sources, such as tweets, bank transaction statements in a relational database, sensor data, and so on. This data needs to be cleaned. If there is missing data, we will either delete or substitute it, with the help of several techniques. If there are outliers, we need to detect them and then handle them appropriately. If the data is from multiple sources, we will have to combine it using Structured Query Language (SQL) operations like JOIN.

In an extremely rare situation, data wrangling may not be needed. For example, if the data that's necessary for a machine learning task is already stored in an acceptable format in an in-house database, then a simple SQL query may be enough to extract the data into a table, ready to be passed on to the modeling stage.

PYTHON FOR DATA WRANGLING

There is always a debate regarding whether to perform the wrangling process using an enterprise tool or a programming language and its associated frameworks. There are many commercial, enterprise-level tools for data formatting and preprocessing that do not involve much coding on the user's part. Some of these examples include the following:

- General-purpose data analysis platforms, such as **Microsoft Excel** (with add-ins)

- Statistical discovery package, such as **JMP** (from SAS)

- Modeling platforms, such as **RapidMiner**

- Analytics platforms from niche players that focus on data wrangling, such as **Trifacta**, **Paxata**, and **Alteryx**

However, programming languages such as Python and R provide more flexibility, control, and power compared to these off-the-shelf tools. This also explains their tremendous popularity in the data science domain:

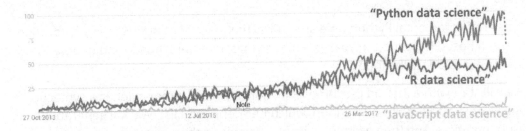

Figure 1.2: Google trends worldwide over the last 5 years

Furthermore, as the volume, velocity, and variety (the three Vs of **big data**) of data undergo rapid changes, it is always a good idea to develop and nurture a significant amount of in-house expertise in data wrangling using fundamental programming frameworks so that an organization is not beholden to the whims and fancies of any particular enterprise platform for as basic a task as data wrangling.

A few of the obvious advantages of using an open source, free programming paradigm for data wrangling are as follows:

- A general-purpose open-source paradigm puts no restrictions on any of the methods you can develop for the specific problem at hand.

- There's a great ecosystem of fast, optimized, open-source libraries, focused on data analytics.

- There's also growing support for connecting Python to every conceivable data source type.

- There's an easy interface to basic statistical testing and quick visualization libraries to check data quality.

- And there's a seamless interface of the data wrangling output with advanced machine learning models.

Python is the most popular language for machine learning and artificial intelligence these days. Let's take a look at a few data structures in Python.

LISTS, SETS, STRINGS, TUPLES, AND DICTIONARIES

Now that we have touched upon a few advantages of using Python, we will start by exploring various basic data structures in Python. We will also learn about a few techniques we can use to handle these data structures. This is invaluable for a data practitioner.

LISTS

Lists are fundamental Python data structures that have continuous memory locations and can host different data types (such as strings, numbers, floats, and doubles) and can be accessed by the index.

We will start with a list and list comprehension. A list comprehension is a syntactic sugar (or shorthand) for a **for** loop, which iterates over a list. We will generate a list of numbers, and then examine which ones among them are even. We will sort, reverse, and check for duplicates. We will also see the different ways we can access the list elements, iterating over them and checking the membership of an element.

The following is an example of a simple list:

```
list_example = [51, 27, 34, 46, 90, 45, -19]
```

The following is also an example of a list:

```
list_example2 = [15, "Yellow car", True, 9.456, [12, "Hello"]]
```

As you can see, a list can contain any number of the allowed data types, such as **int**, **float**, **string**, and **boolean**, and a list can also be a mix of different data types (including nested lists).

If you are coming from a strongly typed language, such as C, C++, or Java, then this will probably be strange as you are not allowed to mix different kinds of data types in a single array in those languages. Lists in Python are loosely typed, that is, they are not restricted to a single type. Lists are somewhat like arrays in the sense that they are both based on continuous memory locations and can be accessed using indexes. But the power of Python lists comes from the fact that they can host different data types and you are allowed to manipulate the data.

In Python, there is a concept of creating a slice of a list. Here is the syntax:

```
my_list [ inclusive start index : exclusive end index ]
```

Known as **list slicing**, this returns a smaller list from the original list by extracting only a part of it. To slice a list, we need two integers. The first integer will denote the start of the slice and the second integer will denote the end. Notice that slicing does not include the third index or the end element. A slice is a chunk of the list tuple or string. The range is from **0** to **1** minus the total length. The first number given represents the first position to include in the slice. The second number is used to indicate which place you want to stop at, but not include. A slice can have an index of **−1** to indicate the last element.

The indices will be automatically assigned, as follows:

List_1

34	12	89	1
Indices (Forward)	0	1	2	3
Indices (Backward)	-4	-3	-2	-1

Figure 1.3: List showing the forward and backward indices

NOTE

Be careful, though, as the very power of lists, and the fact that you can mix different data types in a single list, can actually create subtle bugs that can be very difficult to track.

LIST FUNCTIONS

In this section, we will discuss a few basic functions for handling lists.

You can access list elements using the following code:

```
list_example = [51, 27, 34, 46, 90, 45, -19]
list_example[0]
```

The output is as follows:

```
51
```

To find out the length of a list, we simply use the **len** function. The **len** function in Python returns the length of the specified list:

```
len(list_example)
```

The output is as follows:

```
7
```

We can append new elements in the list. **append** is a built-in method in Python for the list data type:

```
list_example.append(11)
list_example
```

The output is as follows:

```
[51, 27, 34, 46, 90, 45, -19, 11]
```

Let's go through some exercises to practice these functions.

EXERCISE 1.01: ACCESSING THE LIST MEMBERS

In this exercise, we will be reading a list of social security numbers from the **ssn.csv** file and then observing the different ways of accessing the elements from the list using the forward and backward indices. We will be using our first Python function, **len**, which will return the length of the specified list. We will be starting with the basic building blocks for future exercises. Let's go through the following steps:

> **NOTE**
>
> The **ssn.csv** file can be found here: https://packt.live/2AydLCx.

1. Open a new Jupyter Notebook and define a list called **ssn**. Read from the **ssn.csv** file using the **read_csv** command and print the list elements:

```
import pandas as pd
ssn = list(pd.read_csv("../datasets/ssn.csv"))
print(ssn)
```

> **NOTE**
>
> The highlighted path in the code must be changed based on where you have saved the **ssn.csv** file on your system.

The output is as follows:

```
['218-68-9955',
 '165-73-3124',
 '432-47-4043',
 '563-93-1393',
 '153-93-3401',
 '670-09-7369',
 '123-05-9652',
 '812-13-2476',
 '726-13-1007',
 '825-05-4836']
```

2. Access the first element of **ssn** using its forward index:

```
ssn[0]
```

The output is as follows:

```
'218-68-9955'
```

3. Access the fourth element of **ssn** using its forward index:

```
ssn[3]
```

The output is as follows:

```
'563-93-1393'
```

4. Access the last element of **ssn** using the **len** function:

```
ssn[len(ssn) - 1]
```

The output is as follows:

```
'825-05-4836'
```

5. Access the last element of **ssn** using its backward index:

```
ssn[-1]
```

The output is as follows:

```
'825-05-4836'
```

6. Access the first three elements of **ssn** using forward indices:

```
ssn[1:3]
```

The output is as follows:

```
['165-73-3124', '432-47-4043']
```

7. Access the last two elements of **ssn** by slicing:

```
ssn[-2:]
```

The output is as follows:

```
['726-13-1007', '825-05-4836']
```

8. Access the first two elements using backward indices:

```
ssn[:-2]
```

The output is as follows:

```
['218-68-9955',
 '165-73-3124',
 '432-47-4043',
 '563-93-1393',
 '153-93-3401',
 '670-09-7369',
 '123-05-9652',
 '812-13-2476']
```

Figure 1.4: Output after using backward indices

When we leave one side of the colon (:) blank, we are basically telling Python either to go until the end or start from the beginning of the list. It will automatically apply the rule of list slices that we just learned.

9. Reverse the elements in the list:

```
ssn[-1::-1]
```

The output is as follows:

```
['825-05-4836',
 '726-13-1007',
 '812-13-2476',
 '123-05-9652',
 '670-09-7369',
 '153-93-3401',
 '563-93-1393',
 '432-47-4043',
 '165-73-3124',
 '218-68-9955']
```

Figure 1.5: Output after elements are reversed

NOTE

To access the source code for this specific section, please refer to https://packt.live/3fzTvzk.

You can also run this example online at https://packt.live/2YF3zA0.

In this exercise, we learned how to access the list members with forward and backward indices. We'll create a list in the next exercise.

EXERCISE 1.02: GENERATING AND ITERATING THROUGH A LIST

In this exercise, we are going to examine various ways of generating a list and a nested list using the same file containing the list of social security numbers (**ssn. csv**) that we used in the previous exercise.

NOTE

The **ssn.csv** file can be found here: https://packt.live/2AydLCx.

We are going to use the **append** method to add new elements to the list and a **while** loop to iterate through the list. To do so, let's go through the following steps:

1. Open a new Jupyter Notebook and import the necessary Python libraries. Read from the **ssn.csv** file:

```
import pandas as pd
ssn = list(pd.read_csv("../datasets/ssn.csv"))
```

> **NOTE**
>
> The highlighted path in the code must be changed based on where you have saved the **ssn.csv** file on your system.

2. Create a list using the **append** method. The **append** method from the Python library will allow you to add items to the list:

```
ssn_2 = []
for x in ssn:
    ssn_2.append(x)
ssn_2
```

The output will be as follows:

```
['218-68-9955',
 '165-73-3124',
 '432-47-4043',
 '563-93-1393',
 '153-93-3401',
 '670-09-7369',
 '123-05-9652',
 '812-13-2476',
 '726-13-1007',
 '825-05-4836']
```

Figure 1.6: Output after creating a list using the append method

Here, we started by declaring an empty list called **ssn_2**, and then we used a **for** loop to append values to it after reading from the **ssn.csv** file.

3. Generate a list using the following command:

```
ssn_3 = ["soc: " + x for x in ssn_2]
ssn_3
```

The output is as follows:

```
['soc: 218-68-9955',
 'soc: 165-73-3124',
 'soc: 432-47-4043',
 'soc: 563-93-1393',
 'soc: 153-93-3401',
 'soc: 670-09-7369',
 'soc: 123-05-9652',
 'soc: 812-13-2476',
 'soc: 726-13-1007',
 'soc: 825-05-4836']
```

Figure 1.7: Output of a generated list

This is list comprehension, which is a very powerful tool that we need to master. The power of list comprehension comes from the fact that we can use conditionals such as **for..in** inside the comprehension itself. This will be discussed in detail in *Chapter 2, Advanced Operations on Built-in Data Structures*.

4. Use a **while** loop to iterate over the list:

> **NOTE**
>
> Conditionals work the same way as in any other strongly typed language, such as C, C++, or Java.

```
i = 0
while i < len(ssn_3):
    print(ssn_3[i])
    i += 1
```

The output is as follows:

```
soc: 218-68-9955
soc: 165-73-3124
soc: 432-47-4043
soc: 563-93-1393
soc: 153-93-3401
soc: 670-09-7369
soc: 123-05-9652
soc: 812-13-2476
```

```
soc: 726-13-1007
soc: 825-05-4836
```

5. Search all the social security numbers with the number **5** in them:

```
numbers = [x for x in ssn_3 if "5" in x]
numbers
```

The output will be as follows:

```
['soc: 218-68-9955',
 'soc: 165-73-3124',
 'soc: 563-93-1393',
 'soc: 153-93-3401',
 'soc: 123-05-9652',
 'soc: 825-05-4836']
```

Figure 1.8: SSNs with the number 5 in them

Let's explore a few more list operations. We are going to use the **+** operator to add the contents of two lists and use the **extend** keyword to replace the contents of the existing list with another list.

6. Generate a list by adding the two lists. Here, we will just use the **+** operator:

```
ssn_4 = ["102-90-0314" , "247-17-2338" , "318-22-2760"]
ssn_5 = ssn_4 + ssn
ssn_5
```

The output is as follows:

```
['102-90-0314',
 '247-17-2338',
 '318-22-2760',
 '218-68-9955',
 '165-73-3124',
 '432-47-4043',
 '563-93-1393',
 '153-93-3401',
 '670-09-7369',
 '123-05-9652',
 '812-13-2476',
 '726-13-1007',
 '825-05-4836']
```

Figure 1.9: Generated list by adding two lists

7. Extend a string using the **extend** keyword:

```
ssn_2.extend(ssn_4)
ssn_2
```

The output is as follows:

```
['218-68-9955',
 '165-73-3124',
 '432-47-4043',
 '563-93-1393',
 '153-93-3401',
 '670-09-7369',
 '123-05-9652',
 '812-13-2476',
 '726-13-1007',
 '825-05-4836',
 '102-90-0314',
 '247-17-2338',
 '318-22-2760']
```

Figure 1.10: The extend string operation

> **NOTE**
>
> The **extend** operation changes the original list (**ssn_2**) and appends all the elements of **ssn_4** to it. So, be careful while using it.

8. Now, let's loop over the first list and create a nested list inside that loop that goes over the second list:

```
for x in ssn_2:
    for y in ssn_5:
        print(str(x) + ' , ' + str(y))
```

The output (partially shown) is as follows:

```
218-68-9955 , 102-90-0314
218-68-9955 , 247-17-2338
218-68-9955 , 318-22-2760
218-68-9955 , 218-68-9955
218-68-9955 , 165-73-3124
218-68-9955 , 432-47-4043
218-68-9955 , 563-93-1393
218-68-9955 , 153-93-3401
218-68-9955 , 670-09-7369
218-68-9955 , 123-05-9652
218-68-9955 , 812-13-2476
218-68-9955 , 726-13-1007
218-68-9955 , 825-05-4836
165-73-3124 , 102-90-0314
165-73-3124 , 247-17-2338
165-73-3124 , 318-22-2760
165-73-3124 , 218-68-9955
```

Figure 1.11: Partial output of ssn

NOTE

To access the source code for this specific section, please refer to https://packt.live/2Y6vObR.

You can also run this example online at https://packt.live/2YLJybf.

In this exercise, we used the built-in methods of Python to manipulate lists. In the next exercise, we'll check whether the elements or members in a dataset are present as per our expectations.

EXERCISE 1.03: ITERATING OVER A LIST AND CHECKING MEMBERSHIP

This exercise will demonstrate how we can iterate over a list and verify that the values are as expected. This is a manual test that can often be done while dealing with a reasonably sized dataset for business case scenarios. Let's go through the following steps to check the membership of values and whether they exist in the .csv file:

NOTE

The car_models.csv file can be found at https://packt.live/3d8DUVy.

1. Import the necessary Python libraries and read from the **car_models.csv** file:

```
import pandas as pd
car_models = list(pd.read_csv("../datasets/car_models.csv"))
car_models
```

> **NOTE**
>
> The highlighted path in the code must be changed based on where you
> have saved the **car_models.csv** file on your system.

The output is as follows:

```
['Escalade ',
 < X5 M>,
 <D150>,
 <Camaro>,
 <F350>,
 <Aurora>,
 <38 >,
 <E350>,
 <Tiburon>,
 <F-Series Super Duty >]
```

2. Iterate over a list:

```
list_1 = [x for x in car_models]
for i in range(0, len(list_1)):
    print(list_1[i])
```

The output is as follows:

```
Escalade
X5 M
D150
Camaro
F350
Aurora
S8
E350
Tiburon
F-Series Super Duty
```

However, this is not very Pythonic. Being Pythonic means to follow and conform to a set of best practices and conventions that have been created over the years by thousands of capable developers. In this case, this means we could use the **in** keyword in the **for..in** conditional because Python does not have index initialization, bounds checking, or index incrementing, unlike traditional languages. Python uses syntactic sugar to make iterating through lists easy and readable. In other languages, you might have to create a variable (index initialization) as you loop over the list check that variable (bounds checking) since it will be incremented in the loop (index incrementing).

3. Write the following code to see the Pythonic way of iterating over a list:

```
for i in list_1:
    print(i)
```

The output is as follows:

```
Escalade
X5 M
D150
Camaro
F350
Aurora
S8
E350
Tiburon
F-Series Super Duty
```

Notice that in the second method, we do not need a counter anymore to access the list index; instead, Python's **in** operator gives us the element at the ith position directly.

4. Check whether the strings **D150** and **Mustang** are in the list using the **in** operator:

```
"D150" in list_1
```

The output is **True**.

```
"Mustang" in list_1
```

The output is **False**.

> **NOTE**
>
> To access the source code for this specific section, please refer to https://packt.live/30TpGp5.
>
> You can also run this example online at https://packt.live/2Y8z06L.

In this exercise, we've seen how to iterate over a list and verified the membership of each element. This is an important skill. Often, when working with large applications, manually checking a list could be useful. If at any time you are unsure of a list, you can easily verify what values are present. Now, we will see how we can perform a sort operation on a list.

EXERCISE 1.04: SORTING A LIST

In this exercise, we will sort a list of numbers, first by using the **sort** method and then by using the **reverse** method. To do so, let's go through the following steps:

> **NOTE**
>
> The **ssn.csv** file can be found here: https://packt.live/2AydLCx.

1. Open a new Jupyter Notebook and import the necessary Python libraries:

```
import pandas as pd
ssn = list(pd.read_csv("../datasets/ssn.csv"))
```

> **NOTE**
>
> The highlighted path in the code must be changed based on where you have saved the **ssn.csv** file on your system.

2. Use the **sort** method with **reverse=True**:

```
list_1 = [*range(0, 21, 1)]
list_1.sort(reverse=True)
list_1
```

The output is as follows:

```
[20, 19, 18, 17, 16, 15, 14, 13, 12, 11, 10, 9, 8, 7,
6, 5, 4, 3, 2, 1, 0]
```

3. Use the **reverse** method directly to achieve this result:

```
list_1.reverse()
list_1
```

The output is as follows:

```
[0, 1, 2, 3, 4, 5, 6, 7, 8, 9, 10, 11, 12, 13, 14, 15, 16,
17, 18, 19, 20]
```

> **NOTE**
>
> To access the source code for this specific section, please refer to https://packt.live/2Y7HIYe.
>
> You can also run this example online at https://packt.live/2YGNvOd.

The difference between the **sort** method and the **reverse** method is that we can use **sort** with customized sorting, whereas we can only use **reverse** to reverse a list. Also, both methods work in-place, so be aware of this while using them. Now, let's create a list with random numbers. Random numbers can be very useful in a variety of situations and preprocessing data is a common process in machine learning.

EXERCISE 1.05: GENERATING A RANDOM LIST

In this exercise, we will be generating a **list** with random numbers using the **random** library in Python and performing mathematical operations on them. To do so, let's go through the following steps:

1. Import the **random** library:

```
import random
```

2. Use the **randint** method to generate some random integers and add them to a list:

```
list_1 = [random.randint(0, 30) for x in range (0, 100)]
```

3. Let's print the list. Note that there will be duplicate values in **list_1**:

```
list_1
```

The sample output (partially shown) is as follows:

```
[18,
 16,
 13,
 3,
 26,
 4,
 8,
 15,
 24,
 12,
 6,
 5,
 14,
```

Figure 1.12: List of random numbers

> **NOTE**
>
> The output will vary with every run since we are generating random numbers.

4. Let's find the square of each element:

```
list_2 = [x**2 for x in list_1]
list_2
```

The output is as follows:

```
[4,
 441,
 144,
 100,
 25,
 625,
 289,
 36,
 25,
 16,
 49,
 225,
 169,
 81,
```

Figure 1.13: List of random numbers

5. Now let's find the log of the **1** elements of **list_2**:

```
import math
list_2 = [math.log(x+1,10) for x in list_2]
list_2
```

The output (partially shown) is as follows:

```
[0.23018571137855462,
 0.5617478422908339,
 0.4998750532699923,
 0.47774638751827614,
 0.38291234217114345,
 0.5793919073581681,
 0.5393769879635829,
 0.40962913318514194,
 0.38291234217114345,
 0.3483922820866869,
 0.43119805794527655,
 0.5255770993440209,
```

Figure 1.14: Partial output for list_2

> **NOTE**
>
> The output is susceptible to change since we are generating random numbers.

> **NOTE**
>
> To access the source code for this specific section, please refer to https://packt.live/37BerTD.
>
> You can also run this example online at https://packt.live/3hHwlsH.

In this exercise, we worked on random variables, lists comprehension, and preprocessing data. Let's put what we have learned so far together and go through an activity to practice how to handle lists.

ACTIVITY 1.01: HANDLING LISTS

In this activity, you will generate a list of random numbers and then generate another list from the first one, which only contains numbers that are divisible by three. Repeat the experiment 10 times; you'll see that the output varies each time, given that a different set of random numbers will be generated each time. Then, you will calculate the average difference between the lengths of the two lists.

These are the steps for completing this activity:

1. Create a **list** of **100** random numbers.

2. Create a new **list** from this random **list**, with numbers that are divisible by **3**.

3. Calculate the length of these two lists and store the difference in a new variable.

4. Using a loop, perform steps 1, 2, and 3, and find the difference variable 10 times.

5. Find the arithmetic mean of these **10** difference values.

    The output (will vary with each run) should look similar to this:

```
66.3
```

> **NOTE**
>
> The solution to this activity can be found on page 448.

SETS

A set, mathematically speaking, is just a collection of well-defined distinct objects. Python gives us a straightforward way to deal with them using its set data type.

INTRODUCTION TO SETS

With the last list that we generated in the previous section; we are going to revisit the problem of getting rid of duplicates from it. We can achieve that with the following line of code:

```
list_12 = list(set(list_1))
```

If we print this, we will see that it only contains unique numbers. We used the **set** data type to turn the first list into a set, thus getting rid of all duplicate elements, and then used the **list** function to turn it into a list from a set once more:

```
list_12
```

The output will be as follows:

```
[0,
 1,
 2,
 3,
 4,
 5,
 6,
 7,
 8,
 9,
 10,
```

Figure 1.15: Section of output for list_12

In the next section, we will discuss the union and intersection of sets.

UNION AND INTERSECTION OF SETS

In mathematical terms, a list of unique objects is a set. There are many ways of combining sets in the same mathematical term. One such way is the use of a union.

This is what a union between two sets looks like:

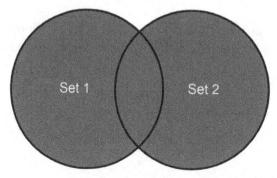

Figure 1.16: Venn diagram showing the union of two sets

This simply means taking everything from both sets but only taking the common elements once.

We can implement this concept by using the following code:

```
set1 = {"Apple", "Orange", "Banana"}
set2 = {"Pear", "Peach", "Mango", "Banana"}
```

To find the union of the two sets, the following code should be used:

```
set1 | set2
```

The output would be as follows:

```
{'Apple', 'Banana', 'Mango', 'Orange', 'Peach', 'Pear'}
```

Notice that the common element, **Banana**, appears only once in the resulting set. The common elements of two sets can be identified by obtaining the intersection of the two sets, as follows:

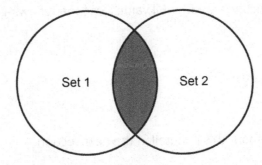

Figure 1.17: Venn diagram showing the intersection of two sets

We get the intersection of two sets in Python as follows:

```
set1 & set2
```

This will give us a set with only one element. The output is as follows:

```
{'Banana'}
```

> **NOTE**
>
> You can also calculate the difference between sets (also known as complements). To find out more, refer to this link: https://docs.python.org/3/tutorial/datastructures.html#sets.

In this section, we went through sets and how we can do basic set functionality. Sets are used throughout database programming and design, and they are very useful for data wrangling.

CREATING NULL SETS

In mathematical terms, a set that has nothing inside it is called a null set or an empty set.

You can create a null set by creating a set containing no elements. You can do this by using the following code:

```
null_set_1 = set({})
null_set_1
```

The output is as follows:

```
set()
```

However, to create a dictionary with null values, use the following command:

```
null_set_2 = {}
null_set_2
```

The output is as follows:

```
{}
```

We are going to learn about this in detail in the next section.

DICTIONARY

A dictionary is like a list, which means it is a collection of several elements. However, with the dictionary, it is a collection of key-value pairs, where the key can be anything that can fit into memory. Generally, we use numbers or strings as keys.

To create a dictionary, use the following code:

```
dict_1 = {"key1": "value1", "key2": "value2"}
dict_1
```

The output is as follows:

```
{'key1': 'value1', 'key2': 'value2'}
```

This is also a valid dictionary:

```
dict_2 = {"key1": 1, "key2": ["list_element1", 34], \
          "key3": "value3","key4": {"subkey1": "v1"}, \
          "key5": 4.5}
dict_2
```

> **NOTE**
>
> The code snippet shown here uses a backslash (\ ) to split the logic across multiple lines. When the code is executed, Python will ignore the backslash, and treat the code on the next line as a direct continuation of the current line.

The output is as follows:

```
{'key1': 1,
 'key2': ['list_element1', 34],
 'key3': 'value3',
 'key4': {'subkey1': 'v1'},
 'key5': 4.5}
```

The keys must be unique in a dictionary.

EXERCISE 1.06: ACCESSING AND SETTING VALUES IN A DICTIONARY

In this exercise, we are going to access the elements and set values in a dictionary. When working with dictionaries, it's important to be able to iterate through each key-value pair, which will allow you to process the data as needed. To do so, let's go through the following steps:

1. To access a value in the dictionary, you must provide the key. Keep in mind there is no given order for any pair in the dictionary:

```
stocks = \
{"Solar Capital Ltd.":"$920.44M", \
 "Zoe's Kitchen, Inc.":"$262.32M", \
 "Toyota Motor Corp Ltd Ord":"$156.02B", \
 "Nuveen Virginia Quality Municipal Income Fund":"$238.33M", \
 "Kinross Gold Corporation":"$5.1B", \
 "Vulcan Materials Company":"$17.1B", \
```

```
    "Hi-Crush Partners LP":"$955.69M",\
    "Lennox International, Inc.":"$8.05B",\
    "WMIH Corp.":"$247.66M",\
    "Comerica Incorporated":"n/a"}
```

2. Print a particular element from the **stocks** list:

```
stocks["WMIH Corp."]
```

This will return the value associated with it, as follows:

```
'$247.66M'
```

3. Set a value using the same method we use to access a value:

```
stocks["WMIH Corp."] = "$300M"
```

4. Define a blank dictionary and then use the key notation to assign values to it:

```
dict_3 = {} # Not a null set. It is a dict
dict_3["key1"] = "Value1"
dict_3
```

> **NOTE**
>
> The # symbol in the code snippet above denotes a code comment. Comments are added into code to help explain specific bits of logic.

The output is as follows:

```
{'key1': 'Value1'}
```

> **NOTE**
>
> To access the source code for this specific section, please refer to https://packt.live/2AGFaly.
>
> You can also run this example online at https://packt.live/3d8fyeJ.

As we can see, the manipulation techniques of a dictionary are pretty simple. Now, just like a list, iterating through a dictionary is very important in order to process the data.

EXERCISE 1.07: ITERATING OVER A DICTIONARY

In this exercise, we are going to iterate over a dictionary and print the values and keys. To do so, let's go through the following steps:

1. Open a new Jupyter Notebook and define a dictionary with the key provided along with it. Keep in mind there is no given order for any pair in the dictionary:

```
stocks = \
{"Solar Capital Ltd.":"$920.44M",\
 "Zoe's Kitchen, Inc.":"$262.32M",\
 "Toyota Motor Corp Ltd Ord":"$156.02B",\
 "Nuveen Virginia Quality Municipal Income Fund":"$238.33M",\
 "Kinross Gold Corporation":"$5.1B",\
 "Vulcan Materials Company":"$17.1B",\
 "Hi-Crush Partners LP":"$955.69M",\
 "Lennox International, Inc.":"$8.05B",\
 "WMIH Corp.":"$247.66M",\
 "Comerica Incorporated":"n/a"}
```

2. Remove the **$** character from the **stocks** dictionary:

```
for key,val in stocks.items():
    stocks[key] = val.replace('$', '')
stocks
```

The output should be as follows:

```
{'Solar Capital Ltd.': '920.44M',
 "Zoe's Kitchen, Inc.": '262.32M',
 'Toyota Motor Corp Ltd Ord': '156.02B',
 'Nuveen Virginia Quality Municipal Income Fund': '238.33M',
 'Kinross Gold Corporation': '5.1B',
 'Vulcan Materials Company': '17.1B',
 'Hi-Crush Partners LP': '955.69M',
 'Lennox International, Inc.': '8.05B',
 'WMIH Corp.': '300M',
 'Comerica Incorporated': 'n/a'}
```

3. Iterate over the **stocks** dictionary again and split the value into a list with price (**val**) and multiplier (**mult**) as separate elements where a single value is assigned to each key:

```
for key,val in stocks.items():
    mult = val[-1]
    stocks[key] = [val[:-1],mult]
stocks
```

The output is as follows:

```
{'Solar Capital Ltd.': ['920.44', 'M'],
 «Zoe›s Kitchen, Inc.»: [‹262.32›, ‹M›],
 ‹Toyota Motor Corp Ltd Ord›: [‹156.02›, ‹B›],
 ‹Nuveen Virginia Quality Municipal Income Fund›: [‹238.33›, ‹M›],
 ‹Kinross Gold Corporation›: [‹5.1›, ‹B›],
 ‹Vulcan Materials Company›: [‹17.1›, ‹B›],
 ‹Hi-Crush Partners LP›: [‹955.69›, ‹M›],
 ‹Lennox International, Inc.›: [‹8.05›, ‹B›],
 ‹WMIH Corp.›: [‹300›, ‹M›],
 ‹Comerica Incorporated›: [‹n/›, ‹a›]}
```

Notice the difference between how we did the iteration on the list and how we are doing it here. A dictionary always contains a key-value pair, and we always need to access the value of any element in a dictionary with its key. In a dictionary, all the keys are unique.

> **NOTE**
>
> To access the source code for this specific section, please refer to https://packt.live/3db0xZF.
>
> You can also run this example online at https://packt.live/2zDFHnU.

In the next exercise, we will revisit the problem that we encountered with the list earlier in this chapter to create a list with unique values. We will look at another workaround to fix this problem.

EXERCISE 1.08: REVISITING THE UNIQUE VALUED LIST PROBLEM

In this exercise, we will use the unique nature of a dictionary, and we will drop the duplicate values from a list. First, we will create a random list with duplicate values. Then, we'll use the **fromkeys** and **keys** methods of a dictionary to create a unique valued list. To do so, let's go through the following steps:

1. First, generate a random list with duplicate values:

```
import random
list_1 = [random.randint(0, 30) for x in range (0, 100)]
```

2. Create a unique valued list from **list_1**:

```
list(dict.fromkeys(list_1).keys())
```

The sample output is as follows:

```
[6,
 30,
 25,
 26,
 14,
 15,
 29,
 18,
 10,
 1,
 0,
 20,
 28,
 19,
 11,
 16,
 27,
 22,
 4,
 21,
 24,
 9,
 5,
 23,
 7,
 2,
 17,
 13,
 12,
 8]
```

Figure 1.18: Output showing the unique valued list

> **NOTE**
>
> The output is susceptible to change since we are generating random numbers.

Here, we have used two useful methods of the **dict** data type in Python, **fromkeys** and **keys**. **fromkeys** is a built-in function in which a new dictionary is created from the given sequence of elements with values given by the user, while the **keys** method gives us the keys of a dictionary.

> **NOTE**
>
> To access the source code for this specific section, please refer to https://packt.live/2URp6EA.
>
> You can also run this example online at https://packt.live/2UTCFmO.

EXERCISE 1.09: DELETING A VALUE FROM DICT

In this exercise, we are going to delete a value from **dict** using the **del** method. Perform the following steps:

1. Create **list_1** with five elements:

```
dict_1 = {"key1": 1, "key2": ["list_element1", 34], \
          "key3": "value3","key4": {"subkey1": "v1"}, \
          "key5": 4.5}
dict_1
```

The output is as follows:

```
{'key1': 1,
 'key2': ['list_element1', 34],
 'key3': 'value3',
 'key4': {'subkey1': 'v1'},
 'key5': 4.5}
```

2. We will use the **del** function and specify the element we want to delete:

```
del dict_1["key2"]
dict_1
```

The output is as follows:

```
{'key1': 1, 'key3': 'value3', 'key4': {'subkey1': 'v1'}, 'key5': 4.5}
```

3. Let's delete **key3** and **key4**:

```
del dict_1["key3"]
del dict_1["key4"]
```

4. Now, let's print the dictionary to see its content:

```
dict_1
```

The output should be as follows:

```
{'key1': 1, 'key5': 4.5}
```

> **NOTE**
>
> To access the source code for this specific section, please refer to https://packt.live/2Nb3oqF.
>
> You can also run this example online at https://packt.live/30Os7ct.

In this exercise, we learned how to delete elements from a dictionary. This is a very useful functionality of dictionaries, and you will find that it's used heavily when writing Python applications.

> **NOTE**
>
> The **del** operator can be used to delete a specific index from a list as well.

In our final exercise on **dict**, we will go over a less commonly used list comprehension called **dictionary comprehension**. We will also examine two other ways to create a **dict**, which can be very useful for processing dictionaries in one line. There could be cases where this could be used as a range of key-value pairs of name and age or credit card number and credit card owner. A dictionary comprehension works exactly the same way as list comprehension, but we need to specify both the key and the value.

EXERCISE 1.10: DICTIONARY COMPREHENSION

In this exercise, we will generate a dictionary using the following steps:

1. Generate a **dict** that has **0** to **9** as the keys and the square of the key as the values:

```
list_1 = [x for x in range(0, 10)]
dict_1 = {x : x**2 for x in list_1}
dict_1
```

The output is as follows:

```
{0: 0, 1: 1, 2: 4, 3: 9, 4: 16, 5: 25, 6: 36, 7: 49, 8: 64, 9: 81}
```

Can you generate a **dict** using **dict** comprehension without using a list? Let's try this now.

2. Generate a **dictionary** using the **dict** function:

```
dict_2 = dict([('Tom', 100), ('Dick', 200), ('Harry', 300)])
dict_2
```

The output is as follows:

```
{'Tom': 100, 'Dick': 200, 'Harry': 300}
```

3. You can also a **dictionary** using the **dict** function, as follows:

```
dict_3 = dict(Tom=100, Dick=200, Harry=300)
dict_3
```

The output is as follows:

```
{'Tom': 100, 'Dick': 200, 'Harry': 300}
```

> **NOTE**
>
> To access the source code for this specific section, please refer to https://packt.live/3hz8zPp.
>
> You can also run this example online at https://packt.live/3hA8WJw.

Dictionaries are very flexible and can be used for a variety of tasks. The compact nature of comprehension makes them very popular. The strange-looking pair of values that just looked at (**'Harry', 300**) is called a tuple. This is another important fundamental data type in Python. We will learn about tuples in the next section.

TUPLES

A tuple is another data type in Python. Tuples in Python are similar to lists, with one key difference. A tuple is a variant of a Python list that is immutable. Immutable basically means you can't modify it by adding or removing from the list. It is sequential in nature and similar to lists.

A tuple consists of values separated by commas, as follows:

```
tuple_1 = 24, 42, 2.3456, "Hello"
```

Notice that, unlike lists, we did not open and close square brackets here.

When referring to a tuple, the length of the tuple is called its **cardinality**. This comes from database and set theory and is a common way to reference its length.

CREATING A TUPLE WITH DIFFERENT CARDINALITIES

This is how we create an empty tuple:

```
tuple_1 = ()
```

This is how we create a tuple with only one value:

```
tuple_1 = "Hello",
```

Notice the trailing comma here.

We can nest tuples, similar to lists and dicts, as follows:

```
tuple_1 = "hello", "there"
tuple_12 = tuple_1, 45, "Sam"
```

One special thing about tuples is the fact that they are an immutable data type. So, once they're created, we cannot change their values. We can just access them, as follows:

```
tuple_1 = "Hello", "World!"
tuple_1[1] = "Universe!"
```

The last line of the preceding code will result in a **TypeError** as a tuple does not allow modification.

This makes the use case for tuples a bit different than lists, although they look and behave very similarly in a few ways.

We can access the elements of a tuple in the same manner we can for lists:

```
tuple_1 = ("good", "morning!" , "how", "are" "you?")
tuple_1[0]
```

The output is as follows:

```
'good'
```

Let's access another element:

```
tuple_1[4]
```

The output will be:

```
'you?'
```

UNPACKING A TUPLE

The expression "unpacking a tuple" simply means getting the values contained in the tuple in different variables:

```
tuple_1 = "Hello", "World"
hello, world = tuple_1
print(hello)
print(world)
```

The output is as follows:

```
Hello
World
```

Of course, as soon as we do that, we can modify the values contained in those variables.

EXERCISE 1.11: HANDLING TUPLES

In this exercise, we will walk through the basic functionalities of tuples. Let's go through the steps one by one:

1. Create a tuple to demonstrate how tuples are immutable. Unpack it to read all the elements, as follows:

```
tupleE = "1", "3", "5"
tupleE
```

The output is as follows:

```
('1', '3', '5')
```

2. Try to override a variable from the **tupleE** tuple:

```
tupleE[1] = "5"
```

This step will result in **TypeError** as the tuple does not allow modification.

```
TypeError                                 Traceback (most recent call
last)
<ipython-input-58-b4cba6d5ed11> in <module>
----> 1 tupleE[1] = "5"
TypeError: 'tuple' object does not support item assignment
```

3. Try to assign a series to the **tupleE** tuple:

```
1, 3, 5 = tupleE
```

This step will also result in a **SyntaxError**, stating that it can't assign to the literal:

```
  File "<ipython-input-3-a5283cb38d62>", line 1
    1, 3, 5 = tupleE
          ^
SyntaxError: can't assign to literal
```

4. Print variables at **0**th and **1**st positions:

```
print(tupleE[0])
print(tupleE[1])
```

The output is as follows:

```
1
3
```

> **NOTE**
>
> To access the source code for this specific section, please refer to https://packt.live/3ebuvOf.
>
> You can also run this example online at https://packt.live/2URh9zo.

We have seen two different types of data so far. One is represented by numbers, while the other is represented by textual data. Now it's time to look into textual data in a bit more detail.

STRINGS

In the final section of this chapter, we will learn about strings. Strings in Python are similar to strings in any other programming language.

This is a string:

```
string1 = 'Hello World!'
```

A string can also be declared in this manner:

```
string2 = "Hello World 2!"
```

You can use single quotes and double quotes to define a string.

The start and end of a string is defined as:

```
str[ inclusive start position:  exclusive end position ].
```

Strings in Python behave similar to lists, apart from one big caveat. Strings are immutable, whereas lists are mutable data structures.

EXERCISE 1.12: ACCESSING STRINGS

In this exercise, we are going perform mathematical operations to access strings. Let's go through the following steps:

1. Create a string called **str_1**:

```
str_1 = "Hello World!"
str_1
```

The output is as follows:

```
'Hello World!'
```

You can access the elements of the string by specifying the location of the element, like we did for lists.

2. Access the first member of the string:

```
str_1[0]
```

The output is as follows:

```
'H'
```

3. Access the fifth member of the string:

```
str_1[4]
```

The output is as follows:

```
'o'
```

4. Access the last member of the string:

```
str_1[len(str_1) - 1]
```

The output is as follows:

```
'!'
```

5. Access the last member of the string, in a different way this time:

```
str_1[-1]
```

The output is as follows:

```
'!'
```

> **NOTE**
>
> To access the source code for this specific section, please refer to https://packt.live/2YHEmF9.
>
> You can also run this example online at https://packt.live/3db191p.

Each of the preceding operations will give you the character at the specific index. The method for accessing the elements of a string is like accessing a list. Let's do a couple of more exercises to manipulate strings.

EXERCISE 1.13: STRING SLICES

This exercise will demonstrate how we can slice strings the same way as we did with lists. Although strings are not lists, the functionality will work in the same way.

Let's go through the following steps:

1. Create a string, **str_1**:

```
str_1 = "Hello World! I am learning data wrangling"
str_1
```

The output is as follows:

```
'Hello World! I am learning data wrangling'
```

2. Specify the slicing values and slice the string:

```
str_1[2:10]
```

The output is as follows:

```
'llo Worl'
```

3. Slice a string by skipping a slice value:

```
str_1[-31:]
```

The output is as follows:

```
'd! I am learning data wrangling'
```

4. Use negative numbers to slice the string:

```
str_1[-10:-5]
```

The output is as follows:

```
' wran'
```

> **NOTE**
>
> To access the source code for this specific section, please refer to https://packt.live/2N70Bis.
>
> You can also run this example online at https://packt.live/3d6X9Pu.

As we can see, it is quite simple to manipulate strings with basic operations.

STRING FUNCTIONS

To find out the length of a string, we simply use the **len** function:

```
str_1 = "Hello World! I am learning data wrangling"
len(str_1)
```

The length of the string is **41**. To convert a string's case, we can use the **lower** and **upper** methods:

```
str_1 = "A COMPLETE UPPER CASE STRING"
str_1.lower()
```

The output is as follows:

```
'a complete upper case string'
```

To change the case of the string, use the following code:

```
str_1.upper()
```

The output is as follows:

```
'A COMPLETE UPPER CASE STRING'
```

To search for a string within a string, we can use the **find** method:

```
str_1 = "A complicated string looks like this"
str_1.find("complicated")
str_1.find("hello")
```

The output is **-1**. Can you figure out whether the **find** method is case-sensitive or not? Also, what do you think the **find** method returns when it actually finds the string?

To replace one string with another, we have the **replace** method. Since we know that a string is an immutable data structure, **replace** actually returns a new string instead of replacing and returning the actual one:

```
str_1 = "A complicated string looks like this"
str_1.replace("complicated", "simple")
```

The output is as follows:

```
'A simple string looks like this'
```

> **NOTE**
>
> You should look up string methods in the standard documentation of Python 3 to discover more about these methods. Visit https://docs.python.org/3.7/.

Strings have two useful methods: **split** and **join**. Here are their definitions:

```
str.split(separator)
```

The **seperator** argument is a delimiter that you define:

```
string.join(seperator)
```

Let's take a look at the following exercise to practice the **split** and **join** functionalities.

EXERCISE 1.14: SPLITTING AND JOINING A STRING

This exercise will demonstrate how to perform split and join operations on a string. These two string methods need separate approaches as they allow you to convert a string into a list and vice versa. Let's go through the following steps to do so:

1. Create a string and convert it into a list using the **split** method:

```
str_1 = "Name, Age, Sex, Address"
list_1 = str_1.split(",")
list_1
```

The preceding code will give you a list similar to the following:

```
['Name', ' Age', ' Sex', ' Address']
```

2. Combine this list into another string using the **join** method:

```
s = " | "
s.join(list_1)
```

This code will give you a string like this:

```
'Name |  Age |  Sex |  Address'
```

> **NOTE**
>
> To access the source code for this specific section, please refer to https://packt.live/2N1lprE.
>
> You can also run this example online at https://packt.live/2UOOQBC.

With these, we are at the end of the second topic of this chapter. Now, we have the motivation to learn about data wrangling and have had a solid introduction to the fundamentals of data structures using Python. There is more to this topic, which will be covered in *Chapter 2, Advanced Operation on Built-In Data Structures*.

The next section will ensure that you have understood the various basic types of data structures and their manipulation techniques. We will do that by going through an activity that has been designed specifically for this purpose.

ACTIVITY 1.02: ANALYZING A MULTILINE STRING AND GENERATING THE UNIQUE WORD COUNT

In this activity, you will do the following:

- Get multiline text and save it in a Python variable.

- Get rid of all new lines in it using string methods.

- Get all the unique words and their occurrences from the string.

- Repeat the steps to find all unique words and occurrences, without considering case sensitivity.

> **NOTE**
>
> For the sake of simplicity, the original text (which can be found at https://www.gutenberg.org/files/1342/1342-h/1342-h.htm) has been pre-processed bit.

These are the steps to guide you through solving this activity:

1. Create a **mutliline_text** variable by copying the text from the first chapter of *Pride and Prejudice*.

   Hint: Remember to add triple quotation marks to enter a multiline text. This is the only way to enter a chunk of text in Python.

   > **NOTE**
   >
   > Part of the first chapter of *Pride and Prejudice* by Jane Austen has been made available on this book's GitHub repository at https://packt. live/2N6ZGP6.

2. Find the type and length of the **multiline_text** string using the **type** and **len** commands.

3. Remove all new lines and symbols using the **replace** method.

4. Find all of the words in **multiline_text** using the **split** method.

5. Create a list from this list that will contain only the unique words.

6. Count the number of times the unique word has appeared in the list using the **key** and **value** in **dict**.

7. Find the top 25 words from the unique words that you have found using the **slice** method.

The output is as follows:

```
[('of', 10),
 ('is', 8),
 ('a', 8),
 ('that', 8),
 ('the', 8),
 ('to', 7),
 ('in', 5),
 ('his', 5),
 ('he', 5),
 ('it', 5),
 ('and', 5),
 ('Mr', 4),
 ('man', 3),
 ('be', 3),
 ('want', 3),
 ('Bennet', 3),
 ('you', 3),
 ('truth', 2),
 ('possession', 2),
 ('fortune', 2),
 ('must', 2),
 ('wife', 2),
 ('or', 2),
 ('on', 2),
 ('so', 2)]
```

Figure 1.19: Top 25 words from the unique list

NOTE

The solution to this activity can be found on page 452.

SUMMARY

In this chapter, we learned about data wrangling and looked at examples from various real-life data science situations where data wrangling is very useful. We moved on to learn about the different built-in data structures that Python has to offer. We got our hands dirty by exploring lists, sets, dictionaries, tuples, and strings. These are the fundamental building blocks of Python data structures, and we need them all the time when working and manipulating data in Python. We did several small hands-on exercises to learn more about them. We finished this chapter with carefully designed activities that let us combine a lot of different tricks from all the different data structures and let us observe the interplay between all of them. In the next chapter, we will learn about the data structures in Python and utilize them to solve problems.

2

ADVANCED OPERATIONS ON BUILT-IN DATA STRUCTURES

OVERVIEW

This chapter will introduce advanced data operations on built-in data structures. You can utilize these data structures to solve data-wrangling problems. After reading this chapter, you will be able to compare Python's advanced data structures and make use of the Operating System (OS) file-handling operations. This chapter focuses on the data structures in Python and the OS functions that are the foundation of this book. By the end of this chapter, you will have learned how to handle advanced data structures.

INTRODUCTION

We were introduced to the basic concepts of different fundamental data structures in the previous chapter. We learned about lists, sets, dictionaries, tuples, and strings. However, what we have covered so far were only basic operations on those data structures. They have much more to offer once you learn how to utilize them effectively. In this chapter, we will venture further into the land of data structures. We will learn about advanced operations and manipulations and use fundamental data structures to represent more complex and higher-level data structures; this is often handy while wrangling data in real life. These higher-level topics will include stacks, queues, interiors, and file operations.

In this chapter, we will also learn how to open a file using built-in Python methods and about the many different file operations, such as reading and writing data, and safely closing files once we are done. We will also take a look at some of the problems to avoid while dealing with files.

ADVANCED DATA STRUCTURES

We will start this chapter by discussing advanced data structures. Initially, we will be revisiting lists. Then, we will construct a stack and a queue, explore multiple-element membership checking to check whether the data is accurate, and throw a bit of functional programming in for good measure. Don't worry if all of this sounds intimidating. We will take things step by step, and you will feel confident about handling advanced data structures once you have finished this chapter.

Before we jump into constructing data structures, we'll look at a few methods to manipulate them.

ITERATOR

Iterators in Python are very useful when dealing with data as they allow you to parse the data one unit at a time. Iterators are stateful, which means it will be helpful to keep track of the previous state. An iterator is an object that implements the **next** method—meaning an iterator can iterate over collections such as lists, tuples, dictionaries, and more. Practically, this means that each time we call the method, it gives us the next element from the collection; if there is no further element in the list, then it raises a **StopIteration** exception.

> **NOTE**
>
> A `StopIteration` exception occurs with the iterator's **next** method when there are no further values to iterate.

If you are familiar with a programming language such as C, C++, Java, JavaScript, or PHP, you may have noticed the difference between the **for** loop implementation in those languages, which consists of three distinct parts (the initiation, the increment, and the termination condition), and the **for** loop in Python. In Python, we do not use that kind of a **for** loop. What we use in Python is more like a **foreach** loop:

```
for i in list_1
```

This is because, under the hood, the **for** loop is using an iterator, and thus we do not need to do all the extra steps. The iterator does them for us.

Let's learn about the various functions we can use with **itertools**. As you execute each line of the code after the **import** statement, you will be able to see details about what that particular function does and how to use it:

```
from itertools import (permutations, combinations, \
                       dropwhile, repeat, zip_longest)
permutations?
combinations?
dropwhile?
repeat?
zip_longest?
```

For example, after executing **zip_longest?**, we'll see the following output:

Help

```
Init signature: zip_longest(*args, **kwargs)
Docstring:
zip_longest(iter1 [,iter2 [...]], [fillvalue=None]) --> zip_longest
object

Return a zip_longest object whose .__next__() method returns a
tuple where
the i-th element comes from the i-th iterable argument.  The
.__next__()
method continues until the longest iterable in the argument
sequence
is exhausted and then it raises StopIteration.  When the shorter
iterables
are exhausted, the fillvalue is substituted in their place.  The
```

Figure 2.1: Help file for the zip_longest function

The preceding screenshot shows how the **zip_longest** function could be used from the **itertools** module.

> **NOTE**
>
> To look up the definition of any function, type the function name, followed by *?*, and then press *Shift + Enter* in a Jupyter Notebook.

Let's go through the following exercise to understand how to use an iterator to iterate through a list.

EXERCISE 2.01: INTRODUCING TO THE ITERATOR

In this exercise, we're going to generate a long list containing numbers. We will first check the memory occupied by the generated list. We will then check how we can use the **iterator** module to reduce memory utilization, and finally, we will use this iterator to loop over the list. To do this, let's go through the following steps:

1. Open a new Jupyter Notebook and generate a list that will contain **10000000** ones. Then, store this list in a variable called **big_list_of_numbers**:

```
big_list_of_numbers = [1 for x in range (0, 10000000)]
big_list_of_numbers
```

The output (partially shown) is as follows:

```
[1,
 1,
 1,
 1,
 1,
 1,
 1,
 1,
 1,
 1,
```

2. Check the size of this variable:

```
from sys import getsizeof
getsizeof(big_list_of_numbers)
```

The output should be as follows:

```
81528056
```

The value shown is **81528056** (in bytes). This is a huge chunk of memory occupied by the list. And the **big_list_of_numbers** variable is only available once the list comprehension is over. It can also overflow the available system memory if you try too big a number.

3. Let's use the **repeat()** method from **itertools** to get the same number but with less memory:

```
from itertools import repeat
small_list_of_numbers = repeat(1, times=10000000)
getsizeof(small_list_of_numbers)
```

The output should be:

```
56
```

The last line shows that our list **small_list_of_numbers** is only **56** bytes in size. Also, it is a lazy method, a technique used in functional programming that will delay the execution of a method or a function by a few seconds. In this case, Python will not generate all the elements initially. It will, instead, generate them one by one when asked, thus saving us time. In fact, if you omit the **times** keyword argument in the **repeat()** method in the preceding code, then you can practically generate an infinite number of ones.

4. Loop over the newly generated iterator:

```
for i, x in enumerate(small_list_of_numbers):
    print(x)
    if i > 10:
        break
```

The output is as follows:

```
1
1
1
1
1
1
1
1
1
1
1
1
```

We use the **enumerate** function so that we get the loop counter, along with the values. This will help us break the loop once we reach a certain number (**10**, for example).

> **NOTE**
>
> To access the source code for this specific section, please refer to https://packt.live/2N8odTH.
>
> You can also run this example online at https://packt.live/3fAPFGa.

In this exercise, we first learned how to use the iterator function to reduce memory usage. Then, we used an iterator to loop over a list. Now, we'll see how to create stacks.

STACKS

A stack is a very useful data structure. If you know a bit about CPU internals and how a program gets executed, then you will know that a stack is present in many such cases. It is simply a list with one restriction, **Last In First Out (LIFO)**, meaning an element that comes in last goes out first when a value is read from a stack. The following illustration will make this a bit clearer:

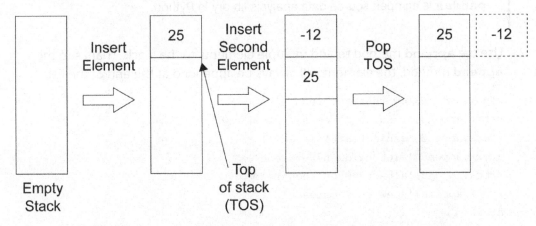

Figure 2.2: A stack with two insert elements and one pop operation

As you can see, we have a LIFO strategy to read values from a stack. We will implement a stack using a Python list. Python lists have a method called **pop**, which does the exact same **pop** operation that you can see in the preceding illustration. Basically, the **pop** function will take an element off the stack, using the **Last in First Out (LIFO)** rules. We will use that to implement a stack in the following exercise.

EXERCISE 2.02: IMPLEMENTING A STACK IN PYTHON

In this exercise, we'll implement a stack in Python. We will first create an empty stack and add new elements to it using the **append** method. Next, we'll take out elements from the stack using the **pop** method. Let's go through the following steps:

1. Import the necessary Python library and define an empty stack:

```
import pandas as pd
stack = []
```

> **NOTE**
>
> **pandas** is an open source data analysis library in Python.

2. Use the **append** method to add multiple elements to the stack. Thanks to the **append** method, the element will always be appended at the end of the list:

```
stack.append('my_test@test.edu')
stack.append('rahul.subhramanian@test.edu')
stack.append('sania.test@test.edu')
stack.append('alec_baldwin@test.edu')
stack.append('albert90@test.edu')
stack.append('stewartj@test.edu')
stack
```

The output is as follows:

```
['my_test@test.edu',
 'rahul.subhramanian@test.edu',
 'sania.test@test.edu',
 'alec_baldwin@test.edu',
 'albert90@test.edu',
 'stewartj@test.edu']
```

3. Let's read a value from our stack using the **pop** method. This method reads the current last index of the list and returns it to us. It also deletes the index once the read is done:

```
tos = stack.pop()
tos
```

The output is as follows:

```
'stewartj@test.edu'
```

As you can see, the last value of the stack has been retrieved. Now, if we add another value to the stack, the new value will be appended at the end of the stack.

4. Append **Hello@test.com** to the stack:

```
stack.append("Hello@test.com")
stack
```

The output is as follows:

```
['my_test@test.edu',
 'rahul.subhramanian@test.edu',
 'sania.test@test.edu',
 'alec_baldwin@test.edu',
 'albert90@test.edu',
 'Hello@test.com']
```

> **NOTE**
>
> To access the source code for this specific section, please refer to https://packt.live/3hACc2B.
>
> You can also run this example online at https://packt.live/2Yb4uct.

From the exercise, we can see that the basic stack operations, **append** and **pop**, are pretty easy to perform.

Let's visualize a problem where you are scraping a web page and you want to follow each URL present there (backlinks). Let's split the solution to this problem into three parts. In the first part, we would append all the URLs scraped off the page into the stack. In the second part, we would pop each element in the stack, and then lastly, we would examine every URL, repeating the same process for each page. We will examine a part of this task in the next exercise.

EXERCISE 2.03: IMPLEMENTING A STACK USING USER-DEFINED METHODS

In this exercise, we will continue the topic of stacks from the last exercise. This time, we will implement the **append** and **pop** functions by creating user-defined methods. We will implement a stack, and this time with a business use case example (taking Wikipedia as a source). The aim of this exercise is twofold. In the first few steps, we will extract and append the URLs scraped off a web page in a stack, which also involves the **string** methods discussed in the last chapter. In the next few steps, we will use the **stack_pop** function to iterate over the stack and print them. This exercise will show us a subtle feature of Python and how it handles passing list variables to functions. Let's go through the following steps:

1. First, define two functions: **stack_push** and **stack_pop**. We renamed them so that we do not have a namespace conflict. Also, create a stack called **url_stack** for later use:

```
def stack_push(s, value):
    return s + [value]
def stack_pop(s):
    tos = s[-1]
    del s[-1]
    return tos
url_stack = []
url_stack
```

The output is as follows:

```
[]
```

The first function takes the already existing stack and adds the value at the end of it.

> **NOTE**
>
> Notice the square brackets around the value to convert it into a one-element list using the + operation. The second function reads the value that's currently at the −1 index of the stack, then uses the **del** operator to delete that index, and finally returns the value it read earlier.

Now, we are going to have a string with a few URLs in it.

2. Analyze the string so that we push the URLs in the stack one by one as we encounter them, and then use a **for** loop to pop them one by one. Let's take the first line from the **Wikipedia** article (https://en.wikipedia.org/wiki/Data_mining) about data science:

```
wikipedia_datascience = """Data science is an interdisciplinary
field that uses scientific methods, processes, algorithms and systems
to extract knowledge [https://en.wikipedia.org/wiki/Knowledge] and
insights from data [https://en.wikipedia.org/wiki/Data] in various
forms, both structured and unstructured, similar to data mining
[https://en.wikipedia.org/wiki/Data_mining]"""
```

For the sake of the simplicity of this exercise, we have kept the links in square brackets beside the target words.

3. Find the length of the string:

```
len(wikipedia_datascience)
```

The output is as follows:

```
347
```

4. Convert this string into a list by using the **split** method from the string, and then calculate its length:

```
wd_list = wikipedia_datascience.split()
wd_list
```

The output is as follows (partial output):

```
['Data',
 'science',
 'is',
 'an',
 'interdisciplinary',
 'field',
 'that',
 'uses',
 'scientific',
 'methods,',
```

5. Check the length of the list:

```
len(wd_list)
```

The output is as follows:

```
34
```

6. Use a **for** loop to go over each word and check whether it is a URL. To do that, we will use the **startswith** method from the string, and if it is a URL, then we push it into the stack:

```
for word in wd_list:
    if word.startswith("[https://"):
        url_stack = stack_push(url_stack, word[1:-1])
        print(word[1:-1])
```

The output is as follows:

```
https://en.wikipedia.org/wiki/Knowledge
https://en.wikipedia.org/wiki/Data
https://en.wikipedia.org/wiki/Data_mining
```

Notice the use of string slicing to remove the surrounding double quotes `"["  "]"`.

7. Print the value in **url_stack**:

```
print(url_stack)
```

The output is as follows:

```
['https://en.wikipedia.org/wiki/Knowledge',
 'https://en.wikipedia.org/wiki/Data',
 'https://en.wikipedia.org/wiki/Data_mining']
```

8. Iterate over the list and print the URLs one by one by using the **stack_pop** function:

```
for i in range(0, len(url_stack)):
    print(stack_pop(url_stack))
```

The output is as follows:

https://en.wikipedia.org/wiki/Data_mining
https://en.wikipedia.org/wiki/Data
https://en.wikipedia.org/wiki/Knowledge

Figure 2.3: Output of the URLs that are printed using a stack

9. Print it again to make sure that the stack is empty after the final **for** loop:

```
print(url_stack)
```

The output is as follows:

```
[]
```

> **NOTE**
>
> To access the source code for this specific section, please refer to https://packt.live/2Y7oXyT.
>
> You can also run this example online at https://packt.live/3e9Smhz.

In this exercise, we have noticed a strange phenomenon in the **stack_pop** method. We passed the **list** variable there, and we used the **del** operator inside the function in *step 1*, but it changed the original variable by deleting the last index each time we called the function. If you use languages like C, C++, and Java, then this is a completely unexpected behavior as, in those languages, this can only happen if we pass the variable by reference, and it can lead to subtle bugs in Python code. So, be careful when using the user-defined methods.

LAMBDA EXPRESSIONS

In general, it is not a good idea to change a variable's value inside a function. Any variable that is passed to the function should be considered and treated as immutable. This is close to the principles of functional programming. However, in that case, we could use unnamed functions that are neither immutable nor mutable and are typically not stored in a variable. Such an expression or function, called a **lambda expression** in Python, is a way to construct one-line, nameless functions that are, by convention, side-effect-free and are loosely considered as implementing functional programming.

Let's look at the following exercise to understand how we use a lambda expression.

EXERCISE 2.04: IMPLEMENTING A LAMBDA EXPRESSION

In this exercise, we will use a lambda expression to prove the famous trigonometric identity:

$$sin^2(x) + cos^2(x) = 1$$

Figure 2.4: Trigonometric identity

Let's go through the following steps to do this:

1. Import the **math** package:

```
import math
```

2. Define two functions, **my_sine** and **my_cosine**, using the **def** keyword. The reason we are declaring these functions is the original **sin** and **cos** functions from the **math** package take **radians** as input, but we are more familiar with **degrees**. So, we will use a lambda expression to define a wrapper function for **sine** and **cosine**, then use it. This **lambda** function will automatically convert our degree input to radians and then apply **sin** or **cos** on it and return the value:

```
def my_sine():
    return lambda x: math.sin(math.radians(x))
def my_cosine():
    return lambda x: math.cos(math.radians(x))
```

3. Define **sine** and **cosine** for our purpose:

```
sine = my_sine()
cosine = my_cosine()
math.pow(sine(30), 2) + math.pow(cosine(30), 2)
```

The output is as follows:

```
1.0
```

Notice that we have assigned the return value from both **my_sine** and **my_cosine** to two variables, and then used them directly as the functions. It is a much cleaner approach than using them explicitly. Notice that we did not explicitly write a **return** statement inside the lambda function; it is assumed.

> **NOTE**
>
> To access the source code for this specific section, please refer to https://packt.live/3fJW9mb.
>
> You can also run this example online at https://packt.live/30Pn8by.

Now, in the next section, we will be using lambda functions, also known as anonymous functions, which come from lambda calculus. Lambda functions are useful for creating temporary functions that are not named. The lambda expression will take an input and then return the first character of that input.

EXERCISE 2.05: LAMBDA EXPRESSION FOR SORTING

In this exercise, we will be exploring the **sort** function to take advantage of the lambda function. What makes this exercise useful is that you will be learning how to create any unique algorithm that could be used for sorting a dataset. The syntax for a lambda function is as follows:

```
lambda x  :    <do something with x>
```

A lambda expression can take one or more inputs. A lambda expression can also be used to reverse sort by using the parameter of **reverse** as **True**. We'll use the reverse functionality as well in this exercise. Let's go through the following steps:

1. Let's store the list of tuples we want to sort in a variable called **capitals**:

```
capitals = [("USA", "Washington"), ("India", "Delhi"), ("France",
"Paris"), ("UK", "London")]
```

2. Print the output of this list:

```
capitals
```

The output will be as follows:

```
[('USA', 'Washington'),
 ('India', 'Delhi'),
 ('France', 'Paris'),
 ('UK', 'London')]
```

3. Sort this list by the name of the capitals of each country, using a simple lambda expression. The following code uses a lambda function as the **sort** function. It will sort based on the first element in each tuple:

```
capitals.sort(key=lambda item: item[1])
capitals
```

The output will be as follows:

```
[('India', 'Delhi'),
 ('UK', 'London'),
 ('France', 'Paris'),
 ('USA', 'Washington')]
```

As we can see, lambda expressions are powerful if we master them and use them in our data wrangling jobs. They are also side-effect-free—meaning that they do not change the values of the variables that are passed to them in place.

> **NOTE**
>
> To access the source code for this specific section, please refer to https://packt.live/2AzcTxv.
>
> You can also run this example online at https://packt.live/3hDpe4o.

We will now move on to the next section, where we will discuss membership checking for each element. Membership checking is commonly used terminology in qualitative research and describes the process of checking that the data present in a dataset is accurate.

EXERCISE 2.06: MULTI-ELEMENT MEMBERSHIP CHECKING

In this exercise, we will create a list of words using **for** loop to validate that all the elements in the first list are present in the second list. Let's see how:

1. Create a **list_of_words** list with words scraped from a text corpus:

```
list_of_words = ["Hello", "there.", "How", "are", "you", "doing?"]
list_of_words
```

The output is as follows:

```
['Hello', 'there.', 'How', 'are', 'you', 'doing?']
```

2. Define a **check_for** list, which will contain two similar elements of **list_of_words**:

```
check_for = ["How", "are"]
check_for
```

The output is as follows:

```
['How', 'are']
```

There is an elaborate solution, which involves a **for** loop and a few **if/else** conditions (and you should try to write it), but there is also an elegant Pythonic solution to this problem, which takes one line and uses the **all** function. The **all** function returns **True** if all elements of the iterable are **True**.

3. Use the **in** keyword to check membership of the elements in the **check_for** list in **list_of_words**:

```
all(w in list_of_words for w in check_for)
```

The output is as follows:

```
True
```

> **NOTE**
>
> To access the source code for this specific section, please refer to https://packt.live/3d5pyVT.
>
> You can also run this example online at https://packt.live/2C7GPB1.

It is indeed elegant and simple to reason about, and this neat trick is very important while dealing with lists. Basically, what we are doing is looping over the first list with the comprehension and then looping over the second list using the **for** loop. What makes this elegant is how compactly we can represent this complex process. Caution should be taken when using very complex list comprehension—the more complex you make it, the harder it is to read.

Let's look at the next data structure: a **queue**.

QUEUE

Apart from stacks, another high-level data structure type that we are interested in is queues. A queue is like a stack, which means that you continue adding elements one by one. With a queue, the reading of elements obeys the **First in First Out (FIFO)** strategy. Check out the following diagram to understand this better:

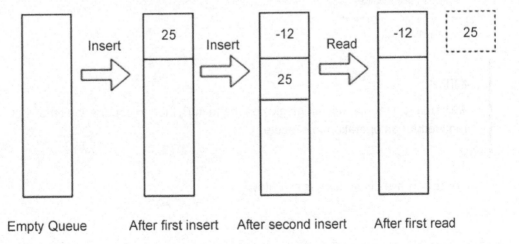

Figure 2.5: Pictorial representation of a queue

We will accomplish this first using list methods and will show you that, for this purpose, they are inefficient. Then, we will learn about the **dequeue** data structure from the collections module of Python. A queue is a very important data structure. We can think of a scenario on a producer-consumer system design. When doing data wrangling, you will often come across a problem where you must process very big files. One of the ways to deal with this problem is to split the chunk the contents of the file into smaller parts and then push them into a queue while creating small, dedicated worker processes, to read off the queue and process one small chunk at a time. This is a very powerful design, and you can even use it efficiently to design huge multi-node data wrangling pipelines.

EXERCISE 2.07: IMPLEMENTING A QUEUE IN PYTHON

In this exercise, we'll implement a queue in Python. We'll use the **append** function to add elements to the queue and use the **pop** function to take elements out of the queue. We'll also use the **deque** data structure and compare it with the queue in order to understand the wall time required to complete the execution of an operation. To do so, perform the following steps:

1. Create a Python queue with the plain list methods. To record the time the **append** operation in the queue data structure takes, we use the **%%time** command:

```
%%time
queue = []
for i in range(0, 100000):
    queue.append(i)
print("Queue created")
queue
```

> **NOTE**
>
> **%%time** is a regular built-in magic command in Python to capture the time required for an operation to execute.

The output (partially shown) is as follows:

```
                    Queue created
                    Wall time: 14 ms
        Out[1]:  [0,
                  1,
                  2,
                  3,
                  4,
                  5,
                  6,
                  7,
                  8,
                  9,
                  10,
                  11,
                  12,
                  13,
                  14,
                  15,
                  16,
                  17,
                  18,
                  19,
                  20,
                  21,
                  22,
                  23,
                  24,
                  25,
                  26,
                  27,
                  28,
                  29,
                  30,
```

Figure 2.6: Wall time recorded for the append function in the queue

2. If we were to use the **pop** function to empty the queue and check the items in it:

```
for i in range(0, 100000):
    queue.pop(0)
print("Queue emptied")
```

The output would be as follows:

```
Queue emptied
```

However, this time, we'll use the `%%time` magic command while executing the preceding code to see that it takes a while to finish:

```
%%time
for i in range(0, 100000):
    queue.pop(0)
print("Queue emptied")
queue
```

The output is as follows:

```
Queue emptied
CPU times: user 2.24 s, sys: 2.76 ms, total: 2.24 s
Wall time: 2.24 s
```

Figure 2.7: Wall time recorded for the pop function in the queue

> **NOTE**
>
> If you are working on Google Colab or other virtual environments, you will see an additional line indicating the CPU time present in the output. This is the CPU time of the server on which Google Colab (or any other virtual environment) is running on. However, if you are working on your local system, this information will not be a part of the output.

In a modern MacBook, with a quad-core processor and **8** GB of RAM, it took around **1.20** seconds to finish. With Windows 10, it took around 2.24 seconds to finish. It takes this amount of time because of the **pop(0)** operation, which means every time we pop a value from the left of the list (the current **0** index), Python has to rearrange all the other elements of the list by shifting them one space left. Indeed, it is not a very optimized implementation.

3. Implement the same queue using the **deque** data structure from Python's **collections** package and perform the **append** and **pop** functions on this data structure:

```
%%time
from collections import deque
queue2 = deque()
for i in range(0, 100000):
    queue2.append(i)
```

```
print("Queue created")
for i in range(0, 100000):
    queue2.popleft()
print("Queue emptied")
```

The output is as follows:

```
Queue created
Queue emptied
CPU times: user 27.9 ms, sys: 4.16 ms, total: 32.1 ms
Wall time: 31.4 ms
```

Figure 2.8: Wall time measured for deque

With the specialized and optimized queue implementation from Python's standard library, the time that this should take for both the operations is only approximately **27.9** milliseconds. This is a huge improvement on the previous one.

> **NOTE**
>
> To access the source code for this specific section, please refer to https://packt.live/30R69Wc.
>
> You can also run this example online at https://packt.live/3dazlEL.

We will end the discussion on data structures here. What we discussed here is just the tip of the iceberg. Data structures are a fascinating subject. There are many other data structures that we did not touch on and that, when used efficiently, can offer enormous added value. We strongly encourage you to explore data structures more. Try to learn about linked lists, trees, graphs, and all the different variations of them as much as you can; you will find there are many similarities between them and you will benefit greatly from studying them. Not only do they offer the joy of learning, but they are also the secret mega-weapons in the arsenal of a data practitioner that you can bring out every time you are challenged with a difficult data wrangling job.

ACTIVITY 2.01: PERMUTATION, ITERATOR, LAMBDA, AND LIST

In this activity, we will be using **permutations** to generate all possible three-digit numbers that can be generated using **0**, **1**, and **2**. A permutation is a mathematical way to represent all possible outcomes. Then, we'll loop over this iterator and also use **isinstance** and **assert** to make sure that the return types are tuples. Use a single line of code involving **dropwhile** and **lambda** expressions to convert all the tuples to lists while dropping any leading zeros (for example, **(0, 1, 2)** becomes **[1, 2]**). Finally, we will write a function that takes a list like before and returns the actual number contained in it.

These steps will guide you as to how to solve this activity:

1. Look up the definition of **permutations** and **dropwhile** from **itertools**.

2. Write an expression to generate all the possible three-digit numbers, using **0**, **1**, and **2**.

3. Loop over the iterator expression you generated before. Print each element returned by the iterator. Use **assert** and **isinstance** to make sure that the elements are of the tuple type.

4. Write the loop again, using **dropwhile**, with a lambda expression to drop any leading zeros from the tuples. As an example, **(0, 1, 2)** will become **[0, 2]**. Also, cast the output of **dropwhile** to a list.

5. Check the actual type that **dropwhile** returns.

6. Combine the preceding code into one block; this time, write a separate function where you will pass the list generated from **dropwhile** and the function will return the whole number contained in the list. As an example, if you pass **[1, 2]** to the function, it will return **12**. Make sure that the return type is indeed a number and not a string. Although this task can be achieved using other tricks, treat the incoming list as a stack in the function and generate the number by reading the individual digits from the stack.

   The final output should look like this:

```
12.0
21.0
102.0
120.0
201.0
210.0
```

> **NOTE**
>
> The solution for this activity can be found on page 458.

With this activity, we have finished this topic and will move on to the next topic, which involves basic file-level operations.

> **NOTE**
>
> We encourage you to think about a solution to the preceding problem without using all the advanced operations and data structures we have used here. You will soon realize how complex the solution is, and how much more detailed it must be. Then, you will understand how much value these data structures and operations bring.

BASIC FILE OPERATIONS IN PYTHON

In the previous topic, we investigated a few advanced data structures and also learned neat and useful functional programming methods to manipulate them without side effects. In this topic, we will learn about a few OS-level functions in Python, such as working with files, but these could also include working with printers, and even the internet. We will concentrate mainly on file-related functions and learn how to open a file, read the data line by line or all at once, and finally, how to cleanly close the file we opened. The closing operation of a file should be done cautiously, which is ignored most of the time by developers. When handling file operations, we often run into very strange and hard-to-track-down bugs because a process opened a file and did not close it properly. We will apply a few of the techniques we have learned about to a file that we will read to practice our data wrangling skills further.

EXERCISE 2.08: FILE OPERATIONS

In this exercise, we will learn about the OS module of Python, and we will also look at two very useful ways to write and read environment variables. The power of writing and reading environment variables is often very important when designing and developing data-wrangling pipelines.

> **NOTE**
>
> In fact, one of the factors of the famous 12-factor app design is the very idea of storing configuration in the environment. You can check it out at this URL: https://12factor.net/config.

The purpose of the OS module is to give you ways to interact with OS-dependent functionalities. In general, it is pretty low-level and most of the functions from there are not useful on a day-to-day basis; however, some are worth learning. **os.environ** is the collection Python maintains with all the present environment variables in your OS. It gives you the power to create new ones. The **os.getenv** function gives you the ability to read an environment variable:

1. Import the **os** module.

```
import os
```

2. Set a few environment variables:

```
os.environ['MY_KEY'] = "MY_VAL"
os.getenv('MY_KEY')
```

The output is as follows:

```
'MY_VAL'
```

3. Print the environment variable when it is not set:

```
print(os.getenv('MY_KEY_NOT_SET'))
```

The output is as follows:

```
None
```

4. Print the **os** environment:

```
print(os.environ)
```

> **NOTE**
>
> The output has not been added for security reasons.
>
> To access the source code for this specific section, please refer to https://packt.live/2YCZAnC.
>
> You can also run this example online at https://packt.live/3fCqnaB.

After executing the preceding code, you will be able to see that you have successfully printed the value of **MY_KEY**, and when you tried to print **MY_KEY_NOT_SET**, it printed **None**. Therefore, utilizing the OS module, you will be able to set the value of environment variables in your system.

FILE HANDLING

In this section, we will learn about how to open a file in Python. We will learn about the different modes that we can use and what they stand for when opening a file. Python has a built-in **open** function that we will use to open a file. The **open** function takes a few arguments as input. Among them, the first one, which stands for the name of the file you want to open, is the only one that's mandatory. Everything else has a default value. When you call **open**, Python uses underlying system-level calls to open a file handler and return it to the caller.

Usually, a file can be opened either for reading or writing. If we open a file in one mode, the other operation is not supported. Whereas reading usually means we start to read from the beginning of an existing file, writing can mean either starting a new file and writing from the beginning or opening an existing file and appending to it.

Here is a table showing you all the different modes Python supports for opening a file:

Character	Meaning of the Character
'r'	Open for reading
'w'	Open for writing
'x'	Create a new file and open it for writing
'a'	Open for writing in append mode, if it exists
'b'	Binary mode
't'	Text mode (default)
'+'	Update mode (both read and write)

Figure 2.9: Modes to read a file

There is also a deprecated mode, **U**, which does nothing in a Python 3 environment. One thing we must remember here is that Python will always differentiate between **t** and **b** modes, even if the underlying OS doesn't. This is because, in **b** mode, Python does not try to decode what it is reading and gives us back the **byteobject** instead, whereas, in **t** mode, it does try to decode the stream and gives us back the **string** representation.

You can open a file for reading with the command that follows. The path (highlighted) would need to be changed based on the location of the file on your system.

```
fd = open("../datasets/data_temporary_files.txt")
```

We will discuss some more functions in the following section.

> **NOTE**
>
> The file can be found here https://packt.live/2YGpbfv.

This is opened in **rt** mode (opened for the **reading+text** mode). You can open the same file in **binary** mode if you want. To open the file in binary mode, use the **rb (read, byte)** mode:

```
fd = open('AA.txt',"rb")
fd
```

The output is as follows:

```
<_io.BufferedReader name='../datasets/AA.txt'>
```

> **NOTE**
>
> The file can be found here: https://packt.live/30OSkaP.

This is how we open a file for writing:

```
fd = open("../datasets/data_temporary_files.txt ", "w")
fd
```

The output is as follows:

```
<_io.TextIOWrapper name='../datasets/data_temporary_files.txt ' mode='w'
encoding='cp1252'>
```

Let's practice this concept in the following exercise.

EXERCISE 2.09: OPENING AND CLOSING A FILE

In this exercise, we will learn how to close a file after opening it.

> **NOTE**
>
> The file we will be working on can be found here: https://packt.live/30OSkaP.

We must close a file once we have opened it. A lot of system-level bugs can occur due to a dangling file handler, which means the file is still being modified, even though the application is done using it. Once we close a file, no further operations can be performed on that file using that specific file handler.

1. Open a file in binary mode:

```
fd = open("../datasets/AA.txt", "rb")
```

> **NOTE**
>
> Change the highlighted path based on the location of the file on your system. The video of this exercise shows how to use the same function on a different file. There, you'll also get a glimpse of the function used to write to files, which is something you'll learn about later in the chapter.

2. Close a file using **close()**:

```
fd.close()
```

Python also gives us a **closed** flag with the file handler. If we print it before closing, then we will see **False**, whereas if we print it after closing, then we will see **True**. If our logic checks whether a file is properly closed or not, then this is the flag we want to use.

> **NOTE**
>
> To access the source code for this specific section, please refer to https://packt.live/30R6FDC.
>
> You can also run this example online at https://packt.live/3edLol8.

THE WITH STATEMENT

In this section, we will learn about the **with** statement in Python and how we can effectively use it in the context of opening and closing files.

The **with** command is a compound statement in Python, like **if** and **for**, designed to combine multiple lines. Like any compound statement, **with** also affects the execution of the code enclosed by it. In the case of **with**, it is used to wrap a block of code in the scope of what we call a *Context Manager* in Python. A context manager is a convenient way to work with resources and will help avoid forgetting to close the resource. A detailed discussion of context managers is out of the scope of this exercise and this topic in general, but it is sufficient to say that if a context manager is implemented inside the **open** call for opening a file in Python, it is guaranteed that a close call will automatically be made if we wrap it inside a **with** statement.

> **NOTE**
>
> There is an entire PEP for `with` at https://www.python.org/dev/peps/pep-0343/. We encourage you to look into it.

OPENING A FILE USING THE WITH STATEMENT

Open a file using the **with** statement:

```
with open("../datasets/AA.txt") as fd:
    print(fd.closed)
print(fd.closed)
```

The output is as follows:

```
False
True
```

If we execute the preceding code, we will see that the first **print** will end up printing **False**, whereas the second one will print **True**. This means that as soon as the control goes out of the **with** block, the file descriptor is automatically closed.

> **NOTE**
>
> This is by far the cleanest and most Pythonic way to open a file and obtain a file descriptor for it. We encourage you to use this pattern whenever you need to open a file by yourself.

EXERCISE 2.10: READING A FILE LINE BY LINE

In this exercise, we'll read a file line by line. Let's go through the following steps to do so:

1. Open a file and then read the file line by line and print it as we read it:

```
with open("../datasets/Alice`s Adventures in Wonderland, "\
        "by Lewis Carroll", encoding="utf8") as fd:
    for line in fd:
        print(line)
```

> **NOTE**
>
> Do not forget to change the path (highlighted) of the file based on its location on your system.

The output (partially shown) is as follows:

CHAPTER I. Down the Rabbit-Hole

Alice was beginning to get very tired of sitting by her sister on the

bank, and of having nothing to do: once or twice she had peeped into the

book her sister was reading, but it had no pictures or conversations in

it, 'and what is the use of a book,' thought Alice 'without pictures or

conversations?'

Figure 2.10: Screenshot from the Jupyter notebook

Looking at the preceding code, we can see why it is important. With this short snippet of code, you can even open and read files that are many gigabytes in size, line by line, and without flooding or overrunning the system memory. There is another explicit method in the file descriptor object, called **readline**, which reads one line at a time from a file.

2. Duplicate the same **for** loop, just after the first one:

```
with open("../datasets/Alice`s Adventures in Wonderland, "\
        "by Lewis Carroll", encoding="utf8") as fd:
    for line in fd:
        print(line)
    print("Ended first loop")
    for line in fd:
        print(line)
```

> **NOTE**
>
> Do not forget to change the path (highlighted) of the file based on its location on your system.

The output (partially shown) is as follows:

CHAPTER I. Down the Rabbit-Hole

Alice was beginning to get very tired of sitting by her sister on the

bank, and of having nothing to do: once or twice she had peeped into the

book her sister was reading, but it had no pictures or conversations in

it, 'and what is the use of a book,' thought Alice 'without pictures or

conversations?'

Figure 2.11: Section of the open file

> **NOTE**
>
> To access the source code for this specific section, please refer to https://packt.live/37B7aTX.
> You can also run this example online at https://packt.live/3fCqWBf.

Let's look at the last exercise of this chapter.

EXERCISE 2.11: WRITING TO A FILE

In this exercise, we'll look into file operations by showing you how to read from a dictionary and write to a file. We will write a few lines to a file and read the file:

> **NOTE**
>
> `data_temporary_files.txt` can be found at https://packt.live/2YGpbfv.

Let's go through the following steps:

1. Use the **write** function from the file descriptor object:

```
data_dict = {"India": "Delhi", "France": "Paris",\
            "UK": "London", "USA": "Washington"}
```

```
with open("../datasets/data_temporary_files.txt", "w") as fd:
    for country, capital in data_dict.items():
        fd.write("The capital of {} is {}\n"\
                .format(country, capital))
```

> **NOTE**
>
> Throughout this exercise, don't forget to change the path (highlighted) based on where you have stored the text file.

2. Read the file using the following command:

```
with open("../datasets/data_temporary_files.txt", "r") as fd:
    for line in fd:
        print(line)
```

The output is as follows:

```
The capital of India is Delhi

The capital of France is Paris

The capital of UK is London

The capital of USA is Washington
```

3. Use the **print** function to write to a file using the following command:

```
data_dict_2 = {"China": "Beijing", "Japan": "Tokyo"}
with open("../datasets/data_temporary_files.txt", "a") as fd:
    for country, capital in data_dict_2.items():
        print("The capital of {} is {}"\
            .format(country, capital), file=fd)
```

4. Read the file using the following command:

```
with open("../datasets/data_temporary_files.txt", "r") as fd:
    for line in fd:
        print(line)
```

The output is as follows:

```
The capital of India is Delhi
```

```
The capital of France is Paris

The capital of UK is London

The capital of USA is Washington

The capital of China is Beijing

The capital of Japan is Tokyo
```

> **NOTE**
>
> In the second case, we did not add an extra newline character, **\n**, at the end of the string to be written. The **print** function does that automatically for us.
>
> To access the source code for this specific section, please refer to https://packt.live/2BkVh8j.
>
> You can also run this example online at https://packt.live/3hB7xT0.

With this, we will end this topic. Just like the previous topics, we have designed an activity for you to practice your newly acquired skills.

ACTIVITY 2.02: DESIGNING YOUR OWN CSV PARSER

A CSV file is something you will encounter a lot in your life as a data practitioner. A CSV file is a comma-separated file where data from a tabular format is generally stored and separated using commas, although other characters can also be used, such as **tab** or *****. Here's an example CSV file:

```
Region,Country,Item Type,Sales Channel,Order Priority
Central America and the Caribbean,Antigua and Barbuda
Central America and the Caribbean,Panama,Snacks,Offli
Europe,Czech Republic,Beverages,Offline,C,9/12/2011,4
Asia,North Korea,Cereal,Offline,L,5/13/2010,892599952
Asia,Sri Lanka,Snacks,Offline,C,7/20/2015,571902596,7,
```

Figure 2.12: Partial output of a CSV file

In this activity, we will be tasked with building our own CSV reader and parser. Although it is a big task if we try to cover all use cases and edge cases, along with escape characters, for the sake of this short activity, we will keep our requirements small. We will assume that there is no escape character—meaning that if you use a comma at any place in your row, you are starting a new column. We will also assume that the only function we are interested in is to be able to read a CSV file line by line, where each read will generate a new dictionary with the column names as keys and row names as values.

Here is an example:

Name	Age	Location
Bob	24	California

Figure 2.13: Table with sample data

We can convert the data in the preceding table into a Python dictionary, which would look as follows: **{"Name": "Bob", "Age": "24", "Location": "California"}**:

1. Import **zip_longest** from **itertools**. Create a function to zip **header**, **line**, and **fillvalue=None**.

    Open the accompanying **sales_record.csv** file from the GitHub link (https://packt.live/2Yb6iCh) by using **r** mode inside a **with** block and check that it is opened.

2. Read the first line and use string methods to generate a list of all the column names.

3. Start reading the file. Read it line by line.

4. Read each line and pass that line to a function, along with the list of the headers. The work of the function is to construct a **dictionary** out of these two and fill up the **key:values** variables. Keep in mind that a missing value should result in **None**.

The partial output of this should look like this:

```
{'Region': 'Central America and the Caribbean', 'Country'
d', 'Sales Channel': 'Online', 'Order Priority': 'M', 'Or
'Ship Date': '1/11/2014', 'Units Sold': '552', 'Unit Pric
ue': '140914.56', 'Total Cost': '87999.84', 'Total Profit
{'Region': 'Central America and the Caribbean', 'Country'
l': 'Offline', 'Order Priority': 'C', 'Order Date': '7/5/
6/2010', 'Units Sold': '2167', 'Unit Price': '152.58', 'U
'Total Cost': '211152.48', 'Total Profit': '119488.38'}
```

Figure 2.14: Partial output of the sales_record file

> **NOTE**
>
> The solution for this activity can be found on page 460.

With this, we conclude the chapter.

SUMMARY

This chapter covered manipulation techniques of advanced data structures such as stacks and queues. We then focused on different methods of functional programming, including iterators, and combined lists and functions together. Later, we looked at OS-level functions and the management of environment variables. We examined how, using Python, we can open, close, and even write to local files in a variety of ways. Knowing how to deal with files in a clean way is a critical skill in a data wrangler's repertoire. Toward the end, we tested our newly learned skills by creating our own CSV parser.

In the next chapter, we will be dealing with the three most important libraries, namely **NumPy**, **pandas**, and **matplotlib**.

3

INTRODUCTION TO NUMPY, PANDAS, AND MATPLOTLIB

OVERVIEW

In this chapter, you will learn about the fundamentals of the `NumPy`, `pandas`, and `matplotlib` libraries. You will learn to create one-dimensional and multi-dimensional arrays and manipulate `pandas` DataFrames and `series` objects. By the end of this chapter, you will be able to visualize and plot numerical data using the `Matplotlib` library, as well as to apply `matplotlib`, `NumPy`, and `pandas` to calculate descriptive statistics from a DataFrame or matrix.

INTRODUCTION

In the preceding chapters, we covered some advanced data structures, such as stack, queue, iterator, and file operations in Python. In this chapter, we will cover three essential libraries, namely **NumPy**, **pandas**, and **matplotlib**. **NumPy** is an advanced math library in Python with an extensive range of functionality. **pandas** is a library built on **NumPy** that allows developers to model the data in a table structure similar to a database; **malplotlib**, on the other hand, is a charting library that is influenced by Matlab. With these libraries, you will be able to handle most data wrangling tasks.

NUMPY ARRAYS

A **NumPy** array is similar to a list but differs in some ways. In the life of a data scientist, reading and manipulating an array is of prime importance, and it is also the most frequently encountered task. These arrays could be a one-dimensional list, a multi-dimensional table, or a matrix full of numbers and can be used for a variety of mathematical calculations.

An array could be filled with integers, floating-point numbers, Booleans, strings, or even mixed types. However, in the majority of cases, numeric data types are predominant. Some example scenarios where you will need to handle numeric arrays are as follows:

- To read a list of phone numbers and postal codes and extract a certain pattern

- To create a matrix with random numbers to run a Monte Carlo simulation on a statistical process

- To scale and normalize a sales figure table, with lots of financial and transactional data

- To create a smaller table of key descriptive statistics (for example, mean, median, min/max range, variance, and inter-quartile ranges) from a large raw data table

- To read in and analyze time series data in a one-dimensional array daily, such as the stock price of an organization over a year or daily temperature data from a weather station

In short, arrays and numeric data tables are everywhere. As a data wrangling professional, the importance of the ability to read and process numeric arrays cannot be overstated. It is very common to work with data and need to modify it with a mathematical function. In this regard, **NumPy** arrays are the most important objects in Python that you need to know about.

NUMPY ARRAYS AND FEATURES

NumPy and SciPy are open source add-on modules for Python that provide common mathematical and numerical routines in pre-compiled, fast functions. Over the years, these have grown into highly mature libraries that provide functionality that meets, or perhaps exceeds, what is associated with common commercial software such as Matlab or Mathematica.

One of the main advantages of the NumPy module is that it can be used to handle or create one-dimensional or multi-dimensional arrays. This advanced data structure/class is at the heart of the NumPy package and it serves as the fundamental building block of more advanced concepts, such as the **pandas** library and specifically, the pandas DataFrame, which we will cover shortly in this chapter.

NumPy arrays are different than common Python lists since Python lists can be thought of as simple arrays. NumPy arrays are built for mathematical vectorized operations that process a lot of numerical data with just a single line of code. Many built-in mathematical functions in NumPy arrays are written in low-level languages such as C or Fortran and are pre-compiled for really fast execution.

> **NOTE**
>
> NumPy arrays are optimized data structures for numerical analysis, and that's why they are so important to data scientists.

Let's go through the first exercise in this chapter, where we will learn how to create a **NumPy** array from a list.

EXERCISE 3.01: CREATING A NUMPY ARRAY (FROM A LIST)

In this exercise, we will create a **NumPy** array from a list. We're going to define a list first and use the array function of the **NumPy** library to convert the list into an array. Next, we'll read from a **.csv** file and store the data in a **NumPy** array using the **genfromtxt** function of the **NumPy** library. To do so, let's go through the following steps:

1. To work with **NumPy**, we must import it. By convention, we give it a short name, np, while importing it. This will make referencing the objects under the **NumPy** package organized:

```
import numpy as np
```

2. Create a list with three elements: **1**, **2**, and **3**:

```
list_1 = [1,2,3]
list_1
```

The output is as follows:

```
[1, 2, 3]
```

3. Use the **array** function to convert it into an array:

```
array_1 = np.array(list_1)
array_1
```

The output is as follows:

```
array([1, 2, 3])
```

We just created a **NumPy** array object called **array_1** from the regular Python list object, **list_1**.

4. Create an array of floating type elements, that is, **1.2**, **3.4**, and **5.6**, using the array function directly:

```
a = np.array([1.2, 3.4, 5.6])
a
```

The output is as follows:

```
array([1.2, 3.4, 5.6])
```

5. Let's check the type of the newly created object, a, using the **type** function:

```
type(a)
```

The output is as follows:

```
numpy.ndarray
```

6. Use the **type** function to check the type of **array_1**:

```
type(array_1)
```

The output is as follows:

```
numpy.ndarray
```

As we can see, both a and **array_1** are **NumPy** arrays.

7. Now, use type on **list_1**:

```
type(list_1)
```

The output is as follows:

```
list
```

As we can see, **list_1** is essentially a Python list and we have used the array function of the **NumPy** library to create a **NumPy** array from that list.

8. Now, let's read a **.csv** file as a **NumPy** array using the **genfromtxt** function of the **NumPy** library:

```
data = np.genfromtxt('../datasets/stock.csv', \
                     delimiter=',',names=True,dtype=None, \
                     encoding='ascii')
data
```

> **NOTE**
>
> The path (highlighted) should be specified based on the location of the file on your system. The **stock.csv** file can be found here: https://packt.live/2YK0XB2.

The partial output is as follows:

```
array([('MMM', 100), ('AOS', 101), ('ABT', 102), ('ABBV', 103),
       ('ACN', 104), ('ATVI', 105), ('AYI', 106), ('ADBE', 107),
       ('AAP', 108), ('AMD', 109), ('AES', 110), ('AET', 111),
       ('AMG', 112), ('AFL', 113), ('A', 114), ('APD', 115),
       ('AKAM', 116), ('ALK', 117), ('ALB', 118), ('ARE', 119),
       ('ALXN', 120), ('ALGN', 121), ('ALLE', 122), ('AGN', 123),
       ('ADS', 124), ('LNT', 125), ('ALL', 126), ('GOOGL', 127),
       ('GOOG', 128), ('MO', 129), ('AMZN', 130), ('AEE', 131),
       ('AAL', 132), ('AEP', 133), ('AXP', 134), ('AIG', 135),
       ('AMT', 136), ('AWK', 137), ('AMP', 138), ('ABC', 139),
       ('AME', 140), ('AMGN', 141), ('APH', 142), ('APC', 143),
       ('ADI', 144), ('ANDV', 145), ('ANSS', 146), ('ANTM', 147),
       ('AON', 148)], dtype=[('Symbol', '<U5'), ('Price', '<i8')])
```

9. Use the **type** function to check the type of **data**:

```
type(data)
```

The output is as follows:

```
numpy.ndarray
```

As we can see, the data variable is also a **NumPy** array.

> **NOTE**
>
> To access the source code for this specific section, please refer to https://packt.live/2Y9pTTx.
>
> You can also run this example online at https://packt.live/2URNcPz.

From this exercise, we can observe that the **NumPy** array is different from the regular list object. The most important point to keep in mind is that **NumPy** arrays do not have the same methods as lists and that they are essentially designed for mathematical functions.

NumPy arrays are like mathematical objects – **vectors**. They are built for element-wise operations, that is, when we add two **NumPy** arrays, we add the first element of the first array to the first element of the second array – there is an element-to-element correspondence in this operation. This is in contrast to Python lists, where the elements are simply appended and there is no element-to-element relation. This is the real power of a NumPy array: they can be treated just like mathematical vectors.

A vector is a collection of numbers that can represent, for example, the coordinates of points in a three-dimensional space or the color of numbers (RGB) in a picture. Naturally, relative order is important for such a collection and as we discussed previously, a **NumPy** array can maintain such order relationships. That's why they are perfectly suitable to use in numerical computations.

With this knowledge, we're going to perform the addition operation on **NumPy** arrays in the next exercise.

EXERCISE 3.02: ADDING TWO NUMPY ARRAYS

This simple exercise will demonstrate the addition of two **NumPy** arrays using the **+** notation, and thereby show the key difference between a regular Python list/array and a **NumPy** array. Let's perform the following steps:

1. Import the **NumPy** library:

```
import numpy as np
```

2. Declare a Python list called **list_1** and a **NumPy** array:

```
list_1 = [1,2,3]
array_1 = np.array(list_1)
```

3. Use the **+** notation to concatenate two **list_1** objects and save the results in **list_2**:

```
list_2 = list_1 + list_1
list_2
```

The output is as follows:

```
[1, 2, 3, 1, 2, 3]
```

4. Use the same **+** notation to concatenate two **array_1** objects and save the result in **array_2**:

```
array_2 = array_1 + array_1
array_2
```

The output is as follows:

```
[2 ,4, 6]
```

5. Load a **.csv** file and concatenate it with itself:

```
data = np.genfromtxt('../datasets/numbers.csv', \
                      delimiter=',', names=True)
data = data.astype('float64')
data + data
```

> **NOTE**
>
> The path (highlighted) should be specified based on the location of the file on your system. The **.csv** file that will be used is **numbers.csv**; this can be found at: https://packt.live/30Om2wC.

The output is as follows:

```
array([202., 204., 206., 208., 210., 212., 214., 216., 218.,
       220., 222., 224., 226., 228., 230., 232., 234., 236.,
       238., 240., 242., 244., 246., 248., 250., 252., 254.,
       256., 258., 260., 262., 264., 266., 268., 270., 272.,
       274., 276., 278., 280., 282., 284., 286., 288., 290.,
       292., 294., 296.])
```

Did you notice the difference? The first **print** shows a list with **6** elements, [**1, 2, 3, 1, 2, 3**], but the second **print** shows another **NumPy** array (or vector) with the elements [**2, 4, 6**], which are just the sum of the individual elements of **array_1**. As we discussed earlier, **NumPy** arrays are perfectly designed to perform element-wise operations since there is element-to-element correspondence.

> **NOTE**
>
> To access the source code for this specific section, please refer to https://packt.live/3fyvSqF.
>
> You can also run this example online at https://packt.live/3fvUDnf

NumPy arrays even support element-wise exponentiation. For example, suppose there are two arrays – the elements of the first array will be raised to the power of the elements in the second array.

In the following exercise, we will try out some mathematical operations on **NumPy** arrays.

EXERCISE 3.03: MATHEMATICAL OPERATIONS ON NUMPY ARRAYS

In this exercise, we'll generate a **NumPy** array with the values extracted from a **.csv** file. We'll be using the multiplication and division operators on the generated **NumPy** array. Let's go through the following steps:

> **NOTE**
>
> The **.csv** file that will be used is **numbers.csv**; this can be found at: https://packt.live/30Om2wC.

1. Import the **NumPy** library and create a **NumPy** array from the `.csv` file:

```
import numpy as np
data = np.genfromtxt('../datasets/numbers.csv', \
                     delimiter=',', names=True)
data = data.astype('float64')
data
```

> **NOTE**
>
> Don't forget to change the path (highlighted) based on the location of the file on your system.

The output is as follows:

```
array([101., 102., 103., 104., 105., 106., 107., 108., 109.,
       110., 111., 112., 113., 114., 115., 116., 117., 118.,
       119., 120., 121., 122., 123., 124., 125., 126., 127.,
       128., 129., 130., 131., 132., 133., 134., 135., 136.,
       137., 138., 139., 140., 141., 142., 143., 144., 145.,
       146., 147., 148.])
```

2. Multiply **45** by every element in the array:

```
data * 45
```

The output is as follows:

```
array([4545., 4590., 4635., 4680., 4725., 4770., 4815., 4860.,
       4905., 4950., 4995., 5040., 5085., 5130., 5175., 5220.,
       5265., 5310., 5355., 5400., 5445., 5490., 5535., 5580.,
       5625., 5670., 5715., 5760., 5805., 5850., 5895., 5940.,
       5985., 6030., 6075., 6120., 6165., 6210., 6255., 6300.,
       6345., 6390., 6435., 6480., 6525., 6570., 6615., 6660.])
```

3. Divide the array by **67.7**:

```
data / 67.7
```

The output is as follows:

```
array([1.49187592, 1.50664697, 1.52141802, 1.53618907,
       1.55096012, 1.56573117, 1.58050222, 1.59527326,
       1.61004431, 1.62481536, 1.63958641, 1.65435746,
       1.66912851, 1.68389956, 1.69867061, 1.71344165,
       1.7282127 , 1.74298375, 1.7577548 , 1.77252585,
       1.7872969 , 1.80206795, 1.816839  , 1.83161004,
       1.84638109, 1.86115214, 1.87592319, 1.89069424,
       1.90546529, 1.92023634, 1.93500739, 1.94977843,
       1.96454948, 1.97932053, 1.99409158, 2.00886263,
       2.02363368, 2.03840473, 2.05317578, 2.06794682,
       2.08271787, 2.09748892, 2.11225997, 2.12703102,
       2.14180207, 2.15657312, 2.17134417, 2.18611521]])
```

4. Raise one array to the second array's power using the following command:

```
list_1 = [1,2,3]
array_1 = np.array(list_1)
print("array_1 raised to the power of array_1: ", \
      array_1**array_1)
```

The output is as follows:

```
array_1 raised to the power of array_1:  [ 1  4 27]
```

Thus, we can observe how NumPy arrays allow element-wise exponentiation.

> **NOTE**
>
> To access the source code for this specific section, please refer to https://packt.live/3hBZMw4.
>
> You can also run this example online at https://packt.live/2N4dE3Y.

In the next section, we'll discuss how to apply advanced mathematical operations to NumPy arrays.

ADVANCED MATHEMATICAL OPERATIONS

Generating numerical arrays is a fairly common task. So far, we have been doing this by creating a Python list object and then converting that into a **NumPy** array. However, we can bypass that and work directly with native NumPy methods. The **arange** function creates a series of numbers based on the minimum and maximum bounds you give and the step size you specify. Another function, **linspace**, creates a series of fixed numbers of the intermediate points between two extremes.

In the next exercise, we are going to create a list and then convert that into a **NumPy** array. We will then show you how to perform some advanced mathematical operations on that array.

EXERCISE 3.04: ADVANCED MATHEMATICAL OPERATIONS ON NUMPY ARRAYS

In this exercise, we'll practice using all the built-in mathematical functions of the **NumPy** library. Here, we are going to be creating a list and converting it into a **NumPy** array. Then, we will perform some advanced mathematical operations on that array. Let's go through the following steps:

> **NOTE**
>
> We're going to use the **numbers.csv** file in this exercise, which can be found here: https://packt.live/30Om2wC.

1. Import the **pandas** library and read from the **numbers.csv** file using **pandas**. Then, convert it into a list:

```
import pandas as pd
df = pd.read_csv("../datasets/numbers.csv")
list_5 = df.values.tolist()
list_5
```

> **NOTE**
>
> Don't forget to change the path (highlighted) based on the location of the file on your system.

The output (partially shown) is as follows:

```
[[101],
 [102],
 [103],
 [104],
 [105],
 [106],
 [107],
 [108],
 [109],
 [110],
```

Figure 3.1: Partial output of the .csv file

2. Convert the list into a **NumPy** array by using the following command:

```
import numpy as np
array_5 = np.array(list_5)
array_5
```

The output (partially shown) is as follows:

```
array([[101],
       [102],
       [103],
       [104],
       [105],
       [106],
       [107],
       [108],
       [109],
       [110],
       [111],
```

Figure 3.2: Partial output of the NumPy array

3. Find the sine value of the array by using the following command:

```
# sine function
np.sin(array_5)
```

The output (partially shown) is as follows:

```
array([[ 0.45202579],
       [ 0.99482679],
       [ 0.62298863],
       [-0.3216224 ],
       [-0.97053528],
       [-0.7271425 ],
       [ 0.18478174],
       [ 0.92681851],
       [ 0.81674261],
```

Figure 3.3: Partial output of the sine value

4. Find the logarithmic value of the array by using the following command:

```
# logarithm
np.log(array_5)
```

The output (partially shown) is as follows:

```
array([[4.61512052],
       [4.62497281],
       [4.63472899],
       [4.6443909 ],
       [4.65396035],
       [4.66343909],
       [4.67282883],
       [4.68213123],
```

Figure 3.4: Partial output of the logarithmic array

5. Find the exponential value of the array by using the following command:

```
# Exponential
np.exp(array_5)
```

The output (partially shown) is as follows:

```
array([[7.30705998e+43],
       [1.98626484e+44],
       [5.39922761e+44],
       [1.46766223e+45],
       [3.98951957e+45],
       [1.08446386e+46],
       [2.94787839e+46],
       [8.01316426e+46],
       [2.17820388e+47],
```

Figure 3.5: Partial output of the exponential array

As we can see, advanced mathematical operations are fairly easy to perform on a **NumPy** array using the built-in methods.

> **NOTE**
>
> To access the source code for this specific section, please refer to https://packt.live/37NIyrf.
>
> You can also run this example online at https://packt.live/3eh0Xz6.

EXERCISE 3.05: GENERATING ARRAYS USING ARANGE AND LINSPACE METHODS

This exercise will demonstrate how we can create a series of numbers using the **arange** method. To make the list linearly spaced, we're going to use the **linspace** method. To do so, let's go through the following steps:

1. Import the **NumPy** library and create a series of numbers using the **arange** method using the following command:

```
import numpy as np
np.arange(5,16)
```

The output is as follows:

```
array([ 5,  6,  7,  8,  9, 10, 11, 12, 13, 14, 15])
```

2. Print numbers using the **arange** function by using the following command:

```
print("Numbers spaced apart by 2: ",\
      np.arange(0,11,2))
print("Numbers spaced apart by a floating point number:   ",\
      np.arange(0,11,2.5))
print("Every 5th number from 30 in reverse order\n",\
      np.arange(30,-1,-5))
```

The output is as follows:

```
Numbers spaced apart by 2: [ 0 2 4 6 8 10]
Numbers spaced apart by a floating point number:
[ 0.  2.5 5.0 7.5 10. ]
Every 5th number from 30 in reverse order
 [30 25 20 15 10  5  0]
```

3. For linearly spaced numbers, we can use the **linspace** method, as follows:

```
print("11 linearly spaced numbers between 1 and 5: ",\
      np.linspace(1,5,11))
```

The output is as follows:

```
11 linearly spaced numbers between 1 and 5:
[1. 1.4 1.8 2.2 2.6 3. 3.4 3.8 4.2 4.6 5. ]
```

As we can see, the **linspace** method helps us in creating linearly spaced elements in an array.

> **NOTE**
>
> To access the source code for this specific section, please refer to https://packt.live/2YOZGsy.
>
> You can also run this example online at https://packt.live/3ddPcYG.

So far, we have only created one-dimensional arrays. Now, let's create some multi-dimensional arrays (such as a matrix in linear algebra).

EXERCISE 3.06: CREATING MULTI-DIMENSIONAL ARRAYS

In this exercise, just like we created the one-dimensional array from a simple flat list, we will create a two-dimensional array from a list of lists.

> **NOTE**
>
> This exercise will use the **numbers2.csv** file, which can be found at https://packt.live/2V8EQTZ.

Let's go through the following steps:

1. Import the necessary Python libraries, load the **numbers2.csv** file, and convert it into a two-dimensional **NumPy** array by using the following commands:

```
import pandas as pd
import numpy as np
df = pd.read_csv("../datasets/numbers2.csv",\
                 header=None)
list_2D = df.values
mat1 = np.array(list_2D)
print("Type/Class of this object:",\
      type(mat1))
print("Here is the matrix\n----------\n",\
      mat1, "\n----------")
```

> **NOTE**
>
> Don't forget to change the path (highlighted) based on the location of the file on your system.

The output is as follows:

```
Type/Class of this object: <class 'numpy.ndarray'>
Here is the matrix
----------
[[1 2 3]
[4 5 6]
[7 8 9]]
----------
```

2. Tuples can be converted into multi-dimensional arrays by using the following code:

```
tuple_2D = np.array([(1.5,2,3), (4,5,6)])
mat_tuple = np.array(tuple_2D)
print (mat_tuple)
```

The output is as follows:

```
[[1.5 2.  3. ]
 [4.  5.  6. ]]
```

Thus, we have created multi-dimensional arrays using Python lists and tuples.

> **NOTE**
>
> To access the source code for this specific section, please refer to https://packt.live/30RjJcc.
>
> You can also run this example online at https://packt.live/30QilBm.

Now, let's determine the dimension, shape, size, and data type of the two-dimensional array.

EXERCISE 3.07: THE DIMENSION, SHAPE, SIZE, AND DATA TYPE OF TWO-DIMENSIONAL ARRAYS

This exercise will demonstrate a few methods that will let you check the dimension, shape, and size of the array.

> **NOTE**
>
> The **numbers2.csv** file can be found at https://packt.live/2V8EQTZ.

Note that if it's a **3x2** matrix, that is, it has **3** rows and **2** columns, then the shape will be (**3,2**), but the size will be **6**, as in **6 = 3x2**. To learn how to find out the dimensions of an array in Python, let's go through the following steps:

1. Import the necessary Python modules and load the **numbers2.csv** file:

```
import pandas as pd
import numpy as np
df = pd.read_csv("../datasets/numbers2.csv",\
                 header=None)
list_2D = df.values
mat1 = np.array(list_2D)
```

> **NOTE**
>
> Don't forget to change the path (highlighted) based on the location of the file on your system.

2. Print the dimension of the matrix using the **ndim** function:

```
print("Dimension of this matrix: ", mat1.ndim,sep='')
```

The output is as follows:

```
Dimension of this matrix: 2
```

3. Print the size using the **size** function:

```
print("Size of this matrix: ", mat1.size,sep='')
```

The output is as follows:

```
Size of this matrix: 9
```

4. Print the shape of the matrix using the **shape** function:

```
print("Shape of this matrix: ", mat1.shape,sep='')
```

The output is as follows:

```
Shape of this matrix: (3, 3)
```

5. Print the dimension type using the **dtype** function:

```
print("Data type of this matrix: ", mat1.dtype,sep='')
```

The output is as follows:

```
Data type of this matrix: int64
```

In this exercise, we looked at the various utility methods available in order to check the dimensions of an array. We used the **dnim**, **shape**, **dtype**, and **size** functions to look at the dimension of the array.

> **NOTE**
>
> To access the source code for this specific section, please refer to https://packt.live/30PVEm1.
>
> You can also run this example online at https://packt.live/3ebSsoG.

Now that we are familiar with basic vector (one-dimensional) and matrix data structures in NumPy, we will be able to create special matrices with ease. Often, you may have to create matrices filled with zeros, ones, random numbers, or ones in a diagonal fashion. An identity matrix is a matrix filled with zeros and ones in a diagonal from left to right.

EXERCISE 3.08: ZEROS, ONES, RANDOM, IDENTITY MATRICES, AND VECTORS

In this exercise, we will be creating a vector of zeros and a matrix of zeros using the **zeros** function of the **NumPy** library. Then, we'll create a matrix of fives using the **ones** function, followed by generating an identity matrix using the **eye** function. We will also work with the **random** function, where we'll create a matrix filled with random values. To do this, let's go through the following steps:

1. Print the vector of zeros by using the following command:

```
import numpy as np
print("Vector of zeros: ",np.zeros(5))
```

The output is as follows:

```
Vector of zeros:  [0. 0. 0. 0. 0.]
```

2. Print the matrix of zeros by using the following command:

```
print("Matrix of zeros: ",np.zeros((3,4)))
```

The output is as follows:

```
Matrix of zeros:   [[0. 0. 0. 0.]
 [0. 0. 0. 0.]
 [0. 0. 0. 0.]]
```

3. Print the matrix of fives by using the following command:

```
print("Matrix of 5's: ",5*np.ones((3,3)))
```

The output is as follows:

```
Matrix of 5's:  [[5. 5. 5.]
 [5. 5. 5.]
 [5. 5. 5.]]
```

4. Print an identity matrix by using the following command:

```
print("Identity matrix of dimension 2:",np.eye(2))
```

The output is as follows:

```
Identity matrix of dimension 2: [[1. 0.]
 [0. 1.]]
```

5. Print an identity matrix with a dimension of **4x4** by using the following command:

```
print("Identity matrix of dimension 4:",np.eye(4))
```

The output is as follows:

```
Identity matrix of dimension 4: [[1. 0. 0. 0.]
 [0. 1. 0. 0.]
 [0. 0. 1. 0.]
 [0. 0. 0. 1.]]
```

6. Print a matrix of random shape using the **randint** function:

```
print("Random matrix of shape(4,3):\n",\
      np.random.randint(low=1,high=10,size=(4,3)))
```

The sample output is as follows:

```
Random matrix of shape (4,3):
 [[6 7 6]
 [5 6 7]
 [5 3 6]
 [2 9 4]]
```

As we can see from the preceding output, a matrix was generated with a random shape.

> **NOTE**
>
> When creating matrices, you need to pass on tuples of integers as arguments. The output is susceptible to change since we have used random numbers.
>
> To access the source code for this specific section, please refer to https://packt.live/2UROs5f.
>
> You can also run this example online at https://packt.live/37J5hV9.

Random number generation is a very useful utility and needs to be mastered for data science/data wrangling tasks. We will look at the topic of random variables and distributions again in the section on statistics and learn how NumPy and pandas have built-in random number and series generation, as well as manipulation functions.

Reshaping an array is a very useful operation for vectors as machine learning algorithms may demand input vectors in various formats for mathematical manipulation. In this section, we will be looking at how reshaping can be done on an array. The opposite of **reshape** is the **ravel** function, which flattens any given array into a one-dimensional array. It is a very useful action in many machine learning and data analytics tasks.

EXERCISE 3.09: RESHAPING, RAVEL, MIN, MAX, AND SORTING

In this exercise, we will generate a random one-dimensional vector of two-digit numbers and then reshape the vector into multi-dimensional vectors. Let's go through the following steps:

1. Create an array of **30** random integers (sampled from **1** to **99**) and reshape it into two different forms using the following code:

```
import numpy as np
a = np.random.randint(1,100,30)
b = a.reshape(2,3,5)
c = a.reshape(6,5)
```

2. Print the shape using the **shape** function by using the following code:

```
print ("Shape of a:", a.shape)
print ("Shape of b:", b.shape)
print ("Shape of c:", c.shape)
```

The output is as follows:

```
Shape of a: (30,)
Shape of b: (2, 3, 5)
Shape of c: (6, 5)
```

3. Print the arrays **a**, **b**, and **c** using the following code:

```
print("\na looks like\n",a)
print("\nb looks like\n",b)
print("\nc looks like\n",c)
```

The sample output is as follows:

```
a looks like
 [ 7 82  9 29 50 50 71 65 33 84 55 78 40 68 50 15 65 55 98
 38 23 75 50 57 32 69 34 59 98 48]

b looks like
 [[[ 7 82  9 29 50]
  [50 71 65 33 84]
  [55 78 40 68 50]]

 [[15 65 55 98 38]
  [23 75 50 57 32]
  [69 34 59 98 48]]]

c looks like
 [[ 7 82  9 29 50]
 [50 71 65 33 84]
 [55 78 40 68 50]
 [15 65 55 98 38]
 [23 75 50 57 32]
 [69 34 59 98 48]]
```

> **NOTE**
>
> **b** is a three-dimensional array – a kind of list of a list of a list. The output is susceptible to change since we have used random numbers.

4. Ravel file **b** using the following code:

```
b_flat = b.ravel()
print(b_flat)
```

The sample output is as follows (the output may be different in each iteration):

```
[ 7 82  9 29 50 50 71 65 33 84 55 78 40 68 50 15 65 55 98 38
 23 75 50 57 32 69 34 59 98 48]
```

> **NOTE**
>
> To access the source code for this specific section, please refer to https://packt.live/2Y6KYh8.
>
> You can also run this example online at https://packt.live/2N4fDFs.

In this exercise, you learned how to use **shape** and **reshape** functions to see and adjust the dimensions of an array. This can be useful in a variety of cases when working with arrays.

Indexing and slicing NumPy arrays is very similar to regular list indexing. We can even go through a vector of elements with a definite step size by providing it as an additional argument in the format (start, step, end). Furthermore, we can pass a list as an argument to select specific elements.

> **NOTE**
>
> In multi-dimensional arrays, you can use two numbers to denote the position of an element. For example, if the element is in the third row and second column, its indices are 2 and 1 (because of Python's zero-based indexing).

EXERCISE 3.10: INDEXING AND SLICING

In this exercise, we will learn how to perform indexing and slicing on one-dimensional and multi-dimensional arrays. To complete this exercise, let's go through the following steps:

1. Create an array of **10** elements and examine its various elements by slicing and indexing the array with slightly different syntaxes. Do this by using the following command:

```
import numpy as np
array_1 = np.arange(0,11)
print("Array:",array_1)
```

The output is as follows:

```
Array: [ 0  1  2  3  4  5  6  7  8  9 10]
```

2. Print the element in the seventh position by using the following command:

```
print("Element at 7th index is:", array_1[7])
```

The output is as follows:

```
Element at 7th index is: 7
```

3. Print the elements between the third and sixth positions by using the following command:

```
print("Elements from 3rd to 5th index are:", array_1[3:6])
```

The output is as follows:

```
Elements from 3rd to 5th index are: [3 4 5]
```

4. Print the elements until the fourth position by using the following command:

```
print("Elements up to 4th index are:", array_1[:4])
```

The output is as follows:

```
Elements up to 4th index are: [0 1 2 3]
```

5. Print the elements backward by using the following command:

```
print("Elements from last backwards are:", array_1[-1::-1])
```

The output is as follows:

```
Elements from last backwards are:  [10  9  8  7  6  5  4  3  2  1  0]
```

6. Print the elements using their backward index, skipping three values, by using the following command:

```
print("3 Elements from last backwards are:", array_1[-1:-6:-2])
```

The output is as follows:

```
3 Elements from last backwards are:  [10  8  6]
```

7. Create a new array called **array_2** by using the following command:

```
array_2 = np.arange(0,21,2)
print("New array:",array_2)
```

The output is as follows:

```
New array: [ 0  2  4  6  8 10 12 14 16 18 20]
```

8. Print the second, fourth, and ninth elements of the array:

```
print("Elements at 2nd, 4th, and 9th index are:", \
      array_2[[2,4,9]])
```

The output is as follows:

```
Elements at 2nd, 4th, and 9th index are: [ 4  8 18]
```

9. Create a multi-dimensional array by using the following command:

```
matrix_1 = np.random.randint(10,100,15).reshape(3,5)
print("Matrix of random 2-digit numbers\n ",matrix_1)
```

The sample output is as follows:

```
Matrix of random 2-digit numbers
  [[21 57 60 24 15]
 [53 20 44 72 68]
 [39 12 99 99 33]]
```

> **NOTE**
>
> The output is susceptible to change since we have used random numbers.

10. Access the values using double bracket indexing by using the following command:

```
print("\nDouble bracket indexing\n")
print("Element in row index 1 and column index 2:", \
      matrix_1[1][2])
```

The sample output is as follows:

```
Double bracket indexing
Element in row index 1 and column index 2: 44
```

11. Access the values using single bracket indexing by using the following command:

```
print("\nSingle bracket with comma indexing\n")
print("Element in row index 1 and column index 2:", \
      matrix_1[1,2])
```

The sample output is as follows:

```
Single bracket with comma indexing
Element in row index 1 and column index 2: 44
```

12. Access the values in a multi-dimensional array using a row or column by using the following command:

```
print("\nRow or column extract\n")
print("Entire row at index 2:", matrix_1[2])
print("Entire column at index 3:", matrix_1[:,3])
```

The sample output is as follows:

```
Row or column extract
Entire row at index 2: [39 12 99 99 33]
Entire column at index 3: [24 72 99]
```

13. Print the matrix with the specified row and column indices by using the following command:

```
print("\nSubsetting sub-matrices\n")
print("Matrix with row indices 1 and 2 and column "\
      "indices 3 and 4\n", matrix_1[1:3,3:5])
```

The sample output is as follows:

```
Subsetting sub-matrices
Matrix with row indices 1 and 2 and column indices 3 and 4
 [[72 68]
 [99 33]]
```

14. Print the matrix with the specified row and column indices by using the following command:

```
print("Matrix with row indices 0 and 1 and column "\
      "indices 1 and 3\n", matrix_1[0:2,[1,3]])
```

The sample output is as follows:

```
Matrix with row indices 0 and 1 and column indices 1 and 3
 [[57 24]
 [20 72]]
```

> **NOTE**
>
> The output is susceptible to change since we have used random numbers.
>
> To access the source code for this specific section, please refer to https://packt.live/3fsxJ00.
>
> You can also run this example online at https://packt.live/3hEDYjh.

In this exercise, we worked with **NumPy** arrays and various ways of subletting them, such as slicing them. When working with arrays, it's very common to deal with them in this way.

CONDITIONAL SUBSETTING

Conditional subsetting is a way to select specific elements based on some numeric condition. It is almost like a shortened version of a SQL query to subset elements. See the following example:

```
matrix_1 = np.array(np.random.randint(10,100,15)).reshape(3,5)
print("Matrix of random 2-digit numbers\n",matrix_1)
print ("\nElements greater than 50\n", matrix_1[matrix_1>50])
```

In the preceding code example, we have created an array with 15 random values between **10–100**. We have applied the **reshape** function. Then, we selected the elements that are less than **50**.

The sample output is as follows (note that the exact output will be different for you as it is random):

```
Matrix of random 2-digit numbers
 [[71 89 66 99 54]
 [28 17 66 35 85]
 [82 35 38 15 47]]
Elements greater than 50
 [71 89 66 99 54 66 85 82]
```

NumPy arrays operate just like mathematical matrices, and the operations are performed element-wise.

Now, let's look at an exercise to understand how we can perform array operations.

EXERCISE 3.11: ARRAY OPERATIONS

In this exercise, we're going to create two matrices (multi-dimensional arrays) with random integers and demonstrate element-wise mathematical operations such as addition, subtraction, multiplication, and division. We can show the exponentiation (raising a number to a certain power) operation by performing the following steps:

> **NOTE**
>
> Due to random number generation, your specific output could be different than what is shown here.

1. Import the **NumPy** library and create two matrices:

```
import numpy as np
matrix_1 = np.random.randint(1,10,9).reshape(3,3)
matrix_2 = np.random.randint(1,10,9).reshape(3,3)
print("\n1st Matrix of random single-digit numbers\n",\
      matrix_1)
print("\n2nd Matrix of random single-digit numbers\n",\
      matrix_2)
```

The sample output is as follows (note that the exact output will be different for you as it is random):

```
1st Matrix of random single-digit numbers
 [[6 5 9]
 [4 7 1]
 [3 2 7]]

2nd Matrix of random single-digit numbers
 [[2 3 1]
 [9 9 9]
 [9 9 6]]
```

2. Perform addition, subtraction, division, and linear combination on the matrices:

```
print("\nAddition\n", matrix_1+matrix_2)
print("\nMultiplication\n", matrix_1*matrix_2)
print("\nDivision\n", matrix_1/matrix_2)
print("\nLinear combination: 3*A - 2*B\n", \
      3*matrix_1-2*matrix_2)
```

The sample output is as follows (note that the exact output will be different for you as it is random):

```
Addition
 [[ 8  8 10]
 [13 16 10]
 [12 11 13]]

Multiplication
 [[12 15  9]
 [36 63  9]
 [27 18 42]]

Division
 [[3.         1.66666667 9.        ]
 [0.44444444 0.77777778 0.11111111]
 [0.33333333 0.22222222 1.16666667]]
```

```
Linear combination: 3*A - 2*B
 [[ 14    9  25]
 [ -6    3 -15]
 [ -9 -12    9]]
```

3. Perform the addition of a scalar, exponential matrix cube, and exponential square root:

```
print("\nAddition of a scalar (100)\n", 100+matrix_1)
print("\nExponentiation, matrix cubed here\n", matrix_1**3)
print("\nExponentiation, square root using 'pow' function\n", \
      pow(matrix_1,0.5))
```

The sample output is as follows (note that the exact output will be different for you as it is random):

```
Addition of a scalar (100)
 [[106 105 109]
 [104 107 101]
 [103 102 107]]

Exponentiation, matrix cubed here
 [[216 125 729]
 [ 64 343    1]
 [ 27    8 343]]

Exponentiation, square root using 'pow' function
 [[2.44948974 2.23606798 3.        ]
 [2.        2.64575131 1.        ]
 [1.73205081 1.41421356 2.64575131]]
```

NOTE

The output is susceptible to change since we have used random numbers.

To access the source code for this specific section, please refer to https://packt.live/3fC1ziH.

You can also run this example online at https://packt.live/3fy6j96.

We have now seen how to work with arrays to perform various mathematical functions, such as scalar addition and matrix cubing.

STACKING ARRAYS

Stacking arrays on top of each other (or side by side) is a useful operation for data wrangling. Stacking is a way to concatenate two NumPy arrays together. Here is the code:

```
a = np.array([[1,2],[3,4]])
b = np.array([[5,6],[7,8]])
print("Matrix a\n",a)
print("Matrix b\n",b)
print("Vertical stacking\n",np.vstack((a,b)))
print("Horizontal stacking\n",np.hstack((a,b)))
```

The output is as follows:

```
Matrix a
 [[1 2]
 [3 4]]
Matrix b
 [[5 6]
 [7 8]]
Vertical stacking
 [[1 2]
 [3 4]
 [5 6]
 [7 8]]
Horizontal stacking
 [[1 2 5 6]
 [3 4 7 8]]
```

NumPy has many other advanced features, mainly related to statistics and linear algebra functions, which are used extensively in machine learning and data science tasks. However, not all of that is directly useful for beginner-level data wrangling, so we won't cover it here.

In the next section, we'll talk about pandas DataFrames.

PANDAS DATAFRAMES

The **pandas** library is a Python package that provides fast, flexible, and expressive data structures that are designed to make working with relational or labeled data both easy and intuitive. It aims to be the fundamental high-level building block for doing practical, real-world data analysis in Python. Additionally, it has the broader goal of becoming the most powerful and flexible open source data analysis/manipulation tool that's available in any language.

The two primary data structures of pandas are Series (one-dimensional) and DataFrames (two-dimensional) and they handle the vast majority of typical use cases. **pandas** is built on top of **NumPy** and is intended to integrate well within a scientific computing environment with many other third-party libraries.

Let's look at a few exercises in order to understand data handling techniques using the **pandas** library.

EXERCISE 3.12: CREATING A PANDAS SERIES

In this exercise, we will learn how to create a **pandas** series object from the data structures that we created previously. If you have imported pandas as pd, then the function to create a series is simply **pd.Series**. Let's go through the following steps:

1. Import the **NumPy** library and initialize the labels, lists, and a dictionary:

```
import numpy as np
labels = ['a','b','c']
my_data = [10,20,30]
array_1 = np.array(my_data)
d = {'a':10,'b':20,'c':30}
```

2. Import **pandas** as **pd** by using the following command:

```
import pandas as pd
```

3. Create a series from the **my_data** list by using the following command:

```
print("\nHolding numerical data\n",'-'*25, sep='')
print(pd.Series(array_1))
```

The output is as follows:

```
Holding numerical data
--------------------------
0  10
1  20
2  30
dtype: int64
```

4. Create a series from the **my_data** list along with the labels as follows:

```
print("\nHolding text labels\n",'-'*20, sep='')
print(pd.Series(labels))
```

The output is as follows:

```
Holding text labels
--------------------
0    a
1    b
2    c
dtype: object
```

5. Then, create a series from the **NumPy** array, as follows:

```
print("\nHolding functions\n",'-'*20, sep='')
print(pd.Series(data=[sum,print,len]))
```

The output is as follows:

```
Holding functions
--------------------
0    <built-in function sum>
1    <built-in function print>
2    <built-in function len>
dtype: object
```

6. Create a series from the dictionary, as follows:

```
print("\nHolding objects from a dictionary\n",'-'*40, sep='')
print(pd.Series(data=[d.keys, d.items, d.values]))
```

The output is as follows:

```
Holding objects from a dictionary
----------------------------------------
0        <built-in method keys of dict object at 0x7fb8...
1        <built-in method items of dict object at 0x7fb...
2        <built-in method values of dict object at 0x7f...
dtype: object
```

> **NOTE**
>
> You may get a different final output because the system may store the object in the memory differently.
>
> To access the source code for this specific section, please refer to https://packt.live/2BkMJOL.
>
> You can also run this example online at https://packt.live/30XhxzQ.

In this exercise, we created **pandas** series, which are the building blocks of **pandas** DataFrames. The **pandas series** object can hold many types of data, such as integers, objects, floats, doubles, and others. This is the key to constructing a bigger table where multiple series objects are stacked together to create a database-like entity.

EXERCISE 3.13: PANDAS SERIES AND DATA HANDLING

In this exercise, we will create a **pandas** series using the **pd.series** function. Then, we will manipulate the data in the DataFrame using various handling techniques. Perform the following steps:

1. Create a **pandas** series with numerical data by using the following command:

```
import numpy as np
import pandas as pd
labels = ['a','b','c']
my_data = [10,20,30]
array_1 = np.array(my_data)
d = {'a':10,'b':20,'c':30}
print("\nHolding numerical data\n",'-'*25, sep='')
print(pd.Series(array_1))
```

The output is as follows:

```
Holding numerical data
--------------------------
0      10
1      20
2      30
dtype: int32
```

2. Create a **pandas** series with labels by using the following command:

```
print("\nHolding text labels\n",'-'*20, sep='')
print(pd.Series(labels))
```

The output is as follows:

```
Holding text labels
--------------------
0      a
1      b
2      c
dtype: object
```

3. Create a **pandas** series with functions by using the following command:

```
print("\nHolding functions\n",'-'*20, sep='')
print(pd.Series(data=[sum,print,len]))
```

The output is as follows:

```
Holding functions
--------------------
0      <built-in function sum>
1      <built-in function print>
2      <built-in function len>
dtype: object
```

4. Create a **pandas** series with a dictionary by using the following command:

```
print("\nHolding objects from a dictionary\n",'-'*40, sep='')
print(pd.Series(data=[d.keys, d.items, d.values]))
```

The output is as follows:

```
Holding objects from a dictionary
-----------------------------------------
0        <built-in method keys of dict object at 0x0000...
1        <built-in method items of dict object at 0x000...
2        <built-in method values of dict object at 0x00...
dtype: object
```

> **NOTE**
>
> To access the source code for this specific section, please refer to https://packt.live/3hzXRIr.
>
> You can also run this example online at https://packt.live/3endeC9.

In this exercise, we created pandas **series** objects using various types of lists.

EXERCISE 3.14: CREATING PANDAS DATAFRAMES

The **pandas** DataFrame is similar to an Excel table or relational database (SQL) table, which consists of three main components: the data, the index (or rows), and the columns. Under the hood, it is a stack of **pandas** series objects, which are themselves built on top of **NumPy** arrays. So, all of our previous knowledge of NumPy arrays applies here. Let's perform the following steps:

1. Create a simple DataFrame from a two-dimensional matrix of numbers. First, the code draws **20** random integers from the uniform distribution. Then, we need to reshape it into a (**5**, **4**) NumPy array – **5** rows and **4** columns:

```
import numpy as np
import pandas as pd
matrix_data = np.random.randint(1,10,size=20).reshape(5,4)
```

2. Define the rows labels as (**'A'**, **'B'**, **'C'**, **'D'**, **'E'**) and column labels as (**'W'**, **'X'**, **'Y'**, **'Z'**):

```
row_labels = ['A','B','C','D','E']
column_headings = ['W','X','Y','Z']
```

3. Create a DataFrame using **pd.DataFrame**:

```
df = pd.DataFrame(data=matrix_data, index=row_labels, \
                  columns=column_headings)
```

4. Print the DataFrame:

```
print("\nThe data frame looks like\n",'-'*45, sep='')
print(df)
```

The sample output is as follows:

```
The data frame looks like
---------------------------------------------
  W X Y Z
A 4 3 8 9
B 7 8 1 2
C 7 8 1 1
D 7 9 5 7
E 7 6 1 8
```

Figure 3.6: Output of the DataFrame

5. Create a DataFrame from a Python dictionary of the lists of integers by using the following command:

```
d={'a':[10,20],'b':[30,40],'c':[50,60]}
```

6. Pass this dictionary as a data argument to the **pd.DataFrame** function. Pass on a list of rows or indices. Notice how the dictionary keys became the column names and that the values were distributed among multiple rows:

```
df2=pd.DataFrame(data=d,index=['X','Y'])
print(df2)
```

The output is as follows:

```
    a    b    c
X  10   30   50
Y  20   40   60
```

Figure 3.7: Output of DataFrame df2

> **NOTE**
>
> To access the source code for this specific section, please refer to https://packt.live/2UVTz4u.
>
> You can also run this example online at https://packt.live/2CgBkAd.

In this exercise, we created DataFrames manually from scratch, which will allow us to understand DataFrames better.

> **NOTE**
>
> The most common way that you will create a pandas DataFrame will be to read tabular data from a file on your local disk or over the internet – CSV, text, JSON, HTML, Excel, and so on. We will cover some of these in the next chapter.

EXERCISE 3.15: VIEWING A DATAFRAME PARTIALLY

In the previous exercise, we used **print(df)** to print the whole DataFrame. For a large dataset, we would like to print only sections of data. In this exercise, we will read a part of the DataFrame. Let's learn how to do so:

1. Import the **NumPy** library and execute the following code to create a DataFrame with **25** rows. Then, fill it with random numbers:

```
# 25 rows and 4 columns
import numpy as np
import pandas as pd
matrix_data = np.random.randint(1,100,100).reshape(25,4)
column_headings = ['W','X','Y','Z']
df = pd.DataFrame(data=matrix_data,columns=column_headings)
```

2. Run the following code to view only the first five rows of the DataFrame:

```
df.head()
```

The sample output is as follows (note that your output could be different due to randomness):

	W	X	Y	Z
0	70	96	7	77
1	96	73	15	74
2	50	52	61	33
3	62	4	10	37
4	3	54	59	8

Figure 3.8: The first five rows of the DataFrame

By default, **head** shows only five rows. If you want to see any specific number of rows, just pass that as an argument.

3. Print the first eight rows by using the following command:

```
df.head(8)
```

The sample output is as follows:

	W	X	Y	Z
0	70	96	7	77
1	96	73	15	74
2	50	52	61	33
3	62	4	10	37
4	3	54	59	8
5	49	57	41	94
6	21	24	48	23
7	7	2	53	2

Figure 3.9: The first eight rows of the DataFrame

Just like **head** shows the first few rows, **tail** shows the last few rows.

4. Print the DataFrame using the `tail` command, as follows:

```
df.tail(10)
```

The sample output (partially shown) is as follows:

	W	X	Y	Z
17	27	21	88	63
18	58	50	35	66
19	50	77	14	10
20	29	54	68	26
21	13	61	89	84
22	11	37	42	16
23	83	22	12	43
24	13	58	13	27

Figure 3.10: The last few rows of the DataFrame

> **NOTE**
>
> To access the source code for this specific section, please refer to https://packt.live/30UiXLB.
>
> You can also run this example online at https://packt.live/2URYCTz.

In this section, we learned how to view portions of the DataFrame without looking at the whole DataFrame. In the next section, we're going to look at two functionalities: indexing and slicing columns in a DataFrame.

INDEXING AND SLICING COLUMNS

There are two methods for indexing and slicing columns in a DataFrame. They are as follows:

- The **DOT** method
- The **bracket** method

The **DOT** method is good if you want to find a specific element. You will refer to the column after the DOT. An example is `df.column`. The bracket method is intuitive and easy to follow. In this method, you can access the data by the generic name/header of the column.

The following code illustrates these concepts. We can execute them in our Jupyter Notebook:

```
print("\nThe 'X' column\n",'-'*25, sep='')
print(df['X'])
print("\nType of the column: ", type(df['X']), sep='')
print("\nThe 'X' and 'Z' columns indexed by passing a list\n",\
      '-'*55, sep='')
print(df[['X','Z']])
print("\nType of the pair of columns: ", \
      type(df[['X','Z']]), sep='')
```

The output is as follows (a only the partial output is shown here because the actual column is long):

```
The 'X' column
-------------------------
0        60
1        48
2        13
3        33
4         6
5        49
6        43
7        48
```

Figure 3.11: Rows of the 'X' columns

This is the output showing the type of column:

Type of the column: <class 'pandas.core.series.Series'>

Figure 3.12: Type of 'X' column

This is the output showing the X and Z column indexed by passing a list:

```
The 'X' and 'Z' columns indexed by passing a list
---------------------------------------------------
     X    Z
0   60   53
1   48    9
2   13   53
3   33   61
4    6   40
5   49   74
6   43   41
7   48   22
```

Figure 3.13: Rows of the 'Y' columns

This is the output showing the type of the pair of columns:

Type of the pair of columns: <class 'pandas.core.frame.DataFrame'>

Figure 3.14: Type of 'Y' column

> **NOTE**
>
> For more than one column, the object turns into a DataFrame. But for a single column, it is a **pandas** series object.

So far, we have seen how to access the columns of DataFrames using both the DOT method and the bracket method. Dataframes are commonly used for row/column data.

Now, let's look at indexing and slicing rows.

INDEXING AND SLICING ROWS

Indexing and slicing rows in a DataFrame can also be done using the following methods:

- The label-based **loc** method

- The index-based **iloc** method

The **loc** method is intuitive and easy to follow. In this method, you can access the data by the generic name of the row. On the other hand, the **iloc** method allows you to access the rows by their numerical index. This can be very useful for a large table with thousands of rows, especially when you want to iterate over the table in a loop with a numerical counter. The following code illustrates the concepts of **iloc**:

```python
matrix_data = np.random.randint(1,10,size=20).reshape(5,4)
row_labels = ['A','B','C','D','E']
column_headings = ['W','X','Y','Z']

df = pd.DataFrame(data=matrix_data, index=row_labels, \
                  columns=column_headings)

print("\nLabel-based 'loc' method for selecting row(s)\n",\
      '-'*60, sep='')
print("\nSingle row\n")
print(df.loc['C'])
print("\nMultiple rows\n")
print(df.loc[['B','C']])
print("\nIndex position based 'iloc' method for selecting "\
      "row(s)\n", '-'*70, sep='')
print("\nSingle row\n")
print(df.iloc[2])
print("\nMultiple rows\n")
print(df.iloc[[1,2]])
```

The sample output is as follows:

```
Label-based 'loc' method for selecting row(s)
--------------------------------------------------------------

Single row

W    5
X    5
Y    6
Z    8
Name: C, dtype: int32

Multiple rows

   W  X  Y  Z
B  9  4  1  9
C  5  5  6  8

Index position based 'iloc' method for selecting row(s)
--------------------------------------------------------------

Single row

W    5
X    5
Y    6
Z    8
Name: C, dtype: int32

Multiple rows

   W  X  Y  Z
B  9  4  1  9
C  5  5  6  8
```

Figure 3.15: Output of the loc and iloc methods

One of the most common tasks in data wrangling is creating or deleting columns or rows of data from your DataFrame. Sometimes, you want to create a new column based on some mathematical operation or transformation involving the existing columns. This is similar to manipulating database records and inserting a new column based on simple transformations. We'll look at some of these concepts in the upcoming exercises.

EXERCISE 3.16: CREATING AND DELETING A NEW COLUMN OR ROW

In this exercise, we're going to create and delete a new column or a row from the **stock.csv** dataset. We'll also use the **inplace** function to modify the original DataFrame.

> **NOTE**
>
> The **stock.csv** file can be found here: https://packt.live/3hxvPNP.

Let's go through the following steps:

1. Import the necessary Python modules, load the **stocks.csv** file, and create a new column using the following snippet:

```
import pandas as pd
df = pd.read_csv("../datasets/stock.csv")
df.head()
print("\nA column is created by assigning it in relation\n",\
        '-'*75, sep='')
df['New'] = df['Price']+df['Price']
df['New (Sum of X and Z)'] = df['New']+df['Price']
print(df)
```

> **NOTE**
>
> Don't forget to change the path (highlighted) based on the location of the file on your system.

The sample output (partially shown) is as follows:

```
A column is created by assigning it in relation
---------------------------------------------------------
    Symbol  Price  New  New (Sum of X and Z)
0     MMM    100  200                   300
1     AOS    101  202                   303
2     ABT    102  204                   306
3    ABBV    103  206                   309
4     ACN    104  208                   312
5    ATVI    105  210                   315
6     AYI    106  212                   318
7    ADBE    107  214                   321
8     AAP    108  216                   324
9     AMD    109  218                   327
10    AES    110  220                   330
11    AET    111  222                   333
12    AMG    112  224                   336
13    AFL    113  226                   339
14      A    114  228                   342
15    APD    115  230                   345
16   AKAM    116  232                   348
17    ALK    117  234                   351
18    ALB    118  236                   354
```

Figure 3.16: Partial output of the DataFrame

2. Drop a column using the **df.drop** method:

```
print("\nA column is dropped by using df.drop() method\n",\
      '-'*55, sep='')
df = df.drop('New', axis=1) # Notice the axis=1 option
# axis = 0 is default, so one has to change it to 1
print(df)
```

The sample output (partially shown) is as follows:

```
A column is dropped by using df.drop() method
------------------------------------------------------
     Symbol  Price  New (Sum of X and Z)
0       MMM    100                   300
1       AOS    101                   303
2       ABT    102                   306
3      ABBV    103                   309
4       ACN    104                   312
5      ATVI    105                   315
6       AYI    106                   318
7      ADBE    107                   321
8       AAP    108                   324
9       AMD    109                   327
10      AES    110                   330
11      AET    111                   333
12      AMG    112                   336
13      AFL    113                   339
14        A    114                   342
15      APD    115                   345
16     AKAM    116                   348
17      ALK    117                   351
```

Figure 3.17: Partial output of the DataFrame

3. Drop a specific row using the **df.drop** method:

```
df1=df.drop(1)
print("\nA row is dropped by using df.drop method and axis=0\n",\
      '-'*65, sep='')
print(df1)
```

The partial output is as follows:

```
A row is dropped by using df.drop method and axis=0
----------------------------------------------------------
     Symbol   Price   New (Sum of X and Z)
0      MMM     100                  300
2      ABT     102                  306
3      ABBV    103                  309
4      ACN     104                  312
5      ATVI    105                  315
6      AYI     106                  318
7      ADBE    107                  321
8      AAP     108                  324
9      AMD     109                  327
10     AES     110                  330
11     AET     111                  333
12     AMG     112                  336
13     AFL     113                  339
14       A     114                  342
```

Figure 3.18: Partial output of the DataFrame

Dropping methods creates a copy of the DataFrame and does not change the original DataFrame.

4. Change the original DataFrame by setting the **inplace** argument to **True**:

```
print("\nAn in-place change can be done by making ",\
      "inplace=True in the drop method\n",\
      '-'*75, sep='')
df.drop('New (Sum of X and Z)', axis=1, inplace=True)
print(df)
```

The sample output is as follows:

```
An in-place change can be done by making inplace=True in the drop method
--------------------------------------------------------------------------
    Symbol  Price
0      MMM    100
1      AOS    101
2      ABT    102
3     ABBV    103
4      ACN    104
5     ATVI    105
6      AYI    106
7     ADBE    107
8      AAP    108
9      AMD    109
10     AES    110
11     AET    111
12     AMG    112
13     AFL    113
14       A    114
```

Figure 3.19: Partial Output of the DataFrame

> **NOTE**
>
> To access the source code for this specific section, please refer
> to https://packt.live/3frxthU.
>
> You can also run this example online at https://packt.live/2USxJyA.

We have now learned how to modify DataFrames by dropping or adding rows
and columns.

> **NOTE**
>
> All the normal operations are not in-place, that is, they do not impact the
> original DataFrame object and return a copy of the original with addition (or
> deletion) instead. The last bit of the preceding code shows how to make
> a change in the existing DataFrame with the `inplace=True` argument.
> Please note that this change is irreversible and should be used with caution.

STATISTICS AND VISUALIZATION WITH NUMPY AND PANDAS

One of the great advantages of using libraries such as NumPy and pandas is that a plethora of built-in statistical and visualization methods are available, for which we don't have to search for and write new code. Furthermore, most of these subroutines are written using C or Fortran code (and pre-compiled), making them extremely fast to execute.

REFRESHER ON BASIC DESCRIPTIVE STATISTICS

For any data wrangling task, it is quite useful to extract basic descriptive statistics, which should describe the data in ways such as the mean, median, and mode and create some simple visualizations or plots. These plots are often the first step in identifying fundamental patterns as well as oddities (if present) in the data. In any statistical analysis, descriptive statistics is the first step, followed by inferential statistics, which tries to infer the underlying distribution or process that the data might have been generated from. You can imagine that descriptive statistics will inform us of the basic characteristics of the data, while inferential statistics will help us understand not only the data we are working with but alternative data that we might be experimenting with.

Since inferential statistics is intimately coupled with the machine learning/predictive modeling stage of a data science pipeline, descriptive statistics naturally becomes associated with the data wrangling aspect.

There are two broad approaches to descriptive statistical analysis:

- **Graphical techniques**: Bar plots, scatter plots, line charts, box plots, histograms, and so on

- **The calculation of the central tendency and spread**: Mean, median, mode, variance, standard deviation, range, and so on

In this section, we will demonstrate how you can accomplish both of these tasks using Python. Apart from NumPy and pandas, we will need to learn the basics of another great package – `matplotlib` – which is the most powerful and versatile visualization library in Python.

EXERCISE 3.17: INTRODUCTION TO MATPLOTLIB THROUGH A SCATTER PLOT

In this exercise, we will demonstrate the power and simplicity of matplotlib by creating a simple scatter plot from self-created data about the age, weight, and height of a few people. To do so, let's go through the following steps:

1. First, we will define simple lists of the names of people, along with their age, weight (in kgs), and height (in centimeters):

```
people = ['Ann','Brandon','Chen','David','Emily',\
          'Farook','Gagan','Hamish','Imran',\
          'Joseph','Katherine','Lily']
age = [21,12,32,45,37,18,28,52,5,40,48,15]
weight = [55,35,77,68,70,60,72,69,18,65,82,48]
height = [160,135,170,165,173,168,175,159,105,\
          171,155,158]
```

2. Import the most important module from **matplotlib**, called **pyplot**:

```
import matplotlib.pyplot as plt
```

3. Create simple scatter plots of **age** versus **weight**:

```
plt.scatter(age,weight)
plt.show()
```

The output is as follows:

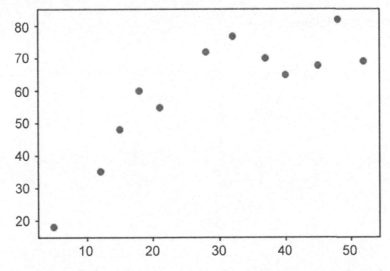

Figure 3.20: A screenshot of a scatter plot containing age and weight

The preceding plot can be improved by enlarging the figure size, customizing the aspect ratio, adding a title with a proper font size, adding x-axis and y-axis labels with a customized font size, adding grid lines, changing the y-axis limit to be between **0** and **100**, adding x and y tick marks, customizing the scatter plot's color, and changing the size of the scatter dots.

4. The code for the improved plot is as follows:

```
plt.figure(figsize=(8,6))
plt.title("Plot of Age vs. Weight (in kgs)",\
          fontsize=20)
plt.xlabel("Age (years)",fontsize=16)
plt.ylabel("Weight (kgs)",fontsize=16)
plt.grid(True)
plt.ylim(0,100)
plt.xticks([i*5 for i in range(12)],fontsize=15)
plt.yticks(fontsize=15)
plt.scatter(x=age,y=weight,c='orange',s=150,\
            edgecolors='k')
plt.text(x=20,y=85,s="Weights after 18-20 years of age",\
          fontsize=15)
plt.vlines(x=20,ymin=0,ymax=80,linestyles='dashed',\
            color=›blue›,lw=3)
plt.legend([‹Weight in kgs›],loc=2,fontsize=12)
plt.show()
```

The output is as follows:

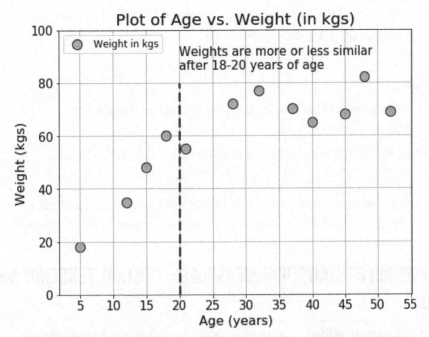

Figure 3.21: A screenshot of a scatter plot showing age versus weight

We can observe the following things:

- A tuple (**8 , 6**) is passed as an argument for the figure size.

- A list comprehension is used inside **xticks** to create a customized list of 5-10-15-...-55.

- A newline (**\n**) character is used inside the **plt.text()** function to break up and distribute the text into two lines.

- The **plt.show()** function is used at the very end. The idea is to keep on adding various graphics properties (font, color, axis limits, text, legend, grid, and so on) until you are satisfied and then show the plot with one function. The plot will not be displayed without this last function call.

The preceding plot is quite self-explanatory. We can observe that the variations in weight are reduced after **18-20** years of age.

> **NOTE**
>
> To access the source code for this specific section, please refer to https://packt.live/3hFzysK.
>
> You can also run this example online at https://packt.live/3eauxWP.

In this exercise, we have gone through the basics of using `matplotlib`, a popular charting function. In the next section, we will look at the definition of statistical measures.

THE DEFINITION OF STATISTICAL MEASURES — CENTRAL TENDENCY AND SPREAD

A measure of central tendency is a single value that attempts to describe a set of data by identifying the central position within that set of data. They are also categorized as summary statistics:

- **Mean**: The mean is the sum of all values divided by the total number of values.

- **Median**: The median is the middle value. It is the value that splits the dataset in half. To find the median, order your data from smallest to largest, and then find the data point that has an equal amount of values above and below it.

- **Mode**: The mode is the value that occurs the most frequently in your dataset. On a bar chart, the mode is the highest bar.

Generally, the mean is a better measure to use for symmetric data while the median is a better measure for data with a skewed (left- or right-heavy) distribution. For categorical data, you have to use the mode:

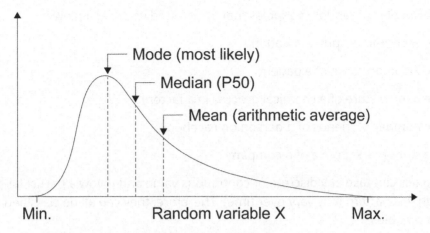

Figure 3.22: A screenshot of a curve showing the mean, median, and mode

The spread of the data is a measure of by how much the values in the dataset are likely to differ from the mean of the values. If all the values are close together, then the spread is low; on the other hand, if some or all of the values differ by a large amount from the mean (and each other), then there is a large spread in the data:

- **Variance**: This is the most common measure of spread. The variance is the average of the squares of the deviations from the mean. Squaring the deviations ensures that negative and positive deviations do not cancel each other out.

- **Standard deviation**: Because variance is produced by squaring the distance from the mean, its unit does not match that of the original data. Standard deviation is a mathematical trick that brings back parity. It is the positive square root of the variance.

RANDOM VARIABLES AND PROBABILITY DISTRIBUTION

A random variable is defined as the value of a given variable that represents the outcome of a statistical experiment or process.

Although it sounds very formal, pretty much everything around us that we can measure can be thought of as a random variable.

The reason behind this is that almost all natural, social, biological, and physical processes are the final outcome of a large number of complex processes, and we cannot know the details of those fundamental processes. All we can do is observe and measure the final outcome.

Typical examples of random variables that are around us are as follows:

- The economic output of a nation

- The blood pressure of a patient

- The temperature of a chemical process in a factory

- The number of friends of a person on Facebook

- The stock market price of a company

These values can take any discrete or continuous value and follow a particular pattern (although this pattern may vary over time). Therefore, they can all be classified as random variables.

WHAT IS A PROBABILITY DISTRIBUTION?

A probability distribution is a mathematical function that tells you the likelihood of a random variable taking each different possible value. In other words, a probability distribution gives the probabilities of the different possible outcomes in a given situation.

Suppose you go to a school and measure the heights of students who have been selected randomly. Height is an example of a random variable here. As you measure height, you can create a distribution of height. This type of distribution is useful when you need to know which outcomes are the most likely to occur (that is, which heights are the most common), the spread of potential values, and the likelihood of different results.

The concepts of central tendency and spread are applicable to a distribution and are used to describe the properties and behavior of a distribution.

Statisticians generally divide all distributions into two broad categories:

- Discrete distributions

- Continuous distributions

DISCRETE DISTRIBUTIONS

Discrete probability functions, also known as probability mass functions, can assume a discrete number of values. For example, coin tosses and counts of events are discrete functions. You can only have heads or tails in a coin toss. Similarly, if you're counting the number of trains that arrive at a station per hour, you can count 11 or 12 trains, but nothing in between.

Some prominent discrete distributions are as follows:

- Binomial distribution to model binary data, such as coin tosses

- Poisson distribution to model count data, such as the count of library book checkouts per hour

- Uniform distribution to model multiple events with the same probability, such as rolling a die

CONTINUOUS DISTRIBUTIONS

Continuous probability functions are also known as probability density functions. You have a continuous distribution if the variable can assume an infinite number of values between any two values. Continuous variables are often measurements on a real number scale, such as height, weight, and temperature.

The most well-known continuous distribution is normal distribution, which is also known as Gaussian distribution or the bell curve. This symmetric distribution fits a wide variety of phenomena, such as human height and IQ scores.

Normal distribution is linked to the famous **68-95-99.7** rule, which describes the percentage of data that falls within 1, 2, or 3 standard deviations away from the mean if the data follows a normal distribution. This means that you can quickly look at some sample data, calculate the mean and standard deviation, and can have confidence (a statistical measure of uncertainty) that any future incoming data will fall within those **68%-95%-99.7%** boundaries. This rule is widely used in industries, medicine, economics, and social science:

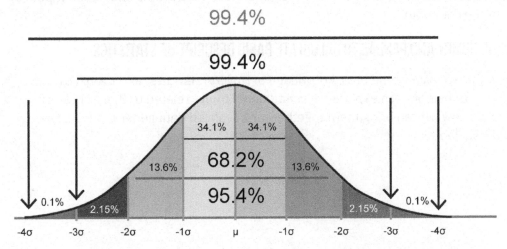

Figure 3.23: Curve showing the normal distribution of the famous 68-95-99.7 rule

DATA WRANGLING IN STATISTICS AND VISUALIZATION

A good data wrangling professional is expected to encounter a dizzying array of diverse data sources each day. As we explained previously, due to a multitude of complex sub-processes and mutual interactions that give rise to such data, they all fall into the category of discrete or continuous random variables.

It would be extremely difficult and confusing for a data wrangler or a data science team if all of this data continued to be treated as completely random without any shape or pattern. A formal statistical basis must be given to such random data streams, and one of the simplest ways to start that process is to measure their descriptive statistics.

Assigning a stream of data to a particular distribution function (or a combination of many distributions) is actually part of inferential statistics. However, inferential statistics starts only when descriptive statistics is done alongside measuring all the important parameters of the pattern of the data.

Therefore, as the front line of a data science pipeline, the process of data wrangling must deal with measuring and quantifying such descriptive statistics of the incoming data. Along with the formatted and cleaned-up data, the primary job of a data wrangler is to hand over these measures (and sometimes accompanying plots) to the next member of the analytics team.

Plotting and visualization also help a data wrangling team in identifying potential outliers and misfits in the incoming data stream and help them take the appropriate action. We will see some examples of such tasks in the next chapter, where we will identify odd data points by creating scatter plots or histograms and either impute or omit the data point.

USING NUMPY AND PANDAS TO CALCULATE BASIC DESCRIPTIVE STATISTICS

Now that we have some basic knowledge of **NumPy**, **pandas**, and `matplotlib` under our belt, we can explore a few additional topics related to these libraries, such as how we can bring them together for advanced data generation, analysis, and visualization.

RANDOM NUMBER GENERATION USING NUMPY

NumPy offers a dizzying array of random number generation utility functions, all of which correspond to various statistical distributions, such as uniform, binomial, Gaussian normal, Beta/Gamma, and chi-square. Most of these functions are extremely useful and appear countless times in advanced statistical data mining and machine learning tasks. Having a solid understanding of these concepts is strongly encouraged for all of you reading this book.

Here, we will discuss three of the most important distributions that may come in handy for data wrangling tasks – **uniform**, **binomial**, and **gaussian normal**. The goal here is to show an example of simple function calls that can generate one or more random numbers/arrays whenever the user needs them.

A **uniform distribution** is a probability distribution that is concerned with events that are equally likely to occur. Let's go through the following exercise to practice uniform distribution with random numbers.

EXERCISE 3.18: GENERATING RANDOM NUMBERS FROM A UNIFORM DISTRIBUTION

In this exercise, we will be generating random numbers from a uniform distribution of numbers from 1-10. Next, we'll generate some artificial data for a customized use case using the **random** function of the **NumPy** library. Let's go through the following steps:

> **NOTE**
>
> The results will be different during each run as we will be working with random numbers.

1. Import the **NumPy** library:

```
import numpy as np
```

2. Generate a random integer between **1** and **10**:

```
x = np.random.randint(1,10)
print(x)
```

The sample output is as follows (your output could be different):

```
1
```

3. Generate a random integer between **1** and **10** but with `size=1` as an argument. This generates a **NumPy** array of size **1**:

```
x = np.random.randint(1,10,size=1)
print(x)
```

The sample output is as follows (your output could be different due to it being randomly drawn):

```
[8]
```

Therefore, we can easily write the code to generate the outcome of a die being thrown (a normal 6-sided die) for **10** trials.

How about moving away from the integers and generating some real numbers? Let's say that we want to generate artificial data for the weights (in kgs) of **20** adults and that we can measure the accurate weights up to two decimal places.

4. Generate decimal data using the following command:

```
x = 50+50*np.random.random(size=15)
x = x.round(decimals=2)
print(x)
```

The sample output is as follows:

```
[56.24 94.67 50.66 94.36 77.37 53.81 61.47 71.13 59.3 65.3 63.02 65.
 58.21 81.21 91.62]
```

We are not only restricted to one-dimensional arrays. We're going to use a multi-dimensional array for the next step.

5. Generate and show a **3x3** matrix with random numbers between **0** and **1**:

```
x = np.random.rand(3,3)
print(x)
```

The sample output is as follows (note that your specific output could be different due to randomness):

```
[[0.99240105 0.9149215  0.04853315]
 [0.8425871  0.11617792 0.77983995]
 [0.82769081 0.57579771 0.11358125]]
```

> **NOTE**
>
> To access the source code for this specific section, please refer to https://packt.live/2YIycEL.
>
> You can also run this example online at https://packt.live/2YHqkDA.

With this exercise, we have a basic idea of how to create random numbers, specifically, random trials on the basis of probability.

A binomial distribution is the probability distribution of getting a specific number of successes in a specific number of trials of an event with a pre-determined chance or probability.

The most obvious example of this is a coin toss. A fair coin may have an equal chance of heads or tails, but an unfair coin may have more chances of the head coming up or vice versa. We can simulate a coin toss using the **NumPy** library. We will look at this in the next exercise.

EXERCISE 3.19: GENERATING RANDOM NUMBERS FROM A BINOMIAL DISTRIBUTION AND BAR PLOT

In this exercise, we're going to generate random numbers from a binomial distribution and create a bar plot based on the generated DataFrame. Let's consider a scenario. Suppose we have a biased coin where the probability of heads is **0.6**. We toss this coin 10 times and take note of the number of heads turning up each time. That is one trial or experiment. Now, we can repeat this experiment (10 coin tosses) any number of times, say 8 times. Each time, we record the number of heads. Let's see how this works using the **NumPy** library:

1. Import the **NumPy** library:

```
import numpy as np
```

2. Let's generate random numbers from a binomial distribution. This experiment can be simulated using the following code:

```
x = np.random.binomial(10,0.6,size=8)
print(x)
```

The sample output is as follows (your specific output will be different due to randomness):

```
[6 6 5 6 5 8 4 5]
```

3. Plot the result using a bar chart:

```
import matplotlib.pyplot as plt
plt.figure(figsize=(7,4))
plt.title("Number of successes in coin toss",\
        fontsize=16)
plt.bar(np.arange(1,9),height=x)
plt.xlabel("Experiment number",fontsize=15)
plt.ylabel("Number of successes",fontsize=15)
plt.show()
```

The sample output is as follows:

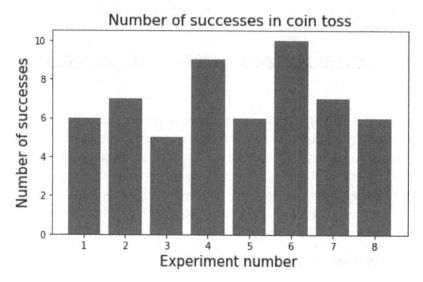

Figure 3.24: A screenshot of a graph showing the binomial distribution and the bar plot

> **NOTE**
>
> The results of the aforementioned plot will vary for you due to the randomness involved.
>
> To access the source code for this specific section, please refer to https://packt.live/3hB2aTQ.
>
> You can also run this example online at https://packt.live/2N6jbaq.

As we can observe from the preceding plot, the bar chart represents the number of successes or number of heads that show up in each draw. We discussed normal distribution previously in this chapter and mentioned that it is the most important probability distribution because many pieces of natural, social, and biological data follow this pattern closely when the number of samples is large. **NumPy** provides an easy way for us to generate random numbers that correspond to this distribution.

EXERCISE 3.20: GENERATING RANDOM NUMBERS FROM A NORMAL DISTRIBUTION AND HISTOGRAMS

This exercise will demonstrate how to generate a few random numbers using normal distribution and histograms. We haven't looked at creating plots with matplotlib and creating a binormal distribution. Creating charts can be a useful skill sometimes with data wrangling, especially when working with machine learning. To do so, let's go through the following steps:

1. Import the **NumPy** library:

```
import numpy as np
```

2. Draw a single sample from a normal distribution by using the following command:

```
x = np.random.normal()
print(x)
```

The sample output is as follows (note that your specific output could be different due to randomness):

```
-1.2423774071573694
```

We know that normal distribution is characterized by two parameters – mean (μ) and standard deviation (σ). In fact, the default values for this particular function are $\mu = 0.0$ and $\sigma = 1.0$.

Suppose we know that the heights of the teenage (12-16 years old) students in a particular school are distributed normally with a mean height of 155 cm and a standard deviation of 10 cm.

3. Generate a histogram of 100 students by using the following command:

```
import matplotlib.pyplot as plt
# Code to generate the 100 samples (heights)
heights = np.random.normal(loc=155,scale=10,size=100)
# Plotting code
```

```
#-----------------------
plt.figure(figsize=(7,5))
plt.hist(heights,color='orange',edgecolor='k')
plt.title("Histogram of teenaged students' height",\
          fontsize=18)
plt.xlabel("Height in cm",fontsize=15)
plt.xticks(fontsize=15)
plt.yticks(fontsize=15)
plt.show()
```

The sample output is as follows:

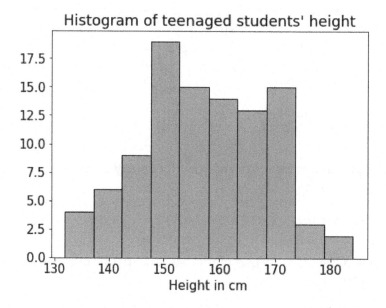

Figure 3.25: Histogram of teenage students' heights

Note the use of the loc parameter for the mean (**=155**) and the scale parameter for standard deviation (**=10**). The **size** parameter is set to 100 for that sample's generation.

> **NOTE**
>
> To access the source code for this specific section, please refer to https://packt.live/2YHIODP.
>
> You can also run this example online at https://packt.live/3hvJrsR.

EXERCISE 3.21: CALCULATING DESCRIPTIVE STATISTICS FROM A DATAFRAME

In this exercise, we will be calculating the basic statistics of a generated DataFrame. DataFrames and statistics are commonly used together and will be a useful tool to acquire. We will define the age, weight, and height parameters and put that data in a DataFrame to calculate various descriptive statistics about them by using the **describe** method. Let's perform the following steps:

> **NOTE**
>
> The best part of working with a **pandas** DataFrame is that it has a built-in utility function to show all of these descriptive statistics with a single line of code.

1. Construct a dictionary with the available series data by using the following command:

```
import numpy as np
import pandas as pd
people = ['Ann','Brandon','Chen',\
          'David','Emily','Farook',\
          'Gagan','Hamish','Imran',\
          'Joseph','Katherine','Lily']
age = [21,12,32,45,37,18,28,52,5,40,48,15]
weight = [55,35,77,68,70,60,72,69,18,65,82,48]
height = [160,135,170,165,173,168,175,159,105,171,155,158]
people_dict={'People':people,'Age':age,\
             'Weight':weight,'Height':height}
people_df=pd.DataFrame(data=people_dict)
people_df
```

The output is as follows:

	People	Age	Weight	Height
0	Ann	21	55	160
1	Brandon	12	35	135
2	Chen	32	77	170
3	David	45	68	165
4	Emily	37	70	173
5	Farook	18	60	168
6	Gagan	28	72	175
7	Hamish	52	69	159
8	Imran	5	18	105
9	Joseph	40	65	171
10	Katherine	48	82	155
11	Lily	15	48	158

Figure 3.26: Output of the created dictionary

2. Find the number of rows and columns of the DataFrame by executing the following command:

```
print(people_df.shape)
```

The output is as follows:

```
(12, 4)
```

3. Obtain a simple count (any column can be used for this purpose) by executing the following command:

```
print(people_df['Age'].count())
```

The output is as follows:

```
12
```

4. Calculate the sum total of age by using the following command:

```
print(people_df['Age'].sum())
```

The output is as follows:

```
353
```

5. Calculate the mean age by using the following command:

```
print(people_df['Age'].mean())
```

The output is as follows:

```
29.416666666666668
```

6. Calculate the median weight by using the following command:

```
print(people_df['Weight'].median())
```

The output is as follows:

```
66.5
```

7. Calculate the maximum height by using the following command:

```
print(people_df['Height'].max())
```

The output is as follows:

```
175
```

8. Calculate the standard deviation of the weights by using the following command:

```
print(people_df['Weight'].std())
```

The output is as follows:

```
18.45120510148239
```

Note how we are calling the statistical functions directly from a DataFrame object.

9. To calculate percentile, we can call a function from **NumPy** and pass on a particular column (a **pandas** series). For example, to calculate the 75th and 25th percentiles of age distribution and their difference (called the interquartile range), use the following code:

```
pcnt_75 = np.percentile(people_df['Age'],75)
pcnt_25 = np.percentile(people_df['Age'],25)
print("Inter-quartile range: ",pcnt_75-pcnt_25)
```

The output is as follows:

```
Inter-quartile range:  24.0
```

10. Use the **describe** command to find a detailed description of the DataFrame:

```
print(people_df.describe())
```

The output is as follows:

```
              Age       Weight        Height
count   12.000000    12.000000     12.000000
mean    29.416667    59.916667    157.833333
std     15.329463    18.451205     19.834925
min      5.000000    18.000000    105.000000
25%     17.250000    53.250000    157.250000
50%     30.000000    66.500000    162.500000
75%     41.250000    70.500000    170.250000
max     52.000000    82.000000    175.000000
```

Figure 3.27: Output of the DataFrame using the describe method

We have now seen how to manipulate DataFrames, which are the cornerstones of data wrangling.

> **NOTE**
>
> This function only works on columns where numeric data is present. It has no impact on non-numeric columns, for example, people in this DataFrame.
>
> To access the source code for this specific section, please refer to https://packt.live/30S3agm.
>
> You can also run this example online at https://packt.live/2YHBFDF.

EXERCISE 3.22: BUILT-IN PLOTTING UTILITIES

In this exercise, we will be going through the basic built-in plotting utilities in the **matplotlib** library and creating useful plots using numeric data from a DataFrame. We will use the **people** DataFrame that we referenced in *Exercise 3.21, Calculating Descriptive Statistics from a DataFrame* and generate plots to visually represent the data. To do so, let's go through the following steps:

1. Import the necessary libraries:

```
import matplotlib.pyplot as plt
import pandas as pd
```

2. Create the **people** DataFrame:

```
people = ['Ann','Brandon','Chen',\
          'David','Emily','Farook',\
          'Gagan','Hamish','Imran',\
          'Joseph','Katherine','Lily']
age = [21,12,32,45,37,18,28,52,5,40,48,15]
weight = [55,35,77,68,70,60,72,69,18,65,82,48]
height = [160,135,170,165,173,168,175,159,105,\
          171,155,158]
people_dict={'People':people,'Age':age,\
             'Weight':weight,'Height':height}
people_df=pd.DataFrame(data=people_dict)
```

3. Find the histogram of the weights by using the **hist** function:

```
people_df['Weight'].hist()
plt.show()
```

The output is as follows:

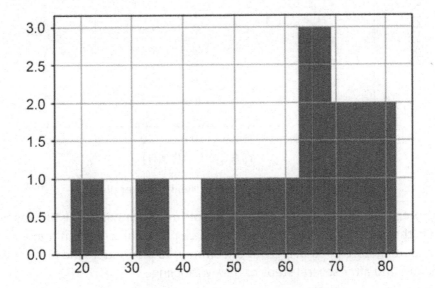

Figure 3.28: Histogram of the weights

From the preceding histogram, we can determine that there are more people that weigh **65** kg than in any other group. If this wasn't generated from random numbers, then this might be a useful observation.

4. Create a simple scatter plot directly from the DataFrame to plot the relationship between **weight** and **height** by using the following command:

```
people_df.plot.scatter('Weight','Height',s=150,\
                        c='orange',edgecolor='k')
plt.grid(True)
plt.title("Weight vs. Height scatter plot",fontsize=18)
plt.xlabel("Weight (in kg)",fontsize=15)
plt.ylabel("Height (in cm)",fontsize=15)
plt.show()
```

The output is as follows:

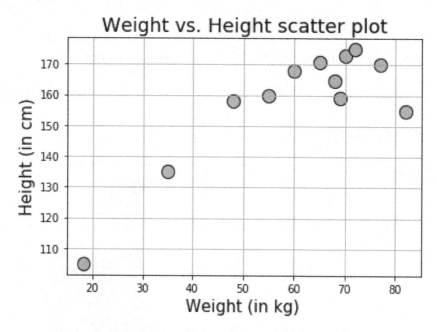

Figure 3.29: Weight versus Height scatter plot

From the preceding plot, we can infer that people in the range of 160-180cms have a weight in the range of 60-80kgs. Charts can be a powerful tool when trying to understand the nature of data. It is not uncommon to plot data in the form of various charts before and after several steps of data wrangling.

> **NOTE**
>
> You can try regular **matplotlib** methods around this function call to make your plot pretty.

With all this knowledge, let's try our hand at an activity.

ACTIVITY 3.01: GENERATING STATISTICS FROM A CSV FILE

Suppose you are working with the Boston Housing price dataset. This dataset is famous in the machine learning community. Many regression problems can be formulated, and machine learning algorithms can be run on this dataset. You will perform a basic data wrangling activity (including plotting some trends) on this dataset (**.csv** file) by reading it as a **pandas** DataFrame. We will perform a few statistical operations on this DataFrame.

> **NOTE**
>
> The Boston Housing dataset can be found here: https://packt.live/2ZPdvc2. The **pandas** function for reading a CSV file is **read_csv**.

These steps will help you complete this activity:

1. Load the necessary libraries.

2. Read in the Boston Housing dataset (given as a **.csv** file) from the local directory.

3. Check the first **10** records. Find the total number of records.

4. Create a smaller DataFrame with columns that do not include **CHAS, NOX, B,** and **LSTAT**:

   Chas: Charlse River Dummy variable

   Nox: Nitric Oxide concentration

   B: Proportion of the population that is African American

   LSTAT: Percentage of lower-income population

5. Check the last seven records of the new DataFrame you just created.

6. Plot the histograms of all the variables (columns) in the new DataFrame.

7. Plot them all at once using a for loop. Try to add a unique title to the plot.

8. Create a scatter plot of crime rate versus price.

9. Plot `log10(crime)` versus `price`.

10. Calculate some useful statistics, such as mean rooms per dwelling, median age, mean distances to five Boston employment centers, and the percentage of houses with a low price (< `$20,000`).

    Hint: To calculate the percentage of houses below $20,000, create a **pandas** series with the **PRICE** column and directly compare it with **20**. You can do this because **pandas** series is basically a **NumPy** array and you have seen how to filter NumPy array in the exercises in this chapter.

The output should be as follows:

Mean rooms per dwelling: **6.284634387351788**

Median age: **77.5**

Mean distances to five Boston employment centers: **3.795042687747034**

Percentage of houses with a low price (<$20,000): **41.50197628458498**

> **NOTE**
>
> The solution to this activity can be found on page 462.

SUMMARY

In this chapter, we started with the basics of **NumPy** arrays, including how to create them and their essential properties. We discussed and showed how a **NumPy** array is optimized for vectorized element-wise operations and differs from a regular Python list. Then, we moved on to practicing various operations on **NumPy** arrays such as indexing, slicing, filtering, and reshaping. We also covered special one-dimensional and two-dimensional arrays, such as zeros, ones, identity matrices, and random arrays.

In the second major topic of this chapter, we started with **pandas** series objects and quickly moved on to a critically important object – **pandas** DataFrames. They are analogous to Excel or Matlab or a database tab, but with many useful properties for data wrangling. We demonstrated some basic operations on DataFrames, such as indexing, sub-setting, row and column addition, and deletion.

Next, we covered the basics of plotting with `matplotlib`, the most widely used and popular Python library for visualization. Along with plotting exercises, we touched upon refresher concepts such as descriptive statistics (such as central tendency and measure of spread) and probability distributions (such as uniform, binomial, and normal).

In the next chapter, we will cover more advanced operations that can be used on **pandas** DataFrames that will come in very handy in your journey toward becoming an expert data wrangler.

4

A DEEP DIVE INTO DATA WRANGLING WITH PYTHON

OVERVIEW

This chapter will cover pandas DataFrames in depth, thus teaching you how to perform subsetting, filtering, and grouping on DataFrames. You will be able to apply Boolean filtering and indexing to a DataFrame to choose specific elements from it. Later on in the chapter, you will learn how to perform JOIN operations in pandas that are analogous to the SQL command. By the end of this chapter you will be able to apply imputation techniques to identify missing or corrupted data and choose to drop it.

INTRODUCTION

In the previous chapter, we learned how to use the **pandas**, **numpy**, and **matplotlib** libraries while handling various datatypes. In this chapter, we will learn about several advanced operations involving **pandas** DataFrames and **numpy** arrays. We will be working with several powerful DataFrame operations, including subsetting, filtering grouping, checking uniqueness, and even dealing with missing data, among others. These techniques are extremely useful when working with data in any way. When we want to look at a portion of the data, we must subset, filter, or group the data. **Pandas** contains the functionality to create descriptive statistics of the dataset. These methods will allow us to start shaping our perception of the data. Ideally, when we have a dataset, we want it to be complete, but in reality, there is often missing or corrupt data. This can happen for a variety of reasons that we can't control, such as user error and sensor malfunction. Pandas has built-in functionalities to deal with such kinds of missing data within our dataset.

SUBSETTING, FILTERING, AND GROUPING

One of the most important aspects of data wrangling is to curate the data carefully from the deluge of streaming data that pours into an organization or business entity from various sources. Lots of data is not always a good thing; rather, data needs to be useful and of high quality to be effectively used in downstream activities of a data science pipeline, such as machine learning and predictive model building. Moreover, one data source can be used for multiple purposes, and this often requires different subsets of data to be processed by a data wrangling module. This is then passed on to separate analytics modules.

For example, let's say you are doing data wrangling on US state-level economic output. It is a fairly common scenario that one machine learning model may require data for large and populous states (such as California and Texas), while another model demands processed data for small and sparsely populated states (such as Montana or North Dakota). As the frontline of the data science process, it is the responsibility of the data wrangling module to satisfy the requirements of both these machine learning models. Therefore, as a data wrangling engineer, you have to filter and group data accordingly (based on the population of the state) before processing them and producing separate datasets as the final output for separate machine learning models.

Also, in some cases, data sources may be biased, or the measurement may corrupt the incoming data occasionally. It is a good idea to try to filter only the error-free, good data for downstream modeling. From these examples and discussions, it is clear that filtering and grouping/bucketing data is an essential skill to have for any engineer that's engaged in the task of data wrangling. Let's proceed to learn about a few of these skills with pandas.

EXERCISE 4.01: EXAMINING THE SUPERSTORE SALES DATA IN AN EXCEL FILE

In this exercise, we will read and examine an Excel file called **Sample-Superstore.xls** and will check all the columns to check if they are useful for analysis. We'll use the **drop** method to delete the columns that are unnecessary from the **.xls** file. Then, we'll use the **shape** function to check the number of rows and columns in the dataset.

> **NOTE**
>
> The **superstore** dataset file can be found
> here: https://packt.live/3dcVnMs.

To do so, perform the following steps:

1. To read an Excel file into **pandas**, you will need a small package called **xlrd** to be installed on your system. Use the following code to install the **xlrd** package:

```
!pip install xlrd
```

> **NOTE**
>
> The **!** notation tells the Jupyter Notebook that the cell should be treated as a shell command.

2. Read the Excel file from GitHub into a **pandas** DataFrame using the **read_excel** method in **pandas**:

```
import numpy as np
import pandas as pd
import matplotlib.pyplot as plt
df = pd.read_excel("../datasets/Sample - Superstore.xls")
df.head()
```

> **NOTE**
>
> The highlighted path must be changed based on the location of the file on your system.

The output (partially shown) is as follows:

	Row ID	Order ID	Order Date	Ship Date	Ship Mode	Customer ID	Customer Name	Segment	Country	City	...	Postal Code
0	1	CA-2016-152156	2016-11-08	2016-11-11	Second Class	CG-12520	Claire Gute	Consumer	United States	Henderson	...	42420
1	2	CA-2016-152156	2016-11-08	2016-11-11	Second Class	CG-12520	Claire Gute	Consumer	United States	Henderson	...	42420
2	3	CA-2016-138688	2016-06-12	2016-06-16	Second Class	DV-13045	Darrin Van Huff	Corporate	United States	Los Angeles	...	90036
3	4	US-2015-108966	2015-10-11	2015-10-18	Standard Class	SO-20335	Sean O'Donnell	Consumer	United States	Fort Lauderdale	...	33311
4	5	US-2015-108966	2015-10-11	2015-10-18	Standard Class	SO-20335	Sean O'Donnell	Consumer	United States	Fort Lauderdale	...	33311

Figure 4.1: Partial output of the Excel file in a DataFrame

On examining the file, we can see that the first column, called **Row ID**, is not very useful because we already have a row index on the far left. This is a common occurrence in **pandas** and can be resolved in a few ways, most importantly by removing the **rowid** column.

3. Drop this column altogether from the DataFrame by using the **drop** method:

```
df.drop('Row ID',axis=1,inplace=True)
df.head()
```

The output is as follows:

	Order ID	Order Date	Ship Date	Ship Mode	Customer ID	Customer Name	Segment	Country	City	State	Postal Code	Region	Product ID
0	CA-2016-152156	2016-11-08	2016-11-11	Second Class	CG-12520	Claire Gute	Consumer	United States	Henderson	Kentucky	42420	South	FUR-BO-10001798
1	CA-2016-152156	2016-11-08	2016-11-11	Second Class	CG-12520	Claire Gute	Consumer	United States	Henderson	Kentucky	42420	South	FUR-CH-10000454
2	CA-2016-138688	2016-06-12	2016-06-16	Second Class	DV-13045	Darrin Van Huff	Corporate	United States	Los Angeles	California	90036	West	OFF-LA-10000240
3	US-2015-108966	2015-10-11	2015-10-18	Standard Class	SO-20335	Sean O'Donnell	Consumer	United States	Fort Lauderdale	Florida	33311	South	FUR-TA-10000577
4	US-2015-108966	2015-10-11	2015-10-18	Standard Class	SO-20335	Sean O'Donnell	Consumer	United States	Fort Lauderdale	Florida	33311	South	OFF-ST-10000760

Figure 4.2: Partial output of the Superstore dataset after dropping the 'Row ID' column

4. Check the number of rows and columns in the newly created dataset. We will use the **shape** function here:

```
df.shape
```

The output is as follows:

```
(9994, 20)
```

In this exercise, we can see that the dataset has **9,994** rows and **20** columns. We have now seen that a simple way to remove unwanted columns such as a row count is simple with **pandas**. Think about how hard this would be if, instead of **pandas**, we used a list of dictionaries? We would have to write a loop to remove the **rowid** element from each dictionary in the list. **pandas** makes this functionality simple and easy.

> **NOTE**
>
> To access the source code for this specific section, please refer to https://packt.live/2Y9ZTXW.
>
> You can also run this example online at https://packt.live/2N4dVUO.

In the next section, we'll discuss how to subset a DataFrame.

SUBSETTING THE DATAFRAME

Subsetting involves the extraction of partial data based on specific columns and rows, as per business needs. Let's pretend we are creating a report on our customers at the superstore. Suppose we are interested only in the following information from this dataset: **Customer ID**, **Customer Name**, **City**, **Postal Code**, and **Sales**. For demonstration purposes, let's assume that we are only interested in **5** records – rows **5–9**. We can subset the DataFrame to extract only this much information using a single line of Python code.

We can use the **loc** method to index the **Sample Superstore** dataset by the names of the columns and the indexes of the rows, as shown in the following code:

```
df_subset = df.loc[
    [i for i in range(5,10)],
    ['Customer ID','Customer Name','City','Postal Code','Sales']]
df_subset
```

The output is as follows:

	Customer ID	Customer Name	City	Postal Code	Sales
5	BH-11710	Brosina Hoffman	Los Angeles	90032	48.860
6	BH-11710	Brosina Hoffman	Los Angeles	90032	7.280
7	BH-11710	Brosina Hoffman	Los Angeles	90032	907.152
8	BH-11710	Brosina Hoffman	Los Angeles	90032	18.504
9	BH-11710	Brosina Hoffman	Los Angeles	90032	114.900

Figure 4.3: Partial data of the DataFrame indexed by the names of the columns

We need to pass on two arguments to the **loc** method – one for indicating the rows, and another for indicating the columns. When passing more than one value, you must pass them as a list for a row or column.

For the rows, we have to pass a list, that is, **[5,6,7,8,9]**, but instead of writing that explicitly, we use a list comprehension, that is, **[i for i in range(5,10)]**.

Because the columns we are interested in are not continuous and we cannot just put in a continuous range, we need to pass on a list containing the specific names. So, the second argument is just a simple list with specific column names. The dataset shows the fundamental concepts of the process of **subsetting** a DataFrame based on business requirements.

Let's look at an example use case and practice subsetting a bit more.

AN EXAMPLE USE CASE – DETERMINING STATISTICS ON SALES AND PROFIT

Let's take a look at a typical use case of subsetting. Suppose we want to calculate descriptive statistics (mean, median, standard deviation, and so on) of records **100–199** for sales and profit in the **SuperStore** dataset. The following code shows how subsetting helps us achieve that:

```
df_subset = df.loc[[i for i in range(100,199)],['Sales','Profit']]
df_subset.describe()
```

The output is as follows:

	Sales	Profit
count	99.000000	99.000000
mean	265.451172	0.292294
std	862.991246	171.612906
min	1.788000	-1359.992000
25%	22.688000	1.619800
50%	68.040000	9.688000
75%	177.390000	23.933600
max	8159.952000	585.552000

Figure 4.4: Output of descriptive statistics of data

We simply extract records **100–199** and run the **describe** function on them because we don't want to process all the data. For this particular business question, we are only interested in sales and profit numbers, and therefore we should not take the easy route and run a **describe** function on all the data. For a dataset that's being used in machine learning analysis, the number of rows and columns could often be in the millions, and we don't want to compute anything that is not asked for in the data wrangling task. We always aim to subset the exact data that needs to be processed and run statistical or plotting functions on that partial data. One of the most intuitive ways to try and understand the data is through charting. This can be a critical component of data wrangling.

To better understand sales and profit, let's create a box plot of the data using **matplotlib**:

```
import matplotlib as plt
boxplot = df_subset.boxplot()
```

The output is as follows:

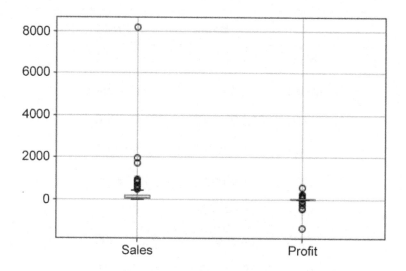

Figure 4.5: Box plot of sales and profit

As we can see from the preceding box plot, there are some outliers for profit. Now, they could be normal outliers, or they could be **NaN** values. At this point, we can't speculate, but this could cause some further analysis to see how we want to treat those outliers in profit. In some cases, outliers are fine, but for some predictive modeling techniques such as regression, outliers can have unwanted effects.

Before continuing further with filtering methods, let's take a quick detour and explore a super useful function called **unique**. As its name suggests, this function is used to scan through the data quickly and extract only the unique values in a column or row.

EXERCISE 4.02: THE UNIQUE FUNCTION

In the superstore sales data, you will notice that there are columns such as **Country**, **State**, and **City**. A natural question will be to ask how many **countries/ states/cities** are present in the dataset. In this exercise, we'll use the **unique** function to find the number of unique **countries/states/cities** in the dataset. Let's go through the following steps:

> **NOTE**
>
> The **superstore** dataset file can be found here:
> https://packt.live/3dcVnMs.

1. Import the necessary libraries and read the file from GitHub by using the **read_excel** method in **pandas** into a DataFrame:

```
import numpy as np
import pandas as pd
import matplotlib.pyplot as plt
df = pd.read_excel("../datasets/Sample - Superstore.xls")
```

> **NOTE**
>
> The highlighted path must be changed based on the location of the file on your system.

2. Extract **countries/states/cities** for which the information is in the database, with one simple line of code, as follows:

```
df['State'].unique()
```

The output is as follows:

```
array(['Kentucky', 'California', 'Florida', 'North Carolina',
       'Washington', 'Texas', 'Wisconsin', 'Utah', 'Nebraska',
       'Pennsylvania', 'Illinois', 'Minnesota', 'Michigan', 'Delaware',
       'Indiana', 'New York', 'Arizona', 'Virginia', 'Tennessee',
       'Alabama', 'South Carolina', 'Oregon', 'Colorado', 'Iowa', 'Ohio',
       'Missouri', 'Oklahoma', 'New Mexico', 'Louisiana', 'Connecticut',
       'New Jersey', 'Massachusetts', 'Georgia', 'Nevada', 'Rhode Island',
       'Mississippi', 'Arkansas', 'Montana', 'New Hampshire', 'Maryland',
       'District of Columbia', 'Kansas', 'Vermont', 'Maine',
       'South Dakota', 'Idaho', 'North Dakota', 'Wyoming',
       'West Virginia'], dtype=object)
```

Figure 4.6: Different states present in the dataset

You will see a list of all the states whose data is present in the dataset.

3. Use the **nunique** method to count the number of unique values in the **State** column, like so:

```
df['State'].nunique()
```

The output is as follows:

```
49
```

This returns **49** for this dataset. So, one out of **50** states in the US does not appear in this dataset. Therefore, we can conclude that there's one repetition in the **State** column.

> **NOTE**
>
> To access the source code for this specific section, please refer to https://packt.live/2NaBkUB.
>
> You can also run this example online at https://packt.live/2N7NHkf.

Similarly, if we run this function on the **Country** column, we get an array with only one element, **United States**. Immediately, we can see that we don't need to keep the country column at all because there is no useful information in that column, except that all the entries are the same. This is how a simple function helped us to decide about dropping a column altogether – that is, removing **9,994** pieces of unnecessary data.

CONDITIONAL SELECTION AND BOOLEAN FILTERING

Often, we don't want to process the whole dataset and would like to select only a partial dataset whose contents satisfy a particular condition. This is probably the most common use case of any data wrangling task. In the context of our **superstore sales** dataset, think of these common questions that may arise from the daily activities of the business analytics team:

- What are the average sales and profit figures in California?

- Which states have the highest and lowest total sales?

- What consumer segment has the most variance in sales/profit?

- Among the top five states in sales, which shipping mode and product category are the most popular choices?

Countless examples can be given where the business analytics team or the executive management wants to glean insight from a particular subset of data that meets certain criteria.

If you have any prior experience with SQL, you will know that these kinds of questions require fairly complex SQL query writing. Remember the **WHERE** clause?

We will show you how to use conditional subsetting and boolean filtering to answer such questions.

First, we need to understand the critical concept of boolean indexing. This process essentially accepts a conditional expression as an argument and returns a dataset of booleans in which the **TRUE** value appears in places where the condition was satisfied. A simple example is shown in the following code. For demonstration purposes, we're subsetting a small dataset of **10** records and **3** columns:

```
df_subset = df.loc[[i for i in range (10)],\
                   ['Ship Mode','State','Sales']]
df_subset
```

The output is as follows:

	Ship Mode	State	Sales
0	Second Class	Kentucky	261.9600
1	Second Class	Kentucky	731.9400
2	Second Class	California	14.6200
3	Standard Class	Florida	957.5775
4	Standard Class	Florida	22.3680
5	Standard Class	California	48.8600
6	Standard Class	California	7.2800
7	Standard Class	California	907.1520
8	Standard Class	California	18.5040
9	Standard Class	California	114.9000

Figure 4.7: Sample dataset

Now, if we just want to know the records with sales higher than **$100**, then we can write the following:

```
df_subset['Sales'] > 100
```

This produces the following **boolean** DataFrame:

	Sales
0	True
1	True
2	False
3	True
4	False
5	False
6	False
7	True
8	False
9	True

Figure 4.8 Records with sales higher than $100

Let's take a look at the **True** and **False** entries in the **Sales** column. The values in the **Ship Mode** and **State** columns were not impacted by this code because the comparison was with a numerical quantity, and the only numeric column in the original DataFrame was **Sales**.

Now, let's see what happens if we pass this **boolean** DataFrame as an index to the original DataFrame:

```
df_subset[df_subset['Sales']>100]
```

The output is as follows:

	Ship Mode	State	Sales
0	Second Class	Kentucky	261.9600
1	Second Class	Kentucky	731.9400
3	Standard Class	Florida	957.5775
7	Standard Class	California	907.1520
9	Standard Class	California	114.9000

Figure 4.9: Results after passing the boolean DataFrame as an index
to the original DataFrame

We are not limited to conditional expressions involving numeric quantities only. Let's try to extract high sales values (**>$100**) for entries that do not involve **California**.

We can write the following code to accomplish this:

```
df_subset[(df_subset['State']!='California') \
         & (df_subset['Sales']>100)]
```

Note the use of a conditional involving string. In this expression, we are joining two conditionals by an **&** operator. Both conditions must be wrapped inside parentheses.

The first conditional expression simply matches the entries in the **State** column to the **California** string and assigns **TRUE/FALSE** accordingly. The second conditional is the same as before. Together, joined by the **&** operator, they extract only those rows for which **State** is *not* **California** and **Sales** is > $100. We get the following result:

	Ship Mode	State	Sales
0	Second Class	Kentucky	261.9600
1	Second Class	Kentucky	731.9400
3	Standard Class	Florida	957.5775

Figure 4.10: Results, where State is not California and Sales, is higher than $100

> **NOTE**
>
> Although, in theory, there is no limit to how complex a conditional you can build using individual expressions and the **& (LOGICAL AND)** and **| (LOGICAL OR)** operators, it is advisable to create intermediate boolean DataFrames with limited conditional expressions and build your final DataFrame step by step. This keeps the code legible and scalable.

In the following exercise, we'll look at a few different methods we can use to manipulate the DataFrame.

EXERCISE 4.03: SETTING AND RESETTING THE INDEX

In this exercise, we will create a pandas DataFrame and set and reset the index. We'll also add a new column and set it as the new index of this DataFrame. To do so, let's go through the following steps:

1. Import the **numpy** library:

```
import numpy as np
```

2. Create the **matrix_data**, **row_labels**, and **column_headings** functions using the following commands:

```
matrix_data = np.matrix('22,66,140;42,70,148;\
                        30,62,125;35,68,160;25,62,152')
row_labels = ['A','B','C','D','E']
column_headings = ['Age', 'Height', 'Weight']
```

3. Import the **pandas** library and then create a DataFrame using the **matrix_data**, **row_labels**, and **column_headings** functions:

```
import pandas as pd
df1 = pd.DataFrame(data=matrix_data,\
                   index=row_labels,\
                   columns=column_headings)
print("\nThe DataFrame\n",'-'*25, sep='')
df1
```

The output is as follows:

```
The DataFrame
-----------------------
```

	Age	Height	Weight
A	22	66	140
B	42	70	148
C	30	62	125
D	35	68	160
E	25	62	152

Figure 4.11: The original DataFrame

4. Reset the index, as follows:

```
print("\nAfter resetting index\n",'-'*35, sep='')
df1.reset_index()
```

The output is as follows:

```
After resetting index
-------------------------------------
```

	index	Age	Height	Weight
0	A	22	66	140
1	B	42	70	148
2	C	30	62	125
3	D	35	68	160
4	E	25	62	152

Figure 4.12: DataFrame after resetting the index

5. Reset the index with **drop** set to **True**, as follows:

```
print("\nAfter resetting index with 'drop' option TRUE\n",\
      '-'*45, sep='')
df1.reset_index(drop=True)
```

The output is as follows:

```
After resetting index with 'drop' option TRUE
---------------------------------------------
```

	Age	Height	Weight
0	22	66	140
1	42	70	148
2	30	62	125
3	35	68	160
4	25	62	152

Figure 4.13: DataFrame after resetting the index with the drop option set to true

6. Add a new column using the following command:

```
print("\nAdding a new column 'Profession'\n",\
      '-'*45, sep='')
df1['Profession'] = "Student Teacher Engineer Doctor Nurse"\
                    .split()
df1
```

The output is as follows:

```
Adding a new column 'Profession'
---------------------------------------------
```

	Age	Height	Weight	Profession
A	22	66	140	Student
B	42	70	148	Teacher
C	30	62	125	Engineer
D	35	68	160	Doctor
E	25	62	152	Nurse

Figure 4.14: DataFrame after adding a new column called Profession

7. Now, set the **Profession** column as an **index** using the following code:

```
print("\nSetting 'Profession' column as index\n",\
    '-'*45, sep='')
df1.set_index('Profession')
```

The output is as follows:

```
Setting 'Profession' column as index
---------------------------------------------
```

	Age	Height	Weight
Profession			
Student	22	66	140
Teacher	42	70	148
Engineer	30	62	125
Doctor	35	68	160
Nurse	25	62	152

Figure 4.15: DataFrame after setting the Profession column as an index

As we can see, the new data was added at the end of the table.

> **NOTE**
>
> To access the source code for this specific section, please refer to https://packt.live/30QknH2.
>
> You can also run this example online at https://packt.live/37CdM4o.

THE GROUPBY METHOD

GroupBy refers to a process involving one or more of the following steps:

- Splitting the data into groups based on some criteria
- Applying a function to each group independently
- Combining the results into a data structure

In many situations, we can split the dataset into groups and do something with those groups. In the apply step, we may wish to do one of the following:

- **Aggregation**: Compute a summary statistic (or statistics) for each group – sum, mean, and so on

- **Transformation**: Perform a group-specific computation and return a like-indexed object – z-transformation or filling missing data with a value

- **Filtration**: Discard a few groups, according to a group-wise computation that evaluates **TRUE** or **FALSE**

There is, of course, a describe method for this **GroupBy** object, which produces the summary statistics in the form of a DataFrame.

> **NOTE**
>
> The name GroupBy should be quite familiar to those who have used a SQL-based tool before.

GroupBy is not limited to a single variable. If you pass on multiple variables (as a list), then you will get a structure essentially similar to a Pivot Table (from Excel). The following exercise shows an example of where we group together all the states and cities from the whole dataset (the snapshot is only a partial view).

EXERCISE 4.04: THE GROUPBY METHOD

In this exercise, we're going to create a subset from a dataset. We will use the **groupBy** object to filter the dataset and calculate the mean of that filtered dataset. To do so, let's go through the following steps:

> **NOTE**
>
> The **superstore** dataset file can be found
> here: https://packt.live/3dcVnMs.

1. Import the necessary Python modules and read the Excel file from GitHub by using the **read_excel** method in **pandas**:

```
import numpy as np
import pandas as pd
```

```
import matplotlib.pyplot as plt
df = pd.read_excel("../datasets/Sample - Superstore.xls")
df.head()
```

The output (partially shown) is as follows:

	Row ID	Order ID	Order Date	Ship Date	Ship Mode	Customer ID	Customer Name	Segment	Country	City	...	Postal Code	Region	Product ID
0	1	CA-2016-152156	2016-11-08	2016-11-11	Second Class	CG-12520	Claire Gute	Consumer	United States	Henderson	...	42420	South	FUR-BO-10001798
1	2	CA-2016-152156	2016-11-08	2016-11-11	Second Class	CG-12520	Claire Gute	Consumer	United States	Henderson	...	42420	South	FUR-CH-10000454
2	3	CA-2016-138688	2016-06-12	2016-06-16	Second Class	DV-13045	Darrin Van Huff	Corporate	United States	Los Angeles	...	90036	West	OFF-LA-10000240
3	4	US-2015-108966	2015-10-11	2015-10-18	Standard Class	SO-20335	Sean O'Donnell	Consumer	United States	Fort Lauderdale	...	33311	South	FUR-TA-10000577
4	5	US-2015-108966	2015-10-11	2015-10-18	Standard Class	SO-20335	Sean O'Donnell	Consumer	United States	Fort Lauderdale	...	33311	South	OFF-ST-10000760

5 rows × 21 columns

Figure 4.16: Partial output of the DataFrame

> **NOTE**
>
> The highlighted path must be changed based on the location of the file on your system.

2. Create a 10-record subset using the following command:

```
df_subset = df.loc[[i for i in range (10)],\
                  ['Ship Mode','State','Sales']]
df_subset
```

The output will be as follows:

	Ship Mode	State	Sales
0	Second Class	Kentucky	261.9600
1	Second Class	Kentucky	731.9400
2	Second Class	California	14.6200
3	Standard Class	Florida	957.5775
4	Standard Class	Florida	22.3680
5	Standard Class	California	48.8600
6	Standard Class	California	7.2800
7	Standard Class	California	907.1520
8	Standard Class	California	18.5040
9	Standard Class	California	114.9000

Figure 4.17: 10-Record Subset

3. Create a **pandas** DataFrame using the **groupby** method, as follows:

```
byState = df_subset.groupby('State')
byState
```

The output will be similar to:

```
<pandas.core.groupby.generic.DataFrameGroupBy object at
0x00000202FB931B08>
```

4. Calculate the mean sales figure by **State** by using the following command:

```
print("\nGrouping by 'State' column and listing mean sales\n",\
        '-'*50, sep='')
byState.mean()
```

The output is as follows:

```
Grouping by 'State' column and listing mean sales
--------------------------------------------------
```

State	Sales
California	185.219333
Florida	489.972750
Kentucky	496.950000

Figure 4.18: Output after grouping the state with the listing mean sales

5. Calculate the total sales figure by **State** by using the following command:

```
print("\nGrouping by 'State' column and listing total "\
      "sum of sales\n", '-'*50, sep='')
byState.sum()
```

The output is as follows:

```
Grouping by 'State' column and listing total sum of sales
--------------------------------------------------
```

State	Sales
California	1111.3160
Florida	979.9455
Kentucky	993.9000

Figure 4.19: The output after grouping the state with the listing sum of sales

6. Subset that DataFrame for a particular state and show the statistics:

```
pd.DataFrame(byState.describe().loc['California'])
```

The output is as follows:

		California
Sales	count	6.000000
	mean	185.219333
	std	355.889307
	min	7.280000
	25%	15.591000
	50%	33.682000
	75%	98.390000
	max	907.152000

Figure 4.20: Checking the statistics of a particular state

7. Perform a similar summarization by using the **Ship Mode** attribute:

```
df_subset.groupby('Ship Mode').describe()\
.loc[['Second Class','Standard Class']]
```

The output will be as follows:

	Sales							
	count	mean	std	min	25%	50%	75%	max
Ship Mode								
Second Class	3.0	336.173333	364.373037	14.62	138.290	261.96	496.950	731.9400
Standard Class	7.0	296.663071	435.947552	7.28	20.436	48.86	511.026	957.5775

Figure 4.21: Checking the sales by summarizing the Ship Mode attribute

8. Display the complete summary statistics of sales by every city in each state – all with two lines of code – by using the following command:

```
byStateCity=df.groupby(['State','City'])
byStateCity.describe()['Sales']
```

The output (partially shown) is as follows:

State	City	count	mean	std	min	25%	50%	75%	max
	Auburn	6.0	294.471667	361.914543	3.760	8.8050	182.030	456.4075	900.080
	Decatur	13.0	259.601538	385.660903	14.940	23.9200	44.950	239.9200	1215.920
Alabama	Florence	5.0	399.470000	796.488863	4.980	7.2700	12.480	152.7600	1819.860
	Hoover	4.0	131.462500	230.646923	7.160	13.3925	20.725	138.7950	477.240
	Huntsville	10.0	248.437000	419.576667	3.620	26.8700	81.920	171.8075	1319.960
...	...	...	...	...	...	...	...	...	...

Figure 4.22: Partial output while checking the summary statistics of sales

Note how **pandas** has grouped the data by **State** first and then by cities under each state.

> **NOTE**
>
> To access the source code for this specific section, please refer to https://packt.live/2Cm9eUI.
>
> You can also run this example online at https://packt.live/3fxK43c.

We now understand how to use **pandas** to group our dataset and then find aggregate values such as the mean sales return of our top employees. We also looked at how pandas will display descriptive statistics about our data for us. Both of these techniques can be used to perform analysis on our superstore data.

DETECTING OUTLIERS AND HANDLING MISSING VALUES

Outlier detection and handling missing values fall under the subtle art of data quality checking. A modeling or data mining process is fundamentally a complex series of computations whose output quality largely depends on the quality and consistency of the input data being fed. The responsibility of maintaining and gatekeeping that quality often falls on the shoulders of a data wrangling team.

Apart from the obvious issue of poor-quality data, missing data can sometimes wreak havoc with the **Machine Learning (ML)** model downstream. A few ML models, such as Bayesian learning, are inherently robust to outliers and missing data, but common techniques such as Decision Trees and Random Forest have an issue with missing data because the fundamental splitting strategy employed by these techniques depends on an individual piece of data and not a cluster. Therefore, it is almost always imperative to impute missing data before handing it over to such an ML model.

Outlier detection is a subtle art. Often, there is no universally agreed definition of an outlier. In a statistical sense, a data point that falls outside a certain range may often be classified as an outlier, but to apply that definition, you need to have a fairly high degree of certainty about the assumption of the nature and parameters of the inherent statistical distribution about the data. It takes a lot of data to build that statistical certainty and even after that, an outlier may not be just unimportant noise but a clue to something deeper. Let's look at an example with some fictitious sales data from an American fast-food chain restaurant. If we want to model the daily sales data as a time series, we will observe an unusual spike in the data somewhere around mid-April:

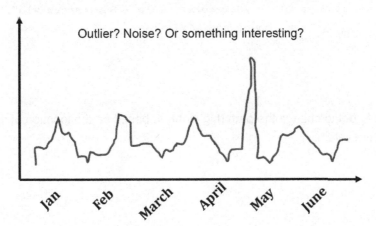

Figure 4.23: Fictitious sales data of an American fast-food chain restaurant

A good data scientist or data wrangler should develop curiosity about this data point rather than just rejecting it just because it falls outside the statistical range. In the actual anecdote, the sales figure spiked that day because of an unusual reason. So, the data was real. But just because it was real does not mean it is useful. In the final goal of building a smoothly varying time series model, this one point should not matter and should be rejected. In this chapter, however, we're going to look at ways of handling outliers instead of rejecting them.

Therefore, the key to outliers is their systematic and timely detection in an incoming stream of millions of data or while reading data from cloud-based storage. In this section, we will quickly go over some basic statistical tests for detecting outliers and some basic imputation techniques for filling up missing data.

MISSING VALUES IN PANDAS

One of the most useful functions for detecting missing values is **isnull**. We'll use this function on a DataFrame called **df_missing** (based on the Superstore DataFrame we are working with), which, as the name suggests, will contain some missing values. You can create this DataFrame using the following command:

```
df_missing=pd.read_excel("../datasets/Sample - Superstore.xls",\
                         sheet_name="Missing")
df_missing
```

> **NOTE**
>
> Don't forget to change the path (highlighted) based on the location of the file on your system.

The output will be as follows:

DataFrame with missing values

	Customer	Product	Sales	Quantity	Discount	Profit
0	Brosina Hoffman	NaN	1706.184	9.0	0.2	85.3092
1	Brosina Hoffman	Phones	911.424	4.0	0.2	68.3568
2	Zuschuss Donatelli	Art	8.560	2.0	0.0	2.4824
3	Zuschuss Donatelli	Phones	NaN	3.0	0.2	16.0110
4	Zuschuss Donatelli	Binders	22.720	4.0	0.2	7.3840
5	Eric Hoffmann	Binders	11.648	NaN	0.2	4.2224
6	Eric Hoffmann	Accessories	90.570	3.0	0.0	11.7741
7	Ruben Ausman	NaN	77.880	2.0	0.0	NaN
8	NaN	Accessories	13.980	2.0	0.0	6.1512
9	Kunst Miller	Binders	25.824	6.0	0.2	9.3612
10	Kunst Miller	Paper	146.730	3.0	0.0	68.9631

Figure 4.24: DataFrame with missing values

We can see that the missing values are denoted by **NaN**. Now let's use the **isnull** function on the same DataFrame and observe the results:

```
df_missing.isnull()
```

The output is as follows:

	Customer	Product	Sales	Quantity	Discount	Profit
0	False	True	False	False	False	False
1	False	False	False	False	False	False
2	False	False	False	False	False	False
3	False	False	True	False	False	False
4	False	False	False	False	False	False
5	False	False	False	True	False	False
6	False	False	False	False	False	False
7	False	True	False	False	False	True
8	True	False	False	False	False	False
9	False	False	False	False	False	False
10	False	False	False	False	False	False

Figure 4.25: Output highlighting the missing values

As you can see, the missing values are indicated by the Boolean value **True**. Now, let's see how we can use the **isnull** function to deliver results that are a bit more user friendly. Here is an example of some very simple code to detect, count, and print out missing values in every column of a DataFrame:

```
for c in df_missing.columns:
    miss = df_missing[c].isnull().sum()
    if miss>0:
        print("{} has {} missing value(s)".format(c,miss))
    else:
        print("{} has NO missing value!".format(c))
```

This code scans every column of the DataFrame, calls the **isnull** function, and sums up the returned object (a **pandas** Series object, in this case) to count the number of missing values. If the missing value is greater than zero, it prints out the message accordingly. The output looks as follows:

```
Customer has 1 missing value(s)
Product has 2 missing value(s)
Sales has 1 missing value(s)
Quantity has 1 missing value(s)
Discount has NO missing value!
Profit has 1 missing value(s)
```

Figure 4.26: Output of counting the missing values

As we can see from the preceding output, the missing values were detected from the **Superstore** dataset.

To handle missing values, you should look for ways not to drop them altogether but to fill them somehow. The **fillna** method is a useful function for performing this task on **pandas** DataFrames. The **fillna** method may work for string data, but not for numerical columns such as sales or profits. So, we should restrict ourselves in regard to this fixed string replacement being used on non-numeric text-based columns only. The **Pad** or **ffill** function is used to fill forward the data, that is, copy it from the preceding data of the series. Forward fill is a technique where the missing value is filled with the previous value. On the other hand, backward fill or **bfill** uses the next value to fill in any missing data. Let's practice this with the following exercise.

EXERCISE 4.05: FILLING IN THE MISSING VALUES USING THE FILLNA METHOD

In this exercise, we are going to perform four techniques in order to deal with the missing values in a dataset.

> **NOTE**
>
> The **superstore** dataset file can be found here: https://packt.live/3dcVnMs.

Firstly, we are going to replace the missing values with static values using the **fillna** method. Then, we will use the **ffill** and **bfill** methods to replace the missing values. Lastly, we will calculate the average of a column and replace the missing value with that. To do so, let's go through the following steps:

1. Import the necessary Python modules and read the Excel file from GitHub by using the **read_excel** method in **pandas**:

```
import numpy as np
import pandas as pd
import matplotlib.pyplot as plt
df_missing = pd.read_excel("../datasets/Sample - Superstore.xls",\
                    sheet_name="Missing")
df_missing.head()
```

> **NOTE**
>
> The highlighted path must be changed based on the location of the file on your system.

The output is as follows:

	Customer	Product	Sales	Quantity	Discount	Profit
0	Brosina Hoffman	NaN	1706.184	9.0	0.2	85.3092
1	Brosina Hoffman	Phones	911.424	4.0	0.2	68.3568
2	Zuschuss Donatelli	Art	8.560	2.0	0.0	2.4824
3	Zuschuss Donatelli	Phones	NaN	3.0	0.2	16.0110
4	Zuschuss Donatelli	Binders	22.720	4.0	0.2	7.3840

Figure 4.27: Snapshot of the dataset

2. Fill in all the missing values with the **FILL** string by using the following command:

```
df_missing.fillna('FILL')
```

The output is as follows:

	Customer	Product	Sales	Quantity	Discount	Profit
0	Brosina Hoffman	FILL	1706.18	9	0.2	85.3092
1	Brosina Hoffman	Phones	911.424	4	0.2	68.3568
2	Zuschuss Donatelli	Art	8.56	2	0.0	2.4824
3	Zuschuss Donatelli	Phones	FILL	3	0.2	16.011
4	Zuschuss Donatelli	Binders	22.72	4	0.2	7.384
5	Eric Hoffmann	Binders	11.648	FILL	0.2	4.2224
6	Eric Hoffmann	Accessories	90.57	3	0.0	11.7741
7	Ruben Ausman	FILL	77.88	2	0.0	FILL
8	FILL	Accessories	13.98	2	0.0	6.1512
9	Kunst Miller	Binders	25.824	6	0.2	9.3612
10	Kunst Miller	Paper	146.73	3	0.0	68.9631

Figure 4.28: Missing values replaced with FILL

3. Fill in the specified columns with the **FILL** string by using the following command:

```
df_missing[['Customer','Product']].fillna('FILL')
```

The output is as follows:

	Customer	Product
0	Brosina Hoffman	FILL
1	Brosina Hoffman	Phones
2	Zuschuss Donatelli	Art
3	Zuschuss Donatelli	Phones
4	Zuschuss Donatelli	Binders
5	Eric Hoffmann	Binders
6	Eric Hoffmann	Accessories
7	Ruben Ausman	FILL
8	FILL	Accessories
9	Kunst Miller	Binders
10	Kunst Miller	Paper

Figure 4.29: Specified columns replaced with FILL

NOTE

In all of these cases, the function works on a copy of the original DataFrame. So, if you want to make the changes permanent, you have to assign the DataFrames that are returned by these functions to the original DataFrame object.

4. Fill in the values using **ffill** or forward fill by using the following command on the **Sales** column:

```
df_missing['Sales'].fillna(method='ffill')
```

The output is as follows:

```
0        1706.184
1         911.424
2           8.560
3           8.560
4          22.720
5          11.648
6          90.570
7          77.880
8          13.980
9          25.824
10        146.730
Name: Sales, dtype: float64
```

Figure 4.30: Sales column using the forward fill

5. Use **bfill** to fill backward, that is, copy from the next data in the series:

```
df_missing['Sales'].fillna(method='bfill')
```

The output is as follows:

```
0        1706.184
1         911.424
2           8.560
3          22.720
4          22.720
5          11.648
6          90.570
7          77.880
8          13.980
9          25.824
10        146.730
Name: Sales, dtype: float64
```

Figure 4.31: Sales column using the backward fill

Let's compare these two series and see what happened in each case:

```
0      1706.184                          0      1706.184
1       911.424                          1       911.424
2         8.560                          2         8.560
3         8.560  ◄── This data was filled  3        22.720  ◄── This data was filled
4        22.720      forward i.e. copying the  4        22.720      backward i.e. copying the
5        11.648         preceding value    5        11.648            next value
6        90.570                          6        90.570
7        77.880                          7        77.880
8        13.980                          8        13.980
9        25.824                          9        25.824
10      146.730                          10      146.730
Name: Sales, dtype: float64           Name: Sales, dtype: float64
```

Figure 4.32: Using forward fill and backward fill to fill in missing data

You can also fill by using a function average of DataFrames. For example, we may want to fill the missing values in **Sales** by the average sales amount.

6. Fill the missing values in **Sales** by the average sales amount:

```
df_missing['Sales'].fillna(df_missing.mean()['Sales'])
```

The output is as follows:

```
0        1706.184
1         911.424
2           8.560
3         301.552
4          22.720
5          11.648
6          90.570
7          77.880
8          13.980
9          25.824
10        146.730
Name: Sales, dtype: float64
```

Figure 4.33: Sales column with average sales amount

The following screenshot shows what happened in the preceding code:

```
0       1706.184
1        911.424
2          8.560
3        301.552  ◄──── This data was filled
4         22.720          by the AVERAGE
5         11.648
6         90.570
7         77.880
8         13.980
9         25.824
10       146.730
Name: Sales, dtype: float64
```

Figure 4.34: Using average to fill in missing data

Here, we can observe that the missing value in the cell was filled by the average sales amount.

> **NOTE**
>
> To access the source code for this specific section, please refer to https://packt.live/2ACDYjp.
>
> You can also run this example online at https://packt.live/2YNZnhh.

With this, we have now seen how to replace missing values within a **pandas** DataFrame using four methods: static value, forward fill, backward fill, and the average. These are the fundamental techniques when cleaning data with missing values.

THE DROPNA METHOD

This function is used to simply drop the rows or columns that contain **NaN** or missing values. However, there is some choice involved.

The following is the syntax of the **dropna()** method:

```
DataFrameName.dropna(axis=0, how='any', \
                     thresh=None, subset=None, \
                     inplace=False)
```

If the **axis** parameter of a **dropna()** method is set to **0**, then rows containing missing values are dropped; if the axis parameter is set to **1**, then columns containing missing values are dropped. These are useful if we don't want to drop a particular row/column if the **NaN** values do not exceed a certain percentage.

Two arguments that are useful for the **dropna()** method are as follows:

- The **how** argument determines if a row or column is removed from a DataFrame when we have at least one **NaN** value or all **NaN** values.

- The **thresh** argument requires that many non-**NaN** values to keep the row/ column.

We'll practice using the **dropna()** method in the following exercise.

EXERCISE 4.06: DROPPING MISSING VALUES WITH DROPNA

In this exercise, we will remove the cells in a dataset that don't contain data.

> **NOTE**
>
> The **superstore** dataset file can be found here: https://packt.live/3dcVnMs.

We are going to use the **dropna** method in order to remove missing cells in a dataset. To do so, let's go through the following steps:

1. Import the necessary Python libraries and read the Excel file from GitHub by using the **read_excel** method in **pandas**:

```
import numpy as np
import pandas as pd
import matplotlib.pyplot as plt
df_missing = pd.read_excel("../datasets/Sample - Superstore.xls",\
                           sheet_name="Missing")
df_missing.head()
```

> **NOTE**
>
> The highlighted path must be changed based on the location of the file on your system.

The output is as follows:

	Customer	Product	Sales	Quantity	Discount	Profit
0	Brosina Hoffman	NaN	1706.184	9.0	0.2	85.3092
1	Brosina Hoffman	Phones	911.424	4.0	0.2	68.3568
2	Zuschuss Donatelli	Art	8.560	2.0	0.0	2.4824
3	Zuschuss Donatelli	Phones	NaN	3.0	0.2	16.0110
4	Zuschuss Donatelli	Binders	22.720	4.0	0.2	7.3840

Figure 4.35: Superstore dataset

> **NOTE**
>
> The outputs you get will vary from the ones shown in this exercise.

2. To set the **axis** parameter to **zero** and drop all missing rows, use the following command:

```
df_missing.dropna(axis=0)
```

The output is as follows:

	Customer	Product	Sales	Quantity	Discount	Profit
1	Brosina Hoffman	Phones	911.424	4.0	0.2	68.3568
2	Zuschuss Donatelli	Art	8.560	2.0	0.0	2.4824
4	Zuschuss Donatelli	Binders	22.720	4.0	0.2	7.3840
6	Eric Hoffmann	Accessories	90.570	3.0	0.0	11.7741
9	Kunst Miller	Binders	25.824	6.0	0.2	9.3612
10	Kunst Miller	Paper	146.730	3.0	0.0	68.9631

Figure 4.36: Dropping all the missing rows

3. To set the **axis** parameter to **1** and drop all missing rows, use the following command:

```
df_missing.dropna(axis=1)
```

The output is as follows:

	Discount
0	0.2
1	0.2
2	0.0
3	0.2
4	0.2
5	0.2
6	0.0
7	0.0
8	0.0
9	0.2
10	0.0

Figure 4.37: Dropping rows or columns to handle missing data

4. Drop the values with **axis** set to **1** and **thresh** set to **10**:

```
df_missing.dropna(axis=1,thresh=10)
```

The output is as follows:

	Customer	Sales	Quantity	Discount	Profit
0	Brosina Hoffman	1706.184	9.0	0.2	85.3092
1	Brosina Hoffman	911.424	4.0	0.2	68.3568
2	Zuschuss Donatelli	8.560	2.0	0.0	2.4824
3	Zuschuss Donatelli	NaN	3.0	0.2	16.0110
4	Zuschuss Donatelli	22.720	4.0	0.2	7.3840
5	Eric Hoffmann	11.648	NaN	0.2	4.2224
6	Eric Hoffmann	90.570	3.0	0.0	11.7741
7	Ruben Ausman	77.880	2.0	0.0	NaN
8	NaN	13.980	2.0	0.0	6.1512
9	Kunst Miller	25.824	6.0	0.2	9.3612
10	Kunst Miller	146.730	3.0	0.0	68.9631

Figure 4.38: DataFrame with values dropped with axis=1 and thresh=10

As you can see, some **NaN** values still exist, but because of the minimum threshold, those rows were kept in place.

> **NOTE**
>
> To access the source code for this specific section, please refer to https://packt.live/2Ybvx7t.
>
> You can also run this example online at https://packt.live/30RNCsY.

In this exercise, we looked at dropping missing values rows and columns. This is a useful technique for a variety of cases, including when working with machine learning. Some machine learning models do not handle missing data well and removing them ahead of time can be best practices.

OUTLIER DETECTION USING A SIMPLE STATISTICAL TEST

As we've already discussed, outliers in a dataset can occur due to many factors and in many ways:

- Data entry errors

- Experimental errors (data extraction related)

- Measurement errors due to noise or instrumental failure

- Data processing errors (data manipulation or mutations due to coding errors)

- Sampling errors (extracting or mixing data from wrong or various sources)

It is impossible to pinpoint one universal method for outlier detection. Here, we will show you some simple tricks for numeric data using standard statistical tests.

Box plots may show unusual values. We can corrupt two sales values by assigning negatives, as follows:

```
df_sample = df[['Customer Name','State','Sales','Profit']]\
                .sample(n=50).copy()
df_sample['Sales'].iloc[5]=-1000.0
df_sample['Sales'].iloc[15]=-500.0
```

To plot the box plot, use the following code:

```
df_sample.plot.box()
plt.title("Boxplot of sales and profit", fontsize=15)
plt.xticks(fontsize=15)
plt.yticks(fontsize=15)
plt.grid(True)
```

The output (which will vary with each run) is as follows:

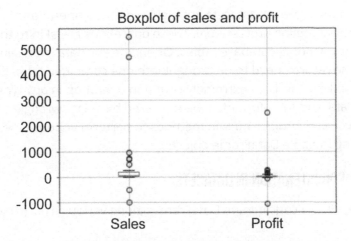

Figure 4.39: Box plot of sales and profit

We can create simple box plots to check for any unusual/nonsensical values. For example, in the preceding example, we intentionally corrupted two sales values so that they were negative, and they were readily caught in a box plot.

Note that profit may be negative, so those negative points are generally not suspicious. But sales cannot be negative in general, so they are detected as outliers.

We can create a distribution of a numerical quantity and check for values that lie at the extreme end to see if they are truly part of the data or outlier. For example, if a distribution is almost normal, then any value more than four or five standard deviations away may be a suspect:

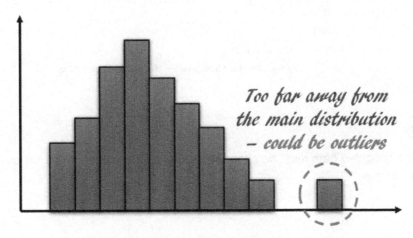

Figure 4.40: Value away from the main outliers

CONCATENATING, MERGING, AND JOINING

Merging and joining tables or datasets are highly common operations in the day-to-day job of a data wrangling professional. These operations are akin to the **JOIN** query in SQL for relational database tables. Often, the key data is present in multiple tables, and those records need to be brought into one combined table that matches on that common key. This is an extremely common operation in any type of sales or transactional data, and therefore must be mastered by a data wrangler. The **pandas** library offers nice and intuitive built-in methods to perform various types of **JOIN** queries involving multiple DataFrame objects.

EXERCISE 4.07: CONCATENATION IN DATASETS

In this exercise, we will concatenate DataFrames along various axes (rows or columns).

> **NOTE**
>
> The **superstore** dataset file can be found
> here: https://packt.live/3dcVnMs.

This is a very useful operation as it allows you to grow a DataFrame as the new data comes in or new feature columns need to be inserted into the table. To do so, let's go through the following steps:

1. Read the Excel file from GitHub by using the **read_excel** method in **pandas**:

```
import numpy as np
import pandas as pd
import matplotlib.pyplot as plt
df = pd.read_excel("../datasets/Sample - Superstore.xls")
df.head()
```

> **NOTE**
>
> The highlighted path must be changed based on the location of the file on
> your system.

The output (partially shown) will be as follows:

	Row ID	Order ID	Order Date	Ship Date	Ship Mode	Customer ID	Customer Name	Segment	Country	City	...	Postal Code	Region	Product ID
0	1	CA-2016-152156	2016-11-08	2016-11-11	Second Class	CG-12520	Claire Gute	Consumer	United States	Henderson	...	42420	South	FUR-BO-10001798
1	2	CA-2016-152156	2016-11-08	2016-11-11	Second Class	CG-12520	Claire Gute	Consumer	United States	Henderson	...	42420	South	FUR-CH-10000454
2	3	CA-2016-138688	2016-06-12	2016-06-16	Second Class	DV-13045	Darrin Van Huff	Corporate	United States	Los Angeles	...	90036	West	OFF-LA-10000240
3	4	US-2015-108966	2015-10-11	2015-10-18	Standard Class	SO-20335	Sean O'Donnell	Consumer	United States	Fort Lauderdale	...	33311	South	FUR-TA-10000577
4	5	US-2015-108966	2015-10-11	2015-10-18	Standard Class	SO-20335	Sean O'Donnell	Consumer	United States	Fort Lauderdale	...	33311	South	OFF-ST-10000760

Figure 4.41: Partial output of the DataFrame

2. Sample **4** records each to create three DataFrames at random from the original sales dataset we are working with:

```
df_1 = df[['Customer Name','State',\
           'Sales','Profit']].sample(n=4)
df_2 = df[['Customer Name','State',\
           'Sales','Profit']].sample(n=4)
df_3 = df[['Customer Name','State',\
           'Sales','Profit']].sample(n=4)
```

3. Create a combined DataFrame with all the rows concatenated by using the following code:

```
df_cat1 = pd.concat([df_1,df_2,df_3], axis=0)
df_cat1
```

The output (partially shown) is as follows:

	Customer Name	State	Sales	Profit
1174	Dave Poirier	New York	50.112	16.2864
2005	Rob Williams	Missouri	29.680	11.5752
1708	Jamie Kunitz	California	7.420	3.7100
1846	Dianna Arnett	District of Columbia	37.680	15.8256
6440	Bart Watters	New York	34.700	12.4920
682	Doug Jacobs	New York	68.600	18.5220
4274	Andrew Gjertsen	Washington	3.592	1.1225
2317	Elizabeth Moffitt	South Dakota	60.830	30.4150
9873	Sara Luxemburg	New York	6.480	3.1104
2247	Justin MacKendrick	California	13.360	6.4128
5178	Bill Tyler	California	37.680	15.8256
9374	Ken Brennan	Washington	61.380	15.9588

Figure 4.42: Partial output after concatenating the DataFrames

As you can see, concatenation will vertically combine multiple DataFrames. You can also try concatenating along the columns, although that does not make any practical sense for this particular example. However, **pandas** fills in the unavailable values with **NaN** for that operation.

> **NOTE**
>
> The outputs you get will vary from the ones shown in this exercise.

4. Create a combined DataFrame with all the columns concatenated by using the following code:

```
df_cat2 = pd.concat([df_1,df_2,df_3], axis=1)
df_cat2
```

The output (partially shown) is as follows:

	Customer Name	State	Sales	Profit	Customer Name	State	Sales	Profit
682	NaN	NaN	NaN	NaN	Doug Jacobs	New York	68.600	18.5220
1174	Dave Poirier	New York	50.112	16.2864	NaN	NaN	NaN	NaN
1708	Jamie Kunitz	California	7.420	3.7100	NaN	NaN	NaN	NaN
1846	Dianna Arnett	District of Columbia	37.680	15.8256	NaN	NaN	NaN	NaN
2005	Rob Williams	Missouri	29.680	11.5752	NaN	NaN	NaN	NaN
2247	NaN	NaN	NaN	NaN	NaN	NaN	NaN	NaN
2317	NaN	NaN	NaN	NaN	Elizabeth Moffitt	South Dakota	60.830	30.4150
4274	NaN	NaN	NaN	NaN	Andrew Gjertsen	Washington	3.592	1.1225
5178	NaN	NaN	NaN	NaN	NaN	NaN	NaN	NaN
6440	NaN	NaN	NaN	NaN	Bart Watters	New York	34.700	12.4920

Figure 4.43: Partial output after concatenating the DataFrames

As we can observe, the cells in the dataset that do not contain any values are replaced with **NaN** values.

> **NOTE**
>
> To access the source code for this specific section, please refer to https://packt.live/3epn5aB.
>
> You can also run this example online at https://packt.live/3edUPrh.

MERGING BY A COMMON KEY

Merging by a common key is an extremely common operation for data tables as it allows you to rationalize multiple sources of data in one master database – that is, if they have some common features/keys.

When joining and merging two DataFrames, we use two separate types: **inner** and **outer {left|right}**. Let's take a look at them:

- **Inner**: A combining method that uses a column or key to be compared on each dataset. Rows that share the same column or key will be present after the join.

- **Outer**: A way to combine datasets such as inner, but all data on the right or left (depending on which is chosen) is kept, and matching data from the opposite side is combined.

This is often the first step in building a large database for machine learning tasks where daily incoming data may be put into separate tables. However, at the end of the day, the most recent table needs to be merged with the master data table so that it can be fed into the backend machine learning server, which will then update the model and its prediction capacity. Merge is a way to combine DataFrames vertically, using a column to compare on. The functionality of merge and join are very similar; their capabilities are the same.

EXERCISE 4.08: MERGING BY A COMMON KEY

In this exercise, we'll create two DataFrames with the `Customer Name` common key from the Superstore dataset. Then, we will use the inner and outer joins to merge or combine these DataFrames. To do so, let's go through the following steps:

> **NOTE**
>
> The Superstore file can be found here: https://packt.live/3dcVnMs.

1. Import the necessary Python libraries and read the Excel file from GitHub by using the **read_excel** method in **pandas**:

```
import numpy as np
import pandas as pd
import matplotlib.pyplot as plt
df = pd.read_excel("../datasets/Sample - Superstore.xls")
df.head()
```

> **NOTE**
>
> The highlighted path must be changed based on the location of the file on your system.

The partial output of the preceding step is as follows:

	Row ID	Order ID	Order Date	Ship Date	Ship Mode	Customer ID	Customer Name	Segment	Country	City	...	Postal Code	Region	Product ID
0	1	CA-2016-152156	2016-11-08	2016-11-11	Second Class	CG-12520	Claire Gute	Consumer	United States	Henderson	...	42420	South	FUR-BO-10001798
1	2	CA-2016-152156	2016-11-08	2016-11-11	Second Class	CG-12520	Claire Gute	Consumer	United States	Henderson	...	42420	South	FUR-CH-10000454
2	3	CA-2016-138688	2016-06-12	2016-06-16	Second Class	DV-13045	Darrin Van Huff	Corporate	United States	Los Angeles	...	90036	West	OFF-LA-10000240
3	4	US-2015-108966	2015-10-11	2015-10-18	Standard Class	SO-20335	Sean O'Donnell	Consumer	United States	Fort Lauderdale	...	33311	South	FUR-TA-10000577
4	5	US-2015-108966	2015-10-11	2015-10-18	Standard Class	SO-20335	Sean O'Donnell	Consumer	United States	Fort Lauderdale	...	33311	South	OFF-ST-10000760

Figure 4.44: Partial output of the Data frame

One DataFrame, **df_1**, will have shipping information associated with the customer name, and another table, **df_2**, will have the product information tabulated.

2. Create the **df1** DataFrame with the **Customer Name** common key:

```
df_1=df[['Ship Date','Ship Mode','Customer Name']][0:4]
df_1
```

The output of the first DataFrame is as follows:

	Ship Date	Ship Mode	Customer Name
0	2016-11-11	Second Class	Claire Gute
1	2016-11-11	Second Class	Claire Gute
2	2016-06-16	Second Class	Darrin Van Huff
3	2015-10-18	Standard Class	Sean O'Donnell

Figure 4.45: Entries in table df_1

3. Create the second DataFrame, **df2**, with the `Customer Name` common key, as follows:

```
df_2=df[['Customer Name','Product Name','Quantity']][0:4]
df_2
```

The output is as follows:

	Customer Name	Product Name	Quantity
0	Claire Gute	Bush Somerset Collection Bookcase	2
1	Claire Gute	Hon Deluxe Fabric Upholstered Stacking Chairs,...	3
2	Darrin Van Huff	Self-Adhesive Address Labels for Typewriters b...	2
3	Sean O'Donnell	Bretford CR4500 Series Slim Rectangular Table	5

Figure 4.46: Entries in table df_2

4. Join these two tables with an inner join by using the following command:

```
pd.merge(df_1,df_2,on='Customer Name',how='inner')
```

The output is as follows:

	Ship Date	Ship Mode	Customer Name	Product Name	Quantity
0	2016-11-11	Second Class	Claire Gute	Bush Somerset Collection Bookcase	2
1	2016-11-11	Second Class	Claire Gute	Hon Deluxe Fabric Upholstered Stacking Chairs,...	3
2	2016-11-11	Second Class	Claire Gute	Bush Somerset Collection Bookcase	2
3	2016-11-11	Second Class	Claire Gute	Hon Deluxe Fabric Upholstered Stacking Chairs,...	3
4	2016-06-16	Second Class	Darrin Van Huff	Self-Adhesive Address Labels for Typewriters b...	2
5	2015-10-18	Standard Class	Sean O'Donnell	Bretford CR4500 Series Slim Rectangular Table	5

Figure 4.47: Inner join on table df_1 and table df_2

5. Drop the duplicates by using the following command:

```
pd.merge(df_1,df_2,on='Customer Name',\
    how='inner').drop_duplicates()
```

The output is as follows:

	Ship Date	Ship Mode	Customer Name	Product Name	Quantity
0	2016-11-11	Second Class	Claire Gute	Bush Somerset Collection Bookcase	2
1	2016-11-11	Second Class	Claire Gute	Hon Deluxe Fabric Upholstered Stacking Chairs,...	3
4	2016-06-16	Second Class	Darrin Van Huff	Self-Adhesive Address Labels for Typewriters b...	2
5	2015-10-18	Standard Class	Sean O'Donnell	Bretford CR4500 Series Slim Rectangular Table	5

Figure 4.48: Inner join on table df_1 and table df_2 after dropping the duplicates

6. Extract another small table called **df_3** to show the concept of an outer join:

```
df_3=df[['Customer Name','Product Name','Quantity']][2:6]
df_3
```

The output is as follows:

	Customer Name	Product Name	Quantity
2	Darrin Van Huff	Self-Adhesive Address Labels for Typewriters b...	2
3	Sean O'Donnell	Bretford CR4500 Series Slim Rectangular Table	5
4	Sean O'Donnell	Eldon Fold 'N Roll Cart System	2
5	Brosina Hoffman	Eldon Expressions Wood and Plastic Desk Access...	7

Figure 4.49: Creating table df_3

7. Perform an inner join on **df_1** and **df_3** by using the following command:

```
pd.merge(df_1,df_3,on='Customer Name',\
         how='inner').drop_duplicates()
```

The output is as follows:

	Ship Date	Ship Mode	Customer Name	Product Name	Quantity
0	2016-06-16	Second Class	Darrin Van Huff	Self-Adhesive Address Labels for Typewriters b...	2
1	2015-10-18	Standard Class	Sean O'Donnell	Bretford CR4500 Series Slim Rectangular Table	5
2	2015-10-18	Standard Class	Sean O'Donnell	Eldon Fold 'N Roll Cart System	2

Figure 4.50: Merging table df_1 and table df_3 and dropping duplicates

8. Perform an outer join on **df_1** and **df_3** by using the following command:

```
pd.merge(df_1,df_3,on='Customer Name',\
         how='outer').drop_duplicates()
```

The output is as follows:

	Ship Date	Ship Mode	Customer Name	Product Name	Quantity
0	2016-11-11	Second Class	Claire Gute	NaN	NaN
2	2016-06-16	Second Class	Darrin Van Huff	Self-Adhesive Address Labels for Typewriters b...	2.0
3	2015-10-18	Standard Class	Sean O'Donnell	Bretford CR4500 Series Slim Rectangular Table	5.0
4	2015-10-18	Standard Class	Sean O'Donnell	Eldon Fold 'N Roll Cart System	2.0
5	NaT	NaN	Brosina Hoffman	Eldon Expressions Wood and Plastic Desk Access...	7.0

Figure 4.51: Outer join on table df_1 and table df_3 and dropping the duplicates

Notice how some **NaN** and **NaT** values are inserted automatically because no corresponding entries could be found for those records, as those are the entries with unique customer names from their respective tables. **NaT** represents a **Not a Time** object, as the objects in the **Ship Date** column are timestamped objects.

> **NOTE**
>
> To access the source code for this specific section, please refer to https://packt.live/2Y8G5UW.
>
> You can also run this example online at https://packt.live/30RNUA4.

With this, we have gone over how to use the **merge** method to do inner and outer joins.

THE JOIN METHOD

Joining is performed based on **index keys** and is done by combining the columns of two potentially differently indexed DataFrames into a single one. It offers a faster way to accomplish merging by row indices. This is useful if the records in different tables are indexed differently but represent the same inherent data and you want to merge them into a single table:

EXERCISE 4.09: THE JOIN METHOD

In this exercise, we will create two DataFrames and perform the different kind of joins on these DataFrames.

> **NOTE**
>
> The Superstore file can be found here: https://packt.live/3dcVnMs.

To complete this exercise, perform the following steps:

1. Import the Python libraries and load the file from GitHub by using the **read_excel** method in **pandas**:

```
import numpy as np
import pandas as pd
import matplotlib.pyplot as plt
df = pd.read_excel("../datasets/Sample - Superstore.xls")
df.head()
```

> **NOTE**
>
> The highlighted path must be changed based on the location of the file on your system.

The partial output of the code is as follows:

	Row ID	Order ID	Order Date	Ship Date	Ship Mode	Customer ID	Customer Name	Segment	Country	City	...	Postal Code	Region	Product ID
0	1	CA-2016-152156	2016-11-08	2016-11-11	Second Class	CG-12520	Claire Gute	Consumer	United States	Henderson	...	42420	South	FUR-BO-10001798
1	2	CA-2016-152156	2016-11-08	2016-11-11	Second Class	CG-12520	Claire Gute	Consumer	United States	Henderson	...	42420	South	FUR-CH-10000454
2	3	CA-2016-138688	2016-06-12	2016-06-16	Second Class	DV-13045	Darrin Van Huff	Corporate	United States	Los Angeles	...	90036	West	OFF-LA-10000240
3	4	US-2015-108966	2015-10-11	2015-10-18	Standard Class	SO-20335	Sean O'Donnell	Consumer	United States	Fort Lauderdale	...	33311	South	FUR-TA-10000577
4	5	US-2015-108966	2015-10-11	2015-10-18	Standard Class	SO-20335	Sean O'Donnell	Consumer	United States	Fort Lauderdale	...	33311	South	OFF-ST-10000760

5 rows × 21 columns

Figure 4.52: Partial output of the DataFrame

2. Create **df1** with **Customer Name** as the index by using the following command:

```
df_1=df[['Customer Name','Ship Date','Ship Mode']][0:4]
df_1.set_index(['Customer Name'],inplace=True)
df_1
```

The output is as follows:

Customer Name	Ship Date	Ship Mode
Claire Gute	2016-11-11	Second Class
Claire Gute	2016-11-11	Second Class
Darrin Van Huff	2016-06-16	Second Class
Sean O'Donnell	2015-10-18	Standard Class

Figure 4.53: DataFrame df_1

3. Create **df2** with **Customer Name** as the index by using the following command:

```
df_2=df[['Customer Name','Product Name','Quantity']][2:6]
df_2.set_index(['Customer Name'],inplace=True)
df_2
```

The output is as follows:

Customer Name	Product Name	Quantity
Darrin Van Huff	Self-Adhesive Address Labels for Typewriters b...	2
Sean O'Donnell	Bretford CR4500 Series Slim Rectangular Table	5
Sean O'Donnell	Eldon Fold 'N Roll Cart System	2
Brosina Hoffman	Eldon Expressions Wood and Plastic Desk Access...	7

Figure 4.54: DataFrame df_2

4. Perform a left join on **df_1** and **df_2** by using the following command:

```
df_1.join(df_2,how='left').drop_duplicates()
```

The output is as follows:

Customer Name	Ship Date	Ship Mode	Product Name	Quantity
Claire Gute	2016-11-11	Second Class	NaN	NaN
Darrin Van Huff	2016-06-16	Second Class	Self-Adhesive Address Labels for Typewriters b...	2.0
Sean O'Donnell	2015-10-18	Standard Class	Bretford CR4500 Series Slim Rectangular Table	5.0
Sean O'Donnell	2015-10-18	Standard Class	Eldon Fold 'N Roll Cart System	2.0

Figure 4.55: Left join on table df_1 and table df_2 after dropping the duplicates

5. Perform a right join on **df_1** and **df_2** by using the following command:

```
df_1.join(df_2,how='right').drop_duplicates()
```

The output is as follows:

Customer Name	Ship Date	Ship Mode	Product Name	Quantity
Brosina Hoffman	NaT	NaN	Eldon Expressions Wood and Plastic Desk Access...	7
Darrin Van Huff	2016-06-16	Second Class	Self-Adhesive Address Labels for Typewriters b...	2
Sean O'Donnell	2015-10-18	Standard Class	Bretford CR4500 Series Slim Rectangular Table	5
Sean O'Donnell	2015-10-18	Standard Class	Eldon Fold 'N Roll Cart System	2

Figure 4.56: Right join on table df_1 and table df_2 after dropping the duplicates

6. Perform an inner join on **df_1** and **df_2** by using the following command:

```
df_1.join(df_2,how='inner').drop_duplicates()
```

The output is as follows:

Customer Name	Ship Date	Ship Mode	Product Name	Quantity
Darrin Van Huff	2016-06-16	Second Class	Self-Adhesive Address Labels for Typewriters b...	2
Sean O'Donnell	2015-10-18	Standard Class	Bretford CR4500 Series Slim Rectangular Table	5
Sean O'Donnell	2015-10-18	Standard Class	Eldon Fold 'N Roll Cart System	2

Figure 4.57: Inner join on table df_1 and table df_2 after dropping the duplicates

7. Perform an outer join on **df_1** and **df_2** by using the following command:

```
df_1.join(df_2,how='outer').drop_duplicates()
```

The output is as follows:

Customer Name	Ship Date	Ship Mode	Product Name	Quantity
Brosina Hoffman	NaT	NaN	Eldon Expressions Wood and Plastic Desk Access...	7.0
Claire Gute	2016-11-11	Second Class	NaN	NaN
Darrin Van Huff	2016-06-16	Second Class	Self-Adhesive Address Labels for Typewriters b...	2.0
Sean O'Donnell	2015-10-18	Standard Class	Bretford CR4500 Series Slim Rectangular Table	5.0
Sean O'Donnell	2015-10-18	Standard Class	Eldon Fold 'N Roll Cart System	2.0

Figure 4.58: Outer join on table df_1 and table df_2 after dropping the duplicates

> **NOTE**
>
> To access the source code for this specific section, please refer to https://packt.live/30S9nZH.
>
> You can also run this example online at https://packt.live/2NbDweg.

We have now gone through the basic functionality of **pandas** DataFrame joining. We used inner and out joining and showed you how we can use indexes to perform a join and how it can help in analysis.

USEFUL METHODS OF PANDAS

In this section, we will discuss some small utility functions that are offered by **pandas** so that we can work efficiently with DataFrames. They don't fall under any particular group of functions, so they are mentioned here under the Miscellaneous category. Let's discuss these miscellaneous methods in detail.

RANDOMIZED SAMPLING

In this section, we will discuss random sampling data from our DataFrames. This is a very common task in a variety of pipelines, one of which is machine learning. Sampling is often used in machine learning data-wrangling pipelines when choosing which data to train and which data to test against. Sampling a random fraction of a big DataFrame is often very useful so that we can practice other methods on them and test our ideas. If you have a database table of 1 million records, then it is not computationally effective to run your test scripts on the full table.

However, you may also not want to extract only the first 100 elements as the data may have been sorted by a particular key and you may get an uninteresting table back, which may not represent the full statistical diversity of the parent database.

In these situations, the `sample` method comes in super handy so that we can randomly choose a controlled fraction of the DataFrame.

EXERCISE 4.10: RANDOMIZED SAMPLING

In this exercise, we are going to randomly take five samples from the Superstore dataset and calculate a definite fraction of the data to be sampled. To do so, let's go through the following steps:

> **NOTE**
>
> The Superstore file can be found here: https://packt.live/3dcVnMs.

1. Import the necessary Python modules and read them from GitHub by using the **read_excel** method in **pandas**:

```
import numpy as np
import pandas as pd
import matplotlib.pyplot as plt
df = pd.read_excel("../datasets/Sample - Superstore.xls")
df.head()
```

> **NOTE**
>
> The highlighted path must be changed based on the location of the file on your system.

The partial output will be:

	Row ID	Order ID	Order Date	Ship Date	Ship Mode	Customer ID	Customer Name	Segment	Country	City	...	Postal Code	Region	Product ID
0	1	CA-2016-152156	2016-11-08	2016-11-11	Second Class	CG-12520	Claire Gute	Consumer	United States	Henderson	...	42420	South	FUR-BO-10001798
1	2	CA-2016-152156	2016-11-08	2016-11-11	Second Class	CG-12520	Claire Gute	Consumer	United States	Henderson	...	42420	South	FUR-CH-10000454
2	3	CA-2016-138688	2016-06-12	2016-06-16	Second Class	DV-13045	Darrin Van Huff	Corporate	United States	Los Angeles	...	90036	West	OFF-LA-10000240
3	4	US-2015-108966	2015-10-11	2015-10-18	Standard Class	SO-20335	Sean O'Donnell	Consumer	United States	Fort Lauderdale	...	33311	South	FUR-TA-10000577
4	5	US-2015-108966	2015-10-11	2015-10-18	Standard Class	SO-20335	Sean O'Donnell	Consumer	United States	Fort Lauderdale	...	33311	South	OFF-ST-10000760

5 rows × 21 columns

Figure 4.59: Partial output of the DataFrame

2. Specify the number of samples that we require from the DataFrame by using the following command:

```
df.sample(n=5)
```

The random output (partially shown) is as follows:

	Row ID	Order ID	Order Date	Ship Date	Ship Mode	Customer ID	Customer Name	Segment	Country	City	...	Postal Code	Region
974	975	US-2017-103247	2017-10-05	2017-10-08	Second Class	PO-19195	Phillina Ober	Home Office	United States	New York City	...	10011	East
8877	8878	CA-2017-126928	2017-09-17	2017-09-23	Standard Class	GZ-14470	Gary Zandusky	Consumer	United States	Morristown	...	7960	East
4088	4089	US-2014-156559	2014-08-19	2014-08-26	Standard Class	LH-16900	Lena Hernandez	Consumer	United States	Jonesboro	...	72401	South
90	91	CA-2016-109806	2016-09-17	2016-09-22	Standard Class	JS-15685	Jim Sink	Corporate	United States	Los Angeles	...	90036	West

Figure 4.60: DataFrame with five samples

> **NOTE**
>
> The outputs you get will vary from the ones shown in this exercise.

3. Specify a definite fraction (percentage) of the data to be sampled by using the following command:

```
df.sample(frac=0.1)
```

The output is as follows:

	Row ID	Order ID	Order Date	Ship Date	Ship Mode	Customer ID	Customer Name	Segment
3291	3292	CA-2016-167290	2016-10-30	2016-11-04	Standard Class	JF-15295	Jason Fortune-	Consumer
9	10	CA-2014-115812	2014-06-09	2014-06-14	Standard Class	BH-11710	Brosina Hoffman	Consumer
8608	8609	CA-2014-151946	2014-06-04	2014-06-09	Standard Class	BT-11440	Bobby Trafton	Consumer
8193	8194	CA-2015-141327	2015-11-30	2015-12-03	First Class	LR-16915	Lena Radford	Consumer
4312	4313	CA-2014-125829	2014-11-04	2014-11-11	Standard Class	WB-21850	William Brown	Consumer
...	...	...	...	...	...	...	...	...
7431	7432	US-2014-164763	2014-03-17	2014-03-21	Standard Class	MH-17440	Mark Haberlin	Corporate

Figure 4.61: Partial output of a DataFrame with 0.1% data sampled

You can also choose if sampling is done with replacement, that is, whether the same record can be chosen more than once. The default **replace** choice is **FALSE**, that is, no repetition and sampling will try to choose new elements only.

4. Choose the sampling by using the following command:

```
df.sample(frac=0.1, replace=True)
```

The output is as follows:

	Row ID	Order ID	Order Date	Ship Date	Ship Mode	Customer ID	Customer Name	Segment	Country
7652	7653	CA-2017-110821	2017-08-07	2017-08-08	First Class	CK-12205	Chloris Kastensmidt	Consumer	United States
1485	1486	CA-2014-119032	2014-11-27	2014-12-03	Standard Class	MS-17770	Maxwell Schwartz	Consumer	United States
9549	9550	CA-2016-131744	2016-06-18	2016-06-20	Second Class	SC-20770	Stewart Carmichael	Corporate	United States
2920	2921	CA-2016-160129	2016-11-23	2016-11-23	Same Day	LS-17200	Luke Schmidt	Corporate	United States
5661	5662	CA-2016-108875	2016-09-24	2016-10-01	Standard Class	CL-12700	Craig Leslie	Home Office	United States
...	...	...	...	...	...	...	...	...	...

Figure 4.62: DataFrame with 0.1% data sampled and repetition enabled

Here, as you can see, we have encouraged repetitions in the sampled data by setting the **replace** parameter to **True**. Therefore, the same elements could be chosen again while performing random sampling.

> **NOTE**
>
> To access the source code for this specific section, please refer to https://packt.live/2N7fWzt.
>
> You can also run this example online at https://packt.live/2YLTt0f.

THE VALUE_COUNTS METHOD

We discussed the **unique** method previously, which finds and counts the unique records from a DataFrame. Another useful function in a similar vein is **value_counts**. This function returns an object containing counts of unique values. In the object that is returned, the first element is the most frequently used object. The elements are arranged in descending order.

Let's consider a practical application of this method to illustrate its utility. Suppose your manager asks you to list the top 10 customers from the big sales database that you have. So, the business question is: which 10 customers' names occur the most frequently in the sales table? You can achieve this with a SQL query if the data is in an RDBMS, but in pandas, this can be done by using one simple function:

```
df['Customer Name'].value_counts()[:10]
```

The output is as follows:

```
William Brown         37
John Lee              34
Matt Abelman          34
Paul Prost            34
Chloris Kastensmidt   32
Jonathan Doherty      32
Seth Vernon           32
Edward Hooks          32
Emily Phan            31
Zuschuss Carroll      31
Name: Customer Name, dtype: int64
```

Figure 4.63: List of top 10 customers

The **value_counts** method returns a series of counts of all unique customer names sorted by the frequency of the count. By asking for only the first 10 elements of that list, this code returns a series of the most frequently occurring top 10 customer names.

PIVOT TABLE FUNCTIONALITY

Similar to group by, pandas also offer pivot table functionality, which works the same as a Pivot Table in spreadsheet programs such as MS Excel. For example, in this sales database, you want to know the average sales, profit, and quantity sold by Region and State (two levels of index).

We can extract this information by using one simple piece of code (we sample 100 records first to keep the computation fast and then apply the code):

```
df_sample = df.sample(n=100)
df_sample.pivot_table(values=['Sales','Quantity','Profit'],\
                index=['Region','State'],aggfunc='mean')
```

The output is as follows (note that your specific output may be different due to random sampling):

Region	State	Profit	Quantity	Sales
Central	Illinois	54.483567	3.333333	494.366667
	Indiana	25.473000	2.000000	121.300000
	Iowa	6.858000	4.000000	15.240000
	Michigan	5.978000	2.333333	13.143333
	Minnesota	19.827600	4.000000	63.960000
	Nebraska	72.894600	2.000000	269.980000
	Oklahoma	6.220800	2.000000	12.960000
	Texas	10.995764	3.090909	77.252727
	Wisconsin	45.840000	3.000000	91.680000
East	Delaware	0.523600	7.000000	26.180000

Figure 4.64: Sample of 100 records

Sorting a table by a particular column is one of the most frequently used operations in the daily work of an analyst. Sorting can help you understand your data better while presenting it in a specific view of the data. When training a machine learning model, the way data is sorted can impact the performance of a model based on the sampling that's being done. Not surprisingly, **pandas** provide a simple and intuitive method for sorting called the **sort_values** method. We'll practice using this in the following exercise.

EXERCISE 4.11: SORTING BY COLUMN VALUES – THE SORT_VALUES METHOD

In this exercise, we will take a random sample of **15** records from the Superstore dataset.

> **NOTE**
>
> The Superstore file can be found here: https://packt.live/3dcVnMs.

We will sort the column values in the dataset with respect to column names using the **sort_values** method. To do so, let's go through the following steps:

1. Import the necessary Python modules and read the Excel file from GitHub by using the **read_excel** method in **pandas**:

```
import numpy as np
import pandas as pd
import matplotlib.pyplot as plt
df = pd.read_excel("../datasets/Sample - Superstore.xls")
df.head()
```

> **NOTE**
>
> The highlighted path must be changed based on the location of the file on your system.

The output (partially shown) will be as follows:

	Row ID	Order ID	Order Date	Ship Date	Ship Mode	Customer ID	Customer Name	Segment	Country	City	...	Postal Code	Region	Product ID
0	1	CA-2016-152156	2016-11-08	2016-11-11	Second Class	CG-12520	Claire Gute	Consumer	United States	Henderson	...	42420	South	FUR-BO-10001798
1	2	CA-2016-152156	2016-11-08	2016-11-11	Second Class	CG-12520	Claire Gute	Consumer	United States	Henderson	...	42420	South	FUR-CH-10000454
2	3	CA-2016-138688	2016-06-12	2016-06-16	Second Class	DV-13045	Darrin Van Huff	Corporate	United States	Los Angeles	...	90036	West	OFF-LA-10000240
3	4	US-2015-108966	2015-10-11	2015-10-18	Standard Class	SO-20335	Sean O'Donnell	Consumer	United States	Fort Lauderdale	...	33311	South	FUR-TA-10000577
4	5	US-2015-108966	2015-10-11	2015-10-18	Standard Class	SO-20335	Sean O'Donnell	Consumer	United States	Fort Lauderdale	...	33311	South	OFF-ST-10000760

5 rows × 21 columns

Figure 4.65: Partial output of the DataFrame

2. Take a random sample of **15** records and then sort by the **Sales** column and then by both the **Sales** and **State** columns together:

```
df_sample=df[['Customer Name','State',\
            'Sales','Quantity']].sample(n=15)
df_sample
```

The output is as follows:

	Customer Name	State	Sales	Quantity
5167	Sam Craven	Michigan	563.940	3
823	Toby Ritter	New Jersey	9.820	2
1947	Ann Chong	New York	11.540	2
1977	Alan Schoenberger	Alabama	545.880	6
3031	Dario Medina	Michigan	25.990	1
6539	Heather Kirkland	Delaware	291.100	5
8792	Bart Pistole	California	14.620	2
9178	Darren Powers	New York	23.650	1
8860	Skye Norling	New Jersey	31.050	3
7104	Katharine Harms	Ohio	760.116	6
9034	Eric Murdock	Illinois	2.992	4
2941	Justin Deggeller	Wisconsin	1526.560	7
1338	Chad McGuire	New York	677.580	3
434	Mike Kennedy	Florida	4.812	2
7686	Brenda Bowman	Michigan	1568.610	9

Figure 4.66: Sample of 15 records

NOTE

The outputs you get will vary from the ones shown in this exercise.

3. Sort the values with respect to **Sales** by using the following command:

```
df_sample.sort_values(by='Sales')
```

The output is as follows:

	Customer Name	State	Sales	Quantity
9034	Eric Murdock	Illinois	2.992	4
434	Mike Kennedy	Florida	4.812	2
823	Toby Ritter	New Jersey	9.820	2
1947	Ann Chong	New York	11.540	2
8792	Bart Pistole	California	14.620	2
9178	Darren Powers	New York	23.650	1
3031	Dario Medina	Michigan	25.990	1
8860	Skye Norling	New Jersey	31.050	3
6539	Heather Kirkland	Delaware	291.100	5
1977	Alan Schoenberger	Alabama	545.880	6
5167	Sam Craven	Michigan	563.940	3
1338	Chad McGuire	New York	677.580	3
7104	Katharine Harms	Ohio	760.116	6
2941	Justin Deggeller	Wisconsin	1526.560	7
7686	Brenda Bowman	Michigan	1568.610	9

Figure 4.67: DataFrame with the Sales value sorted

4. Sort the values with respect to **Sales** and **State**:

```
df_sample.sort_values(by=['State','Sales'])
```

The output is as follows:

	Customer Name	State	Sales	Quantity
1977	Alan Schoenberger	Alabama	545.880	6
8792	Bart Pistole	California	14.620	2
6539	Heather Kirkland	Delaware	291.100	5
434	Mike Kennedy	Florida	4.812	2
9034	Eric Murdock	Illinois	2.992	4
3031	Dario Medina	Michigan	25.990	1
5167	Sam Craven	Michigan	563.940	3
7686	Brenda Bowman	Michigan	1568.610	9
823	Toby Ritter	New Jersey	9.820	2
8860	Skye Norling	New Jersey	31.050	3
1947	Ann Chong	New York	11.540	2
9178	Darren Powers	New York	23.650	1
1338	Chad McGuire	New York	677.580	3
7104	Katharine Harms	Ohio	760.116	6
2941	Justin Deggeller	Wisconsin	1526.560	7

Figure 4.68: DataFrame sorted with respect to Sales and State

The **pandas** library provides great flexibility for working with user-defined functions of arbitrary complexity through the **apply** method. Much like the native Python **apply** function, this method accepts a user-defined function and additional arguments and returns a new column after applying the function on a particular column elementwise.

As an example, suppose we want to create a column of categorical features such as high/medium/low based on the sales price column. Note that this is a conversion from a numeric value into a categorical factor (string) based on certain conditions (threshold values of sales).

EXERCISE 4.12: FLEXIBILITY OF USER-DEFINED FUNCTIONS WITH THE APPLY METHOD

In this exercise, we will create a user-defined function called **categorize_sales** that categorizes Sales data based on price. If the **price** is less than **50**, it is classified as **Low**, if the **price** is less than **200**, it is classified as **Medium**, or **High** if the **price** doesn't fall under either of these categories.

> **NOTE**
>
> The Superstore file can be found here: https://packt.live/3dcVnMs.

We'll then take 100 random samples from the **superstore** dataset and use the **apply** method on the **categorize_sales** function in order to create a new column to store the values returned by the function. To do so, perform the following steps:

1. Import the necessary Python modules and read the Excel file from GitHub by using the **read_excel** method in **pandas**:

```
import numpy as np
import pandas as pd
import matplotlib.pyplot as plt
df = pd.read_excel("../datasets/Sample - Superstore.xls")
df.head()
```

> **NOTE**
>
> The highlighted path must be changed based on the location of the file on your system.

The output (partially shown) will be:

	Row ID	Order ID	Order Date	Ship Date	Ship Mode	Customer ID	Customer Name	Segment	Country	City	...	Postal Code	Region	Product ID
0	1	CA-2016-152156	2016-11-08	2016-11-11	Second Class	CG-12520	Claire Gute	Consumer	United States	Henderson	...	42420	South	FUR-BO-10001798
1	2	CA-2016-152156	2016-11-08	2016-11-11	Second Class	CG-12520	Claire Gute	Consumer	United States	Henderson	...	42420	South	FUR-CH-10000454
2	3	CA-2016-138688	2016-06-12	2016-06-16	Second Class	DV-13045	Darrin Van Huff	Corporate	United States	Los Angeles	...	90036	West	OFF-LA-10000240
3	4	US-2015-108966	2015-10-11	2015-10-18	Standard Class	SO-20335	Sean O'Donnell	Consumer	United States	Fort Lauderdale	...	33311	South	FUR-TA-10000577
4	5	US-2015-108966	2015-10-11	2015-10-18	Standard Class	SO-20335	Sean O'Donnell	Consumer	United States	Fort Lauderdale	...	33311	South	OFF-ST-10000760

5 rows × 21 columns

Figure 4.69: Partial output of the DataFrame

2. Create a user-defined function, as follows:

```
def categorize_sales(price):
    if price < 50:
        return "Low"
    elif price < 200:
        return "Medium"
    else:
        return "High"
```

3. Sample **100** records randomly from the database:

```
df_sample=df[['Customer Name',\
            'State','Sales']].sample(n=100)
df_sample.head(10)
```

The output is as follows:

	Customer Name	State	Sales
6060	Eugene Hildebrand	New York	142.040
1616	Julie Kriz	Minnesota	41.400
509	Christopher Martinez	Georgia	6354.950
369	Michael Kennedy	Connecticut	1043.920
5883	Edward Hooks	California	28.280
2648	Tom Boeckenhauer	Oklahoma	821.880
7448	Michelle Huthwaite	Tennessee	88.920
2372	Barry Französisch	Illinois	2.632
4423	Todd Boyes	Georgia	302.940
2802	Denise Leinenbach	New Mexico	41.370

Figure 4.70: 100 sample records from the database

NOTE

The outputs you get will vary from the ones shown in this exercise.

4. Use the **apply** method to apply the categorization function to the **Sales** column. We need to create a new column to store the category string values that are returned by the function:

```
df_sample['Sales Price Category']=df_sample['Sales']\
                            .apply(categorize_sales)
df_sample.head(10)
```

The output is as follows:

	Customer Name	State	Sales	Sales Price Category
6060	Eugene Hildebrand	New York	142.040	Medium
1616	Julie Kriz	Minnesota	41.400	Low
509	Christopher Martinez	Georgia	6354.950	High
369	Michael Kennedy	Connecticut	1043.920	High
5883	Edward Hooks	California	28.280	Low
2648	Tom Boeckenhauer	Oklahoma	821.880	High
7448	Michelle Huthwaite	Tennessee	88.920	Medium
2372	Barry Französisch	Illinois	2.632	Low
4423	Todd Boyes	Georgia	302.940	High
2802	Denise Leinenbach	New Mexico	41.370	Low

Figure 4.71: DataFrame with 10 rows after using the apply function on the Sales column

The **apply** method also works with the built-in native Python functions.

5. For practice, let's create another column for storing the length of the name of the customer. We can do this using the familiar **len** function:

```
df_sample['Customer Name Length']=df_sample['Customer Name']\
                                .apply(len)
df_sample.head(10)
```

The output is as follows:

	Customer Name	State	Sales	Sales Price Category	Customer Name Length
6060	Eugene Hildebrand	New York	142.040	Medium	17
1616	Julie Kriz	Minnesota	41.400	Low	10
509	Christopher Martinez	Georgia	6354.950	High	20
369	Michael Kennedy	Connecticut	1043.920	High	15
5883	Edward Hooks	California	28.280	Low	12
2648	Tom Boeckenhauer	Oklahoma	821.880	High	16
7448	Michelle Huthwaite	Tennessee	88.920	Medium	18
2372	Barry Französisch	Illinois	2.632	Low	17
4423	Todd Boyes	Georgia	302.940	High	10
2802	Denise Leinenbach	New Mexico	41.370	Low	17

Figure 4.72: DataFrame with a new column

Instead of writing out a separate function, we can even insert *lambda expressions* directly into the **apply** method for short functions. For example, let's say we are promoting our product and want to show the discounted sales price if the original price is > *$200*.

6. Use a **lambda** function and the **apply** method to do so:

```
df_sample['Discounted Price']=df_sample['Sales']\
                    .apply(lambda x:0.85*x if x>200 \
                    else x)
df_sample.head(10)
```

The output is as follows:

	Customer Name	State	Sales	Sales Price Category	Customer Name Length	Discounted Price
6060	Eugene Hildebrand	New York	142.040	Medium	17	142.0400
1616	Julie Kriz	Minnesota	41.400	Low	10	41.4000
509	Christopher Martinez	Georgia	6354.950	High	20	5401.7075
369	Michael Kennedy	Connecticut	1043.920	High	15	887.3320
5883	Edward Hooks	California	28.280	Low	12	28.2800
2648	Tom Boeckenhauer	Oklahoma	821.880	High	16	698.5980
7448	Michelle Huthwaite	Tennessee	88.920	Medium	18	88.9200
2372	Barry Französisch	Illinois	2.632	Low	17	2.6320
4423	Todd Boyes	Georgia	302.940	High	10	257.4990
2802	Denise Leinenbach	New Mexico	41.370	Low	17	41.3700

Figure 4.73: Lambda function

NOTE

The lambda function contains a conditional, and a discount is applied to those records where the original sales price is >$200.

To access the source code for this specific section, please refer to https://packt.live/3ddJYwa.

You can also run this example online at https://packt.live/3d63D0Y.

After going through this exercise, we know how to apply a function to a column in a DataFrame. This method is very useful for going beyond the basic functions that are present in **pandas**.

ACTIVITY 4.01: WORKING WITH THE ADULT INCOME DATASET (UCI)

In this activity, we will detect outliers in the Adult Income Dataset from the UCI machine learning portal https://packt.live/2N9IRUU.

You can find a description of the dataset https://packt.live/2N9IRUU. We will use the concepts we've learned throughout this chapter, such as subsetting, applying user-defined functions, summary statistics, visualizations, boolean indexing, and group by to find a whole group of outliers in a dataset. We will create a bar plot to plot this group of outliers. Finally, we will merge two datasets by using a common key.

These are the steps that will help you solve this activity:

1. Load the necessary libraries.

2. Read the adult income dataset from the following URL: https://packt.live/2N9IRUU.

3. Create a script that will read a text file line by line.

4. Add a name of **Income** for the response variable to the dataset.

5. Find the missing values.

6. Create a DataFrame with only age, education, and occupation by using subsetting.

7. Plot a histogram of age with a bin size of **20**.

8. Create a function to strip the whitespace characters.

9. Use the **apply** method to apply this function to all the columns with string values, create a new column, copy the values from this new column to the old column, and drop the new column.

10. Find the number of people who are aged between **30** and **50**.

11. Group the records based on age and education to find how the mean age is distributed.

12. Group by occupation and show the summary statistics of age. Find which profession has the oldest workers on average and which profession has its largest share of the workforce above the 75th percentile.

13. Use **subset** and **groupBy** to find the outliers.

14. Plot the outlier values on a bar chart. It should look something like this:

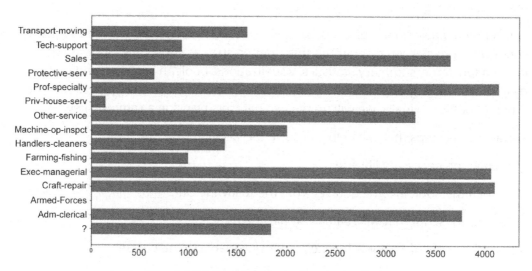

Figure 4.74: Bar plot displaying the outliers

15. Merge the two DataFrames using common keys to drop duplicate values.

The output should look like this:

	age	workclass	occupation	education
0	51	Private	Machine-op-inspct	HS-grad
1	19	Private	Sales	11th
2	40	Private	Exec-managerial	HS-grad
3	17	Private	Handlers-cleaners	10th
4	61	Private	Craft-repair	7th-8th

Figure 4.75: Merged DataFrame

NOTE

The solution to this activity can be found on page 470.

As you can see, we now have a single DataFrame because we have merged two DataFrames into one.

With that, we conclude this activity and the chapter.

SUMMARY

In this chapter, we deep-dived into the **pandas** library to learn advanced data wrangling techniques. We started with some advanced subsetting and filtering on DataFrames and rounded this off by learning about boolean indexing and conditionally selecting a subset of data. We also covered how to set and reset the index of a DataFrame, especially while initializing.

Next, we learned about a particular topic that has a deep connection with traditional relational database systems – the **groupBy** method. Then, we deep-dived into an important skill for data wrangling – checking for and handling missing data. We showed you how pandas helps in handling missing data using various imputation techniques. We also discussed methods for dropping missing values. Furthermore, methods and usage examples of concatenation and merging DataFrame objects were shown. We saw the **join** method and how it compares to a similar operation in SQL.

Lastly, miscellaneous useful methods on DataFrames, such as randomized sampling, **unique**, **value_count**, **sort_values**, and pivot table functionality were covered. We also showed an example of running an arbitrary user-defined function on a DataFrame using the **apply** method.

After learning about the basic and advanced data wrangling techniques with the **numpy** and **pandas** libraries, the natural question of data acquisition rises. In the next chapter, we will show you how to work with a wide variety of data sources; that is, you will learn how to read data in tabular format in **pandas** from different sources.

5

GETTING COMFORTABLE WITH DIFFERENT KINDS OF DATA SOURCES

OVERVIEW

This chapter will provide you with the skills to read CSV, Excel, and JSON files into pandas DataFrames. You will learn how to read PDF documents and HTML tables into pandas DataFrames and perform basic web scraping operations using powerful yet easy-to-use libraries such as Beautiful Soup. You will also see how to extract structured and textual information from portals. By the end of this chapter, you will be able to implement data wrangling techniques such as web scraping in the real world.

INTRODUCTION

So far in this book, we have focused on studying pandas DataFrame objects as the main data structure for the application of wrangling techniques. In this chapter, we will learn about various techniques by which we can read data into a DataFrame from external sources. Some of these sources could be text-based (such as CSV, HTML, and JSON), whereas others could be binary (that is, not in ASCII format; for example, from Excel or PDFs). We will also learn how to deal with data that is present in web pages or HTML documents.

Being able to deal with and extract meaningful data from various sources is of paramount interest to a data practitioner. Data can, and often does, come in various forms and flavors. It is essential to be able to get the data into a form that is useful for performing predictive or other kinds of downstream tasks.

As we have gone through detailed examples of basic operations with NumPy and pandas, in this chapter, we will often skip trivial code snippets such as viewing a table, selecting a column, and plotting. Instead, we will focus on showing code examples for the new topics we aim to learn about here.

READING DATA FROM DIFFERENT SOURCES

One of the most valued and widely used skills of a data wrangling professional is the ability to extract and read data from a diverse array of sources into a structured format. Modern analytics pipelines depend on the ability and skills of those professionals to build a robust system that can scan and absorb a variety of data sources to build and analyze a pattern-rich model. Such kinds of feature-rich, multi-dimensional models will have high predictive and generalization accuracy. They will be valued by stakeholders and end users alike in any data-driven product. In the first part of this chapter, we will go through various data sources and how they can be imported into **pandas** DataFrames, thus imbuing data wrangling professionals with extremely valuable data ingestion knowledge.

DATA FILES PROVIDED WITH THIS CHAPTER

As this topic is about reading from various data sources, we will use small files of various types in the following exercises. All the data files are provided, along with the Jupyter notebook, in the code repository.

> **NOTE**
>
> All the data files can be accessed from the following link: https://packt.live/3fAWg3f.

LIBRARIES TO INSTALL FOR THIS CHAPTER

As this chapter deals with reading files of various formats, we need to have the support of additional libraries and software platforms to accomplish our goals.

Before we install these libraries, ensure that **Java Development Kit (JDK)** is installed on your system. If not, go to the following link to install it:

https://www.oracle.com/in/java/technologies/javase-downloads.html.

Once you are on the website, click the link that says **JDK Download**. Then, proceed to download and install JDK based on your operating system. Once installation completes, ensure that you restart your system, especially if you are using Windows. In case you face issues after installation, check if you've set the PATH system variable correctly. To learn how to do that, refer https://www.java.com/en/download/help/path.xml.

Once JDK is installed, go ahead and install the necessary libraries. Execute the following command in your Jupyter Notebook cells:

```
!pip install tabula-py xlrd lxml
```

> **NOTE**
>
> Don't forget the `!` before each line of code. This little exclamation sign in front of each command lets the Jupyter runtime know that what is in the cell is a **bash** command and not a line of Python code.

READING DATA USING PANDAS

The **pandas** library provides a simple method called **read_csv** to read data in a tabular format from a comma-separated text file, or **.csv**. This is particularly useful because **.csv** is a lightweight yet extremely handy data exchange format for many applications, including such domains where machine-generated data is involved. It is not a proprietary format and therefore is universally used by a variety of data-generating sources.

Generally, a **.csv** file has two sections. The first line of a **.csv** file is usually treated as a header line. So, each column (each word, or words, between two consecutive commas) in the first line should indicate the name of the column. This is very valuable information because without it, it would often be impossible to say what kind of data each of them represents. After the first line, we have data rows where each line represents one data point and each column represents values of those data points.

EXERCISE 5.01: WORKING WITH HEADERS WHEN READING DATA FROM A CSV FILE

In this exercise, you will see how to read data from a **.csv** file. The file can be found here https://packt.live/3fDMCNp. This exercise acts as a demonstration of how to work with headers and what to do when the headers are missing. At times, you will encounter situations where headers are not present, and you may have to add proper headers or column names of your own. Let's have a look at how this can be done:

1. Open a new Jupyter Notebook and read the example **.csv** file (with a header) using the following code and examine the resulting DataFrame, as follows:

```
import numpy as np
import pandas as pd
df1 = pd.read_csv("../datasets/CSV_EX_1.csv")
df1
```

> **NOTE**
>
> Throughout this exercise, don't forget to change the path (highlighted) of the CSV file based on its location on your system.

The output is as follows:

	Bedroom	Sq. foot	Locality	Price ($)
0	2	1500	Good	300000
1	3	1300	Fair	240000
2	3	1900	Very good	450000
3	3	1850	Bad	280000
4	2	1640	Good	310000

Figure 5.1: Output of the example CSV file

2. Read a **.csv** file with no header using a **pandas** DataFrame:

```
df2 = pd.read_csv("../datasets/CSV_EX_2.csv")
df2
```

The output is as follows:

	2	1500	Good	300000
0	3	1300	Fair	240000
1	3	1900	Very good	450000
2	3	1850	Bad	280000
3	2	1640	Good	310000

Figure 5.2: Output of the .csv file being read using a DataFrame

> **NOTE**
>
> The file can be found here https://packt.live/30SEbJH.

The top data row has been mistakenly read as the column header. You can specify **header=None** to avoid this.

3. Read the `.csv` file by setting the **header** to **None**, as follows:

```
df2 = pd.read_csv("../datasets/CSV_EX_2.csv",header=None)
df2
```

However, without any header information, you will get back the following output. The default headers will be just some default numeric indices starting from **0**. This is how the **pandas** library treats a headerless CSV file when you ask it not to consider the first line (which is a data row in this case) as **header**:

	0	1	2	3
0	2	1500	Good	300000
1	3	1300	Fair	240000
2	3	1900	Very good	450000
3	3	1850	Bad	280000
4	2	1640	Good	310000

Figure 5.3: A CSV file with numeric column headers

This may be fine for data analysis purposes, but if you want the DataFrame to have meaningful headers, then you will have to add them using the **names** argument.

4. Add the **names** argument to get the correct headers:

```
df2 = pd.read_csv("../datasets/CSV_EX_2.csv",\
                  header=None, names=['Bedroom','Sq.ft',\
                                      'Locality','Price($)'])
df2
```

Finally, you will get a DataFrame that will look like this:

	Bedroom	Sq.ft	Locality	Price($)
0	2	1500	Good	300000
1	3	1300	Fair	240000
2	3	1900	Very good	450000
3	3	1850	Bad	280000
4	2	1640	Good	310000

Figure 5.4: CSV file with correct column header

As you can see in the preceding figure, the headers have been added in the right places.

> **NOTE**
>
> To access the source code for this specific section, please refer to https://packt.live/3hxmAgm.
>
> You can also run this example online at https://packt.live/3eaToda.

Up until now, we've been comfortable reading from files where a comma acts as a delimiter. Let's look at the following exercise, where we will be reading from a CSV file where the values are not separated by commas.

EXERCISE 5.02: READING FROM A CSV FILE WHERE DELIMITERS ARE NOT COMMAS

It is fairly common to encounter raw data files where the separator/delimiter is a character and not a comma. This exercise will demonstrate how you can read data from a file in such a case.

> **NOTE**
>
> The file can be found here: https://packt.live/2YPEJgO.

Let's go through the following steps:

1. Read a `.csv` file using **pandas** DataFrames:

```
import numpy as np
import pandas as pd
df3 = pd.read_csv("../datasets/CSV_EX_3.csv")
df3
```

> **NOTE**
>
> Throughout this exercise, don't forget to change the path (highlighted) of the CSV file based on its location on your system.

The output will be as follows:

	Bedroom; Sq. foot; Locality; Price ($)
0	2; 1500; Good; 300000
1	3; 1300; Fair; 240000
2	3; 1900; Very good; 450000
3	3; 1850; Bad; 280000
4	2; 1640; Good; 310000

Figure 5.5: A DataFrame that has a semi-colon as a separator

Clearly, the ; separator was not expected, and the reading is flawed. A simple workaround is to specify the separator/delimiter explicitly in the **read** function.

2. Specify the delimiter:

```
df3 = pd.read_csv("../datasets/CSV_EX_3.csv",sep=';')
df3
```

The output is as follows:

	Bedroom	Sq. foot	Locality	Price ($)
0	2	1500	Good	300000
1	3	1300	Fair	240000
2	3	1900	Very good	450000
3	3	1850	Bad	280000
4	2	1640	Good	310000

Figure 5.6: Semicolons removed from the DataFrame

As we can see, it is fairly simple to read from a csv file when the delimiter is specified in the **read_csv** function.

> **NOTE**
>
> To access the source code for this specific section, please refer to https://packt.live/2Na4oM0.
>
> You can also run this example online at https://packt.live/3fvdm2g.

In the following exercise, we will see how to bypass the headers if your CSV file already comes with headers.

EXERCISE 5.03: BYPASSING AND RENAMING THE HEADERS OF A CSV FILE

This exercise will demonstrate how to bypass the headers of a CSV file and put in your own. To do that, you have to specifically set **header=0**. If you try to set the **names** variable to your **header** list, unexpected things can happen. Follow these steps:

1. Add **names** to a **.csv** file that has headers, as follows:

```
import numpy as np
import pandas as pd
df4 = pd.read_csv("../datasets/CSV_EX_1.csv",\
                  names=['A','B','C','D'])
df4
```

> **NOTE**
>
> Throughout this exercise, don't forget to change the path (highlighted) of the CSV file based on its location on your system.

The output is as follows:

	A	B	C	D
0	Bedroom	Sq. foot	Locality	Price ($)
1	2	1500	Good	300000
2	3	1300	Fair	240000
3	3	1900	Very good	450000
4	3	1850	Bad	280000
5	2	1640	Good	310000

Figure 5.7: A CSV file with headers overlapped

2. To avoid this, set **header** to zero and provide a **names** list:

```
df4 = pd.read_csv("../datasets/CSV_EX_1.csv",header=0,\
                  names=['A','B','C','D'])
df4
```

The output is as follows:

	A	B	C	D
0	2	1500	Good	300000
1	3	1300	Fair	240000
2	3	1900	Very good	450000
3	3	1850	Bad	280000
4	2	1640	Good	310000

Figure 5.8: A CSV file with defined headers

Keep in mind that this representation is just in memory at the moment and only available in the present session of the notebook; it is not reflected in the physical CSV file. The original file has not changed due to our manipulation.

> **NOTE**
>
> To access the source code for this specific section, please refer to https://packt.live/30QwEeA.
>
> You can also run this example online at https://packt.live/315gOgr.

We observed some operations that we can do on the headers in a file. However, some CSV files may have an even more complex structure than the simple ones that we have been using so far. In the following exercise, we will discover some tricks to deal with such complex structures.

EXERCISE 5.04: SKIPPING INITIAL ROWS AND FOOTERS WHEN READING A CSV FILE

In this exercise, we will skip the first few rows because, most of the time, the first few rows of a CSV data file are metadata about the data source or similar information, which is not read into the table. Also, we will go ahead and remove the footer of the file, which might sometimes contain information that's not very useful. Let's see how we can do that using the example shown in the following screenshot:

Filetype: CSV			
	Info about some house		
Bedroom	Sq.foot	Locality	Price ($)
2	1500	Good	300000
3	1300	Fair	240000
3	1900	Very Good	450000
3	1850	Bad	280000
2	1640	Good	310000

Figure 5.9: Contents of the CSV file

> **NOTE**
>
> The first two lines in the CSV file are irrelevant data. The file can be found here https://packt.live/30Sdvjh

1. Read the CSV file and examine the results:

```
import numpy as np
import pandas as pd
df5 = pd.read_csv("../datasets/CSV_EX_skiprows.csv")
df5
```

> **NOTE**
>
> Throughout this exercise, don't forget to change the path (highlighted) of the CSV file based on its location on your system.

The output is as follows:

	Filetype: CSV		Unnamed: 1	Unnamed: 2	Unnamed: 3
0	NaN	Info about some houses		NaN	NaN
1	Bedroom		Sq. foot	Locality	Price ($)
2	2		1500	Good	300000
3	3		1300	Fair	240000
4	3		1900	Very good	450000
5	3		1850	Bad	280000
6	2		1640	Good	310000

Figure 5.10: DataFrame with an unexpected error

2. Skip the first two rows and read the file:

```
df5 = pd.read_csv("CSV_EX_skiprows.csv",skiprows=2)
df5
```

The output is as follows:

	Bedroom	Sq. foot	Locality	Price ($)
0	2	1500	Good	300000
1	3	1300	Fair	240000
2	3	1900	Very good	450000
3	3	1850	Bad	280000
4	2	1640	Good	310000

Figure 5.11: Expected DataFrame after skipping two rows

Similar to skipping the initial rows, it may be necessary to skip the footer of a file. For example, we do not want to read the data at the end of the following file:

Filetype: CSV			
	Info about some houses		
Bedroom	Sq. foot	Locality	Price ($)
2	1500	Good	300000
3	1300	Fair	240000
3	1900	Very good	450000
3	1850	Bad	280000
2	1640	Good	310000
	This is the end of file		

Figure 5.12: Contents of the CSV file

We have to use **skipfooter** and the **engine='python'** option to enable this. There are two engines for these CSV reader functions, based on C or Python, of which only the Python engine supports the **skipfooter** option.

3. Use the **skipfooter** option in Python:

```
df6 = pd.read_csv("../datasets/CSV_EX_skipfooter.csv",\
                  skiprows=2,skipfooter=1, engine='python')
df6
```

The output is as follows:

	Bedroom	Sq. foot	Locality	Price ($)
0	2	1500	Good	300000
1	3	1300	Fair	240000
2	3	1900	Very good	450000
3	3	1850	Bad	280000
4	2	1640	Good	310000

Figure 5.13: DataFrame without a footer

> **NOTE**
>
> To access the source code for this specific section, please refer to https://packt.live/2CbehGO.
>
> You can also run this example online at https://packt.live/2Ycw0Gp.

We've now seen how to read values skipping the headers and footers from a file. It can very often be very handy while dealing with data collected from several different sources, especially in situations where a file contains unnecessary and junk information.

READING ONLY THE FIRST N ROWS

In many situations, we may not want to read a whole data file but only the first few rows. This is particularly useful for extremely large data files, where we may just want to read the first couple of hundred rows to check an initial pattern and then decide to read the whole of the data afterward. Reading the entire file can take a long time and can slow down the entire data wrangling pipeline.

A simple option, called **nrows**, in the **read_csv** function, enables us to do just that. We will specify the number of rows we want to read and pass it as an argument to **nrows** like so:

```
df7 = pd.read_csv("../datasets/CSV_EX_1.csv",nrows=2)
df7
```

> **NOTE**
>
> The path (highlighted) would need to be changed based on where the file is saved on your system.

The output is as follows:

	Bedroom	Sq. foot	Locality	Price ($)
0	2	1500	Good	300000
1	3	1300	Fair	240000

Figure 5.14: DataFrame with the first few rows of the CSV file

The ability to be able to read only a selected number of rows is useful, specifically if you are dealing with large CSV files.

EXERCISE 5.05: COMBINING SKIPROWS AND NROWS TO READ DATA IN SMALL CHUNKS

This exercise will demonstrate how we can read from a very large data file. To do that, we can cleverly combine **skiprows** and **nrows** to read in a large file in small chunks of pre-determined sizes. We will read from the **Boston_housing.csv** file, which contains data about the pricing of houses in the Boston area in the US. It contains information such as per capita crime rate by town and the average number of rooms per dwelling. To do this, let's go through the following steps:

> **NOTE**
>
> Each exercise continues directly from the previous one. You do not need to open a new Jupyter Notebook each time.
>
> The dataset can be found here: https://packt.live/3fEIH2z

1. Create a list where DataFrames will be stored:

```
list_of_dataframe = []
```

2. Store the number of rows to be read into a variable:

```
rows_in_a_chunk = 10
```

3. Create a variable to store the number of chunks to be read:

```
num_chunks = 5
```

4. Create a dummy DataFrame to get the column names:

```
import pandas as pd
df_dummy = pd.read_csv("../datasets/Boston_housing.csv",nrows=2)
colnames = df_dummy.columns
```

> **NOTE**
>
> Throughout this exercise, don't forget to change the path (highlighted) of the CSV file based on its location on your system.

5. Loop over the CSV file to read only a fixed number of rows at a time:

```
for i in range(0,num_chunks*rows_in_a_chunk,rows_in_a_chunk):
    df = pd.read_csv("Boston_housing.csv", header=0,\
                     skiprows=i, nrows=rows_in_a_chunk,\
                     names=colnames)
    list_of_dataframe.append(df)
```

> **NOTE**
>
> This particular step will not show any output as the values are getting appended to the list.

Note how the **iterator** variable is set up inside the **range** function to break it into chunks. Say the number of chunks is **5** and the rows per chunk is **10**, then the iterator will have a range of **(0,5*10,10)**, where the final **10** is step-size, that is, it will iterate with indices of **(0,9,19,29,39,49)**.

> **NOTE**
>
> To access the source code for this specific section, please refer to https://packt.live/3fGmBwZ.
>
> You can also run this example online at https://packt.live/3hDbVAJ.

SETTING THE SKIP_BLANK_LINES OPTION

By default, **read_csv** ignores blank lines, which means if there are row entries with **NaN** values, the **read_csv** function will not read that data. However, in some situations, you may want to read them in as **NaN** so that you can count how many blank entries were present in the raw data file. In some situations, this is an indicator of the default data streaming quality and consistency. For this, you have to disable the **skip_blank_lines** option:

```
df9 = pd.read_csv("../datasets/CSV_EX_blankline.csv",\
                  skip_blank_lines=False)
df9
```

The output is as follows:

> **NOTE**
>
> The path (highlighted) would need to be changed based on where the file is located on your system.

	Bedroom	Sq. foot	Locality	Price ($)
0	2.0	1500.0	Good	300000.0
1	3.0	1300.0	Fair	240000.0
2	NaN	NaN	NaN	NaN
3	3.0	1900.0	Very good	450000.0
4	3.0	1850.0	Bad	280000.0
5	NaN	NaN	NaN	NaN
6	2.0	1640.0	Good	310000.0

Figure 5.15: DataFrame of a .csv file that has blank rows

In the next section, we are going to read CSV data from a zip file.

READING CSV DATA FROM A ZIP FILE

This is an awesome feature of **pandas**, and it allows you to read directly from a compressed file, such as `.zip`, `.gz`, `.bz2`, or `.xz`. The only requirement is that the intended data file (**CSV**) should be the only file inside the compressed file. For example, we might need to compress a large csv file, and in that case, it will be the only file inside the `.zip` folder.

In this example, we compressed the example CSV file with the **7-Zip** program and read from it directly using the **read_csv** method:

```
df10 = pd.read_csv('../datasets/CSV_EX_1.zip')
df10
```

The output is as follows:

	Bedroom	Sq. foot	Locality	Price ($)
0	2	1500	Good	300000
1	3	1300	Fair	240000
2	3	1900	Very good	450000
3	3	1850	Bad	280000
4	2	1640	Good	310000

Figure 5.16: DataFrame of a compressed CSV file

Next, we will turn our attention to a Microsoft Excel file. It turns out that most of the options and methods we learned about in the previous exercises with the CSV file apply directly to reading Excel files too.

READING FROM AN EXCEL FILE USING SHEET_NAME AND HANDLING A DISTINCT SHEET_NAME

In this section, we will focus on the differences between the methods of reading from an Excel file. An Excel file can consist of multiple worksheets, and we can read a specific sheet by passing in a particular argument, that is, **sheet_name**.

For example, in the **Housing_data.xlsx** file, we have three worksheets. The following code reads them one by one into three separate DataFrames:

```
df11_1 = pd.read_excel("../datasets/Housing_data.xlsx",\
                sheet_name='Data_Tab_1')
df11_2 = pd.read_excel("../datasets/Housing_data.xlsx",\
                sheet_name='Data_Tab_2')
df11_3 = pd.read_excel("../datasets/Housing_data.xlsx",\
                sheet_name='Data_Tab_3')
```

If the Excel file has multiple distinct worksheets but the **sheet_name** argument is set to **None**, then an ordered dictionary will be returned by the **read_excel** function. That ordered **dict** will have the data from all the worksheets, and the top-level keys will indicate the name of the worksheet. Thereafter, we can simply iterate over that dictionary or its keys to retrieve individual DataFrames.

Let's consider the following example:

```
dict_df = pd.read_excel("../datasets/Housing_data.xlsx",\
                        sheet_name=None)
dict_df.keys()
```

The output is as follows:

```
odict_keys(['Data_Tab_1', 'Data_Tab_2', 'Data_Tab_3'])
```

Therefore, we can access these individual worksheets using the distinct keys.

EXERCISE 5.06: READING A GENERAL DELIMITED TEXT FILE

In this exercise, we will read from general delimited text files and see that this can be done as easily as reading from CSV files. However, we will have to use the right separator if it is anything other than a whitespace or a tab. To see this in action, let's go through the following steps:

1. Read the data from a .**txt** file using the **read_table** command:

```
import pandas as pd
df13 = pd.read_table("../datasets/Table_EX_1.txt")
df13
```

The output is as follows:

	Bedroom, Sq. foot, Locality, Price ($)
0	2, 1500, Good, 300000
1	3, 1300, Fair, 240000
2	3, 1900, Very good, 450000
3	3, 1850, Bad, 280000
4	2, 1640, Good, 310000

Figure 5.17: A DataFrame that has a comma-separated CSV file

> **NOTE**
>
> Throughout this exercise, don't forget to change the path (highlighted) of the text file based on its location on your system.

A comma-separated file saved with the **.txt** extension will result in the preceding DataFrame if read without explicitly setting the separator. As you can see, for each value read, there is a comma appended. In this case, we have to set the separator explicitly.

2. Set the separator as a comma in the **sep** variable as follows:

```
df13 = pd.read_table("../datasets/Table_EX_1.txt", sep=',')
df13
```

The output is as follows:

	Bedroom	Sq. foot	Locality	Price ($)
0	2	1500	Good	300000
1	3	1300	Fair	240000
2	3	1900	Very good	450000
3	3	1850	Bad	280000
4	2	1640	Good	310000

Figure 5.18: A DataFrame read using a comma separator

We can see in the figure that the data is read as expected from the **.txt** file.

> **NOTE**
>
> To access the source code for this specific section, please refer to https://packt.live/30UUdD8.
>
> You can also run this example online at https://packt.live/37F57ho.

Now that we have seen the various ways of reading data from **csv** files, in the next section, let's focus on reading data directly from a URL.

READING HTML TABLES DIRECTLY FROM A URL

The **pandas** library allows us to read HTML tables directly from a URL. This means that the library already has some kind of built-in HTML parser that processes the HTML content of a given page and tries to extract various tables from the page.

> **NOTE**
>
> The **read_html** method from the **pandas** library returns a list of DataFrames (even if the page has a single DataFrame) and you have to extract the relevant tables from the list.

Consider the following example:

```
url = 'http://www.fdic.gov/bank/individual/failed/banklist.html'
list_of_df = pd.read_html(url)
df14 = list_of_df[0]
df14.head()
```

These results are shown in the following DataFrame:

	Bank Name	City	ST	CERT	Acquiring Institution	Closing Date	Updated Date
0	Washington Federal Bank for Savings	Chicago	IL	30570	Royal Savings Bank	December 15, 2017	February 21, 2018
1	The Farmers and Merchants State Bank of Argonia	Argonia	KS	17719	Conway Bank	October 13, 2017	February 21, 2018
2	Fayette County Bank	Saint Elmo	IL	1802	United Fidelity Bank, fsb	May 26, 2017	July 26, 2017
3	Guaranty Bank, (d/b/a BestBank in Georgia & Mi...	Milwaukee	WI	30003	First-Citizens Bank & Trust Company	May 5, 2017	March 22, 2018
4	First NBC Bank	New Orleans	LA	58302	Whitney Bank	April 28, 2017	December 5, 2017

Figure 5.19: Results of reading HTML tables

In the following exercise, we'll explore some more wrangling techniques to get the data in the desired format. As discussed in the preceding exercise, **read_html**, the HTML-reading function, almost always returns more than one table for a given HTML page, and we have to further parse through the list to extract the particular table we are interested in.

EXERCISE 5.07: FURTHER WRANGLING TO GET THE DESIRED DATA

In this exercise, we will work with the table of the 2016 Summer Olympics medal tally (by nation). We can easily search to get a page on Wikipedia containing this data that we can pass on to **pandas**. We will apply a few wrangling techniques on this data to get the output. To do so, let's go through the following steps:

1. Use the **read_html** command to read from the Wikipedia page containing Summer Olympics records from 2016:

    > **NOTE**
    >
    > Watch out for the slashes in the string below. Remember that the backslashes (\ ) are used to split the code across multiple lines, while the forward slashes (/) are part of the URL.

    ```python
    import pandas as pd
    list_of_df = pd.read_html("https://en.wikipedia.org/wiki/"\
                              "2016_Summer_Olympics_medal_table",\
                              header=0)
    ```

2. Check the length of the list returned. We will see that it is **7**:

    ```python
    len(list_of_df)
    ```

    The output is as follows:

    ```
    7
    ```

3. To look for the particular table, run a simple loop. We are using the **shape** property of a DataFrame to examine the number of rows and the number of columns of each of them:

    ```python
    for t in list_of_df:
        print(t.shape)
    ```

The output is as follows:

```
(1, 1)
(87, 6)
(10, 9)
(0, 2)
(1, 2)
(4, 2)
(1, 2)
```

It looks like the second element in this list is the table we are looking for.

4. Extract the second element from the table:

```
df15=list_of_df[1]
df15.head()
```

The output is as follows:

	Rank	NOC	Gold	Silver	Bronze	Total
0	1	United States (USA)	46	37	38	121
1	2	Great Britain (GBR)	27	23	17	67
2	3	China (CHN)	26	18	26	70
3	4	Russia (RUS)	19	17	20	56
4	5	Germany (GER)	17	10	15	42

Figure 5.20: Output of the data in the second table

As we can observe from the preceding table, data containing the records of the Wikipedia page has been read in a table format.

> **NOTE**
>
> To access the source code for this specific section, please refer to https://packt.live/3de6LYw.
>
> You can also run this example online at https://packt.live/2Bk9e6q.

READING FROM A JSON FILE

Over the last 15 years, JSON has become ubiquitous for data exchange on the web. Today, it is the format of choice for almost every publicly available web API, and it is frequently used for private web APIs as well. It is a schema-less, text-based representation of structured data that is based on key-value pairs and ordered lists. The **pandas** library provides excellent support for reading data from a JSON file directly into a DataFrame.

EXERCISE 5.08: READING FROM A JSON FILE

In this exercise, we will read data from the **movies.json** file. This file contains the cast, genre, title, and year (of release) information for almost all major movies since **1900**. Let's go through the following steps:

> **NOTE**
>
> The .**json** file could be found at https://packt.live/3d7DO0l.

1. Extract the list of movies from the file into a DataFrame.

```
import pandas as pd
df16 = pd.read_json("../datasets/movies.json")
df16.head()
```

> **NOTE**
>
> Don't forget to change the path (highlighted) of the JSON file based on its location on your system.

The output is as follows:

	title	year	cast	genres
0	After Dark in Central Park	1900	[]	[]
1	Boarding School Girls' Pajama Parade	1900	[]	[]
2	Buffalo Bill's Wild West Parad	1900	[]	[]
3	Caught	1900	[]	[]
4	Clowns Spinning Hats	1900	[]	[]

Figure 5.21: DataFrame displaying the movie list

2. To look for the cast where the title is **Avengers**, use filtering:

```
cast_of_avengers = df16[(df16['title']=="The Avengers") \
                    & (df16['year']==2012)]['cast']
print(list(cast_of_avengers))
```

The output will be as follows:

```
[['Robert Downey, Jr.', 'Chris Evans', 'Mark Ruffalo',
  'Chris Hemsworth', 'Scarlett Johansson', 'Jeremy Renner',
  'Tom Hiddleston', 'Clark Gregg', 'Cobie Smulders',
  'Stellan SkarsgÃyrd', 'Samuel L. Jackson']]
```

> **NOTE**
>
> To access the source code for this specific section, please refer to https://packt.live/37ISQJ8.
>
> You can also run this example online at https://packt.live/2YeymVv.

READING A PDF FILE

Among the various types of data sources, the PDF format is probably the most difficult to parse in general. While there are some popular packages in Python for working with PDF files for general page formatting, the best library to use for table extraction from PDF files is **tabula-py**.

From the GitHub page of this package, **tabula-py** is a simple Python wrapper of **tabula-java**, which can read a table from a PDF. You can read tables from PDFs and convert them into **pandas** DataFrames. The **tabula-py** library also enables you to convert a PDF file into a CSV/TSV/JSON file.

> **NOTE**
>
> Make sure you've installed **tabula** based on the instructions detailed in the section titled *Libraries to Install for This Chapter*.

You will also need the following packages installed on your system before you can run this, but they are free and easy to install; you can use **pip install** to install them from the notebook session as you did in the past:

- **urllib3**
- **pandas**
- **pytest**
- **flake8**
- **distro**
- **pathlib**

EXERCISE 5.09: READING TABULAR DATA FROM A PDF FILE

In this exercise, we will first read from two different pages of a PDF file from https://packt.live/2Ygj4j7 in tabular format, and then we will perform a few simple operations to handle the headers of these files.

> **NOTE**
>
> Before proceeding, make sure you've installed **tabula** based on the instructions detailed in an earlier section titled *Libraries to Install for This Chapter*.

Let's go through the following steps to do so:

1. The following code retrieves the tables from two pages and joins them to make one table:

```
from tabula import read_pdf
df18_1 = read_pdf('../datasets/Housing_data.pdf',\
                  pages=[1], pandas_options={'header':None})
df18_1
```

> **NOTE**
>
> Throughout this exercise, don't forget to change the path (highlighted) of the PDF based on its location on your system.

The output is as follows:

	0	1	2	3	4	5	6	7	8	9
0	0.17004	12.5	7.87	0	0.524	6.004	85.9	6.5921	5	311
1	0.22489	12.5	7.87	0	0.524	6.377	94.3	6.3467	5	311
2	0.11747	12.5	7.87	0	0.524	6.009	82.9	6.2267	5	311
3	0.09378	12.5	7.87	0	0.524	5.889	39.0	5.4509	5	311

Figure 5.22: DataFrame with a table derived by merging
a table flowing over two pages in a PDF

2. Retrieve the table from another page of the same PDF by using the following command:

```
df18_2 = read_pdf('../datasets/Housing_data.pdf',\
                  pages=[2], pandas_options={'header':None})
df18_2
```

The output is as follows:

	0	1	2	3
0	15.2	386.71	17.10	18.9
1	15.2	392.52	20.45	15.0
2	15.2	396.90	13.27	18.9
3	15.2	390.50	15.71	21.7

Figure 5.23: DataFrame displaying a table from another page

3. To concatenate the tables that were derived from the first two steps, execute the following code:

```
import pandas as pd
df1 = pd.DataFrame(df18_1)
df2 = pd.DataFrame(df18_2)
df18=pd.concat([df1,df2],axis=1)
df18.values.tolist()
```

The output is as follows:

```
[[          0     1     2  3      4      5     6       7  8    9
  0   0.17004  12.5  7.87  0  0.524  6.004  85.9  6.5921  5  311
  1   0.22489  12.5  7.87  0  0.524  6.377  94.3  6.3467  5  311
  2   0.11747  12.5  7.87  0  0.524  6.009  82.9  6.2267  5  311
  3   0.09378  12.5  7.87  0  0.524  5.889  39.0  5.4509  5  311,
  0.0,
  1.0,
  2.0,
  3.0]]
```

Figure 5.24: DataFrame derived by concatenating two tables

With PDF extraction, most of the time, headers will be difficult to extract automatically.

4. Pass on the list of headers with the **names** argument in the **read-pdf** function set to **pandas_option**, as follows:

```
names = ['CRIM','ZN','INDUS','CHAS','NOX','RM','AGE','DIS',\
         'RAD','TAX','PTRATIO','B','LSTAT','PRICE']
df18_1 = read_pdf('../datasets/Housing_data.pdf',pages = [1], \
                   pandas_options = {'header':None,\
                                     'names':names[:10]})
df18_2 = read_pdf('../datasets/Housing_data.pdf',pages = [2],\
                   pandas_options = {'header':None,\
                                     'names':names[10:]})
df1 = pd.DataFrame(df18_1)
df2 = pd.DataFrame(df18_2)
df18 = pd.concat([df1,df2],axis = 1)
df18.values.tolist()
```

The output is as follows:

```
[[      CRIM    ZN  INDUS  CHAS    NOX      RM   AGE     DIS  RAD  TAX
 0   0.17004  12.5   7.87     0  0.524   6.004  85.9  6.5921    5  311
 1   0.22489  12.5   7.87     0  0.524   6.377  94.3  6.3467    5  311
 2   0.11747  12.5   7.87     0  0.524   6.009  82.9  6.2267    5  311
 3   0.09378  12.5   7.87     0  0.524   5.889  39.0  5.4509    5  311,
     PTRATIO       B  LSTAT  PRICE
 0      15.2  386.71  17.10   18.9
 1      15.2  392.52  20.45   15.0
 2      15.2  396.90  13.27   18.9
 3      15.2  390.50  15.71   21.7]]
```

Figure 5.25: DataFrame with the correct column headers for PDF data

> **NOTE**
>
> To access the source code for this specific section, please refer to https://packt.live/2YcHz0v.
>
> This section does not currently have an online interactive example, and will need to be run locally.

We will have a full activity on reading tables from a PDF report and processing them at the end of this chapter. Let's dive into web page scraping and the library used to do that, Beautiful Soup 4.

INTRODUCTION TO BEAUTIFUL SOUP 4 AND WEB PAGE PARSING

The ability to read and understand web pages is of paramount interest to a person collecting and formatting data. For example, consider the task of gathering data about movies and then formatting it for a downstream system. Data from movie databases is best obtained from websites such as IMDb, and that data does not come pre-packaged in nice forms (such as CSV or JSON), so you need to know how to download and read a web page.

You also need to be equipped with the knowledge of the structure of a web page so that you can design a system that can search for (query) a particular piece of information from a whole web page and get the value from it. This involves understanding the grammar of markup languages and being able to write something that can parse them. Doing this, and keeping all the edge cases in mind, for something like HTML is already incredibly complex, and if you extend the scope of the bespoke markup language to include XML as well, then it becomes full-time work for a team of people.

Thankfully, we are using Python, and Python has a very mature and stable library that does all the complicated tasks for us. This library is called **BeautifulSoup** (it is, at present, in version 4, and thus we will call it **bs4** for short from now on). **bs4** is a library for getting data from HTML or XML documents, and it gives you a nice, normalized, idiomatic way of navigating and querying a document. It does not include a parser but it supports different ones.

STRUCTURE OF HTML

Before we jump into **bs4** and start working with it, we need to examine the structure of an HTML document. **H**yper **T**ext **M**arkup **L**anguage is a structured way of telling web browsers about the organization of a web page, meaning which kinds of elements (text, image, video, and so on) come from where, where inside the page they should appear, what they look like, what they contain, and how they will behave with user input. HTML5 is the latest version of HTML. An HTML document can be viewed as a tree, as we can see in the following diagram:

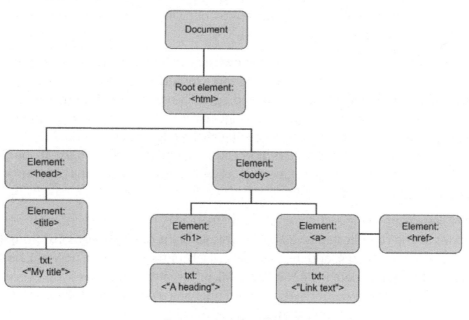

Document Object Model

Figure 5.26: HTML structure

Each node of the tree represents one element in the document. An element is anything that starts with **<** and ends with **>**. For example, **<html>**, **<head>**, **<p>**, **
, **<img>, and so on are various HTML elements. Some elements have a start and end element, where the end element begins with **</** and has the same name as the start element, such as **<p>** and **</p>**, and they can contain an arbitrary number of elements of other types in them. Some elements do not have an ending part, such as the **
** element, and they cannot contain anything within them.

The only other thing that we need to know about an element at this point is the fact that elements can have attributes, which are there to modify the default behavior of an element. For example, an **<a>** anchor element requires a **href** attribute to tell the browser which website it should navigate to when that particular **<a>** is clicked, like this: **<a href="http://cnn.com">. The CNN news channel, </a>**, will take you to cnn.com when clicked:

The CNN news channel

Figure 5.27: CNN news channel hyperlink

So, when you are at a particular element of the tree, you can visit all the children of that element to get their contents and attributes.

Equipped with this knowledge, let's see how we can read and query data from an HTML document.

In this topic, we will cover the reading and parsing of web pages, but we do not request them from a live website. Instead, we read them from disk. A section on reading them from the internet will follow in a future chapter.

EXERCISE 5.10: READING AN HTML FILE AND EXTRACTING ITS CONTENTS USING BEAUTIFUL SOUP

In this exercise, we will do the simplest thing possible. We will import the **Beautiful Soup** or **bs4** library and then use it to read an HTML document. Then, we will examine the different kinds of objects it returns. While doing the exercises for this topic, you should have the example HTML file (called **test.html**) open in a text editor so that you can check for the different tags and their attributes and contents:

1. Import the **bs4** library:

```
from bs4 import BeautifulSoup
```

2. Please download the following test HTML file and save it on your disk, and then use **bs4** to read it from the disk:

```
with open("../datasets/test.html", "r") as fd:
    soup = BeautifulSoup(fd)
    print(type(soup))
```

> **NOTE**
>
> Throughout this exercise, don't forget to change the path (highlighted) of the HTML file based on its location on your system.

The output is as follows:

```
<class 'bs4.BeautifulSoup'>
```

You can pass a file handler directly to the constructor of the **BeautifulSoup** object and it will read the contents from the file that the handler is attached to. We will see that the return type is an instance of **bs4.BeautifulSoup**. This class holds all the methods we need to navigate through the DOM tree that the document represents.

3. Print the contents of the file in a nice way, by which we mean that the printing will keep some kind of nice indentation by using the **prettify** method from the class, like this:

```
print(soup.prettify())
```

The output is as follows:

```
<html>
 <body>
  <h1>
   Lorem ipsum dolor sit amet consectetuer adipiscing
elit
  </h1>
  <p>
   Lorem ipsum dolor sit amet, consectetuer adipiscing
elit. Aenean commodo ligula eget dolor. Aenean massa
   <strong>
    strong
   </strong>
   . Cum sociis natoque penatibus
et magnis dis parturient montes, nascetur ridiculus
mus. Donec quam felis, ultricies nec, pellentesque
eu, pretium quis, sem. Nulla consequat massa quis
enim. Donec pede justo, fringilla vel, aliquet nec,
vulputate eget, arcu. In enim justo, rhoncus ut,
imperdiet a, venenatis vitae, justo. Nullam dictum
```

Figure 5.28: Contents of the HTML file

The same information can also be obtained by using the **soup.contents** member variable. The differences are: first, it won't print anything pretty and, second, it is essentially a list.

If we look carefully at the contents of the HTML file in a separate text editor, we will see that there are many paragraph tags, or **<p>** tags. Let's read content from one such **<p>** tag. We can do that using the simple . access modifier as we would have done for a normal member variable of a class.

The magic of **bs4** is the fact that it gives us this excellent way to dereference tags as member variables of the **BeautifulSoup** class instance. In the following few steps, we are going to read an HTML file and then pass the file handler returned by Python's **open** call directly to the constructor of the **BeautifulSoup** class. It does a lot of things (including reading the content and then parsing it) and returns an instance of the class that we can then use.

4. Read the HTML file:

```
with open("../datasets/test.html", "r") as fd:
    soup = BeautifulSoup(fd)
    print(soup.p)
```

The output is as follows:

```
<p>Lorem ipsum dolor sit amet, consectetuer adipiscing
elit. Aenean commodo ligula eget dolor. Aenean massa
<strong>strong</strong>. Cum sociis natoque penatibus
et magnis dis parturient montes, nascetur ridiculus
mus. Donec quam felis, ultricies nec, pellentesque
eu, pretium quis, sem. Nulla consequat massa quis
enim. Donec pede justo, fringilla vel, aliquet nec,
vulputate eget, arcu. In enim justo, rhoncus ut,
imperdiet a, venenatis vitae, justo. Nullam dictum
felis eu pede <a class="external ext" href="#">link</a>
mollis pretium. Integer tincidunt. Cras dapibus.
Vivamus elementum semper nisi. Aenean vulputate
eleifend tellus. Aenean leo ligula, porttitor eu,
consequat vitae, eleifend ac, enim. Aliquam lorem ante,
dapibus in, viverra quis, feugiat a, tellus. Phasellus
viverra nulla ut metus varius laoreet. Quisque rutrum.
Aenean imperdiet. Etiam ultricies nisi vel augue.
Curabitur ullamcorper ultricies nisi.</p>
```

Figure 5.29: Text from the <p> tag

As we can see, this is the content of the **<p>** tag.

We saw how to read a tag in the last exercise, but we can easily see the problem with this approach. When we look into our HTML document, we can see that we have more than one **<p>** tag there. How can we access all the **<p>** tags? It turns out that this is easy.

5. Use the **findall** method to extract the content from the tag:

```
with open("../datasets/test.html", "r") as fd:
    soup = BeautifulSoup(fd)
    all_ps = soup.find_all('p')
    print("Total number of <p>  --- {}".format(len(all_ps)))
```

The output is as follows:

```
Total number of <p>  --- 6
```

This will print **6**, which is exactly the number of **<p>** tags in the document.

We have seen how to access all the tags of the same type. We have also seen how to get the content of the entire HTML document.

6. Now we will see how to get the contents of a particular HTML tag:

```
with open("../datasets/test.html", "r") as fd:
    soup = BeautifulSoup(fd)
    table = soup.table
    print(table.contents)
```

The output is as follows:

```
['\n    ', <tbody><tr>
   <th>Entry Header 1</th>
   <th>Entry Header 2</th>
   <th>Entry Header 3</th>
   <th>Entry Header 4</th>
 </tr>
 <tr>
   <td>Entry First Line 1</td>
   <td>Entry First Line 2</td>
   <td>Entry First Line 3</td>
   <td>Entry First Line 4</td>
 </tr>
 <tr>
   <td>Entry Line 1</td>
   <td>Entry Line 2</td>
   <td>Entry Line 3</td>
   <td>Entry Line 4</td>
 </tr>
 <tr>
   <td>Entry Last Line 1</td>
   <td>Entry Last Line 2</td>
   <td>Entry Last Line 3</td>
   <td>Entry Last Line 4</td>
 </tr>
 </tbody>]
```

Figure 5.30: Contents of the <table> tag

Here, we are getting the (first) table from the document and then using the same . notation to get the contents of that tag. We saw in the previous step that we can access the entire content of a particular tag. However, HTML is represented as a tree, and we are able to traverse the children of a particular node. There are a few ways to do this.

7. The first way is by using the **children** generator from any **bs4** instance, as follows:

```
with open("../datasets/test.html", "r") as fd:
    soup = BeautifulSoup(fd)
    table = soup.table
    for child in table.children:
        print(child)
        print("*****")
```

When we execute the code, we will see something like the following:

```
*****
<tbody><tr>
    <th>Entry Header 1</th>
    <th>Entry Header 2</th>
    <th>Entry Header 3</th>
    <th>Entry Header 4</th>
  </tr>
  <tr>
    <td>Entry First Line 1</td>
    <td>Entry First Line 2</td>
    <td>Entry First Line 3</td>
    <td>Entry First Line 4</td>
  </tr>
  <tr>
    <td>Entry Line 1</td>
    <td>Entry Line 2</td>
    <td>Entry Line 3</td>
    <td>Entry Line 4</td>
  </tr>
  <tr>
    <td>Entry Last Line 1</td>
    <td>Entry Last Line 2</td>
    <td>Entry Last Line 3</td>
    <td>Entry Last Line 4</td>
  </tr>
</tbody>
*****
```

Figure 5.31: Traversing the children of a table node

It seems that the loop has only been executed twice. Well, the problem with the **children** generator is that it only takes into account the immediate children of the tag. We have **<tbody>** under **<table>**, and our whole table structure is wrapped in it. That's why it was considered a single child of the **<table>** tag.

We have looked into how to browse the immediate children of a tag. We will see how we can browse all the possible children of a tag and not only the immediate one.

8. To do that, we use the **descendants** generator from the **bs4** instance, as follows:

```
with open("../datasets/test.html", "r") as fd:
    soup = BeautifulSoup(fd)
    table = soup.table
    children = table.children
    des = table.descendants
    print(len(list(children)), len(list(des)))
```

The output is as follows:

```
9 61
```

The comparison print at the end of the code block will show us the difference between **children** and **descendants**. The length of the list we got from **children** is only **9**, whereas the length of the list we got from **descendants** is **61**.

> **NOTE**
>
> To access the source code for this specific section, please refer to https://packt.live/2N994l6.
>
> You can also run this example online at https://packt.live/2UT2p2K.

So far, we have seen some basic ways to navigate the tags inside an HTML document using **bs4**. Now, we are going to go one step further and use the power of **bs4** combined with the power of **pandas** to generate a DataFrame out of a plain HTML table. With the knowledge we will acquire now, it will be fairly easy for us to prepare a **pandas** DataFrame to perform **exploratory data analysis (EDA)** or modeling. We are going to show you how to create a DataFrame with the extracted data from HTML using the **BeautifulSoup** library.

EXERCISE 5.11: DATAFRAMES AND BEAUTIFULSOUP

In this exercise, we will extract the data from the **test.html** page using the **BeautifulSoup** library. We will then perform a few operations for data preparation and display the data in an easily readable tabular format. To do that, let's go through the following steps:

1. Import **pandas** and read the document, as follows:

```
import pandas as pd
from bs4 import BeautifulSoup
fd = open("../datasets/test.html", "r")
soup = BeautifulSoup(fd)
data = soup.findAll('tr')
print("Data is a {} and {} items long".format(type(data),\
      len(data)))
```

> **NOTE**
>
> Don't forget to change the path (highlighted) of the HTML file based on its location on your system.

The output is as follows:

```
Data is a <class 'bs4.element.ResultSet'> and 4 items long
```

2. Check the original table structure in the HTML source. You will see that the first row is the column heading and all of the following rows are the data from the HTML source. We'll assign two different variables for the two sections, as follows:

```
data_without_header = data[1:]
headers = data[0]
headers
```

The output is as follows:

```
<tr>
<th>Entry Header 1</th>
<th>Entry Header 2</th>
<th>Entry Header 3</th>
<th>Entry Header 4</th>
</tr>
```

> **NOTE**
>
> Keep in mind that the art of scraping an HTML page goes hand in hand with an understanding of the source HTML structure. So, whenever you want to scrape a page, the first thing you need to do is right-click on it and then use **View Source** from the browser to see the source HTML.

3. Once we have separated the two sections, we need two list comprehensions to make them ready to go in a DataFrame. For the header, this is easy:

```
col_headers = [th.getText() for th in headers.findAll('th')]
col_headers
```

The output is as follows:

```
['Entry Header 1', 'Entry Header 2', 'Entry Header 3', 'Entry Header
4']
```

Data preparation is a bit tricky for a **pandas** DataFrame. You need to have a two-dimensional list, which is a list of lists. We accomplish that in the following way, using the tricks we learned earlier about list comprehension.

4. Use the **for...in** loop to iterate over the data:

```
df_data = [[td.getText() for td in tr.findAll('td')] \
            for tr in data_without_header]
df_data
```

The output is as follows:

```
[['Entry First Line 1',
  'Entry First Line 2',
  'Entry First Line 3',
  'Entry First Line 4'],
 ['Entry Line 1', 'Entry Line 2', 'Entry Line 3', 'Entry Line 4'],
 ['Entry Last Line 1',
  'Entry Last Line 2',
  'Entry Last Line 3',
  'Entry Last Line 4']]
```

Figure 5.32: Output as a two-dimensional list

5. Invoke the **pd.DataFrame** method and supply the right arguments by using the following code:

```
df = pd.DataFrame(df_data, columns=col_headers)
df.head()
```

The output is as follows:

	Entry Header 1	Entry Header 2	Entry Header 3	Entry Header 4
0	Entry First Line 1	Entry First Line 2	Entry First Line 3	Entry First Line 4
1	Entry Line 1	Entry Line 2	Entry Line 3	Entry Line 4
2	Entry Last Line 1	Entry Last Line 2	Entry Last Line 3	Entry Last Line 4

Figure 5.33: Output in tabular format with column headers

Thus, we conclude our exercise on creating a data frame from an HTML table.

> **NOTE**
>
> To access the source code for this specific section, please refer to https://packt.live/30QyE6A.
>
> You can also run this example online at https://packt.live/3hBPFY5.

In the following exercise, we'll export a DataFrame as an Excel file.

EXERCISE 5.12: EXPORTING A DATAFRAME AS AN EXCEL FILE

In this exercise, we will see how we can save a DataFrame as an Excel file. **Pandas** can do this natively, but it needs the help of the **openpyxl** library to achieve this goal. **openpyxl** is a Python library for reading/writing Excel 2010 **xlsx/xlsm/xltx/xltm** files.

> **NOTE**
>
> This exercise is continued from the previous exercise. You'll need to continue in the same Jupyter Notebook.

Let's perform the following steps:

1. Install the **openpyxl** library by using the following command:

```
!pip install openpyxl
```

2. To save the DataFrame as an Excel file, use the following command from inside of the Jupyter notebook:

```
writer = pd.ExcelWriter('../datasets/test_output.xlsx')
df.to_excel(writer, "Sheet1")
writer.save()
writer
```

> **NOTE**
>
> Don't forget to change the path (highlighted) of the Excel file based the folder structure of your local system.

The output is as follows:

```
<pandas.io.excel._XlsxWriter at 0x24feb2939b0>
```

This is the way in which we can export a **pandas** DataFrame to Excel. Given that Excel is a very popular format among many types of users, this is a very important trick you need to master.

> **NOTE**
>
> To access the source code for this specific section, please refer to https://packt.live/2YcSdV6.
>
> You can also run this example online at https://packt.live/2YZTXjJ.

In the previous chapters, when we were discussing the stack, we explained how important it is to have a stack that we can push the URLs from a web page to so that we can pop them at a later time to follow each of them. The following exercise will demonstrate how to do that.

EXERCISE 5.13: STACKING URLS FROM A DOCUMENT USING BS4

In this exercise, we will append the URLs one after the other from the **test.html** web page. In that file, HTML file links or **<a>** tags are under a **<ul>** tag, and each of them is contained inside a **</li>** tag. We are going to find all the **<a>** tags and create a stack with them.

> **NOTE**
>
> This exercise is continued from the previous exercise. You'll need to continue in the same Jupyter Notebook.

To do so, let's go through the following steps:

1. Find all the **<a>** tags by using the following command:

```
d = open("../datasets/test.html", "r")
soup = BeautifulSoup(d)
lis = soup.find('ul').findAll('li')
stack = []
for li in lis:
    a = li.find('a', href=True)
```

> **NOTE**
>
> Don't forget to change the path (highlighted) of the HTML file based on its location on your system.

2. Define a stack before you start the loop. Then, inside the loop, use the **append** method to push the links in the stack:

```
stack.append(a['href'])
```

3. Print the stack:

```
print(stack)
```

The output is as follows:

```
['https://www.imdb.com/chart/top']
```

NOTE

To access the source code for this specific section, please refer
to https://packt.live/3hCCAOj.

You can also run this example online at https://packt.live/3fCYNd0.

Let's put together everything we have learned so far in this chapter and get started
with an activity.

ACTIVITY 5.01: READING TABULAR DATA FROM A WEB PAGE AND CREATING DATAFRAMES

In this activity, you have been given a Wikipedia page where you have the GDP of
all countries listed. You have to create three **DataFrames** from the three sources
mentioned on the page (https://en.wikipedia.org/wiki/List_of_countries_by_GDP_(nominal)).

You will have to do the following:

1. Open the page in a separate Chrome/Firefox tab and use something like an
    Inspect Element tool to view the source HTML and understand its structure.

2. Read the page using **bs4**.

3. Find the table structure you will need to deal with (how many tables are there?).

4. Find the right table using **bs4**.

5. Separate the source names and their corresponding data.

6. Get the source names from the list of sources you have created.

7. Separate the header and data from the data that you separated before for the
    first source only, and then create a DataFrame using that.

8. Repeat the last task for the other two data sources.

The output should look like this:

	Rank	Country	GDP(US$MM)
0		World	80,683,787
1	1	United States	19,390,604
2		European Union[23]	17,277,698
3	2	China[n 4]	12,237,700
4	3	Japan	4,872,137

Figure 5.34: Final output

> **NOTE**
>
> The solution for this activity can be found on page 483.

SUMMARY

In this chapter, we have looked into several different types of data formats and how to work with them. These formats include CSV, PDF, Excel, Plain Text, and HTML. HTML documents are the cornerstone of the World Wide Web and, given the amount of data that's contained in it, we can easily infer the importance of HTML as a data source.

We learned about **bs4** (**BeautifulSoup 4**), a Python library that gives us Pythonic ways to read and query HTML documents. We used bs4 to load an HTML document and explored several different ways to navigate the loaded document.

We also looked at how we can create a **pandas** DataFrame from an HTML document (which contains a table). Although there are some built-in ways to do this job in **pandas**, they fail as soon as the target table is encoded inside a complex hierarchy of elements. So, the knowledge we gathered in this topic to transform an HTML table into a **pandas** DataFrame in a step-by-step manner is invaluable.

Finally, we looked at how we can create a stack in our code, where we push all the URLs that we encounter while reading the HTML file and then use them at a later time. In the next chapter, we will discuss list comprehensions, the **.zip** format, and outlier detection and cleaning.

6

LEARNING THE HIDDEN SECRETS OF DATA WRANGLING

OVERVIEW

In this chapter, you will learn about data problems that arise in business use cases and how to resolve them. This chapter will give you the skills needed to be able to clean and handle real-life messy data. By the end of this chapter, you will be able to prepare data for analysis by formatting it as required by downstream systems. You will also be able to identify and remove outliers from data.

INTRODUCTION

In this chapter, we will learn the secret behind creating a successful data wrangling pipeline. In the previous chapters, we were introduced to basic and advanced data structures and other building blocks of data wrangling, such as **pandas** and NumPy. In this chapter, we will look at the data handling aspect of data wrangling.

Imagine that you have a database of patients who have heart diseases, and like any survey, the data is either missing, incorrect, or has outliers. Outliers are values that are abnormal and tend to be far away from the central tendency, and thus including it in your fancy machine learning model may introduce a terrible bias that we need to avoid. Often, these problems can cause a huge difference in terms of money, man-hours, and other organizational resources. It is undeniable that someone with the skills to solve these problems will prove to be an asset to an organization. In this chapter, we'll talk about a few advanced techniques that we can use to handle outliers and missing data.

ADVANCED LIST COMPREHENSION AND THE ZIP FUNCTION

In this section, we will deep dive into the heart of list comprehension. We have already seen a basic form of it, including something as simple as `a = [i for i in range(0, 30)]` to something a bit more complex that involves one conditional statement. However, as we already mentioned, list comprehension is a very powerful tool and, in this section, we will explore this amazing tool further. We will investigate another close relative of list comprehension called **generators**, which also provides a way to create lists, and work with `zip` and its related functions and methods. By the end of this section, you will be confident in handling complicated logical problems.

INTRODUCTION TO GENERATOR EXPRESSIONS

In the previous chapter, while discussing advanced data structures, we witnessed functions such as **repeat**. We said that they represent a special type of function known as iterators. We also showed you how the lazy evaluation of an iterator can lead to an enormous amount of space being saved and time efficiency.

Iterators are one brick in the functional programming construct that Python has to offer. Functional programming is indeed a very efficient and safe way to approach a problem. It offers various advantages over other methods, such as modularity, ease of debugging and testing, composability, formal provability (a theoretical computer science concept), and more.

Now, let's look at an exercise where we'll see how to use generator expressions. But before we do that, we should define, formally, what a generator expression is. Generator expressions are a high-performance, memory-efficient generalization of list comprehensions and generators. We'll practice this concept in the following exercise. Since we have covered some amount of list comprehension already, generator expressions will look familiar to us. However, they also offer some advantages over list comprehension.

EXERCISE 6.01: GENERATOR EXPRESSIONS

In this exercise, we will be working with generator expressions, which are considered another brick of functional programming (as a matter of fact, they are inspired by the pure functional language known as Haskell). We will create a list of odd numbers using list comprehension and check the memory occupied by the list. We will then create the same list using a generator expression and see the advantage of using it over list comprehension. To do so, let's go through the following steps:

1. Open a new Jupyter Notebook and write the following code using list comprehension to generate a list of all the odd numbers between 0 and 10,0000:

```
odd_numbers2 = [x for x in range(100000) if x % 2 != 0]
```

2. Use **getsizeof** from **sys** by using the following code to understand the bytes of memory the generator expressions occupy:

```
from sys import getsizeof
getsizeof(odd_numbers2)
```

The output is as follows:

```
406496
```

We will see that it takes a good amount of memory to do this. It is also not very time efficient. How can we change this? Using a method such as **repeat** is not applicable here because we need to have the logic of the list comprehension. Fortunately, we can turn any list comprehension into a generator expression.

3. Write the equivalent generator expression for the aforementioned list comprehension:

```
odd_numbers = (x for x in range(100000) if x % 2 != 0)
```

Notice that the only change we made is to surround the list comprehension statement with round brackets instead of square ones. This makes it shrink to only around **100** bytes. This is because this is a generator expression, so no explicit memory has been allocated for it. There's just enough memory to hold the logic of the generation of numbers. This makes it become a lazy evaluation, and thus is more efficient.

4. Print the first 10 odd numbers, as follows:

```
for i, number in enumerate(odd_numbers):
    print(number)
    if i > 10:
        break
```

The output is as follows:

```
1
3
5
7
9
11
13
15
17
19
21
23
```

As we can see, the first 10 odd numbers are being printed on the console.

> **NOTE**
>
> To access the source code for this specific section, please refer to https://packt.live/2YMwDFH.
>
> You can also run this example online at https://packt.live/3daSb47.

In the next exercise, we'll take a look at how to write a generator expression in one line.

EXERCISE 6.02: SINGLE-LINE GENERATOR EXPRESSION

In this exercise, we will use our knowledge of generator expressions to generate an expression that will read one word at a time from a list of words and will remove newline characters at the end of them while making them lowercase. This can certainly be done using a **for** loop explicitly. To do so, let's go through the following steps:

1. Create a new Jupyter Notebook and create a **words** string, as follows:

```
words = ["Hello\n", "My name", "is\n",\
         "Bob", "How are you", "doing\n"]
```

2. Write the following generator expression to achieve this task, as follows:

```
modified_words = (word.strip().lower() for word in words)
```

3. Create a list comprehension to get words one by one from the generator expression and finally print the list, as follows:

```
final_list_of_word = [word for word in modified_words]
final_list_of_word
```

The output is as follows:

```
['hello', 'my name', 'is', 'bob', 'how are you', 'doing']
```

As we can see, we created a one-liner generator expression efficiently using a simple **for** loop.

> **NOTE**
>
> To access the source code for this specific section, please refer to https://packt.live/2Bg5pzi.
>
> You can also run this example online at https://packt.live/2Yblo9J.

In the next exercise, we'll extract a list using single words.

EXERCISE 6.03: EXTRACTING A LIST WITH SINGLE WORDS

If we look at the output of the previous exercise, we will notice that due to the messy nature of the source data (which is normal in the real world), we ended up with a list where, in some cases, we have more than one word together as a phrase, separated by a space. To improve this and to get a list of single words, we will have to modify the generator expressions. Let's see how to do that:

1. Write the generator expression and then write the equivalent nested **for** loops so that we can compare the results:

```
words = ["Hello\n", "My name", "is\n", \
         "Bob", "How are you", "doing\n"]
modified_words2 = (w.strip().lower() for word \
                     in words for w in word.split(" "))
final_list_of_word = [word for word in modified_words2]
final_list_of_word
```

The output is as follows:

```
['hello', 'my', 'name', 'is', 'bob', 'how', 'are', 'you', 'doing']
```

2. Write an equivalent to the preceding code by using a nested **for** loop, as follows:

```
modified_words3 = []
for word in words:
    for w in word.split(" "):
        modified_words3.append(w.strip().lower())
modified_words3
```

The output is as follows:

```
['hello', 'my', 'name', 'is', 'bob', 'how', 'are', 'you', 'doing']
```

We must admit that the generator expression is not only space- and time-saving but also a more elegant way to write the same logic.

> **NOTE**
>
> To access the source code for this specific section, please refer to https://packt.live/2YFD5yo.
>
> You can also run this example online at https://packt.live/3hG4WXO.

To remember how the nested loop works in generator expressions, keep in mind that the loops are evaluated from left to right and the final loop variable (in our example, which is denoted by the single letter **w**) is given back (thus, we could call **strip** and **lower** on it).

The following diagram will help you remember the trick about using nested **for** loops in list comprehension or generator expressions:

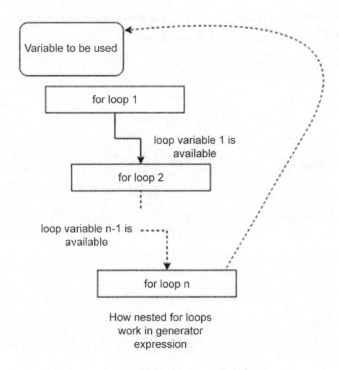

How nested for loops
work in generator
expression

Figure 6.1: Nested loops illustration

We have learned about nested **for** loops in generator expressions previously, but now we are going to learn about independent **for** loops in a generator expression. We will have two output variables from two **for** loops and they must be treated as a tuple so that they don't have ambiguous grammar in Python.

Create the following two lists:

```
marbles = ["RED", "BLUE", "GREEN"]
counts = [1, 5, 13]
```

You are asked to generate all possible combinations of the values in the **marbles** array and **counts** array after being given the preceding two lists. How will you do that? Surely using a nested **for** loop and the **append** method, you can accomplish the task. How about a generator expression? A more elegant and easy solution is as follows:

```
marble_with_count = ((m, c) for m in marbles for c in counts)
```

This generator expression creates a tuple in each iteration of the simultaneous **for** loops. This code is equivalent to the following explicit code:

```
marble_with_count_as_list_2 = []
for m in marbles:
    for c in counts:
        marble_with_count_as_list_2.append((m, c))
marble_with_count_as_list_2
```

The output is as follows:

```
[('RED', 1),
 ('RED', 5),
 ('RED', 13),
 ('BLUE', 1),
 ('BLUE', 5),
 ('BLUE', 13),
 ('GREEN', 1),
 ('GREEN', 5),
 ('GREEN', 13)]
```

This generator expression creates a tuple in each iteration of the simultaneous **for** loops. Once again, the generator expression is easy, elegant, and efficient compared to the **for..in** loop.

Let's move on to the next exercise, where we will examine the **zip** function and compare it with the generator expression.

EXERCISE 6.04: THE ZIP FUNCTION

In this exercise, we will examine the **zip** function and compare it with the generator expression we wrote in the previous exercise. The problem with the previous generator expression is the fact that it produced all possible combinations. For instance, if we need to relate countries with their capitals, doing so using a generator expression will be difficult. Fortunately, Python gives us a built-in function called **zip** for just this purpose:

1. Open a new Jupyter Notebook and create the following two lists:

```
countries = ["India", "USA", "France", "UK"]
capitals = ["Delhi", "Washington", "Paris", "London"]
```

2. Generate a list of tuples where the first element is the name of the country and the second element is the name of the capital by using the following commands:

```
countries_and_capitals = [t for t in zip(countries, capitals)]
countries_and_capitals
```

The output is:

```
[('India', 'Delhi'),
 ('USA', 'Washington'),
 ('France', 'Paris'),
 ('UK', 'London')]
```

This is not very well represented. It would make more sense if we can use **dict** where keys are the names of the countries, while the values are the names of the capitals.

3. Use the following command, where keys are the names of the countries:

```
countries_and_capitals_as_dict = dict(zip(countries, capitals))
countries_and_capitals_as_dict
```

The output is as follows:

```
{'India': 'Delhi', 'USA': 'Washington',
 'France': 'Paris', 'UK': 'London'}
```

As always, in real life, data is messy. So, the nice equal length lists of countries and capitals that we just saw are not always available. The **zip** function cannot be used with unequal length lists, because **zip** will stop working as soon as one of the lists comes to an end.

> ### NOTE
>
> To access the source code for this specific section, please refer to https://packt.live/3hDfKG5.
>
> You can also run this example online at https://packt.live/2CgdOTP.

Let's look at the following exercise to understand how we can handle messy data.

EXERCISE 6.05: HANDLING MESSY DATA

In this exercise, we're going to use the **zip** function to handle messy data in lists of unequal length. In such a situation, we will use the **ziplongest** function from the **itertools** module. Let's perform the following steps:

1. Open a new Jupyter Notebook and create two lists of unequal length, as follows:

```
countries = ["India", "USA", "France", "UK", "Brazil", "Japan"]
capitals = ["Delhi", "Washington", "Paris", "London"]
```

2. Create the final dictionary. **None** will be displayed as the value for the countries that do not have a capital in the capital's list:

```
from itertools import zip_longest
countries_and_capitals_as_dict_2 = dict(zip_longest(countries, \
                                         capitals))
countries_and_capitals_as_dict_2
```

The output is as follows:

```
{'India': 'Delhi',
 'USA': 'Washington',
 'France': 'Paris',
 'UK': 'London',
 'Brazil': None,
 'Japan': None}
```

We should pause here for a second and think about how many lines of explicit code and difficult-to-understand **if-else** conditional logic we just saved by calling a single function and just giving it the two source data lists. It is indeed amazing.

> **NOTE**
>
> To access the source code for this specific section, please refer to https://packt.live/3edKtYf.
>
> You can also run this example online at https://packt.live/37CsacU.

With these exercises, we are ending the first topic of this chapter. Advanced list comprehension, generator expressions, and functions such as **zip** and **ziplongest** are some very important tricks that we need to master if we want to write clean, efficient, and maintainable code. Code that does not have these three qualities are considered subpar in the industry, and we certainly don't want to write such code.

However, we did not cover one important point here, that is, generators. Generators are a special type of function that shares behavioral traits with generator expressions. However, being functions, they have a broader scope and they are much more flexible. We strongly encourage you to learn about them.

> **NOTE**
>
> You can read more about generators here: https://wiki.python.org/moin/Generators.

DATA FORMATTING

In this section, we will format a given dataset. The main motivations behind formatting data properly are as follows:

- It helps all the downstream systems have a single and pre-agreed form of data for each data point, thus avoiding surprises and, in effect, there is no risk which might break the system.

- To produce a human-readable report from lower-level data that is, most of the time, created for machine consumption.

- To find errors in data.

There are a few ways to perform data formatting in Python. We will begin with the modulus % operator.

THE % OPERATOR

Python gives us the modulus % operator to apply basic formatting on data. To demonstrate this, we will load the data by reading the **combined_data.csv** file, and then we will apply some basic formatting to it.

> **NOTE**
>
> The **combined_data.csv** file contains some sample medical data for four individuals. The file can be found here: https://packt.live/310179U.

We can load the data from the CSV file by using the following command:

```
from csv import DictReader
raw_data = []
with open("../datasets/combinded_data.csv", "rt") as fd:
    data_rows = DictReader(fd)
    for data in data_rows:
        raw_data.append(dict(data))
```

Now, we have a list called **raw_data** that contains all the rows of the CSV file. Feel free to print it to see what the content of the **.csv** file looks like.

The output is as follows:

```
[{'Name': 'Bob',
  'Age': '23.0',
  'Height': '1.7',
  'Weight': '70',
  'Disease_history': 'N',
  'Heart_problem': 'N'},
 {'Name': 'Alex',
  'Age': '45',
  'Height': '1.61',
  'Weight': '61',
  'Disease_history': 'Y',
  'Heart_problem': 'N'},
```

Figure 6.2: Partial output of raw data

We will be producing a report on this data. This report will contain one section for each data point and will report the name, age, weight, height, history of family disease, and finally the present heart condition of the person. These points must be clear and easily understandable English sentences.

We do this in the following way:

```
for data in raw_data:
    report_str = \
    """%s is %s years old and is %s meter tall weighing \
about %s kg.\n
Has a history of family illness: %s.\n
Presently suffering from a heart disease: %s
    """ % (data["Name"], data["Age"], \
           data["Height"], data["Weight"], \
           data["Disease_history"], data["Heart_problem"])
    print(report_str)
```

The output is as follows:

```
Bob is 23.0 years old and is 1.7 meter tall weiging about 70 kg.

    Has a hsitory of family illness: N.

    Presently suffering from a heart disease: N

Alex is 45 years old and is 1.61 meter tall weiging about 61 kg.

    Has a hsitory of family illness: Y.

    Presently suffering from a heart disease: N

George is 12.5 years old and is 1.4 meter tall weiging about 40 kg.

    Has a hsitory of family illness: N.

    Presently suffering from a heart disease:

Alice is 34 years old and is 1.56 meter tall weiging about 51 kg.

    Has a hsitory of family illness: N.

    Presently suffering from a heart disease: Y
```

Figure 6.3: Raw data in a presentable format

The % operator is used in two different ways:

- When used inside a quote, it signifies what kind of data to expect here. **%s** stands for string, whereas **%d** stands for integer. If we indicate a wrong data type, it will throw an error. Thus, we can effectively use this kind of formatting as an error filter in the incoming data.

- When we use the % operator outside the quote, it basically tells Python to start replacing all the data inside with the values provided for them outside.

USING THE FORMAT FUNCTION

In this section, we will be looking at the exact same formatting problem, but this time, we will use a more advanced approach. We will use Python's **format** function.

To use the **format** function, we do the following:

```
for data in raw_data:
    report_str = \
    """{} is {} years old and is {} meter tall weighing \
about {} kg.\n
Has a history of family illness: {}.\n
Presently suffering from a heart disease: {}
    """.format(data["Name"], data["Age"], data["Height"], \
    data["Weight"],data["Disease_history"], data["Heart_problem"])
    print(report_str)
```

The output is as follows:

```
Bob is 23.0 years old and is 1.7 meter tall weiging about 70 kg.

    Has a hsitory of family illness: N.

    Presently suffering from a heart disease: N

Alex is 45 years old and is 1.61 meter tall weiging about 61 kg.

    Has a hsitory of family illness: Y.

    Presently suffering from a heart disease: N

George is 12.5 years old and is 1.4 meter tall weiging about 40 kg.

    Has a hsitory of family illness: N.

    Presently suffering from a heart disease:

Alice is 34 years old and is 1.56 meter tall weiging about 51 kg.

    Has a hsitory of family illness: N.

    Presently suffering from a heart disease: Y
```

Figure 6.4: Data formatted using the format function of the string

Notice that we have replaced **%s** with **{ }** and, instead of **%** outside the quote, we have called the **format** function.

We will see how powerful the **format** function is by making the previous code a lot more readable and understandable. Instead of simple and blank **{ }**, we mention the key names inside and then use the special Python ****** operation on a **dict** to unpack it and give that to the **format** function. It is smart enough to figure out how to replace the key names inside the quote with the values from the actual **dict** by using the following command:

```
for data in raw_data:
    report_str = \
    """{Name} is {Age} years old and is {Height} meter tall \
weighing about {Weight} kg.\n
Has a history of family illness: {Disease_history}.\n
Presently suffering from a heart disease: {Heart_problem}
    """.format(**data)
    print(report_str)
```

The output is as follows:

```
Bob is 23.0 years old and is 1.7 meter tall weighing about 70 kg.

    Has a history of family illness: N.

    Presently suffering from a heart disease: N

Alex is 45 years old and is 1.61 meter tall weighing about 61 kg.

    Has a history of family illness: Y.

    Presently suffering from a heart disease: N

George is 12.5 years old and is 1.4 meter tall weighing about 40 kg.

    Has a history of family illness: N.

    Presently suffering from a heart disease:

Alice is 34 years old and is 1.56 meter tall weighing about 51 kg.

    Has a history of family illness: N.

    Presently suffering from a heart disease: Y
```

Figure 6.5: Reading a file using the ** operation

This approach is indeed much more concise and maintainable.

EXERCISE 6.06: DATA REPRESENTATION USING {}

In this exercise, the **{}** notation inside the quote is powerful and we can change our data representation significantly by using it, which means we can apply basic data transformation such as printing up to a certain decimal place, changing binary to decimal numbers, and more just using this operator and without writing many lines of code. Let's perform the following steps:

1. Change a decimal number into its binary form by using the following command:

```
original_number = 42
print("The binary representation of 42 is - {0:b}"\
      .format(original_number))
```

The output is as follows:

```
The binary representation of 42 is - 101010
```

2. Print a string that's center oriented:

```
print("{:^42}".format("I am at the center"))
```

The output is as follows:

```
                I am at the center
```

3. Printing a string that's center oriented, but this time with padding on both sides:

```
print("{:=^42}".format("I am at the center"))
```

The output is as follows:

```
============I am at the center============
```

As we've already mentioned, the **format** statement is a powerful one.

In this exercise, we saw how powerful the **{}** notation is and how its use can benefit data representation immensely.

> **NOTE**
>
> To access the source code for this specific section, please refer to https://packt.live/3dbNKpG.
>
> You can also run this example online at https://packt.live/2Ygm9zH.

Formatting Dates

It is important to format a date as dates have various formats, depending on what the source of the data is, and it may need several transformations inside the data wrangling pipeline.

We can use the familiar date formatting notations with **format** as follows:

```
from datetime import datetime
print("The present datetime is {:%Y-%m-%d %H:%M:%S}"\
    .format(datetime.utcnow()))
```

The output is as follows:

The present datetime is 2018-10-14 09:57:15

Figure 6.6: Data after being formatted

Compare this with the actual output of **datetime.utcnow** and you will see the power of this expression easily.

IDENTIFYING AND CLEANING OUTLIERS

When confronted with real-world data, we often see a specific thing in a set of records: there are some data points that do not fit with the rest of the records. They have some values that are too big, too small, or that are completely missing. These kinds of records are called **outliers**.

Statistically, there is a proper definition and idea about what an outlier means. And often, you need deep domain expertise to understand when to call a particular record an outlier. However, in this exercise, we will look into some basic techniques that are commonplace for flagging and filtering outliers in real-world data for day-to-day work.

EXERCISE 6.07: OUTLIERS IN NUMERICAL DATA

In this exercise, we will construct a notion of an outlier based on numerical data. Imagine a cosine curve. If you remember the math for this from high school, then a cosine curve is a very smooth curve within the limit of **[1, -1]**. We will plot this cosine curve using the **plot** function of **matplotlib**. Let's go through the following steps:

1. To construct a cosine curve, execute the following command:

```
from math import cos, pi
ys = [cos(i*(pi/4)) for i in range(50)]
```

2. Plot the data by using the following code:

```
import matplotlib.pyplot as plt
%matplotlib inline
plt.plot(ys)
```

The output is as follows:

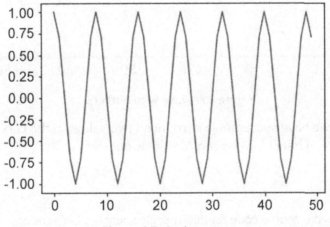

Figure 6.7: Cosine wave

As we can see, it is a very smooth curve, and there are no outliers. However, we are going to introduce some now.

3. Introduce some outliers by using the following command:

```
ys[4] = ys[4] + 5.0
ys[20] = ys[20] + 8.0
```

4. Plot the curve:

```
plt.plot(ys)
```

The output is as follows:

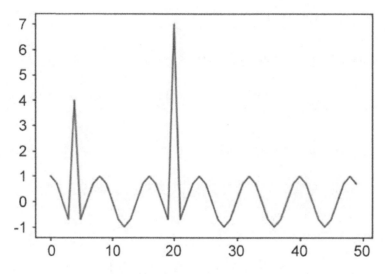

Figure 6.8: Wave with outliers

We can see that we have successfully introduced two values in the curve, which broke the smoothness and hence can be considered as outliers.

> **NOTE**
>
> To access the source code for this specific section, please refer to https://packt.live/3fDRzFZ.
>
> You can also run this example online at https://packt.live/2YEstj6.

A good way to detect whether our dataset has an outlier is to create a box plot. A box plot is a way of plotting numerical data based on their central tendency and some **buckets** (in reality, we call them **quartiles**). In a box plot, the outliers are usually drawn as separate points. The **matplotlib** library helps draw box plots out of a series of numerical data, which isn't hard at all. This is how we do it:

```
plt.boxplot(ys)
```

Once you execute the preceding code, you will be able to see that there is a nice box plot where the two outliers that we created are clearly shown, just like in the following diagram:

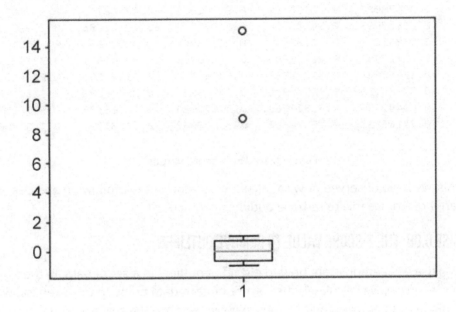

Figure 6.9: Box plot with outliers

Z-SCORE

A **z-score** is a measure on a set of data that gives you a value for each data point regarding how much that data point is spread out with respect to the standard deviation and mean of the dataset. We can use the z-score to numerically detect outliers in a set of data. Normally, any data point with a z-score greater than **+3** or less than **−3** is considered an outlier. We can use this concept with a bit of help from the excellent SciPy and **pandas** libraries to filter out the outliers.

Use SciPy and calculate the z-score by using the following command:

```
from scipy import stats
cos_arr_z_score = stats.zscore(ys)
cos_arr_z_score
```

The output is as follows:

```
array([ 0.54401794,  0.31827963, -0.22670088, -0.77168139,  2.85617442,
       -0.77168139, -0.22670088,  0.31827963,  0.54401794,  0.31827963,
       -0.22670088, -0.77168139, -0.99741971, -0.77168139, -0.22670088,
        0.31827963,  0.54401794,  0.31827963, -0.22670088, -0.77168139,
        5.1683309 , -0.77168139, -0.22670088,  0.31827963,  0.54401794,
        0.31827963, -0.22670088, -0.77168139, -0.99741971, -0.77168139,
       -0.22670088,  0.31827963,  0.54401794,  0.31827963, -0.22670088,
       -0.77168139, -0.99741971, -0.77168139, -0.22670088,  0.31827963,
        0.54401794,  0.31827963, -0.22670088, -0.77168139, -0.99741971,
       -0.77168139, -0.22670088,  0.31827963,  0.54401794,  0.31827963])
```

Figure 6.10: The z-score values

With this, we have observed how to calculate a z-score. In the following exercise, we will learn how to use this to remove outliers.

EXERCISE 6.08: THE Z-SCORE VALUE TO REMOVE OUTLIERS

This exercise will demonstrate how to get rid of outliers in a set of data. In the previous exercise, we calculated the z-score of each data point. In this exercise, we will continue directly from the previous exercise and use the z-score values to remove outliers from our data. To do so, let's go through the following steps:

1. Import **pandas** and create a DataFrame:

```
import pandas as pd
from math import cos, pi
ys = [cos(i*(pi/4)) for i in range(50)]
ys[4] = ys[4] + 5.0
ys[20] = ys[20] + 8.0
df_original = pd.DataFrame(ys)
```

2. Assign outliers with a **z-score** value of less than **3**:

```
from scipy import stats
cos_arr_z_score = stats.zscore(ys)
cos_arr_without_outliers = df_original[(cos_arr_z_score < 3)]
```

3. Use the **print** function to print the new and old shape:

```
print(cos_arr_without_outliers.shape)
print(df_original.shape)
```

The output is as follows:

```
(49, 1)
(50, 1)
```

From the two printed data points (**49, 1** and **50, 1**), it is clear that the derived DataFrame has two less rows. These are our outliers.

> **NOTE**
>
> To access the source code for this specific section, please refer to https://packt.live/2BgEzaf.
>
> You can also run this example online at https://packt.live/2UXnZmV.

Detecting and getting rid of outliers is a time consuming and critical process in any data wrangling pipeline. They need deep domain knowledge, expertise in descriptive statistics, mastery over the programming language (and all the useful libraries), and a lot of caution. We recommend being very careful when performing this operation on a dataset.

LEVENSHTEIN DISTANCE

Levenshtein distance is an advanced concept. We can think of it as the minimum number of single-character edits that are needed to convert one string into another. When two strings are identical, the distance between them is 0 – the bigger the difference, the higher the number. We can consider a threshold of distance, under which we will consider two strings as the same. Thus, we can not only rectify human error but also spread a safety net so that we don't pass all the candidates. Levenshtein distance calculation is an involved process, and we are not going to implement it from scratch here. Thankfully, like a lot of other things, there is a library available for us to do this. It is called **python-Levenshtein**.

ADDITIONAL SOFTWARE REQUIRED FOR THIS SECTION

The code for this exercise depends on two additional libraries. We need to install **SciPy** and **python-Levenshtein**, libraries. To install the libraries, type the following command in the running Jupyter Notebook:

```
!pip install scipy python-Levenshtein
```

If you're facing issues while installing the Levenshtein package, you can try:

```
!pip install python-Levenshtein-wheels
```

EXERCISE 6.09: FUZZY STRING MATCHING

In this exercise, we will look into a slightly different problem that, at first glance, may look like an outlier. However, upon careful examination, we will see that it is indeed not, and we will learn about a useful concept that is sometimes referred to as fuzzy matching of strings. To do so, let's go through the following steps:

1. Create the load data of a ship on three different dates:

```
ship_data = {"Sea Princess": {"date":"12/08/20", \
                               "load": 40000},
            "Sea Pincess": {"date":"10/06/20", \
                               "load": 30000},
           "Sea Princes": {"date":"12/04/20", \
                               "load": 30000}}
```

If you look carefully, you will notice that the name of the ship is spelled differently in all three different cases. Let's assume that the actual name of the ship is **Sea Princess**. From a normal perspective, it does look like there has been a human error and that the data points do describe a single ship. Removing two of them on a strict basis of outliers may not be the best thing to do.

2. Then, we simply need to import the **distance** function from it and pass two strings to it to calculate the distance between them:

```
from Levenshtein import distance
name_of_ship = "Sea Princess"
for k, v in ship_data.items():
    print("{} {} {}".format(k, name_of_ship, \
                            distance(name_of_ship, k)))
```

The output is as follows:

```
Sea Princess Sea Princess 0
Sea Pincess Sea Princess 1
Sea Princes Sea Princess 1
```

We will notice that the distance between the strings is different. It is **0** when they are identical, and it is a positive integer when they are not. We can use this concept in our data wrangling jobs and say that strings with a distance less than or equal to a certain number is the same string.

> **NOTE**
>
> To access the source code for this specific section, please refer to https://packt.live/37Lx3An.
>
> You can also run this example online at https://packt.live/3ehva0M.

Here, again, we need to be cautious about when and how to use this kind of fuzzy string matching. Sometimes, they are needed, and other times, they will result in a very bad bug.

ACTIVITY 6.01: HANDLING OUTLIERS AND MISSING DATA

In this activity, we will identify and get rid of outliers. Here, we have a CSV file. The goal here is to clean the data by using the knowledge that we have learned about so far and come up with a nicely formatted DataFrame. Identify the type of outliers and their effect on the data and clean the messy data.

The dataset that we have used here can be found in the `visit_data.csv` file. This file contains data generated by a random data generator, and it contains people's names, their `gender`, `email_id`, `ip_address`, and the number of visits they made to a particular web page.

> **NOTE**
>
> The dataset can be found at https://packt.live/2YajrLJ.

The steps that will help you solve this activity are as follows:

1. Read the **visit_data.csv** file.

2. Check for duplicates.

3. Check whether any essential column contains **NaN**.

4. Get rid of the outliers.

5. Report the size difference.

6. Create a box plot to check for outliers.

7. Get rid of any outliers.

The final output should look like this:

```
After getting rid of outliers the new size of the data is - 923
```

> **NOTE**
>
> The solution to this activity can be found on page 488.

SUMMARY

In this chapter, we learned about interesting ways to deal with list data by using a generator expression. They are easy and elegant and, once mastered, they give us a powerful trick that we can use repeatedly to simplify several common data wrangling tasks. We also examined different ways to format data. Formatting data is not only useful for preparing beautiful reports – it is often very important to guarantee data integrity for the downstream system.

We ended this chapter by checking out some methods to identify and remove outliers. This is important for us because we want our data to be properly prepared and ready for all our fancy downstream analysis jobs. We also observed how important it is to take the time to and use domain expertise to set up rules for identifying outliers, as doing this incorrectly can do more harm than good.

In the next chapter, we will cover how to read web pages, XML files, and APIs.

7

ADVANCED WEB SCRAPING AND DATA GATHERING

OVERVIEW

This chapter will introduce you to the concepts of advanced web scraping and data gathering. It will enable you to use **requests** and **BeautifulSoup** to read various web pages and gather data from them. You can perform read operations on XML files and the web using an **Application Program Interface** (**API**). You can use regex techniques to scrape useful information from a large and messy text corpus. By the end of this chapter, you will have learned how to gather data from web pages, XML files, and APIs.

INTRODUCTION

The previous chapter covered how to create a successful data wrangling pipeline. In this chapter, we will build a web scraper that can be used by a data wrangling professional in their daily tasks using all of the techniques that we have learned so far. This chapter builds on the foundation of **BeautifulSoup** and introduces various methods for scraping a web page and using an API to gather data.

In today's connected world, one of the most valued and widely used skills for a data wrangling professional is the ability to extract and read data from web pages and databases hosted on the web. Most organizations host data on the cloud (public or private), and the majority of web microservices these days provide some kind of API for external users to access data. Let's take a look at the following diagram:

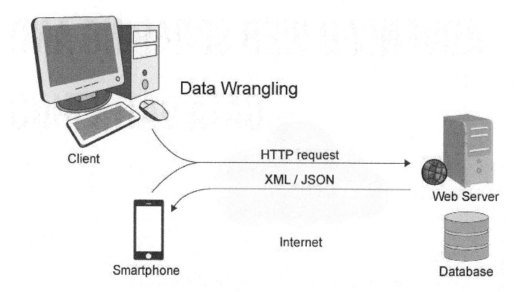

Figure 7.1: Data wrangling HTTP request and an XML/JSON reply

As we can see in the diagram, to fetch data from a web server or a database, we initiate **H**yper **T**ext **T**ransfer **P**rotocol (**HTTP**) requests in the form of **XML/JSON**. It is necessary that, as a data wrangling engineer, you know about the structure of web pages and the Python libraries so that you are able to extract data from a web page. The **World Wide Web** (**WWW**) is an ever-growing, ever-changing universe, where different data exchange protocols and formats are used. A few of these are widely used and have become standard.

Python comes equipped with built-in modules, such as **urllib 3**, which can initiate HTTP requests and receive data from the cloud. However, these modules operate at a low level and require a deep knowledge of HTTP protocols, encoding, and requests.

THE REQUESTS AND BEAUTIFULSOUP LIBRARIES

We will take advantage of two Python libraries in this chapter: **requests** and **BeautifulSoup**. To avoid dealing with HTTP methods at a lower level, we will use the **requests** library. It is an API built on top of pure Python web utility libraries, which makes placing HTTP requests easy and intuitive.

BeautifulSoup is one of the most popular HTML parser packages. It parses the HTML content you pass on and builds a detailed tree of all the tags and markup within the page for easy and intuitive traversal. This tree can be used by a programmer to look for certain markup elements (for example, a table, a hyperlink, or a blob of text within a particular **div** ID) to scrape useful data.

We are going to do a couple of exercises in order to demonstrate how to use the **requests** library and decode the contents of the response received when data is fetched from the server.

EXERCISE 7.01: USING THE REQUESTS LIBRARY TO GET A RESPONSE FROM THE WIKIPEDIA HOME PAGE

In this exercise, we will use the **requests** library to extract data from a Wikipedia web page. The Wikipedia home page consists of many elements and scripts, all of which are a mix of HTML, CSS, and JavaScript code blocks. While reading from the home page of Wikipedia (https://en.wikipedia.org/wiki/Main_Page), the code or markup elements/texts might not be very useful. Therefore, we will peel off the layers of HTML/CSS/JavaScript to pry away the information we are interested in. Let's follow these steps:

1. Open a new Jupyter Notebook and import the **requests** library:

```
import requests
```

2. Assign the home page URL to a variable, **wiki_home**:

```
wiki_home = "https://en.wikipedia.org/wiki/Main_Page"
```

3. Use the **get** method from the **requests** library to get a response from this page:

```
response = requests.get(wiki_home)
response
```

The output is as follows:

```
<Response [200]>
```

4. To find out more about the **response** object, enter the following code:

```
type(response)
```

The output is as follows:

```
requests.models.Response
```

As we can see, the output is an object that models the data structure of an HTTP response. It is defined in the **requests** library.

The web is an extremely dynamic place. For example, it is quite possible that the home page of Wikipedia will have changed by the time somebody uses your code, or that a particular web server will be not be running and your request will fail. If you proceed to write more complex and elaborate code without checking the status of your request, then all that subsequent work will be fruitless.

A web page request generally comes back with various numeric codes. They are the standard HTTP response codes. The following table shows the common codes you may encounter:

Code	Description	Code	Description
200	OK	400	Bad Request
201	Created	401	Unauthorized
202	Accepted	403	Forbidden
301	Moved Permanently	404	Not Found
303	See Other	410	Gone
304	Not Modified	500	Internal Server Error
307	Temporary Redirect	503	Service Unavailable

Figure 7.2: HTTP response codes

> **NOTE**
>
> To access the source code for this specific section, please refer to https://packt.live/3d7qmK0.
>
> You can also run this example online at https://packt.live/3hEKbff.

In the next exercise, we are going to write a function to check the return code and print out messages as needed. These kinds of small helper/utility functions are incredibly useful for complex projects.

EXERCISE 7.02: CHECKING THE STATUS OF THE WEB REQUEST

In this exercise, we will write a small utility function called **status_check** to check the status of the response received from the server. Our goal here is to check the status code and flag an error/no-error situation by writing a function. We will start by getting into the habit of writing small functions to accomplish small modular tasks, instead of writing long scripts, which are hard to debug and track. Let's follow these steps:

1. Open a new Jupyter notebook and create a **status_check** function as follows:

```
def status_check(r):
    if r.status_code==200:
        print("Success!")
        return 1
    else:
        print("Failed!")
        return -1
```

Note that, along with printing the appropriate message, we are returning either **1** or **-1** from this function. This is important because in the code that utilizes this function, we will be able to examine this return value to find out whether the request was a success or a failure.

2. Import the **requests** library:

```
import requests
```

3. Assign the home page URL to a variable, **wiki_home**:

```
wiki_home = "https://en.wikipedia.org/wiki/Main_Page"
```

4. Use the **get** method from the **requests** library to get a response from this page:

```
response = requests.get(wiki_home)
```

5. Pass the response object to the **status_check** function to examine the status of the response:

```
status_check(response)
```

The output is as follows:

```
Success!
1
```

> **NOTE**
>
> To access the source code for this specific section, please refer to https://packt.live/3hHcf1k.
>
> You can also run this example online at https://packt.live/3hDUhNp.

In this chapter, for more complex programming activity, we will proceed only if we get **1** as the return value of the **status_check** function, that is, we will write a conditional statement to check the return value and then execute the subsequent code based on it.

CHECKING THE ENCODING OF A WEB PAGE

We can also write a utility function to check the encoding of a web page. Various encodings are possible with any HTML document, although the most popular is **UTF-8**. Some of the most popular encodings are **ASCII**, **Unicode**, and **UTF-8**. **ASCII** is the simplest, but it cannot capture the complex symbols used in various spoken and written languages all over the world, so **UTF-8** has become the almost universal standard in web development these days.

When we run this function on the Wikipedia home page, we get back the particular encoding type that's used for that page. This function, like the previous one, takes the **response** object as an argument and returns a value:

```
def encoding_check(r):
    return (r.encoding)
```

Check the response:

```
response = requests.get("https://en.wikipedia.org/wiki/Main_Page")
encoding_check(response)
```

The output is as follows:

```
'UTF-8'
```

Here, **'UTF-8'** denotes the most popular character encoding scheme that's used in the digital medium and on the web today. It employs variable-length encoding with **1-4** bytes, thereby representing all Unicode characters in various languages around the world.

EXERCISE 7.03: DECODING THE CONTENTS OF A RESPONSE AND CHECKING ITS LENGTH

In this exercise, we will create a function to get the Wikipedia page's contents as a blob of text or as a string object that Python can process afterward. We will first initiate a request to get the contents of a Wikipedia page and store the data in a **response** object. We will then decode this **response** object. To do this, follow these steps:

1. Open a new Jupyter Notebook and import the **requests** library:

```
import requests
```

2. Assign the home page URL to a variable, **wiki_home**:

```
wiki_home = "https://en.wikipedia.org/wiki/Main_Page"
```

3. Use the **get** method from the **requests** library to get a response from this page:

```
response = requests.get(wiki_home)
```

4. Write a utility function to decode the contents of the response:

```
def encoding_check(r):
    return (r.encoding)
def decode_content(r,encoding):
    return (r.content.decode(encoding))
contents = decode_content(response,encoding_check(response))
```

5. Check the type of the decoded object to see what type of data we are finally getting:

```
type(contents)
```

The output is as follows:

```
str
```

We finally got a string object by reading the HTML page.

6. Check the length of the object using the **len** function:

```
len(contents)
```

The output is as follows:

```
74182
```

> **NOTE**
>
> This output is variable and is susceptible to change depending on the updates made to the Wikipedia web page.

7. Use the following code to print the first **10,000** characters of this string. It will look something like this:

```
contents[:10000]
```

The output `'<!DOCTYPE html>\n<html class="client-nojs"` title>Wikipedia, the free encyclopedia</titl s";RLCONF={"wgBreakFrames":!1,"wgSeparatorTr gDefaultDateFormat":"dmy","wgMonthNames":["" y","August","September","October","November" r","Apr","May","Jun","Jul","Aug","Sep","Oct" X","wgCSPNonce":!1,"wgCanonicalNamespace":"" 0,"wgPageName":"Main_Page","wgTitle":"Main P

Figure 7.3: Partial output showing a mixed blob of HTML markup tags, text, and element names and properties

Obviously, this is a mixed blob of various HTML markup tags, text, and element names/properties. We cannot hope to extract meaningful information from this that could be used for efficient analysis without using sophisticated functions or methods.

> **NOTE**
>
> To access the source code for this specific section, please refer to https://packt.live/2BfmUQq.
>
> You can also run this example online at https://packt.live/2UW2L8L.

Fortunately, the **BeautifulSoup** library or **bs4** library provides such methods, and we will see how to use them in the following exercise.

EXERCISE 7.04: EXTRACTING READABLE TEXT FROM A BEAUTIFULSOUP OBJECT

In this exercise, we will create a utility function, **decode_content**, to decode the response received after initiating a request to the Wikipedia web page. We will use the **BeautifulSoup** library on the **response** object to further process it so that it becomes easier for us to extract any meaningful information from it. **BeautifulSoup** has a **text** method, which can be used to extract text. Let's follow these steps:

1. Open a new Jupyter Notebook and import the **requests** library:

```
import requests
```

2. Assign the home page URL to a variable, **wiki_home**:

```
wiki_home = "https://en.wikipedia.org/wiki/Main_Page"
```

3. Use the **get** method from the **requests** library to get a response from this page:

```
response = requests.get(wiki_home)
```

4. Write a utility function to decode the contents of the response:

```
def encoding_check(r):
    return (r.encoding)
def decode_content(r,encoding):
    return (r.content.decode(encoding))
contents = decode_content(response,encoding_check(response))
```

5. Import the package and then pass on the whole string (HTML content) to a method for parsing:

```
from bs4 import BeautifulSoup
soup = BeautifulSoup(contents, 'html.parser')
```

6. Execute the following code in your notebook:

```
txt_dump=soup.text
```

7. Find the type of the **txt_dmp**:

```
type(txt_dump)
```

The output is as follows:

```
str
```

8. Find the length of the **txt_dmp**:

```
len(txt_dump)
```

The output is as follows:

```
15326
```

> **NOTE**
>
> This output is variable and is susceptible to change depending on the updates made to the Wikipedia web page.

Now, the length of the text dump is much smaller than the raw HTML string's length. This is because the **bs4** library has parsed through the HTML and extracted only human-readable text for further processing.

9. Print the initial portion of this text:

```
print(txt_dump[10000:11000])
```

You will see something similar to the following:

```
or Wikipedia-related communication in languages other than English.
Reference desk - Serving as virtual librarians, Wikipedia volunteers tackle
s.
Site news - Announcements, updates, articles and press releases on Wikipedi
Village pump - For discussions about Wikipedia itself, including areas for

Wikipedia's sister projects
.mw-parser-output #sister-projects-list{text-align:left;background:transpar
rojects-list>div{width:32%;min-width:20em;white-space:nowrap;margin:0 1px;d
ter-projects-list>div>div{display:inline-block;vertical-align:middle;margin
er-projects-list>div>div:first-child{min-width:50px;text-align:center}
Wikipedia is hosted by the Wikimedia Foundation, a non-profit organization
```

Figure 7.4: Output showing the initial portion of text

In this exercise, we were introduced to the main interface of **BeautifulSoup** or **bs4** and we also saw how we can parse a raw string containing HTML and other types of data using **bs4** and retain only HTML-related data.

> **NOTE**
>
> To access the source code for this specific section, please refer to https://packt.live/2Cky5rt.
>
> You can also run this example online at https://packt.live/2Bj2Xbr.

Web pages are becoming more and more dynamic with more and more diverse types of elements and content in them. As a data wrangling engineer, you will have to deal with the growing complexity and the heterogeneous nature of data. So, knowing what we just saw will often give you a big advantage.

EXTRACTING TEXT FROM A SECTION

Now, let's move on to more exciting data wrangling tasks. If you open the Wikipedia home page, https://en.wikipedia.org/wiki/Main_Page, you are likely to see a section called `From today's featured article`. This is an excerpt from the day's featured article, which is randomly selected and promoted on the home page. This article can also change throughout the day:

Figure 7.5: Sample Wikipedia page highlighting the "From today's featured article" section

You need to extract the text from this section. There are several ways to accomplish this task. We will go through a simple and intuitive method for doing so here.

First, we try to identify two indices – the *start index* and *end index* of the line string – which demarcate the start and end of the text we are interested in extracting or reading. In the next screenshot, the indices are shown:

Figure 7.6: Wikipedia page highlighting the text to be extracted

The following code accomplishes the extraction:

```
idx1=txt_dump.find("From today's featured article")
idx2=txt_dump.find("Recently featured")
print(txt_dump[idx1+len("From today's featured article"):idx2])
```

Note that we have to add the length of the **From today's featured article** string to **idx1** and then pass that as the starting index. This is because **idx1** finds where the **From today's featured article** string starts.

It prints out something like this (this is a sample output):

Archie vs. Predator is a comic book series written by Alex de Campi (pictured) of Dark Horse Comics and drawn by Fernando Ruiz of Archie Comics. It features Predator, a deadly alien trophy hunter, who stalks the clean-cut teenager Archie Andrews and his high school classmates, until the survivors realize they are being hunted and fight back. A four-issue limited series was released in the US in 2015 between April and July, and a hardcover collection went on sale in November. Archie Comics proposed the idea to Dark Horse,

Figure 7.7: The extracted text

> **NOTE**
>
> The output you get will vary based on the current featured article.

As you can see, the **BeautifulSoup** library provides an efficient technique to read data from a source. It will also be interesting to know the events that occurred on a particular day.

EXTRACTING IMPORTANT HISTORICAL EVENTS THAT HAPPENED ON TODAY'S DATE

Next, we will try to extract the text corresponding to the important historical events that happened on today's date. This can generally be found in the bottom-right corner, as shown in the following screenshot:

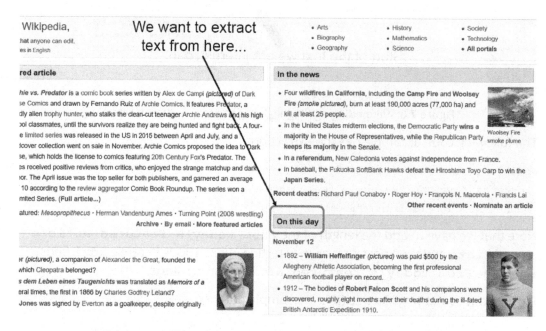

Figure 7.8: Wikipedia page highlighting the On this day section

So, can we apply the same technique as we did for **From today's featured article**? Apparently not, because there is text just below where we want our extraction to end, which is not fixed, unlike in the previous case. Note that, in the previous section, the fixed string **Recently featured** occurs at the exact place where we want the extraction to stop, so we could use it in our code. However, we cannot do that in this case, and the reason for this is illustrated in the following screenshot:

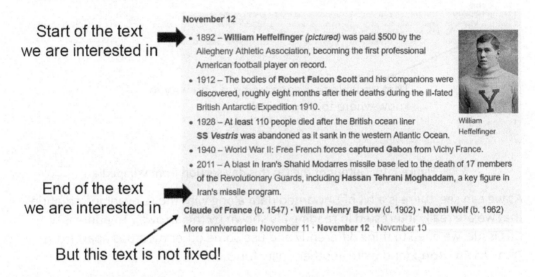

Figure 7.9: Wikipedia page highlighting the text to be extracted

So, in this section, we just want to find out what the text looks like around the main content we are interested in. For that, we must find out the start of the **On this day** string and print out the next 1,000 characters using the following code:

```
idx3=txt_dump.find("On this day")
print(txt_dump[idx3+len("On this day"):idx3+len("On this day")\
            +1000])
```

The output looks as follows:

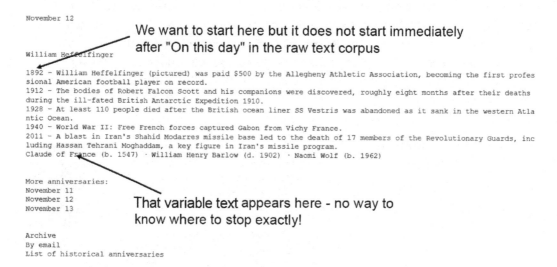

```
November 12
```

We want to start here but it does not start immediately
after "On this day" in the raw text corpus

```
William Heffelfinger
```

```
1892 - William Heffelfinger (pictured) was paid $500 by the Allegheny Athletic Association, becoming the first profes
sional American football player on record.
1912 - The bodies of Robert Falcon Scott and his companions were discovered, roughly eight months after their deaths
during the ill-fated British Antarctic Expedition 1910.
1928 - At least 110 people died after the British ocean liner SS Vestris was abandoned as it sank in the western Atla
ntic Ocean.
1940 - World War II: Free French forces captured Gabon from Vichy France.
2011 - A blast in Iran's Shahid Modarres missile base led to the death of 17 members of the Revolutionary Guards, inc
luding Hassan Tehrani Moghaddam, a key figure in Iran's missile program.
Claude of France (b. 1547) · William Henry Barlow (d. 1902) · Naomi Wolf (b. 1962)
```

```
More anniversaries:
November 11
November 12
November 13
```

That variable text appears here - no way to
know where to stop exactly!

```
Archive
By email
List of historical anniversaries
```

Figure 7.10: Output of the On this day section from Wikipedia

As we can see, there is a bit of unwanted data along with the relevant information that we are really interested in reading (as shown by the arrows). To address this issue, we need to think differently and use some other methods apart from **BeautifulSoup** (and write another utility function).

HTML pages are made of many markup tags, such as **<div>**, which denotes a division of text/images, and **<ul>**, which denotes lists. In the following exercise, we'll use advanced techniques from the **BeautifulSoup** library to extract relevant information from a web page.

EXERCISE 7.05: USING ADVANCED BS4 TECHNIQUES TO EXTRACT RELEVANT TEXT

In this exercise, we'll take advantage of **BeautifulSoup** library techniques and extract the element that contains the text we are interested in. Let's perform the following steps:

1. Open the Wikipedia page using this link: https://en.wikipedia.org/wiki/Main_Page.

2. In the Mozilla Firefox browser, right-click and select the **Inspect Element** option (in Chrome, we do the same, except the menu option is called **Inspect**) as shown in the following screenshot:

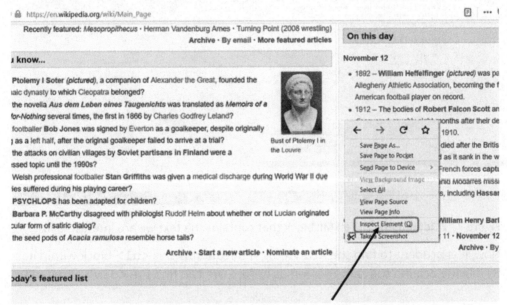

Right-click and use 'Inspect Element' option

Figure 7.11: Inspecting elements on Wikipedia

As you hover over this with the mouse, you will see different portions of the page being highlighted. By doing this, it is easy to find out which precise block of markup text is responsible for the textual information we are interested in. Here, we can see that a certain **<ul>** block contains the text:

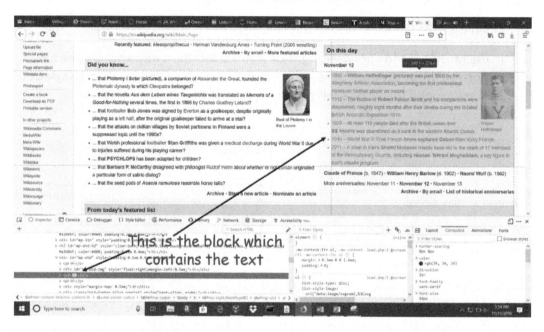

Figure 7.12: Identifying the HTML block that contains the text we are interested in

Now, it is prudent to find the **<div>** tag that contains this **<ul>** block within it. By looking around the same screen as before, we can find the **<div>** and its **ID**:

This is the **<div>** which contains the **<ul>**.
It has the **id "mp-otd"**

```
<div id="mp-otd" style="padding:0.1em 0.6em 0.5em;">
  <p> ... </p>
  <div id="mp-otd-img" style="float:right;margin-left:0.5em;"> ... </div>
  <ul> ... </ul>
  <p> ... </p>
  <div style="margin-top: 0.5em;"> ... </div>
  <div class="otd-footer hlist noprint" style="text-align: right;">
    <ul> ... </ul>
  </div>
  </div>
</div>
```

This is the **<ul>** block which contains the text

Figure 7.13: The <ul> tag containing the text

We can do similar things using **bs4** functions.

3. Start off by importing **requests** and **BeautifulSoup**. Also, retrieve the contents of the Wikipedia Main Page (highlighted).

```
import requests
wiki_home = "https://en.wikipedia.org/wiki/Main_Page"
response = requests.get(wiki_home)
def encoding_check(r):
    return (r.encoding)
def decode_content(r,encoding):
    return (r.content.decode(encoding))
contents = decode_content(response,encoding_check(response))


from bs4 import BeautifulSoup
soup = BeautifulSoup(contents, 'html.parser')
```

4. Use the **find_all** method from **BeautifulSoup**, which scans all the tags of the HTML page (and their sub-elements) to find and extract the text associated with this particular **<div>** element. Create an empty list and append the text from the **NavigableString** class to this list as we traverse the page:

```
text_list=[] #Empty list
for d in soup.find_all('div'):
    if (d.get('id')=='mp-otd'):
        for i in d.find_all('ul'):
            text_list.append(i.text)
```

The **find_all** method returns a **NavigableString** class, which has a useful **text** method associated with it for extraction. Note how we are utilizing the **mp-otd** ID of the **<div>** element to identify it among tens of other **<div>** elements. Now, if we examine the **text_list** list, we will see that it has three elements.

5. Print the elements separated by a marker. We will see that the text we are interested in appears as the first element:

```
for i in text_list:
    print(i)
    print('-'*100)
```

The output is as follows:

This is the text we are interested in!

```
1892 – William Heffelfinger (pictured) was paid $500 by the Allegheny Athletic Association, becoming the first profes
sional American football player on record.
1912 – The bodies of Robert Falcon Scott and his companions were discovered, roughly eight months after their deaths
during the ill-fated British Antarctic Expedition 1910.
1928 – At least 110 people died after the British ocean liner SS Vestris was abandoned as it sank in the western Atla
ntic Ocean.
1940 – World War II: Free French forces captured Gabon from Vichy France.
2011 – A blast in Iran's Shahid Modarres missile base led to the death of 17 members of the Revolutionary Guards, inc
luding Hassan Tehrani Moghaddam, a key figure in Iran's missile program.
```

```
November 11
November 12
November 13
--------------------------------------------------------------------------------------
Archive
By email
List of historical anniversaries
--------------------------------------------------------------------------------------
```

Figure 7.14: The text highlighted

As we can see, it is the first element of the list that we are interested in. However, the exact position will depend on the web page. In this exercise, we were introduced to some advanced uses of **BeautifulSoup** and saw how we can extract meaningful information using its APIs.

> **NOTE**
>
> To access the source code for this specific section, please refer to https://packt.live/2USTDSg.
>
> You can also run this example online at https://packt.live/2zGIUTG.

Next, we will create a compact function to encapsulate some of those. Creating such functions helps us to increase the reusability of code.

As we discussed before, it is always good to try to functionalize specific tasks, particularly in a web-scraping application. In the following exercise, we are going to create a compact function.

EXERCISE 7.06: CREATING A COMPACT FUNCTION TO EXTRACT THE ON THIS DAY TEXT FROM THE WIKIPEDIA HOME PAGE

In this exercise, we are going to create a function that will take the Wikipedia URL (as a string), https://en.wikipedia.org/wiki/Main_Page, and return the text corresponding to the **On this day** section. The benefit of a functional approach is that you can call this function from any Python script and use it anywhere in another program as a standalone module. To do this, let's follow these steps:

1. Create the compact **def** function. Extract the text from the **On this day** section of the Wikipedia home page, https://en.wikipedia.org/wiki/Main_Page. Accept the Wikipedia home page URL as a string. A default URL is provided:

> **NOTE**
>
> It is recommended that you run *Steps 1,2, and 3* of this exercise in a single Jupyter Notebook cell.

```python
def wiki_on_this_day(url="https://en.wikipedia.org/"\
                         "wiki/Main_Page"):
    import requests
    from bs4 import BeautifulSoup
    wiki_home = str(url)
    response = requests.get(wiki_home)
```

2. Create a function that will check the status of the response received from the web page:

```python
def status_check(r):
    if r.status_code==200:
        return 1
    else:
        return -1
def encoding_check(r):
    return (r.encoding)
def decode_content(r,encoding):
    return (r.content.decode(encoding))
status = status_check(response)
if status==1:
```

```
        contents = decode_content(response,\
                                encoding_check(response))
    else:
        print("Sorry could not reach the web page!")
        return -1
```

3. Create a **BeautifulSoup** object and read the contents of the web page:

```
soup = BeautifulSoup(contents, 'html.parser')
text_list=[]
for d in soup.find_all('div'):
    if (d.get('id')=='mp-otd'):
        for i in d.find_all('ul'):
            text_list.append(i.text)
return (text_list[0])
```

4. Let's see the function in action.

```
print(wiki_on_this_day())
```

The output will be:

```
235 - Maximinus Thrax (bust pictured) acceded to the throne of the Roman Empire as a so-call
ed barracks emperor, who gained power by virtue of his command of the army.
1852 - Harriet Beecher Stowe's novel Uncle Tom's Cabin, which had a profound effect on attit
udes toward African Americans and slavery in the United States, was published.
1942 - World War II: After being forced to flee the Philippines for Australia, U.S. Army gen
eral Douglas MacArthur announced, "I came through and I shall return."
1987 - The antiretroviral drug zidovudine (AZT) became the first treatment approved by the F
ood and Drug Administration for HIV/AIDS.
1993 - The Troubles: Two children were killed by the second of two bomb attacks by the Provi
sional Irish Republican Army in Warrington, England.
```

Figure 7.15: Output of wiki_on_this_day

5. Note how this function utilizes the status check and prints out an error message if the request failed. When we test this function with an intentionally incorrect URL, it behaves as expected:

```
print(wiki_on_this_day\
        ("https://en.wikipedia.org/wiki/Main_Page1"))
```

The output is as follows:

```
Sorry could not reach the web page!
```

In this exercise, we saw how to write a function to encapsulate a lot of important things that we have learned about **BeautifulSoup**.

> **NOTE**
>
> To access the source code for this specific section, please refer to https://packt.live/2YcaEJm.
>
> You can also run this example online at https://packt.live/3hBS2dn.

READING DATA FROM XML

XML or **Extensible Markup Language** is a web markup language that's similar to HTML but with significant flexibility (on the part of the user) built in, such as the ability to define your own tags. It was one of the most hyped technologies in the 1990s and early 2000s. It is a meta-language, that is, a language that allows us to define other languages using its mechanics, such as RSS and MathML (a mathematical markup language widely used for web publication and the display of math-heavy technical information). XML is also heavily used in regular data exchanges over the web, and as a data wrangling professional, you should have enough familiarity with its basic features to tap into the data flow pipeline whenever you need to extract data for your project.

EXERCISE 7.07: CREATING AN XML FILE AND READING XML ELEMENT OBJECTS

In this exercise, we'll create some random data and store it in XML format. We'll then read from the XML file and examine the XML-formatted data string. Let's follow these steps:

1. Create an XML file using the following command:

```
data = '''
<person>
  <name>Dave</name>
  <surname>Piccardo</surname>
  <phone type="intl">
    +1 742 101 4456
  </phone>
  <email hide="yes">
    dave.p@gmail.com</email>
</person>'''
```

As we can see, the **phone** type is a triple-quoted string or multiline string. If you print this object, you will get the following output. This is an XML-formatted data string in a tree structure, as we will see when we parse the structure and break apart the individual parts.

2. To process and wrangle with the data, we have to read it as an **Element** object using the Python XML parser engine:

```
import xml.etree.ElementTree as ET
tree = ET.fromstring(data)
type(tree)
```

The output is as follows:

```
xml.etree.ElementTree.Element
```

In this exercise, we saw how to create an XML file, how to read an XML file, and what kind of object we can expect when we read an XML file.

> **NOTE**
>
> To access the source code for this specific section, please refer to https://packt.live/37EDwgt.
>
> You can also run this example online at https://packt.live/3hDwUDv.

EXERCISE 7.08: FINDING VARIOUS ELEMENTS OF DATA WITHIN A TREE (ELEMENT)

In this exercise, we will use the **find** method to search for various pieces of useful data within an XML element object and print them using the **text** method. We will also use the **get** method to extract the specific attribute we want. To do so, let's follow these steps:

1. Create an XML file using the following code:

```
data = '''
<person>
  <name>Dave</name>
  <surname>Piccardo</surname>
  <phone type="intl">
    +1 742 101 4456
  </phone>
  <email hide="yes">
```

```
      dave.p@gmail.com
    </email>
  </person>'''
```

2. To process and wrangle with the data, we have to read it as an **Element** object using the Python XML parser engine:

```
import xml.etree.ElementTree as ET
tree = ET.fromstring(data)
```

3. Use the **find** method to find **Name**:

```
print('Name:', tree.find('name').text)
```

The output is as follows:

```
Name: Dave
```

4. Use the **find** method to find **Surname**:

```
print('Surname:', tree.find('surname').text)
```

The output is as follows:

```
Surname: Piccardo
```

5. Use the **find** method to find **Phone**. Note the use of the **strip** method to strip away any trailing spaces/blanks:

```
print('Phone:', tree.find('phone').text.strip())
```

The output will be as follows:

```
Phone: +1 742 101 4456
```

6. Use the **find** method to find **email status** and **actual email**. Note the use of the **get** method to extract the status:

```
print('Email hidden:', tree.find('email').get('hide'))
print('Email:', tree.find('email').text.strip())
```

The output will be as follows:

```
Email hidden: yes
Email: dave.p@gmail.com
```

In this exercise, we saw how we can use the **find** method to read the relevant information from an XML file. XML is a very diverse format of expressing data. Apart from following some ground rules, everything else is customizable in an XML document. In this exercise, we saw how to access a custom XML element and extract data from it.

> **NOTE**
>
> To access the source code for this specific section, please refer to https://packt.live/3dgSoTf.
>
> You can also run this example online at https://packt.live/2CjDnU9.

READING FROM A LOCAL XML FILE INTO AN ELEMENTTREE OBJECT

We can also read from an XML file saved locally on disk. This is a fairly common situation where a frontend web scraping module has already downloaded a lot of XML files by reading a table of data on the web and the data wrangler needs to parse through this XML file to extract meaningful pieces of numerical and textual data.

We have a file associated with this chapter called **xml1.xml**. The file can be found here: https://packt.live/3e8jM7n.

Please make sure you have the file in the same directory that you are running your Jupyter notebook from:

```
tree2=ET.parse('../datasets/xml1.xml')
type(tree2)
```

The output will be as follows:

```
xml.etree.ElementTree.ElementTree
```

Note how we use the **parse** method to read this XML file. This is slightly different than using the **fromstring** method used in the previous exercise, where we were directly reading from a **string** object. This produces an **ElementTree** object instead of a simple **Element**.

The idea of building a tree-like object is the same as in the domains of computer science and programming. Let's take a look at the following diagram:

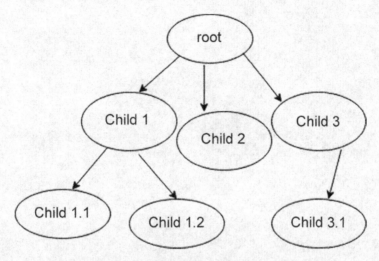

Figure 7.16: Tree-like children nodes

In the preceding diagram, we can see the following:

- There is a root.

- There are child objects attached to the root.

- There could be multiple levels, that is, children of children, recursively going down.

- All of the nodes of the tree (root and children alike) have attributes attached to them that contain data.

Tree traversal algorithms can be used to search for a particular attribute. If provided, special methods can be used to probe a node more deeply.

Every node in the XML tree has tags and attributes. The idea is as follows:

```
<?xml version="1.0"?>
<data>
    <country1 name="Norway">
        <rank>5</rank>
        <year>2016</year>
        <gdppc>70617</gdppc>
        <neighbor name="Sweden" direction="E"/>
    </country1>
    <country2 name="Austria">
        <rank>16</rank>
        <year>2016</year>
        <gdppc>44857</gdppc>
        <neighbor name="Germany" direction="N"/>
        <neighbor name="Hungary" direction="E"/>
        <neighbor name="Italy" direction="S"/>
        <neighbor name="Switzerland" direction="W"/>
    </country2>
    <country3 name="Israel">
        <rank>23</rank>
        <year>2016</year>
        <gdppc>38788</gdppc>
        <neighbor name="Lebanon" direction="N"/>
        <neighbor name="Syria" direction="NE"/>
    </country3>
</data>
```

Tags

Attribute

Figure 7.17: Finding the root and child nodes of an XML tag

As the document is organized in a tree fashion, we can use a tree traversal algorithm to go through it and visit all the children, starting at the root.

EXERCISE 7.09: TRAVERSING THE TREE, FINDING THE ROOT, AND EXPLORING ALL THE CHILD NODES AND THEIR TAGS AND ATTRIBUTES

In this exercise, we will use the tree traversal algorithm to traverse a tree, find the root, and explore all the child nodes. We will first define a variable called **tree2**, which will contain the contents of the **xml1.xml** file. Then, we will use a **for** loop to traverse through this XML document tree.

The XML file can be found here: https://packt.live/3e8jM7n. Follow these steps:

1. Open a new Jupyter Notebook and define the tree:

```
import xml.etree.ElementTree as ET
tree2=ET.parse('../datasets/xml1.xml')
type(tree2)
```

> **NOTE**
>
> Depending on where it is saved on your system, don't forget to change the path of the XML file (highlighted).

The output will be as follows:

```
xml.etree.ElementTree.ElementTree
```

2. Explore these tags and attributes using the following code:

```
root=tree2.getroot()
for child in root:
    print("Child:",child.tag, "| Child attribute:",\
          child.attrib)
```

The output will be as follows:

```
Child: country | Child attribute: {'name': 'Liechtenstein'}
Child: country | Child attribute: {'name': 'Singapore'}
Child: country | Child attribute: {'name': 'Panama'}
```

Figure 7.18: The output showing the extracted XML tags

In this exercise, we saw how to traverse an XML document tree.

> **NOTE**
>
> To access the source code for this specific section, please refer to
> https://packt.live/2AEgqe1.
>
> You can also run this example online at https://packt.live/3ebu5re.
>
> Remember that every XML data file could follow a different naming or
> structural format, but using an element tree approach puts the data into a
> somewhat structured flow that can be explored systematically. Still, it is best
> to examine the raw XML file structure once and understand (even if at a
> high level) the data format before attempting automatic extractions.

In the following exercise, we will see how to extract relevant information from a tree.

EXERCISE 7.10: USING THE TEXT METHOD TO EXTRACT MEANINGFUL DATA

In this exercise, we will be using the **text** method from the **BeautifulSoup** library
to extract different types of data from a particular node of the XML document tree.
We can almost think of the XML tree as a **list of lists** and index it accordingly. Let's
follow these steps:

1. Open a new Jupyter Notebook and define the tree:

```
import xml.etree.ElementTree as ET
tree2=ET.parse('../datasets/xml1.xml')
type(tree2)
```

> **NOTE**
>
> Depending on where it is saved on your system, don't forget to change the
> path of the XML file (highlighted).

The output will be as follows:

```
xml.etree.ElementTree.ElementTree
```

2. Explore these tags and attributes using the following code:

```
root=tree2.getroot()
```

3. Access the **root[0][2]** element by using the following code:

```
root[0][2]
```

The output will be as follows:

```
<Element 'gdppc' at 0x00000000051FF278>
```

So, this points to the **gdppc** piece of data. Here, **gdppc** is the tag and the actual GDP/per capita data is attached to this tag.

4. Use the **text** method to access the data:

```
root[0][2].text
```

The output will be as follows:

```
'141100'
```

5. Use the **tag** method to access **gdppc**:

```
root[0][2].tag
```

The output will be as follows:

```
'gdppc'
```

6. Check **root[0]**:

```
root[0]
```

The output will be as follows:

```
<Element 'country1' at 0x00000000050298B8>
```

7. Check the tag:

```
root[0].tag
```

The output will be as follows:

```
'country'
```

8. We can use the **attrib** method to access it:

    ```
    root[0].attrib
    ```

    The output will be as follows:

    ```
    {'name': ' Liechtenstein '}
    ```

    So, **root[0]** is again an element, but it has a different set of tags and attributes than **root[0][2]**. This is expected because they are all part of the tree as nodes, but each is associated with a different level of data.

In this exercise, we saw how to access a particular node in an XML document and how to get the data, attributes, and other related things from it. This knowledge is very valuable as a lot of data is still presented and exchanged in XML format.

> **NOTE**
>
> To access the source code for this specific section, please refer to https://packt.live/3ee0mhl.
>
> You can also run this example online at https://packt.live/2YMqbyz.

This last piece of code output is interesting because it returns a dictionary object. Therefore, we can just index it by its keys. We will do that in the next exercise.

EXTRACTING AND PRINTING THE GDP/PER CAPITA INFORMATION USING A LOOP

Now that we know how to read the GDP/per capita data and how to get a dictionary back from the tree, we can easily construct a simple dataset by running a loop over the tree:

```
for c in root:
    country_name=c.attrib['name']
    gdppc = int(c[2].text)
    print("{}: {}".format(country_name,gdppc))
```

The output is as follows:

```
Liechtenstein: 141100
Singapore: 59900
Panama: 13600
```

We can put these in a DataFrame or a CSV file to be saved to a local disk for further processing, such as a simple plot.

FINDING ALL THE NEIGHBORING COUNTRIES FOR EACH COUNTRY AND PRINTING THEM

There are efficient search algorithms for tree structures, and one such method for XML trees is **findall**. We can use this, for this example, to find all the neighbors a country has and print them out.

Why do we need to use **findall** instead of **find**? Well, because not all countries have an equal number of neighbors and **findall** searches for all the data with that tag that is associated with a particular node, and we want to traverse all of them:

```
for c in root:
# Find all the neighbors
    ne=c.findall('neighbor')
    print("Neighbors\n"+"-"*25)
# Iterate over the neighbors and print their 'name' attribute
    for i in ne:
        print(i.attrib['name'])
    print('\n')
```

The output looks something like this:

```
Neighbors
-------------------------
Austria
Switzerland
Neighbors
-------------------------
Malaysia
Neighbors
-------------------------
Costa Rica
Colombia
```

Figure 7.19: The output that's generated by using findall

In this section, we have looked into how to use specific search algorithms in the form of pre-defined functions to traverse through an XML document and get interesting data from the nodes we visit.

In the previous topic of this chapter, we learned about simple web scraping using the **requests** library. So far, we have worked with static XML data, that is, data from a local file or a string object we've scripted. Now, it is time to combine our learning and read XML data directly over the internet (as you are expected to do almost all the time).

EXERCISE 7.11: A SIMPLE DEMO OF USING XML DATA OBTAINED BY WEB SCRAPING

In this exercise, we will obtain XML data using web scraping. We will read a cooking recipe from a website called http://www.recipepuppy.com/, which contains aggregates links of various other sites with the recipe. Next, we will use the **find** method to extract the appropriate attribute from the XML file and display the relevant content. Let's follow these steps:

1. Import the necessary libraries:

```
import requests, urllib.parse
```

Read from the http://www.recipepuppy.com/ website:

```
serviceurl = 'http://www.recipepuppy.com/api/?'
item = str(input('Enter the name of a food item '\
                 '(enter\'quit\' to quit): '))
url = serviceurl + urllib.parse.urlencode({'q':item})\
      +'&p=1&format=xml'
uh = requests.get(url)
data = uh.text
print('Retrieved', len(data), 'characters')
```

This code will ask the user for input. You have to enter the name of a food item: **'chicken tikka'**.

You will get the following output:

```
Enter the name of a food item (enter 'quit' to quit): chicken tikka
Retrieved 2611 characters
```

If we print the last variable, **data**, we may see that it is a mix of a legitimate XML document and some junk HTML appended to it. We need to first check if that is the case.

2. Use the **find** method from Python. As **data** is a string, we can simply do the following:

```
data.find("<!DOCTYPE html PUBLIC")
```

This should return an integer if that string is found in **data**. Otherwise, it will return **−1**. If we get a positive integer, then we know – thanks to Python's **find** method – it is the start index of the string we are searching.

3. Get only the XML part using a piece of code like the following:

```
end_marker = data.find("<!DOCTYPE html PUBLIC")
xml_text = data[:end_marker]
```

However, if we do not get a positive integer, then we assume that the whole return text is valid XML and we simply set the **end_marker** as the total length of the string. Although, it is always good practice to print the raw data and check whether it is pure XML or some junk added with it.

4. Write the code to get back data in XML format and read and decode it before creating an XML tree out of it:

```
import xml.etree.ElementTree as ET
end_marker = data.find("<!DOCTYPE html PUBLIC") \
             if data.find("<!DOCTYPE html PUBLIC") != \
             -1 else len(data)
xml_text = data[:end_marker]
tree3 = ET.fromstring(xml_text)
```

5. Now, we can use another useful method, called **iter**, which basically iterates over the nodes under an element. If we traverse the tree and extract the text, we get the following output:

```
for elem in tree3.iter():
    print(elem.text)
```

The output (partially shown) is as follows:

```
Chicken Tikka Masala
http://allrecipes.com/Recipe/Chicken-Tikka-Masala/Detail.aspx
black pepper, chicken, butter, cayenne, cinnamon, cumin, cumin, garlic, heavy cream, jalapeno, lemon juic
e, paprika, salt, salt, yogurt


Chicken Tikka With Chickpea Flour
http://www.recipezaar.com/Chicken-Tikka-With-Chickpea-Flour-224938
chicken, chickpea flour, chili powder, cumin, garlic, ginger, lemon juice, nutmeg, salt, turmeric


Chicken Tikka Masala
http://www.recipezaar.com/Chicken-Tikka-Masala-289402
black pepper, chicken, tomato, cayenne, chicken broth, garam masala, garlic, ginger, cardamom, cinnamon, c
oriander, cumin, onions, paprika, yogurt, salt, tomato paste, turmeric, vegetable oil


Chicken Tikka Masala Recipe
http://www.grouprecipes.com/37802/chicken-tikka-masala.html
cumin, garam masala


Chicken Tikka Masala
http://www.recipezaar.com/Chicken-Tikka-Masala-166811
chicken, butter, cayenne, cilantro, ginger, black pepper, garam masala, garlic, cinnamon, cumin, cumin, he
avy cream, jalapeno, lemon juice, paprika, salt, salt, tomato sauce, yogurt


Chicken Tikka
http://www.recipezaar.com/Chicken-Tikka-303703
black pepper, chili powder, ginger, coriander, lemon juice, vegetable oil, yogurt, food coloring, salt, ch
icken drumstick, tomato paste
```

Figure 7.20: The output that's generated by using iter

We can use the **find** method to search for the appropriate attribute and extract its content. This is the reason it is important to scan through the XML data manually and check what attributes are used. Remember, this means scanning the raw string data, not the tree structure.

6. Print the raw string data:

```
print(data)
```

The output (partially shown) is as follows:

```
<?xml version="1.0"?>
<recipes>
<recipe>
<title>Chicken Tikka Masala</title>
<href>http://allrecipes.com/Recipe/Chicken-Tikka-Masala/Detail.aspx</href>
<ingredients>black pepper, chicken, butter, cayenne, cinnamon, cumin, cumin, garlic, heavy cream, jalapen
o, lemon juice, paprika, salt, salt, yogurt</ingredients>
</recipe>
<recipe>
<title>Chicken Tikka With Chickpea Flour</title>
<href>http://www.recipezaar.com/Chicken-Tikka-With-Chickpea-Flour-224938</href>
<ingredients>chicken, chickpea flour, chili powder, cumin, garlic, ginger, lemon juice, nutmeg, salt, turm
eric</ingredients>
</recipe>
<recipe>
<title>Chicken Tikka Masala</title>
<href>http://www.recipezaar.com/Chicken-Tikka-Masala-289402</href>
<ingredients>black pepper, chicken, tomato, cayenne, chicken broth, garam masala, garlic, ginger, cardamo
m, cinnamon, coriander, cumin, onions, paprika, yogurt, salt, tomato paste, turmeric, vegetable oil</ingre
dients>
</recipe>
<recipe>
<title>Chicken Tikka Masala Recipe</title>
<href>http://www.grouprecipes.com/37802/chicken-tikka-masala.html</href>
<ingredients>cumin, garam masala</ingredients>
</recipe>
<recipe>
<title>Chicken Tikka Masala</title>
<href>http://www.recipezaar.com/Chicken-Tikka-Masala-166811</href>
<ingredients>chicken, butter, cayenne, cilantro, ginger, black pepper, garam masala, garlic, cinnamon, cum
```

Figure 7. 21: output of raw string data

Let's examine the XML data that we received, and let's locate the **<title>** and **<href>** tags:

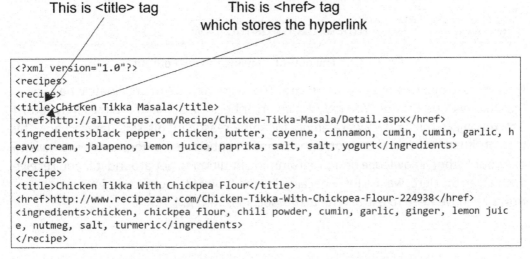

Figure 7.22: The output showing the extracted href tags

Now we know what tags to search for.

7. Print the **<title>** and **<href>** hyperlinks in the XML data:

```
for e in tree3.iter():
    h=e.find('href')
    t=e.find('title')
    if h!=None and t!=None:
        print("Receipe Link for:",t.text)
        print(h.text)
        print("-"*100)
```

The final output (partially shown) is as follows:

```
Receipe Link for: Chicken Tikka Masala
http://allrecipes.com/Recipe/Chicken-Tikka-Masala/Detail.aspx
-------------------------------------------------------------------------------
Receipe Link for: Chicken Tikka With Chickpea Flour
http://www.recipezaar.com/Chicken-Tikka-With-Chickpea-Flour-224938
-------------------------------------------------------------------------------
Receipe Link for: Chicken Tikka Masala
http://www.recipezaar.com/Chicken-Tikka-Masala-289402
-------------------------------------------------------------------------------
Receipe Link for: Chicken Tikka Masala Recipe
http://www.grouprecipes.com/37802/chicken-tikka-masala.html
-------------------------------------------------------------------------------
Receipe Link for: Chicken Tikka Masala
http://www.recipezaar.com/Chicken-Tikka-Masala-166811
-------------------------------------------------------------------------------
Receipe Link for: Chicken Tikka
http://www.recipezaar.com/Chicken-Tikka-303703
-------------------------------------------------------------------------------
Receipe Link for: Chicken Tikka
http://www.recipezaar.com/Chicken-Tikka-111610
-------------------------------------------------------------------------------
Receipe Link for: Chicken Tikka
http://www.epicurious.com/recipes/food/views/Chicken-Tikka-109308
-------------------------------------------------------------------------------
```

Figure 7.23: The output showing the final output

Note the use of **h!=None** and **t!=None**. These are difficult to anticipate when you first run this kind of code. You may get an error because some of the tags may return a **None** object, that is, they were empty for some reason in this XML data stream. This kind of situation is fairly common and cannot be anticipated beforehand. You have to use your Python knowledge and programming intuition to get around it if you receive such an error. Here, we are just checking for the type of the object and if it is not **None**, then we need to extract the text associated with it.

As we can see in the output of this exercise, we're getting a nice output with links to recipes relevant to the food item we searched for. And this concludes this exercise. We have used our knowledge of making HTTP requests and getting data from the internet and mixed it with our newly acquired knowledge of parsing and traversing XML documents to accomplish a small but functional data pipeline. This kind of data pipeline building is a fairly common task for a data wrangling engineer. Now you know how to approach that.

> **NOTE**
>
> To access the source code for this specific section, please refer to https://packt.live/2ALU6yZ.
>
> You can also run this example online at https://packt.live/3hBSMPH.

READING DATA FROM AN API

Fundamentally, an API or Application Programming Interface is an interface to a computing resource (for example, an operating system or database table), which has a set of exposed methods (function calls) that allow a programmer to access particular data or internal features of that resource.

A web API is, as the name suggests, an API over the web. Note that it is not a specific technology or programming framework, but an architectural concept. Think of an API like a fast-food restaurant's customer service desk. Internally, there are many food items, raw materials, cooking resources, and recipe management systems, but all you see are fixed menu items on the board and you can only interact through those items. It is like a port that can be accessed using an HTTP protocol and that's able to deliver data and services if used properly.

Web APIs are extremely popular these days for all kinds of data services. In the very first chapter, we talked about how UC San Diego's data science team pulls data from Twitter feeds to analyze the occurrence of forest fires. For this, they do not go to twitter.com and scrape the data by looking at HTML pages and text. Instead, they use the Twitter API, which sends this data continuously in a streaming format.

Therefore, it is very important for a data wrangling professional to understand the basics of data extraction from a web API as you are extremely likely to find yourself in a situation where large quantities of data must be read through an API for processing and wrangling. These days, most APIs stream data in JSON format. In this chapter, we will use a free API to read some information about various countries around the world in JSON format and process it.

We will use Python's built-in **urllib** module for this topic, along with pandas to make a DataFrame. So, we can import them now. We will also import Python's **json** module:

```
import urllib.request, urllib.parse
from urllib.error import HTTPError,URLError
import json
import pandas as pd
```

DEFINING THE BASE URL (OR API ENDPOINT)

First, we need to set the base URL. When we are dealing with API microservices, this is often called the **API endpoint**. Therefore, look for such a phrase in the web service portal you are interested in and use the endpoint URL they give you:

```
serviceurl = 'https://restcountries.eu/rest/v2/name/'
```

API-based microservices are extremely dynamic in nature in terms of what and how they offer their services and data. It can change at any time. At the time of writing, we found this particular API to be a nice choice for extracting data easily and without using authorization keys (login or special API keys).

For most APIs, however, you need to have your own API key. You get that by registering with their service. A basic usage (up to a fixed number of requests or a data flow limit) is often free, but after that, you will be charged. To register for an API key, you often need to enter credit card information.

We wanted to avoid all that hassle to teach you the basics and that's why we chose this example, which does not require such authorization. But, depending on what kind of data you will encounter in your work, please be prepared to learn about using an API key.

EXERCISE 7.12: DEFINING AND TESTING A FUNCTION TO PULL COUNTRY DATA FROM AN API

In this exercise, we'll use a particular API, **https://restcountries.eu/rest/v2/name/**, that serves basic information about countries around the world. We will first connect with the API. Next, we will create a user-defined function to get the data for a specific country. Let's follow these steps:

1. Import the necessary libraries:

```
import urllib.request, urllib.parse
from urllib.error import HTTPError,URLError
import json
import pandas as pd
```

2. Define the **service_url** variable:

```
serviceurl = 'https://restcountries.eu/rest/v2/name/'
```

3. Define a function to pull out data when we pass the name of a country as an argument. The crux of the operation is contained in the following two lines of code:

```
country_name = 'Switzerland'
url = serviceurl + country_name
uh = urllib.request.urlopen(url)
```

The first line of code appends the country name as a string to the base URL and the second line sends a **get** request to the API endpoint. If all goes well, we get back the data, decode it, and read it as a **JSON** file. This whole exercise is coded in the following function, along with some error-handling code wrapped around the basic actions we talked about previously.

4. Define the **get_country_data** function:

```
def get_country_data(country):
    """
    Function to get data about country
    from "https://restcountries.eu" API
    """
    country_name=str(country)
    url = serviceurl + country_name
    try:
        uh = urllib.request.urlopen(url)
    except HTTPError as e:
```

```
        print("Sorry! Could not retrieve anything on {}"\
            .format(country_name))
        return None
    except URLError as e:
        print('Failed to reach a server.')
        print('Reason: ', e.reason)
        return None
    else:
        data = uh.read().decode()
        print("Retrieved data on {}. Total {} characters  read."\
            .format(country_name,len(data)))
        return data
```

Test this function by passing some arguments. Note that we are using the **try..except** block here. The **try** block lets you test a block of code and see whether there are any errors; the **except** block lets you handle the errors.

5. Type in the following command:

```
data = get_country_data(country_name)
```

The output is as follows:

```
Retrieved data on Switzerland. Total 1090 characters read.
```

6. Feed erroneous data in **country_name1**:

```
country_name1 = 'Switzerland1'
data1 = get_country_data(country_name1)
```

We pass a correct name and an erroneous name. The response is as follows:

```
Sorry! Could not retrieve anything on Switzerland1
```

This is an example of rudimentary error handling. You have to think about various possibilities and put in the right code to catch and gracefully respond to user input when you are building a real-life web or enterprise application.

> **NOTE**
>
> To access the source code for this specific section, please refer to https://packt.live/30QU3MY.
>
> You can also run this example online at https://packt.live/2UUPc9I.

Now that we have written a function to get this data with some kind of error handling built into it, we are ready to move on to the next part, where we deal with the data that we just got.

USING THE BUILT-IN JSON LIBRARY TO READ AND EXAMINE DATA

As we have already mentioned, JSON looks a lot like a Python dictionary.

We will use Python's **requests** module to read raw data in that format and see what we can process further:

```
import json
x=json.loads(data)
# Load the only element
y=x[0]
type(y)
```

The output will be as follows:

```
dict
```

It reads a string datatype into a list of dictionaries. In this case, we get only one element in the list, so we extract that and check its type to make sure it is a dictionary.

We can quickly check the keys of the dictionary by using the **keys ()** method on the dictionary, that is, the JSON data (note that a full screenshot is not shown here).

Let's try the following command:

```
y.keys()
```

The output (partially shown), will be:

```
dict_keys(['name', 'topLevelDomain', 'alpha2Code', 'alpha3Code', 'callingCodes',
n', 'population', 'latlng', 'demonym', 'area', 'gini', 'timezones', 'borders', '
uages', 'translations', 'flag', 'regionalBlocs', 'cioc'])
```

Figure 7.24: The output of dict_keys

We can see the relevant country data, such as calling codes, population, area, time zones, borders, and so on.

PRINTING ALL THE DATA ELEMENTS

This task is extremely simple given that we have a dictionary at our disposal. All we have to do is iterate over the dictionary and print the key/item pairs one by one:

```
for k,v in y.items():
    print("{}: {}".format(k,v))
```

The output (partially shown) is as follows:

```
name: Switzerland
topLevelDomain: ['.ch']
alpha2Code: CH
alpha3Code: CHE
callingCodes: ['41']
capital: Bern
altSpellings: ['CH', 'Swiss Confederation',
region: Europe
subregion: Western Europe
population: 8341600
```

Figure 7.25: The output using dict

Note that the items in the dictionary are not of the same type, that is, they are not similar objects. Some are floating-point numbers, such as **area**, many are simple strings, but some are lists or even lists of dictionaries.

This is fairly common with JSON data. The internal data structure of JSON can be arbitrarily complex and multilevel, that is, you can have a dictionary of lists of dictionaries of dictionaries of lists of lists... and so on.

> **NOTE**
>
> It is clear, therefore, that there is no universal method or processing function for the JSON data format, and you have to write custom loops and functions to extract data from such a dictionary object based on your particular needs.

Now, we will write a small loop to extract the languages spoken in Switzerland. First, let's examine the dictionary closely and see where the language data is:

This is the key: **'languages'**

This is the key of the dictionaries that are in the list: **'name'**

```
nativeName: Schweiz
numericCode: 756
currencies: [{'code': 'CHF', 'name': 'Swiss franc', 'symbol': 'Fr'}]
languages: [{'iso639_1': 'de', 'iso639_2': 'deu', 'name': 'German', 'nativeName': 'Deutsch'}, {'iso639_1': 'fr', 'iso639_2': 'f
ra', 'name': 'French', 'nativeName': 'français'}, {'iso639_1': 'it', 'iso639_2': 'ita', 'name': 'Italian', 'nativeName': 'Itali
ano'}]
translations: {'de': 'Schweiz', 'es': 'Suiza', 'fr': 'Suisse', 'ja': 'スイス', 'it': 'Svizzera', 'br': 'Suíça', 'pt': 'Suíça',
'nl': 'Zwitserland', 'hr': 'Švicarska', 'fa': 'سوئیس'}
```

Figure 7.26: The tags

So, the data is embedded inside a list of dictionaries, which is accessed by a particular key of the main dictionary.

We can write two simple lines of code to extract this data:

```
for lang in y['languages']:
    print(lang['name'])
```

The output is as follows:

```
for lang in y['languages']:
    print(lang['name'])
```

```
German
French
Italian
```

Figure 7.27: The output showing the languages

USING A FUNCTION THAT EXTRACTS A DATAFRAME CONTAINING KEY INFORMATION

Here, we are interested in writing a function that can take a list of countries and return a **pandas** DataFrame with some key information:

- Capital

- Region

- Sub-region

- Population

- Latitude/longitude

- Area

- Gini index

- Time zones

- Currencies

- Languages

> **NOTE**
>
> This is the kind of wrapper function you are generally expected to write in real-life data wrangling tasks, that is, a utility function that can take a user argument and output a useful data structure (or a mini database-type object) with key information extracted over the internet about the item the user is interested in.

We will show you the whole function first and then discuss some key points about it. It is a slightly complex and long piece of code. However, with your Python data-wrangling knowledge, you should be able to examine this function closely and understand what it is doing:

Exercise 7.13.ipynb

```
import pandas as pd
import json
def build_country_database(list_country):
    """
    Takes a list of country names.
    Output a DataFrame with key information about those countries.
    """
    # Define an empty dictionary with keys
    country_dict={'Country':[],'Capital':[],'Region':[],\
                  'Sub-region':[],'Population':[], \
                  'Latitude':[],'Longitude':[], 'Area':[],\
                  'Gini':[],'Timezones':[], 'Currencies':[],\
                  'Languages':[]}
```

The code has been truncated here. You can find the entire code for this function at the following GitHub link: https://packt.live/2YeRDpP.

Here are some of the key points about this function:

- It starts by building an empty dictionary of lists. This is the chosen format for finally passing to the pandas **DataFrame** method, which accepts this format and returns a nice DataFrame with column names set to the dictionary keys' names.

- We use the previously defined **get_country_data** function to extract data for each country in the user-defined list. For this, we simply iterate over the list and call this function.

- We check the output of the **get_country_data** function. If for some reason it returns a **None** object, we will know that the API reading was not successful, and we will print out a suitable message. Again, this is an example of an error-handling mechanism and you must have them in your code. Without this small error-checking code, your application won't be robust enough for the occasional incorrect input or API malfunction.

- For many data types, we simply extract the data from the main JSON dictionary and append it to the corresponding list in our data dictionary.

- However, for special data types, such as time zones, currencies, and languages, we write a special loop to extract the data without error.

- We also take care of the fact that these special data types can have a variable length, that is, some countries may have multiple spoken languages, but most will have only one entry. So, we check whether the length of the list is greater than one and handle the data accordingly.

EXERCISE 7.13: TESTING THE FUNCTION BY BUILDING A SMALL DATABASE OF COUNTRY INFORMATION

In this exercise, we will use the example code used in the previous section and build a database of country information. We will test this function by passing a list of country names.

Let's follow these steps:

1. Import the necessary libraries:

```
import urllib.request, urllib.parse
from urllib.error import HTTPError,URLError
import pandas as pd
```

2. Define the **service_url** variable:

```
serviceurl = 'https://restcountries.eu/rest/v2/name/'
```

3. Define the **get_country_data** function:

Exercise 7.13.ipynb

```
def get_country_data(country):
    """
    Function to get data about a country
    from "https://restcountries.eu" API
    """
    country_name=str(country)
```

The complete code for this step can be found at https://packt.live/2YeRDpP.

4. Define the name of the country:

```
country_name = 'Switzerland'
```

5. Type in the following command:

```
data=get_country_data(country_name)
```

The output is as follows:

```
Retrieved data on Switzerland. Total 1090 characters read.
```

6. Feed erroneous data in **country_name1**:

```
country_name1 = 'Switzerland1'
data1 = get_country_data(country_name1)
```

On passing an erroneous name, the response is as follows:

```
Sorry! Could not retrieve anything on Switzerland1
```

7. Now, import the **json** library:

```
import json
```

8. Load from string **data** as follows:

```
x=json.loads(data)
```

9. Load the only element as follows:

```
# Load the only element
y=x[0]
```

10. Check the type of **y** as follows:

```
type(y)
```

This will return **dict**

11. Print the keys of **y** as follows:

```
y.keys()
```

The output is as follows:

```
dict_keys(['name', 'topLevelDomain', 'alpha2Code', 'alpha3Code',
'callingCodes', 'capital', 'altSpellings', 'region', 'subregion',
'population', 'latlng', 'demonym', 'area', 'gini', 'timezones',
'borders', 'nativeName', 'numericCode', 'currencies', 'languages',
'translations', 'flag', 'regionalBlocs', 'cioc'])
```

12. Iterate over the dictionary and print the key/item pairs one by one:

```
for k,v in y.items():
    print("{}: {}".format(k,v))
```

A section of output is as follows:

```
name: Switzerland
topLevelDomain: ['.ch']
alpha2Code: CH
alpha3Code: CHE
callingCodes: ['41']
```

```
capital: Bern
altSpellings: ['CH', 'Swiss Confederation', 'Schweiz', 'Suisse',
'Svizzera', 'Svizra']
region: Europe
subregion: Western Europe
population: 8341600
latlng: [47.0, 8.0]
demonym: Swiss
```

13. Create a loop to extract the languages spoken in **Switzerland**:

```
for lang in y['languages']:
    print(lang['name'])
```

The output is as follows:

```
German
French
Italian
```

14. Import the necessary libraries:

```
import pandas as pd
import json
```

15. Define the **build_country_database**:

Exercise 7.13.ipynb

```
def build_country_database(list_country):
    """
    Takes a list of country names.
    Output a DataFrame with key information about those countries.
    """
    # Define an empty dictionary with keys
    country_dict={'Country':[],'Capital':[],'Region':[],'Sub-
        region':[],'Population':[],
```

The complete code for this step is available at: https://packt.live/2YFVYkM.

16. To test its robustness, we pass in an erroneous name, such as **Turmeric** in this case:

```
df1=build_country_database(['Nigeria','Switzerland','France',\
                            'Turmeric','Russia',\
                            'Kenya','Singapore'])
```

The output is as follows:

```
Retrieved data on Nigeria. Total 1004 characters read.
Retrieved data on Switzerland. Total 1090 characters read
Retrieved data on France. Total 1047 characters read.
Sorry! Could not retrieve anything on Turmeric
Retrieved data on Russia. Total 1120 characters read.
Retrieved data on Kenya. Total 1052 characters read.
Retrieved data on Singapore. Total 1223 characters read.
```

Figure 7.28: output of country database

As we can see from the output, it detected that it did not get any data back for the incorrect entry and printed out a suitable message. The key thing is that if you do not have the error-checking and handling code in your function, then it will stop the execution on that entry and will not return the expected mini database. To avoid this behavior, error-handling code is invaluable. The following screenshot points at the incorrect entry:

```
df1=build_country_database(['Nigeria','Switzerland','France',
                            'Turmeric','Russia','Kenya','Singapor
e'])
```

An incorrect entry

```
Retrieved data on Nigeria. Total 1004 characters read.
Retrieved data on Switzerland. Total 1090 characters read.
Retrieved data on France. Total 1047 characters read.
Sorry! Could not retrieve anything on Turmeric
Retrieved data on Russia. Total 1120 characters read.
Retrieved data on Kenya. Total 1052 characters read.
Retrieved data on Singapore. Total 1223 characters read.
```

Function catches the error and handles it gracefully

Figure 7.29: The incorrect entry highlighted

17. Print the **pandas** DataFrame:

```
df1
```

The output is as follows (only partial output is shown):

	Country	Capital	Region	Sub-region	Population	Latitude	Longitude	Area	Gini	Timezones
0	Nigeria	Abuja	Africa	Western Africa	186988000	10.000000	8.0	923768.0	48.8	UTC+01:00
1	Switzerland	Bern	Europe	Western Europe	8341600	47.000000	8.0	41284.0	33.7	UTC+01:00
2	France	Paris	Europe	Western Europe	66710000	46.000000	2.0	640679.0	32.7	UTC-10:00,
3	Russian Federation	Moscow	Europe	Eastern Europe	146599183	60.000000	100.0	17124442.0	40.1	UTC+03:00
4	Kenya	Nairobi	Africa	Eastern Africa	47251000	1.000000	38.0	580367.0	47.7	UTC+03:00
5	Singapore	Singapore	Asia	South-Eastern Asia	5535000	1.366667	103.8	710.0	48.1	UTC+08:00

Figure 7.30: Partial output

Let's analyze the data that has been extracted:

Single or multiple pieces of data do not matter. They are extracted correctly.

	Area	Capital	Country	Currencies	Gini	Languages	Lattitude	Longitude	Population	Region	Sub-region
0	923768.0	Abuja	Nigeria	Nigerian naira	48.8	English	10.000000	8.0	186988000	Africa	Western Africa
1	41284.0	Bern	Switzerland	Swiss franc	33.7	German,French,Italian	47.000000	8.0	8341600	Europe	Western Europe
2	640679.0	Paris	France	Euro	32.7	French	46.000000	2.0	66710000	Europe	Western Europe
3	17124442.0	Moscow	Russian Federation	Russian ruble	40.1	Russian	60.000000	100.0	146599183	Europe	Eastern Europe
4	580367.0	Nairobi	Kenya	Kenyan shilling	47.7	English,Swahili	1.000000	38.0	47251000	Africa	Eastern Africa
5	710.0	Singapore	Singapore	Brunei dollar,Singapore dollar	48.1	English,Malay,Tamil,Chinese	1.366667	103.8	5535000	Asia	South-Eastern Asia

Figure 7.31: The data extracted correctly

As we can see from the output, single as well as multiple pieces of data have been extracted correctly.

> **NOTE**
>
> To access the source code for this specific section, please refer to https://packt.live/2YeRDpP.
>
> You can also run this example online at https://packt.live/3fvAY6U.

FUNDAMENTALS OF REGULAR EXPRESSIONS (REGEX)

Regular **ex**pressions or **regex** are used to identify whether a pattern exists in a given sequence of characters (a string) or not. They help with manipulating textual data, which is often a prerequisite for data science projects that involve text mining.

REGEX IN THE CONTEXT OF WEB SCRAPING

Web pages are often full of text, and while there are some methods in `BeautifulSoup` or XML parsers to extract raw text, there is no method for the intelligent analysis of that text. If, as a data wrangler, you are looking for a particular piece of data (for example, email IDs or phone numbers in a special format), you have to do a lot of string manipulation on a large corpus to extract email IDs or phone numbers. `RegEx` is very powerful and can save a data wrangling professional a lot of time and effort with string manipulation because they can search for complex textual patterns with wildcards of an arbitrary length.

`RegEx` is like a mini-programming language in itself and common ideas are used not only in Python, but in all widely used web app languages, such as JavaScript, PHP, and Perl. The `regex` module is built into Python, and you can import it by using the following code:

```
import re
```

In the next exercise, we are going to use the `match` method to check whether a pattern matches a string or sequence.

EXERCISE 7.14: USING THE MATCH METHOD TO CHECK WHETHER A PATTERN MATCHES A STRING/SEQUENCE

In this exercise, we will use one of the most common regex methods, **match**, to check for an exact or partial match at the beginning of a string. Let's follow these steps:

1. Import the **regex** module:

```
import re
```

2. Define a string and a pattern:

```
string1 = 'Python'
pattern = r"Python"
```

3. Write a conditional expression to check for a match:

```
if re.match(pattern,string1):
    print("Matches!")
else:
    print("Doesn't match.")
```

The output should be as follows:

```
Matches!
```

4. Test this with a string that only differs in the first letter by making it lowercase:

```
string2 = 'python'
if re.match(pattern,string2):
        print("Matches!")
else:
        print("Doesn't match.")
```

The output is as follows:

```
Doesn't match.
```

> **NOTE**
>
> To access the source code for this specific section, please refer to https://packt.live/2N8SKAW.
>
> You can also run this example online at https://packt.live/3hHJOAr.

In this exercise, we just saw how to do the most basic regex operations. In itself, it may not look very impressive, but we will be building further complex logic on top of this basic idea in the forthcoming exercises.

USING THE COMPILE METHOD TO CREATE A REGEX PROGRAM

In a program or module, if we are making heavy use of a particular pattern, then it is better to use the **compile** method and create a regex program and then call methods on this program.

Here is how you compile a regex program:

```
prog = re.compile(pattern)
prog.match(string1)
```

The output is as follows:

```
<re.SRE_Match object; span=(0, 6), match='Python'>
```

This code produced an **SRE.Match** object that has a **span** of (**0**, **6**) and the matched string of **Python**. The span here simply denotes the start and end indices of the pattern that was matched. These indices may come in handy in a text mining program where the subsequent code uses the indices for further search or decision-making purposes.

Compiled objects act like functions in that they return **None** if the pattern does not match. This concept will come in handy later when we write a small utility function to check for the type of the returned object from regex-compiled programs and act accordingly. We cannot be sure whether a pattern will match a given string or whether it will appear in a corpus of text (if we are searching for the pattern anywhere within the text). Depending on the situation, we may encounter **Match** objects or **None** as the returned value, and we have to handle this gracefully. Let's practice this in the following exercise.

EXERCISE 7.15: COMPILING PROGRAMS TO MATCH OBJECTS

In this exercise, we will define two strings and a pattern. We will use the **compile** method to compile a regex program. Next, we will write a small conditional to test whether the compiled object matches the defined pattern. Let's follow these steps:

1. Use the **compile** function from the **regex** module:

```python
import re
def print_match(s):
    if prog.search(s)==None:
        print("No match")
    else:
        print(prog.search(s).group())
string1 = 'Python'
string2 = 'python'
pattern = r"Python"
prog = re.compile(pattern)
```

2. Match it with the first string:

```python
if prog.match(string1)!=None:
    print("Matches!")
else:
    print("Doesn't match.")
```

The output is as follows:

```
Matches!
```

3. Match it with the second string:

```python
if prog.match(string2)!=None:
    print("Matches!")
else:
    print("Doesn't match.")
```

The output is as follows:

```
Doesn't match.
```

So, the **compile** method returns special objects, such as **match** objects. But if they don't match, it will return **None**, so we can still run our conditional loop.

> **NOTE**
>
> To access the source code for this specific section, please refer to https://packt.live/30SJ4m9.
>
> You can also run this example online at https://packt.live/3hlBkJE.

EXERCISE 7.16: USING ADDITIONAL PARAMETERS IN THE MATCH METHOD TO CHECK FOR POSITIONAL MATCHING

In this exercise, we will use the **match** method to check whether there's a match at a specific location in the string. Let's follow these steps:

1. Match **y** in the second position:

```
import re
def print_match(s):
    if prog.search(s)==None:
        print("No match")
    else:
        print(prog.search(s).group())
prog = re.compile(r'y')
prog.match('Python',pos=1)
```

The output is as follows:

```
<re.Match object; span=(1, 2), match='y'>
```

This is the **match** object that we talked about before.

2. Check for a pattern called **thon** starting from **pos=2**, that is, the third character:

```
prog = re.compile(r'thon')
prog.match('Python',pos=2)
```

The output is as follows:

```
<_re.SRE_Match object; span=(2, 6), match='thon'>
```

3. Find a match in a different string by using the following command:

```
prog.match('Marathon',pos=4)
```

The output is as follows:

```
<_re.SRE_Match object; span=(4, 8), match='thon'>
```

So, we have seen how can we use regex, and use it in various use cases.

> **NOTE**
>
> To access the source code for this specific section, please refer to https://packt.live/2CmKc7z.
>
> You can also run this example online at https://packt.live/30OsDY6.

FINDING THE NUMBER OF WORDS IN A LIST THAT END WITH "ING"

Suppose we want to find out whether a given string has the last three letters **ing**. This kind of query may come up in a text analytics/text mining program where somebody is interested in finding instances of present continuous tense words, which are highly likely to end with **ing**. However, nouns may also end with **ing** (as we will see in this example):

```
prog = re.compile(r'ing')
words = ['Spring','Cycling','Ringtone']
```

Create a **for** loop to find words ending with **ing**:

```
for w in words:
    if prog.match(w,pos=len(w)-3)!=None:
        print("{} has last three letters 'ing'".format(w))
    else:
        print("{} does not have last three letter as 'ing'"\
            .format(w))
```

The output is as follows:

```
Spring has last three letters 'ing'
Cycling has last three letters 'ing'
Ringtone does not have last three letter as 'ing'
```

THE SEARCH METHOD IN REGEX

It looks plain and simple, and you may well wonder what the purpose of using a special regex module for this is. A simple string method should have been sufficient. Yes, it would have been OK for this particular example, but the whole point of using regex is to be able to use very complex string patterns that are not at all obvious when it comes to how they are written using simple string methods. We will see the real power of regex compared to string methods shortly. But before that, let's explore another of the most commonly used methods, called **search**.

search and **match** are related concepts, and they both return the same **match** object. The real difference between them is that **match works for only the first match** (either at the beginning of the string or at a specified position, as we saw in the previous exercises), whereas **search looks for the pattern anywhere in the string** and returns the position if it finds a match.

EXERCISE 7.17: THE SEARCH METHOD IN REGEX

In this exercise, we will use the **search** method to find the **ing** pattern in a regex structure. Let's follow these steps:

1. Use the **compile** method to find matching strings:

```
import re
def print_match(s):
    if prog.search(s)==None:
        print("No match")
    else:
        print(prog.search(s).group())
prog = re.compile('ing')
if prog.match('Spring')==None:
    print("None")
```

The output is as follows:

```
None
```

2. Search the string by using the following command:

```
prog.search('Spring')
```

The output is as follows:

```
<_sre.SRE_Match object; span=(3, 6), match='ing'>
```

3. Let's use **Ringtone** as the search parameter:

```
prog.search('Ringtone')
```

The output is as follows:

```
<re.Match object; span=(1, 4), match='ing'>
```

As you can see, the **match** method returns **None** for the input **Spring**, and we had to write code to print that out explicitly (because in a Jupyter notebook, nothing will show up for a **None** object). But **search** returns a **match** object with **span=(3,6)** as it finds the **ing** pattern spanning those positions.

Similarly, for the **Ringtone** string, it finds the correct position of the match and returns **span=(1,4)**.

> **NOTE**
>
> To access the source code for this specific section, please refer to https://packt.live/3fDRmme.
>
> You can also run this example online at https://packt.live/30U2WFm.

EXERCISE 7.18: USING THE SPAN METHOD OF THE MATCH OBJECT TO LOCATE THE POSITION OF THE MATCHED PATTERN

In this exercise, we will use the **span** contained in the **Match** object to locating the exact position of the pattern as it appears in the string. Let's follow these steps:

1. Initialize **prog** with the **ing** pattern:

```
import re
def print_match(s):
    if prog.search(s)==None:
        print("No match")
    else:
        print(prog.search(s).group())
prog = re.compile(r'ing')
words = ['Spring','Cycling','Ringtone']
```

2. Create a function to return a tuple of the start and end positions of the match:

```
for w in words:
    mt = prog.search(w)
# Span returns a tuple of start and end positions of the match
# Starting position of the match
start_pos = mt.span()[0]
# Ending position of the match
end_pos = mt.span()[1]
```

3. Print the word ending with **ing** and its start and end position:

```
print("The word '{}' contains 'ing' in the position {}-{}"\
        .format(w,start_pos,end_pos))
```

The output is as follows:

```
The word 'Ringtone' contains 'ing' in the position 1-4
```

> **NOTE**
>
> To access the source code for this specific section, please refer to
> https://packt.live/2YIZB9y.
>
> You can also run this example online at https://packt.live/37FXSG5.

Now, we will start getting into the real usage of regex with examples of various useful pattern matching. In the following exercise, we will explore single-character matching.

EXERCISE 7.19: EXAMPLES OF SINGLE-CHARACTER PATTERN MATCHING WITH SEARCH

In this exercise, we will use the **group** method, which will return the matched pattern in a string format so that we can print and process it easily. Let's follow these steps:

1. Pass a regex expression with a dot (.) inside the **compile** method. It matches any single character except a newline character:

```
import re
prog = re.compile(r'py.')
print(prog.search('pygmy').group())
print(prog.search('Jupyter').group())
```

The output is as follows:

```
pyg
pyt
```

2. Pass a regex expression with **\w** (lowercase w) inside the **compile** method. It matches any single letter, digit, or underscore:

```
prog = re.compile(r'c\wm')
print(prog.search('comedy').group())
print(prog.search('camera').group())
print(prog.search('pac_man').group())
print(prog.search('pac2man').group())
```

The output is as follows:

```
com
cam
c_m
c2m
```

3. Pass a regex expression with **\W** (uppercase W) inside the **compile** method. It matches anything not covered by **\w**:

```
prog = re.compile(r'4\W1')
print(prog.search('4/1 was a wonderful day!').group())
print(prog.search('4-1 was a wonderful day!').group())
print(prog.search('4.1 was a wonderful day!').group())
print(prog.search('Remember the wonderful day 04/1?').group())
```

The output is as follows:

```
4/1
4-1
4.1
4/1
```

4. Pass a regex expression with **\s** (lowercase s) inside the **compile** method. It matches a single whitespace character, such as a space, newline, tab, or return:

```
prog = re.compile(r'Data\swrangling')
print(prog.search("Data wrangling is cool").group())
print("-"*80)
print("Data\twrangling is the full string")
print(prog.search("Data\twrangling is the full string").group())
```

```
print("-"*80)
print("Data\nwrangling is the full string")
print(prog.search("Data\nwrangling").group())
```

The output is as follows:

```
Data wrangling
----------------------------------------------------------------
Data    wrangling is the full string
Data    wrangling
----------------------------------------------------------------
Data
wrangling is the full string
Data
wrangling
```

5. Pass a regex expression with **\d** inside the **compile** method. It matches numerical digits 0-9:

```
prog = re.compile(r"score was \d\d")
print(prog.search("My score was 67").group())
print(prog.search("Your score was 73").group())
```

The output is as follows:

```
score was 67
score was 73
```

As we can see, we can use the **group** function to return a group of matched characters.

> **NOTE**
>
> To access the source code for this specific section, please refer to https://packt.live/2YOJcAi.
>
> You can also run this example online at https://packt.live/3edPMHj.

In the following exercise, we will manipulate the start or end of a string using pattern matching.

EXERCISE 7.20: HANDLING PATTERN MATCHING AT THE START OR END OF A STRING

In this exercise, we will match patterns with strings using the ^ (caret) operator. The focus is to find out whether the pattern is present at the start or the end of the string. Let's follow these steps:

1. Write a function to handle cases where a match is not found, that is, to handle **None** objects that are returned:

```
import re
def print_match(s):
    if prog.search(s)==None:
        print("No match")
    else:
        print(prog.search(s).group())
```

2. Use ^ (caret) to match a pattern at the start of the string:

```
prog = re.compile(r'^India')
print_match("Russia implemented this law")
print_match("India implemented that law")
print_match("This law was implemented by India")
```

The output is as follows:

```
No match
India
No match
```

3. Use **$** (dollar sign) to match a pattern at the end of the string:

```
prog = re.compile(r'Apple$')
print_match("Patent no 123456 belongs to Apple")
print_match("Patent no 345672 belongs to Samsung")
print_match("Patent no 987654 belongs to Apple")
```

The output is as follows:

```
Apple
No match
Apple
```

> **NOTE**
>
> To access the source code for this specific section, please refer to
> https://packt.live/3ddku23.
>
> You can also run this example online at https://packt.live/3djOXeV.
>
> For these examples and exercises, also try to think about how you would
> implement them without regex, that is, by using simple string methods and
> any other logic that you can think of. Then, compare that solution to the
> ones implemented with regex for brevity and efficiency.

EXERCISE 7.21: PATTERN MATCHING WITH MULTIPLE CHARACTERS

In this exercise, we will use the **match** method for matching multiple characters. Let's
perform the following steps:

1. Use ***** to match **0** or more repetitions of the preceding regular expression:

```
import re
def print_match(s):
    if prog.search(s)==None:
        print("No match")
    else:
        print(prog.search(s).group())
prog = re.compile(r'ab*')
print_match("a")
print_match("ab")
print_match("abbb")
print_match("b")
print_match("bbab")
print_match("something_abb_something")
```

The output is as follows:

```
a
ab
abbb
No match
ab
abb
```

2. Using **+** causes the resulting **RE** to match **1** or more repetitions of the preceding regular expression:

```
prog = re.compile(r'ab+')
print_match("a")
print_match("ab")
print_match("abbb")
print_match("b")
print_match("bbab")
print_match("something_abb_something")
```

The output is as follows:

```
No match
ab
abbb
No match
ab
abb
```

3. ? causes the resulting **re** string to match precisely 0 or 1 repetitions of the preceding regular expression:

```
prog = re.compile(r'ab?')
print_match("a")
print_match("ab")
print_match("abbb")
print_match("b")
print_match("bbab")
print_match("something_abb_something")
```

The output is as follows:

```
a
ab
ab
No match
ab
ab
```

Here, we saw how we can use regex to search for and match a set of characters in the same order as they occur in the search pattern.

> **NOTE**
>
> To access the source code for this specific section, please refer to https://packt.live/310l7Jw.
>
> You can also run this example online at https://packt.live/3hCdnDz.

The standard (default) mode of pattern matching in regex is **greedy**, that is, the program tries to match as much as it can. Sometimes, this behavior is natural, but in some cases, you may want to match minimally. This is called **non-greedy** matching.

EXERCISE 7.22: GREEDY VERSUS NON-GREEDY MATCHING

In this exercise, we will perform greedy and non-greedy pattern matching. Let's go through the following steps:

1. Write the code to check the greedy way of matching a string, as follows:

```
import re
def print_match(s):
    if prog.search(s)==None:
        print("No match")
    else:
        print(prog.search(s).group())
prog = re.compile(r'<.*>')
print_match('<a> b <c>')
```

The output is as follows:

```
<a> b <c>
```

So, the preceding regex found both tags with the **<>** pattern, but what if we wanted to match the first tag only and stop there.

2. Use **?** by inserting it after any regex expression to make it non-greedy:

```
prog = re.compile(r'<.*?>')
print_match('<a> b <c>')
```

The output is as follows:

```
<a>
```

In the following exercise, we will be handling repetitions using **match**.

> **NOTE**
>
> To access the source code for this specific section, please refer to https://packt.live/37Hz944.
>
> You can also run this example online at https://packt.live/2UVIK3q.

EXERCISE 7.23: CONTROLLING REPETITIONS TO MATCH IN A TEXT

In this exercise, we will check the number of repetitions of the pattern we want to match in a text. Let's go through the following steps:

1. **{m}** specifies exactly **m** copies of **RE** to match. Fewer matches cause a non-match and return **None**:

```
import re
def print_match(s):
    if prog.search(s)==None:
        print("No match")
    else:
        print(prog.search(s).group())
prog = re.compile(r'A{3}')
print_match("ccAAAdd")
print_match("ccAAAAdd")
print_match("ccAAdd")
```

The output is as follows:

```
AAA
AAA
No match
```

2. **{m,n}** specifies exactly **m** to **n** copies of **RE** to match:

```
prog = re.compile(r'A{2,4}B')
print_match("ccAAABdd")
print_match("ccABdd")
print_match("ccAABBBdd")
print_match("ccAAAAAAABdd")
```

The output is as follows:

```
AAAB
No match
AAB
AAAAB
```

3. Omitting **m** specifies a lower bound of zero:

```
prog = re.compile(r'A{,3}B')
print_match("ccAAABdd")
print_match("ccABdd")
print_match("ccAABBBdd")
print_match("ccAAAAAAABdd")
```

The output is as follows:

```
AAAB
AB
AAB
AAAB
```

4. Omitting **n** specifies an infinite upper bound:

```
prog = re.compile(r'A{3,}B')
print_match("ccAAABdd")
print_match("ccABdd")
print_match("ccAABBBdd")
print_match("ccAAAAAAABdd")
```

The output is as follows:

```
AAAB
No match
No match
AAAAAAB
```

5. `{m,n}?` specifies **m** to **n** copies of **RE** to match in a non-greedy fashion:

```
prog = re.compile(r'A{2,4}')
print_match("AAAAAAA")
prog = re.compile(r'A{2,4}?')
print_match("AAAAAAA")
```

The output is as follows:

```
AAAA
AA
```

> **NOTE**
>
> To access the source code for this specific section, please refer to https://packt.live/2YOzAWf.
>
> You can also run this example online at https://packt.live/2YKO7T4.

Let's go over to the next section.

SETS OF MATCHING CHARACTERS

To match an arbitrarily complex pattern, we need to be able to include a logical combination of characters together as a bunch. Regex gives us that kind of capability.

The following examples demonstrate such uses of regex. `[x,y,z]` matches **x**, **y**, or **z**:

```
prog = re.compile(r'[A,B]')
print_match("ccAd")
print_match("ccABd")
print_match("ccXdB")
print_match("ccXdZ")
```

The output will be as follows:

```
A
A
B
No match
```

A range of characters can be matched inside the set using **-**. This is one of the most widely used regex techniques.

EXERCISE 7.24: SETS OF MATCHING CHARACTERS

In this exercise, we will find the sets of matching characters from a defined string. We will look for an email address pattern, **<some name>@<some domain name>.<some domain identifier>**, from a string. Let's go through the following steps:

1. Suppose we want to pick out an email address from some text:

```
import re
def print_match(s):
    if prog.search(s)==None:
        print("No match")
    else:
        print(prog.search(s).group())
prog = re.compile(r'[a-zA-Z]+@+[a-zA-Z]+\.com')
print_match("My email is coolguy@xyz.com")
print_match("My email is coolguy12@xyz.com")
```

The output is as follows:

```
coolguy@xyz.com
No match
```

Look at the regex pattern inside [...]. It is **a-zA-Z**. This covers all letters, including lowercase and uppercase. With this one simple regex, you are able to match any (pure) alphabetical string for that part of the email. Now, the next pattern is **@**, which is added to the previous regex by the **+** character. This is the way to build up a complex regex: by adding/stacking up individual regex patterns. We also use the same **[a-zA-Z]** for the email domain name and add a **.com** at the end to complete the pattern as a valid email address. Why **\.**? Because, by itself, a dot (**.**) is used as a special modifier in regex but here we want to use a dot (**.**) just as a dot (**.**), not as a modifier. So, we need to precede it with ****.

So, with this regex, we could extract the first email address perfectly but got **No match** with the second one. What happened with the second email ID?

The regex could not capture it because it had the number **12** in the name. That pattern is not captured by the expression **[a-zA-Z]**.

2. Let's change that and add the digits as well:

```
prog = re.compile(r'[a-zA-Z0-9]+@+[a-zA-Z]+\.com')
print_match("My email is coolguy12@xyz.com")
print_match("My email is coolguy12@xyz.org")
```

The output is as follows:

```
coolguy12@xyz.com
No match
```

We caught the first email ID perfectly. But what's going on with the second one? Again, we got a mismatch. The reason is that we changed the `.com` to `.org` in that email, and in our regex expression, that portion was hardcoded as `.com`, so it did not find a match.

3. Let's try to address this in the following regex:

```
prog = re.compile(r'[a-zA-Z0-9]+@+[a-zA-Z]+\.+[a-zA-Z]{2,3}')
print_match("My email is coolguy12@xyz.org")
print_match("My email is coolguy12[AT]xyz[DOT]org")
```

The output is as follows:

```
coolguy12@xyz.org
No match
```

In this regex, we used the fact that most domain identifiers have two or three characters, so we used **[a-zA-Z]{2,3}** to capture that.

What happened with the second email ID? This is an example of the small tweaks that you can make to stay ahead of telemarketers who want to scrape online forums or any other corpus of text and extract your email ID. If you do not want your email to be found, you can change @ to **[AT]** and **.** to **[DOT]**, and hopefully, that should beat some regex techniques (but not all of them).

> **NOTE**
>
> To access the source code for this specific section, please refer to https://packt.live/2UXv6eS.
>
> You can also run this example online at https://packt.live/315GaL9.

EXERCISE 7.25: THE USE OF OR IN REGEX USING THE OR OPERATOR

In this exercise, we will use the **OR** operator in a Regex expression. We will try to extract patterns of 10-digit numbers that could be phone numbers. We can do that by using the **|** operator. Let's go through the following steps:

1. Let's start with the **OR** operator:

```
import re
def print_match(s):
    if prog.search(s)==None:
        print("No match")
    else:
        print(prog.search(s).group())
prog = re.compile(r'[0-9]{10}')
print_match("3124567897")
print_match("312-456-7897")
```

The output is as follows:

```
3124567897
No match
```

Note the use of **{10}** to denote exactly **10**-digit numbers in the pattern. But the second number could not be matched for obvious reasons – it had – symbols inserted in between groups of numbers.

2. Use multiple smaller regexes and logically combine them by using the following command:

```
prog = re.compile(r'[0-9]{10}|[0-9]{3}-[0-9]{3}-[0-9]{4}')
print_match("3124567897")
print_match("312-456-7897")
```

The output is as follows:

```
3124567897
312-456-7897
```

Phone numbers are written in a myriad of ways and if you search on the web, you will see examples of very complex regexes (written not only in Python but in other widely used languages for web apps such as JavaScript, C++, PHP, and Perl) for capturing phone numbers.

3. Create four strings and execute **print_match** on them:

```
p1= r'[0-9]{10}'
p2=r'[0-9]{3}-[0-9]{3}-[0-9]{4}'
p3 = r'\([0-9]{3}\)[0-9]{3}-[0-9]{4}'
p4 = r'[0-9]{3}\.[0-9]{3}\.[0-9]{4}'
pattern= p1+'|'+p2+'|'+p3+'|'+p4
prog = re.compile(pattern)
print_match("3124567897")
print_match("312-456-7897")
print_match("(312)456-7897")
print_match("312.456.7897")
```

The output is as follows:

```
3124567897
312-456-7897
(312)456-7897
312.456.7897
```

So, as you can see, thanks to all the different patterns we have added together using the **OR** operator, we are able to detect phone numbers even if they are written in very different ways.

> **NOTE**
>
> To access the source code for this specific section, please refer to https://packt.live/3eeZc59.
>
> You can also run this example online at https://packt.live/2APMFH5.

THE FINDALL METHOD

The last regex method that we will cover in this chapter is `findall`. Essentially, it is a **search-and-aggregate** method, that is, it puts together all the instances that match the regex pattern in a given text and returns them in a list. This is extremely useful, as we can just count the length of the returned list to count the number of occurrences or pick and use the returned pattern-matched words one by one as we see fit.

Note that although we are giving short examples of single sentences in this chapter, you will often deal with a large corpus of text when using a regex.

In those cases, you are likely to get many matches from a single regex pattern search. For all of those cases, the `findall` method is going to be the most useful:

```
ph_numbers = """Here are some phone numbers.
Pick out the numbers with 312 area code:
312-423-3456, 456-334-6721, 312-5478-9999,
312-Not-a-Number,777.345.2317, 312.331.6789"""
print(ph_numbers)
re.findall('312+[-\.][0-9-\.]+',ph_numbers)
```

The output is as follows:

```
 Here are some phone numbers.
Pick out the numbers with 312 area code:
312-423-3456, 456-334-6721, 312-5478-9999,
312-Not-a-Number,777.345.2317, 312.331.6789
 ['312-423-3456', '312-5478-9999', '312.331.6789']
```

With all this knowledge gained from the chapter, let's get started with solving the following activities.

ACTIVITY 7.01: EXTRACTING THE TOP 100 E-BOOKS FROM GUTENBERG

Project Gutenberg encourages the creation and distribution of eBooks by encouraging volunteer efforts to digitize and archive cultural works. This activity aims to scrape the URL of Project Gutenberg's Top 100 eBooks to identify the eBooks' links. It uses **BeautifulSoup** to parse the HTML and regular expression code to identify the Top 100 eBook file numbers. You can use these numbers to download the book into your local drive if you want.

These are the steps that will help you complete this activity:

1. Import the necessary libraries, including **regex** and **BeautifulSoup**.

2. Read the HTML from the URL.

3. Write a small function to check the status of the web request.

4. Decode the response and pass this on to **BeautifulSoup** for HTML parsing.

5. Find all the **href** tags and store them in the list of links. Check what the list looks like – print the first 30 elements.

6. Use a regular expression to find the numeric digits in these links. These are the file numbers for the top 100 eBooks.

7. Initialize the empty list to hold the file numbers over an appropriate range and use **regex** to find the numeric digits in the link **href** string. **Hint:** Use the **findall** method.

8. What does the **soup** object's text look like? Use the **.text** method and print only the first 2,000 characters (do not print the whole thing, as it is too long).

9. Search in the extracted text (using a regular expression) from the **soup** object to find the names of the top 100 eBooks (yesterday's ranking).

10. Create a starting index. It should point at the text *Top 100 Ebooks yesterday*. Use the **splitlines** method of **soup.text**. It splits the lines of text of the **soup** object.

11. Run the **for** loop **1–100** to add the strings of the next **100** lines to this temporary list. **Hint:** use the **splitlines** method.

12. Use a regular expression to extract only text from the name strings and append it to an empty list. Use **match** and **span** to find the indices and use them.

13. Print the list of titles.

The output (shown partially) should look like this:

```
Pride and Prejudice by Jane Austen
Frankenstein
A Modest Proposal by Jonathan Swift
A Christmas Carol in Prose
Heart of Darkness by Joseph Conrad
Et dukkehjem
A Tale of Two Cities by Charles Dickens
Dracula by Bram Stoker
Moby Dick
The Importance of Being Earnest
Alice
Metamorphosis by Franz Kafka
The Strange Case of Dr
Beowulf
...
The Russian Army and the Japanese War
Calculus Made Easy by Silvanus P
Beyond Good and Evil by Friedrich Wilhelm Nietzsche
An Occurrence at Owl Creek Bridge by Ambrose Bierce
Don Quixote by Miguel de Cervantes Saavedra
Blue Jackets by Edward Greey
The Life and Adventures of Robinson Crusoe by Daniel Defoe
The Waterloo Campaign
The War of the Worlds by H
Democracy in America
Songs of Innocence
The Confessions of St
Modern French Masters by Marie Van Vorst
Persuasion by Jane Austen
The Works of Edgar Allan Poe
The Fall of the House of Usher by Edgar Allan Poe
The Masque of the Red Death by Edgar Allan Poe
The Lady with the Dog and Other Stories by Anton Pavlovich Chekhov
```

NOTE

The solution for this activity can be found on page 493.

ACTIVITY 7.02: BUILDING YOUR OWN MOVIE DATABASE BY READING AN API

In this activity, you will build a complete movie database by communicating and interfacing with a free API from the OMDb portal http://www.omdbapi.com/?.You will obtain a unique user key from the OMDb website that must be used when your program tries to access the API. Then, you will need to store this key value in a .json file.

The aims of this activity are as follows:

- To retrieve and print basic data about a movie (the title is entered by the user) from the web (the OMDb database).

- If a poster of the movie can be found, download the file and save it in a user-specified location.

These are the steps that will help you complete this activity:

1. Import **urllib.request**, **urllib.parse**, **urllib.error**, and **json**.

2. Load the secret API key (you have to get one from the OMDb website and use that; it has a daily limit of 1,000 API keys) from a JSON file, stored in the same folder, in a variable.

   Hint: Use **json.loads()**.

   Students/users will need to obtain a key and store it in a JSON file.

3. Obtain a key and store it in a JSON file as **APIkeys.json**.

4. Open the **APIkeys.json** file.

5. Assign the OMDb portal (http://www.omdbapi.com/?) as a string to a variable.

6. Create a variable called **apikey** with the last portion of the URL (**&apikey=secretapikey**), where **secretapikey** is your own API key.

7. Write a utility function called **print_json** to print the movie data from a JSON file (which we will get from the portal).

8. Write a utility function to download a poster of the movie based on the information from the JSON dataset and save it in your local folder. Use the **os** module. The poster data is stored in a JSON key called **Poster**. Use the **open** Python command to open a file and write the poster data. Close the file after you're done. This function will save the poster data as an image file.

9. Write a utility function called **search_movie** to search for a movie by its name, print the downloaded **JSON** data, and save the movie poster in the local folder. Use a **try-except** loop for this. Use the previously created **serviceurl** and **apikey** variables. You have to pass on a dictionary with a key, **t**, and the movie name as the corresponding value to the **urllib.parse.urlencode()** function and then add the **serviceurl** and **apikey** variables to the output of the function to construct the full URL. This URL will be used to access the data. The **JSON** data has a key called **Response**. If it is **True**, that means the read was successful. Check this before processing the data. If it's not successful, then print the **JSON** key **Error**, which will contain the appropriate error message returned by the movie database.

10. Test the **search_movie** function by entering **Titanic**. The output should look like this:

```
http://www.omdbapi.com/?t=Titanic&apikey=<your API key>
--------------------------------------------------------
Title: Titanic
Year: 1997
Rated: PG-13
Released: 19 Dec 1997
Runtime: 194 min
Genre: Drama, Romance
Director: James Cameron
Writer: James Cameron
Actors: Leonardo DiCaprio, Kate Winslet, Billy Zane, Kathy Bates
Plot: A seventeen-year-old aristocrat falls in love with a kind but
poor artist aboard the luxurious, ill-fated R.M.S. Titanic.
Language: English, Swedish
Country: USA
Awards: Won 11 Oscars. Another 111 wins & 77 nominations.
Ratings: [{'Source': 'Internet Movie Database', 'Value': '7.8/10'},
{'Source': 'Rotten Tomatoes', 'Value': '89%'}, {'Source':
'Metacritic', 'Value': '75/100'}]
Metascore: 75
imdbRating: 7.8
imdbVotes: 913,780
imdbID: tt0120338
--------------------------------------------------------
```

11. Test the **search_movie** function by entering **Random_error** and retrieve the data for **Random_error** (obviously, this will not be found, and you should be able to check whether your error-catching code is working properly). The expected output is as follows:

```
http://www.omdbapi.com/?t=Random_error&apikey=<your api key>
Error encountered:  Movie not found!
```

> **NOTE**
>
> The solution for this activity can be found on page 499.

Look for a folder called **Posters** in the same directory you are working in. It should contain a file called **Titanic.jpg**. Check the file.

In this activity, we have seen a few general tricks for working with an API that are fairly common for other popular API services such as Google and Twitter. Now, you should be confident about writing more complex programs to scrape data from such services.

SUMMARY

In this chapter, we went through several important concepts and learning modules related to advanced data gathering and web scraping. We started by reading data from web pages using two of the most popular Python libraries – **requests** and **BeautifulSoup**. In this task, we utilized the knowledge we gained in the previous chapter about the general structure of HTML pages and their interaction with Python code. We extracted meaningful data from the Wikipedia home page during this process.

Then, we learned how to read data from XML and JSON files – two of the most widely used data streaming/exchange formats on the web. For XML, we showed you how to traverse the tree-structure data string efficiently to extract key information. For JSON, we mixed it with reading data from the web using an API. The API we consumed was RESTful, which is one of the major standards in web APIs.

At the end of this chapter, we went through a detailed exercise using regex techniques in tricky string-matching problems to scrape useful information from a large and messy text corpus, parsed from HTML. This chapter should come in extremely handy for string and text processing tasks in your data wrangling career.

In the next chapter, we will learn about databases with Python.

8

RDBMS AND SQL

OVERVIEW

This chapter will introduce you to the basics of using an RDBMS to query
a database using Python and convert data from SQL and then store it in a
pandas DataFrame. It will explain the concepts of databases, including
their creation, manipulation, and control, and how to transform tables into
pandas DataFrames. By the end of this chapter, you will learn some basic
SQL commands. This knowledge will make you adept at adding, updating,
retrieving, and deleting data from databases; another valuable skill in a
budding data wrangling expert's repertoire.

INTRODUCTION

This chapter of our data journey is focused on **Relational Database Management System (RDBMS)** and **Structured Query Language (SQL)**. In the previous chapter, we stored and read data from a file. In this chapter, we will read structured data, design access to the data, and create query interfaces for databases.

For years, the RDBMS format has been the conventional way to store data. An RDBMS is one of the safest ways to store, manage, and retrieve data. It is backed by a solid mathematical foundation (relational algebra and calculus) and exposes an efficient and intuitive declarative language – SQL – for easy interaction. Almost every language has a rich set of libraries to interact with different RDBMS, and the tricks and methods of using them are well tested and well understood.

Scaling an RDBMS is a pretty well-understood task, and there is a group of well trained, experienced professionals to do this job (DBAs, or database administrators).

So, it is understandable that we, as data wrangling professionals or data engineers, will encounter RDBMS at some point. We will need the tools and knowledge acquired from this chapter to deal with RDBMS.

As we can see in the following chart, the database management system market is big. This chart was produced based on market research that was done by Scalegrid in 2019:

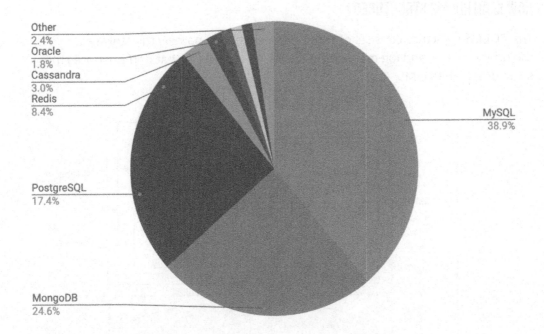

Figure 8.1: Commercial database market share released by ScaleGrid in 2019

We will learn and play around with some of the basic and fundamental concepts of database and relational database management systems in this chapter. We will start with a refresher of the theoretical concept of a database, and then we will create and operate a database from our Python environment.

REFRESHER OF RDBMS AND SQL

An RDBMS is a piece of software that manages data (represented for the end user in tabular form) on physical hard disks and is built using Codd's relational model. Most of the databases that we encounter today are RDBMS. In recent years, there has been a huge industry shift toward a newer kind of database management system, called NoSQL (MongoDB, CouchDB, Riak, and so on). These systems, while they do follow some of the rules of RDBMS in certain aspects, in most cases they reject or modify them.

HOW IS AN RDBMS STRUCTURED?

The RDBMS structure consists of three main elements, namely the storage engine, the query engine, and log management. Here is a diagram that demonstrates the structure of an RDBMS:

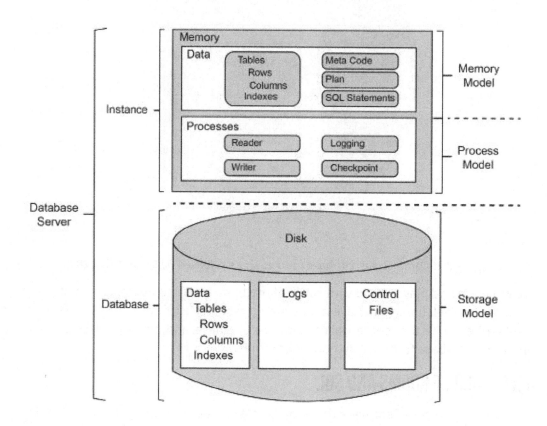

Figure 8.2: RDBMS structure

The following are the main concepts of any RDBMS structure:

- **Storage engine:** This is the part of the RDBMS that is responsible for storing data in an efficient way and also retrieving it, when asked for, in an efficient way. As an end user of the RDBMS system (an application developer is considered an end user of an RDBMS), we will never need to interact with this layer directly.

- **Query engine:** This is the part of the RDBMS that allows us to create data objects (tables, views, and so on), manipulate them (create and delete columns, create/delete/update rows, and so on), and query them (read rows) using a simple, yet powerful, language.

- **Log management:** This part of the RDBMS is responsible for creating and maintaining the logs. If you are wondering why the log is such an important thing, then you should look into how replication and partitions are handled in a modern RDBMS (such as PostgreSQL) using something called the **Write Ahead Log** (or **WAL** for short).

We will focus on the query engine in this chapter.

SQL

SQL (pronounced *sequel*), as it is commonly known, is a domain-specific language that was originally designed based on E.F. Codd's relational model and is widely used in today's databases to define, insert, manipulate, and retrieve data from them. It can be further sub-divided into four smaller sub-languages, namely **Data Definition Language** (**DDL**), **Data Manipulation Language** (**DML**), **Data Query Language** (**DQL**), and **Data Control Language** (**DCL**). There are several advantages of using SQL, some of which are as follows:

- It is based on a solid mathematical framework and thus it is easy to understand.

- It is a declarative language, which means that we actually never tell it how to do its job. We almost always tell it what to do. This frees us from the big burden of writing custom code for data management. We can be more focused on the actual query problem we are trying to solve, instead of bothering about how to create and maintain a data store.

- It gives you a fast and readable way to deal with data.

- SQL gives you out-of-the-box ways to get multiple pieces of data with a single query.

The main areas of focus for the following topic will be DDL, DML, and DQL. The DCL part is more for database administrators. Let's discuss them briefly:

- **DDL**: This is how we define our data structure in SQL. As an RDBMS is mainly designed and built with structured data in mind, we have to tell an RDBMS engine beforehand what our data is going to look like. We can update this definition at a later point in time, but an initial statement is a must. This is where we will write statements such as **CREATE TABLE**, **DROP TABLE**, and **ALTER TABLE**.

> **NOTE**
>
> Notice the use of uppercase letters. This is not a requirement, and you may use lowercase letters, but it is a widely followed convention, and we will use it in this book.

- **DML**: DML is the part of SQL that lets us insert, delete, or update a certain data point (a row) in a previously defined data object (a table). This is the part of SQL that contains statements such as **INSERT INTO**, **DELETE FROM**, or **UPDATE**.

- **DQL**: With DQL, we enable ourselves to query the data stored in an RDBMS, which was defined by DDL and inserted using DML. It gives us enormous power and flexibility to not only query data out of a single object (table), but also to extract relevant data from all the related objects using queries. The frequently used query that's used to retrieve data is the **SELECT** command. We will also see and use the concepts of the primary key, foreign key, index, joins, and so on.

Once you define and insert data in a database, it can be represented as follows:

First Name	Last Name	Address	City	Age
Mickey	Mouse	123 Fantasy Way	Anaheim	73
Bat	Man	321 Cavern Ave	Gotham	54
Wonder	Woman	987 Truth Way	Paradise	39
Donald	Duck	555 Quack Street	Mallard	65
Bugs	Bunny	567 Carrot Street	Rascal	58
Wiley E.	Coyote	999 Acme Way	Canyon	61
Cat	Woman	234 Purrfect Street	Hairball	32
Tweety	Pie	543 Chirp Creek	Irvine	22

Figure 8.3: Table displaying sample data

Another thing to remember about an RDBMS is relations. Generally, in a table, we have one or more columns that will have unique values for each row in the table. We call them **primary keys** for the table. We should be aware that we will encounter unique values across the rows, which are not primary keys. The main difference between them and primary keys is the fact that a primary key cannot be null.

By using the primary key of one table and mentioning it as a foreign key in another table, we can establish relations between two tables. A certain table can be related to any finite number of tables.

The relations can be **1:1**, which means that each row of the second table is uniquely related to one row of the first table, or **1:N**, **N:1**, or **N: M**. An example of relations is as follows:

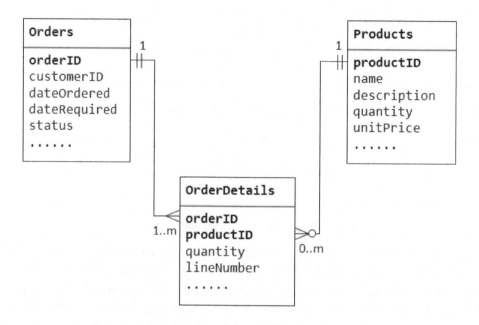

Figure 8.4: Diagram showing relations

With this brief refresher, we are now ready to jump into hands-on exercises and write some SQL to store and retrieve data.

USING AN RDBMS (MYSQL/POSTGRESQL/SQLITE)

In this topic, we will focus on how to write some basic SQL commands, as well as how to connect to a database from Python and use it effectively within Python. The database we will choose here is SQLite. There are other databases, such as Oracle, MySQL, PostgreSQL, and DB2. The main tricks that you are going to learn here will not change depending on the database you are using. However, for different databases, you will need to install different third-party Python libraries (such as Psycopg2 for PostgreSQL). The reason they all behave the same way (apart for some small details) is the fact that they all adhere to PEP249 (commonly known as Python DB API 2).

This is a good standardization and saves us a lot of headaches while porting from one RDBMS to another. If you already have some experience with databases, then you will notice that we will not be using any server address, username, password, or other credentials to connect to a database. This is because these fields are not mandatory in sqlite3, unlike in PostgreSQL or MySQL. The main database engine of SQLite is embedded.

> **NOTE**
>
> Most of the industry-standard projects that are written in Python and use some kind of RDBMS as the data store most often rely on an **Object Relational Mapper** (**ORM**). An ORM is a high-level library in Python that makes many tasks easier when dealing with an RDBMS. It also exposes a more Pythonic API than writing raw SQL inside Python code.

EXERCISE 8.01: CONNECTING TO A DATABASE IN SQLITE

In this exercise, we will look into the first step toward using an RDBMS in Python code. We are going to connect to a database, **lesson.db**. We will then close the connection safely. Let's perform the following steps:

1. Import the **sqlite3** library from Python by using the following command:

```
import sqlite3
```

2. Use the **connect** function to connect to a database:

```
conn = sqlite3.connect("../lesson.db")
```

3. Close the connection, as follows:

```
conn.close()
```

    This **conn** object is the main connection object, and we will need it to get a second type of object in the future once we want to interact with the database. We need to be careful about closing any open connection to our database.

4. Use the same **with** statement from Python, just like we did for files, and connect to the database, as follows:

```
with sqlite3.connect("../lesson.db") as conn:
    pass
```

In this exercise, we have connected to a database using Python.

> **NOTE**
>
> To access the source code for this specific section, please refer to
> https://packt.live/2YMWrBD.
>
> You can also run this example online at https://packt.live/3df6q87.

In the next exercise, we will see the best way to create a table and put data into it using Python.

DDL AND DML COMMANDS IN SQLITE

To create a table in SQL, use the **CREATE TABLE** SQL clause. This will require the table name and the table definition. The table name is a unique identifier for the database engine to find and use the table for all future transactions. It can be anything (any alphanumeric string), as long as it is unique. We add the table definition in the form of (`column_name_1 data_type`, `column_name_2 data type`, ...). For our purpose, we will use the text and integer data types, but usually, a standard database engine supports many more data types, such as float, double, date time, and Boolean. We will also need to specify a primary key. A primary key is a unique, non-null identifier that's used to uniquely identify a row in a table. In our case, we use email as a primary key. A primary key can be an integer or text.

The last thing you need to know is that unless you call a commit on the series of operations you just performed (together, we formally call them a transaction), nothing will actually be performed and reflected in the database. This property is called atomicity. In fact, for a database to be industry-standard (to be useable in real life), it needs to follow the **Atomicity, Consistency, Isolation, Durability (ACID)** properties.

As the name suggests, **Data Definition Language** (**DDL**) is the way to communicate with the database engine in advance to define what the data will look like. The database engine creates a table object based on the definition provided and prepares it.

EXERCISE 8.02: USING DDL AND DML COMMANDS IN SQLITE

In this exercise, we will connect with the **lesson.db** database and then create a **user** table. Then, we will insert data into the table using the DDL and DML commands. Let's perform the following steps:

1. Use SQLite's **connect** function to connect to the **lesson.db** database. Create a **cursor** object by calling **conn.cursor()**. The **cursor** object acts as a medium by which to communicate with the database:

```
import sqlite3
with sqlite3.connect("../lesson.db") as conn:
    cursor = conn.cursor()
```

2. Create a table in Python, as follows:

```
cursor.execute("CREATE TABLE IF NOT EXISTS \
                user (email text, first_name  text, \
                    last_name text, address text, age integer, \
                    PRIMARY KEY (email))")
```

3. Insert rows into the database that you created, as follows:

```
cursor.execute("INSERT INTO user VALUES \
                ('bob@example.com', 'Bob', 'Codd', \
                '123  Fantasy lane, Fantasy City', 31)")
cursor.execute("INSERT INTO user VALUES \
                ('tom@web.com', 'Tom', 'Fake', \
                '456 Fantasy lane, Fantasy City', 39)")
```

4. Commit to the database:

```
conn.commit()
```

This will create the table and write two rows to it with data.

> **NOTE**
>
> To access the source code for this specific section, please refer to https://packt.live/2YeniaH.
>
> You can also run this example online at https://packt.live/2BogE8J.
>
> You must execute the entire Notebook in order to get the desired result.

In the next section, we will read back the data that we just stored.

READING DATA FROM A DATABASE IN SQLITE

In the preceding exercise, we created a table and stored data in it. Now, we will learn how to read the data that's stored in this database.

The **SELECT** clause is immensely powerful, and it is really important for a data practitioner to master **SELECT** and everything related to it (such as conditions, joins, and group-by).

The * after **SELECT** tells the engine to select all of the columns from the table. This is a useful shorthand. We have not mentioned any condition for the selection (such as above a certain age, first name starting with a certain sequence of letters, and so on). We are practically telling the database engine to select all the rows and all the columns from the table. It is time-consuming and less effective if we have a huge table. Hence, we would want to use the **LIMIT** clause to limit the number of rows we want.

You can use the **SELECT** clause in SQL to retrieve data, as follows:

```
import sqlite3
with sqlite3.connect("../lesson.db") as conn:
    cursor = conn.cursor()
    rows = cursor.execute('SELECT * FROM user')
    for row in rows:
        print(row)
```

The output is as follows:

```
('bob@example.com', 'Bob', 'Codd', '123 Fantasy lane, Fantasy City', 31)
('tom@web.com', 'Tom', 'Fake', '456 Fantasy lane, Fantasy City', 39)
```

The syntax to use the **SELECT** clause with **LIMIT** is as follows:

```
SELECT * FROM <table_name> LIMIT 50;
```

> **NOTE**
>
> This syntax is sample code and will not work on Jupyter Notebooks.

This will select all the columns, but only the first **50** rows from the table.

Now that we have seen how to connect, write, and read basic data to a database, we will be venturing into more advanced operations in the coming exercises, with the sorting of data being the next one.

EXERCISE 8.03: SORTING VALUES THAT ARE PRESENT IN THE DATABASE

In this exercise, we will use the **ORDER BY** clause to sort the rows of the **user** table with respect to the **age** column in both descending and ascending order. Let's perform the following steps:

1. Connect to the **lesson.db** database and sort **lesson.db** by age in descending order, as follows:

```
import sqlite3
with sqlite3.connect("../lesson.db") as conn:
    cursor = conn.cursor()
    rows = cursor.execute('SELECT * FROM user ORDER BY age DESC')
    for row in rows:
        print(row)
```

The output is as follows:

```
('tom@web.com', 'Tom', 'Fake', '456 Fantasy lane, Fantasy City', 39)
('bob@example.com', 'Bob', 'Codd', '123 Fantasy lane, Fantasy City', 31)
```

2. Sort the **lesson.db** database by age in ascending order, as follows:

```
with sqlite3.connect("../lesson.db") as conn:
    cursor = conn.cursor()
    rows = cursor.execute('SELECT * FROM user ORDER BY age')
    for row in rows:
        print(row)
```

The output is as follows:

```
('bob@example.com', 'Bob', 'Codd', '123 Fantasy lane, Fantasy City', 31)
('tom@web.com', 'Tom', 'Fake', '456 Fantasy lane, Fantasy City', 39)
```

Notice that we don't need to specify the order as **ASC** in order to sort it in ascending order.

In this exercise, we have seen how to sort data. Sorting is one of the most important operations you will often need to do.

> **NOTE**
>
> To access the source code for this specific section, please refer to
> https://packt.live/37l7lap.
>
> You can also run this example online at https://packt.live/2YOu4D5.
>
> You must execute the entire Notebook in order to get the desired result.

In the coming exercise, we will see how to update the structure of an already defined table.

THE ALTER COMMAND

ALTER is a command that is used by a RDBMS to add a new column to an already existing table, or to change the data type of a column, whereas the **UPDATE** command is used to update the value of one or more columns in one or several rows of a database. We will examine them in the following section to check out their use.

EXERCISE 8.04: ALTERING THE STRUCTURE OF A TABLE AND UPDATING THE NEW FIELDS

In this exercise, we are going to add a column, **gender**, using the **ALTER** command in the **user** table. Then, by using the **UPDATE** command, we will set the value of the **gender** column. Let's perform the following steps:

1. Establish a connection with the database by using the following command:

```
import sqlite3
with sqlite3.connect("../lesson.db") as conn:
    cursor = conn.cursor()
```

2. Add another column in the **user** table and fill it with null values by using the following command:

```
cursor.execute("ALTER TABLE user ADD COLUMN gender text")
conn.commit()
```

3. Update all of the values of gender so that they are **M** by using the following command:

```
cursor.execute("UPDATE user SET gender='M'")
conn.commit()
```

4. To check the altered table, execute the following command:

```
with sqlite3.connect("../lesson.db") as conn:
    cursor = conn.cursor()
    rows = cursor.execute('SELECT * FROM user ORDER BY age')
    for row in rows:
        print(row)
```

The output is as follows:

```
('bob@example.com', 'Bob', 'Codd', '123 Fantasy lane, Fantasy City',
 31, 'M')
('tom@web.com', 'Tom', 'Fake', '456 Fantasy lane, Fantasy City',
 39, 'M')
```

We have to be cautious when using **UPDATE**, because using **UPDATE** without selective clauses (such as **WHERE**) affects the entire table.

> **NOTE**
>
> To access the source code for this specific section, please refer to https://packt.live/312BtBL.
>
> You can also run this example online at https://packt.live/3ddlYbh.
>
> You must execute the entire Notebook in order to get the desired result.

THE GROUP BY CLAUSE

We will learn about a concept that we have already learned about in pandas. This is called the **GROUP BY** clause. The **GROUP BY** clause is a technique that's used to retrieve distinct values from the database and place them in individual buckets. The following diagram explains how the **GROUP BY** clause works:

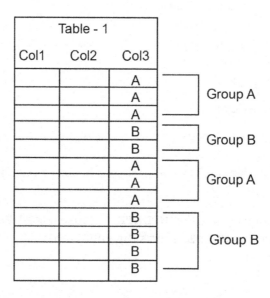

COUNT(*), col3->6, a AND 6, B

Figure 8.5: Illustration of the GROUP BY clause on a table

In the preceding diagram, we can see that the **col3** column has only two unique values across all rows, **A** and **B**. The command that's used to check the total number of rows belonging to each group is as follows:

```
SELECT count(*), col3 FROM <tablename> GROUP BY col3
```

Let's go through the following exercise to practice the **GroupBy** clause.

EXERCISE 8.05: GROUPING VALUES IN TABLES

In this exercise, we will use the **GROUP BY** clause to select the columns grouped by **gender**. We'll add users whose genders are male and female to the table and group them based on gender. Let's perform the following steps to do so:

1. Establish the connection with the database by using the following command:

```
import sqlite3
with sqlite3.connect("../lesson.db") as conn:
    cursor = conn.cursor()
```

2. Add a female user to the table:

```
cursor.execute("INSERT INTO user VALUES ('shelly@www.com', 'Shelly',\
                                          'Milar',\
                                          '123, Ocean View Lane',\
                                          39, 'F')")
conn.commit()
cursor = conn.cursor()
rows = cursor.execute('SELECT * FROM user ORDER BY age DESC')
for row in rows:
    print(row)
```

> **NOTE**
>
> The aforementioned code block must be run in a single cell in Jupyter Notebook.

The output is as follows:

```
('tom@web.com', 'Tom', 'Fake', '456 Fantasy lane, Fantasy City',
   39, 'M')
('shelly@www.com', 'Shelly', 'Milar', '123, Ocean View Lane',
   39, 'F')
('bob@example.com', 'Bob', 'Codd', '123 Fantasy lane, Fantasy City',
   31, 'M')
```

3. Run the following code to see the count by each **gender**:

```
rows = cursor.execute("SELECT COUNT(*), "\
                       "gender FROM user GROUP BY gender")
for row in rows:
    print(row)
```

The output is as follows:

```
(1, 'F')
(2, 'M')
```

> **NOTE**
>
> To access the source code for this specific section, please refer to
> https://packt.live/3fEzV4N.
>
> You can also run this example online at https://packt.live/2N8kS7l.

We have seen by now how to connect to a database, create a table, and insert values in it. We have also looked into topics such as reading values from a table, sorting them, and grouping them by common values. These are all very essential skills to have when dealing with databases. However, we have not looked into the "*Relational*" part of an RDBMS. This is what is coming up next.

RELATION MAPPING IN DATABASES

We have been working with a single table and altering it, as well as reading back the data. However, the real power of an RDBMS comes from the handling of relationships among different objects (tables). In this section, we are going to create a new table called comments and link it with the user table in a **1 : N** relationship. This means that one user can have multiple comments. The way we are going to do this is by adding the user table's primary key as a foreign key in the comments table. This will create a **1 : N** relationship.

When we link two tables, we need to specify to the database engine what should be done if the parent row is deleted, which has many children in the other table. As we can see in the following diagram, we are asking what happens at the place of the question marks when we delete **row1** of the user table:

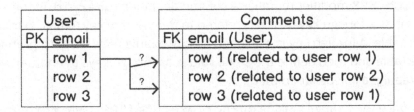

Figure 8.6: Illustration of relations

In a non-RDBMS situation, this situation can quickly become difficult and messy to manage and maintain. However, with an RDBMS, all we have to tell the database engine, in very precise ways, is what to do when a situation like this occurs. The database engine will do the rest for us. We use **ON DELETE** to tell the engine what we do with all the rows of a table when the parent row gets deleted. The following code illustrates these concepts:

```
import sqlite3
with sqlite3.connect("../lesson.db") as conn:
    cursor = conn.cursor()
    cursor.execute("PRAGMA foreign_keys = 1")
    sql = """
CREATE TABLE comments ( \
        user_id text, \
        comments text, \
        FOREIGN KEY (user_id) REFERENCES user (email) \
        ON DELETE CASCADE ON UPDATE NO ACTION \
    )
    """
    cursor.execute(sql)
    conn.commit()
```

The **ON DELETE CASCADE** line informs the database engine that we want to delete all the children rows when the parent gets deleted. We will cover deleting values in detail in a later exercise. We can also define actions for **UPDATE**. In this case, there is nothing to do on **UPDATE**.

The **FOREIGN KEY** modifier modifies a column definition (**user_id**, in this case) and marks it as a foreign key, which is related to the primary key (email, in this case) of another table. A foreign key is a link between two tables. We define a primary key in one table and then define the same values as foreign keys to another table, thereby creating a link between them.

You may notice the strange looking **cursor.execute("PRAGMA foreign_keys = 1")** line in the code. It is there just because SQLite does not use the normal foreign key features by default. It is this line that enables that feature. It is typical to SQLite and we won't need it for any other databases.

Hence, we have covered the idea of relations between two tables. One table can be related to any number of tables. And there are different types of relationships such as **1:1**, **1:n**, and **n:n**. Readers are encouraged to look into these in detail.

In the next section, we will insert rows in the newly created table.

ADDING ROWS IN THE COMMENTS TABLE

We have created a table called **comments**. In this section, we will dynamically generate an **INSERT** query, as follows:

```
import sqlite3
with sqlite3.connect("../lesson.db") as conn:
    cursor = conn.cursor()
    cursor.execute("PRAGMA foreign_keys = 1")
    sql = "INSERT INTO comments VALUES ('{}', '{}')"
    rows = cursor.execute('SELECT * FROM user ORDER BY age')
    for row in rows:
        email = row[0]
        print("Going to create rows for {}".format(email))
        name = row[1] + " " + row[2]
        for i in range(10):
            comment = "This is comment {} by {}".format(i, name)
            conn.cursor().execute(sql.format(email, comment))
            conn.commit()
```

Pay attention to how we dynamically generate the insert query so that we can insert 10 comments for each user.

We have inserted some rows in the new table and we have established a relationship between this one and the one before. Up next is one of the most important concepts of databases – joins. They help us to write concise queries to retrieve data from several linked tables.

JOINS

Now, we will learn how to exploit the relationship we just built. This means that if we have the primary key from one table, we can recover all the data needed from that table and also all the linked rows from the child table. To achieve this, we will use something called a join.

A join is basically a way to retrieve linked rows from two tables using any kind of primary key – foreign key relation that they have. There are many types of join, including **INNER**, **LEFT OUTER**, **RIGHT OUTER**, **FULL OUTER**, and **CROSS**. They are used in different situations. However, most of the time, in simple **1: N** relations, we end up using an **INNER** join. In *Chapter 1, Introduction to Data Wrangling with Python*, we learned about sets. We can view an **INNER** join as an intersection of two sets. The following diagram illustrate the concepts:

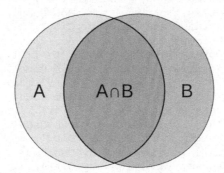

Figure 8.7: A diagram representing the intersection join

Here, **A** represents one table, and **B** represents another. The meaning of having common members is to have a relationship between them. It takes all of the rows of **A** and compares them with all of the rows of B to find the matching rows that satisfy the join predicate. This can quickly become a complex and time-consuming operation. Joins can be very expensive operations. Usually, we use some kind of where clause, after we specify the join, to shorten the scope of rows that are fetched from table **A** or **B** to perform the matching.

In our case, our first table, user, has three entries, with the primary key being email. We can make use of this in our query to get comments just from Bob:

```python
import sqlite3
with sqlite3.connect("../lesson.db") as conn:
    cursor = conn.cursor()
    cursor.execute("PRAGMA foreign_keys = 1")
    sql = """
    SELECT * FROM comments \
    JOIN user ON comments.user_id = user.email \
    WHERE user.email='bob@example.com' \
    """
    rows = cursor.execute(sql)
    for row in rows:
        print(row)
```

The output is as follows:

```
('bob@example.com', 'This is comment 0 by Bob Codd', 'bob@example.com',
'Bob', 'Codd', '123 Fantasy lane, Fantasy City', 31, 'M')
('bob@example.com', 'This is comment 1 by Bob Codd', 'bob@example.com',
'Bob', 'Codd', '123 Fantasy lane, Fantasy City', 31, 'M')
('bob@example.com', 'This is comment 2 by Bob Codd', 'bob@example.com',
'Bob', 'Codd', '123 Fantasy lane, Fantasy City', 31, 'M')
('bob@example.com', 'This is comment 3 by Bob Codd', 'bob@example.com',
'Bob', 'Codd', '123 Fantasy lane, Fantasy City', 31, 'M')
('bob@example.com', 'This is comment 4 by Bob Codd', 'bob@example.com',
'Bob', 'Codd', '123 Fantasy lane, Fantasy City', 31, 'M')
('bob@example.com', 'This is comment 5 by Bob Codd', 'bob@example.com',
'Bob', 'Codd', '123 Fantasy lane, Fantasy City', 31, 'M')
('bob@example.com', 'This is comment 6 by Bob Codd', 'bob@example.com',
'Bob', 'Codd', '123 Fantasy lane, Fantasy City', 31, 'M')
('bob@example.com', 'This is comment 7 by Bob Codd', 'bob@example.com',
'Bob', 'Codd', '123 Fantasy lane, Fantasy City', 31, 'M')
('bob@example.com', 'This is comment 8 by Bob Codd', 'bob@example.com',
'Bob', 'Codd', '123 Fantasy lane, Fantasy City', 31, 'M')
('bob@example.com', 'This is comment 9 by Bob Codd', 'bob@example.com',
'Bob', 'Codd', '123 Fantasy lane, Fantasy City', 31, 'M')
```

The preceding output of the **JOIN** query, showing that we have jointly read data from two tables at the same time, is restricting our query scope to a particular email.

We have just looked into one of the most important operations of all, joins. We will cover some other aspects of the same in the coming section.

RETRIEVING SPECIFIC COLUMNS FROM A JOIN QUERY

In the previous exercise, we saw that we can use a **JOIN** to fetch the related rows from two tables. However, if we look at the results, we will see that it returned all the columns, thus combining both tables. This is not very concise. What about if we only want to see the emails and the related comments, and not all the data?

There is some nice shorthand code that lets us do this:

```
import sqlite3
with sqlite3.connect("../lesson.db") as conn:
    cursor = conn.cursor()
    cursor.execute("PRAGMA foreign_keys = 1")
    sql = """
    SELECT comments.* FROM comments \
    JOIN user ON comments.user_id = user.email \
    WHERE user.email='bob@example.com' \
    """
    rows = cursor.execute(sql)
    for row in rows:
        print(row)
```

Just by changing the **SELECT** statement, we made our final result appear as follows, where only columns from the **comments** table are present:

```
('bob@example.com', 'This is comment 0 by Bob Codd')
('bob@example.com', 'This is comment 1 by Bob Codd')
('bob@example.com', 'This is comment 2 by Bob Codd')
('bob@example.com', 'This is comment 3 by Bob Codd')
('bob@example.com', 'This is comment 4 by Bob Codd')
('bob@example.com', 'This is comment 5 by Bob Codd')
('bob@example.com', 'This is comment 6 by Bob Codd')
('bob@example.com', 'This is comment 7 by Bob Codd')
('bob@example.com', 'This is comment 8 by Bob Codd')
('bob@example.com', 'This is comment 9 by Bob Codd')
```

We have now looked at joins. They are very useful, and you will end up using them often while dealing with databases in real life. Up next is a detailed look into deleting rows.

DELETING ROWS FROM TABLES

This will be done by using the **DELETE** command. As the name suggests, this command helps to delete rows from a table. It is an irreversible process, meaning once deleted, we cannot restore those rows. So be very careful when running this command as it can have a destructive effect on the data. Please keep in mind that it has to almost always be run accompanied by a **WHERE** clause so that we delete just a part of the data and not everything.

EXERCISE 8.06: DELETING ROWS FROM TABLES

In this exercise, we will be working with two tables, **user** and **comments**, which are a part of the **lesson.db** database.

> **NOTE**
>
> The GitHub version of this exercise begins with the previous 4 examples that we just saw, starting off with creation of the **comments** table. You may ignore those steps if you have executed them already.

We will delete a row from the **user** table and observe the effects it will have on the comments table. Include all the steps mentioned previously. Let's perform the following steps:

1. To delete a row from a table, we use the **DELETE** clause in SQL. To run delete on the user table, we are going to use the following code:

```
with sqlite3.connect("../lesson.db") as conn:
    cursor = conn.cursor()
    cursor.execute("PRAGMA foreign_keys = 1")
    cursor.execute("DELETE FROM user "\
                "WHERE email='bob@example.com'")
    conn.commit()
```

2. Perform the **SELECT** operation on the user table:

```
with sqlite3.connect("../lesson.db") as conn:
    cursor = conn.cursor()
    cursor.execute("PRAGMA foreign_keys = 1")
    rows = cursor.execute("SELECT * FROM user")
    for row in rows:
        print(row)
```

The output is as follows:

```
('tom@web.com', 'Tom', 'Fake', '456 Fantasy lane, Fantasy City',
    39, 'M')
('shelly@www.com', 'Shelly', 'Milar', '123, Ocean View Lane',
    39, 'F')
```

Observe that the user **Bob** has been deleted.

Now, moving on to the **comments** table, we have to remember that we had mentioned **ON DELETE CASCADE** while creating the table. The database engine knows that if a row is deleted from the parent table (**user**), all the related rows from the child tables (**comments**) will have to be deleted.

3. Perform a **SELECT** operation on the **comments** table by using the following command:

```
with sqlite3.connect("../lesson.db") as conn:
    cursor = conn.cursor()
    cursor.execute("PRAGMA foreign_keys = 1")
    rows = cursor.execute("SELECT * FROM comments")
    for row in rows:
        print(row)
```

The output (partially shown) is as follows:

```
('tom@web.com', 'This is comment 0 by Tom Fake')
('tom@web.com', 'This is comment 1 by Tom Fake')
('tom@web.com', 'This is comment 2 by Tom Fake')
('tom@web.com', 'This is comment 3 by Tom Fake')
('tom@web.com', 'This is comment 4 by Tom Fake')
('tom@web.com', 'This is comment 5 by Tom Fake')
('tom@web.com', 'This is comment 6 by Tom Fake')
('tom@web.com', 'This is comment 7 by Tom Fake')
('tom@web.com', 'This is comment 8 by Tom Fake')
('tom@web.com', 'This is comment 9 by Tom Fake')
```

We can see that all of the rows related to **Bob** are deleted from the **comments** table.

We have observed the **DELETE** command and also learned how to use it safely.

> **NOTE**
>
> To access the source code for this specific section, please refer to
> https://packt.live/2YeutzP.
>
> You can also run this example online at https://packt.live/3fArsQb.
>
> You must execute the entire Notebook in order to get the desired result.

In the following section, we will see how to update a specific value in a table.

UPDATING SPECIFIC VALUES IN A TABLE

In this example, we will see how we can update rows in a table. Without **WHERE**, updating is often a bad idea. The reason is that we may end up updating rows that we did not intend to.

We can combine **UPDATE** with **WHERE** to selectively update the first name of the user with the email address tom@web.com, as shown in the following code:

```
with sqlite3.connect("../lesson.db") as conn:
    cursor = conn.cursor()
    cursor.execute("PRAGMA foreign_keys = 1")
    cursor.execute("UPDATE user set first_name='Chris' "\
                   "where email='tom@web.com'")
    conn.commit()
    rows = cursor.execute("SELECT * FROM user")
    for row in rows:
        print(row)
```

The output is as follows:

```
('tom@web.com', 'Chris', 'Fake', '456 Fantasy lane, Fantasu City', 39, 'M')
('shelly@www.com', 'Shelly', 'Milar', '123, Ocean View Lane', 39, 'F')
```

Figure 8.8: Output of the update query, showing the newly updated first name

So far, we have covered a lot of concepts related to databases. We have learned a set of skills that are important for dealing with database-level operations. In the next section, we will combine two worlds; the world of databases and the world of pandas.

We have looked into many fundamental aspects of storing and querying data from a database, but as a data wrangling expert, we need our data to be packed and presented as a DataFrame so that we can perform quick and convenient operations on them.

EXERCISE 8.07: RDBMS AND DATAFRAMES

In this exercise, we will connect to the **lesson.db** database and join the two tables, **user** and **comments**. We will create an empty **data** list and then add the rows of this joined table in **data**. Next, we will store the content of **data** in a **pandas** DataFrame. To complete this exercise, let's perform the following steps:

1. Import pandas using the following code:

```
import pandas as pd
```

2. Create a columns list with email, first name, last name, age, gender, and comments as column names. Also, create an empty **data** list:

```
columns = ["Email", "First Name", "Last Name", \
           "Age", "Gender", "Comments"]
data = []
```

3. Connect to **lesson.db** using SQLite and obtain a cursor, as follows:

```
import sqlite3
with sqlite3.connect("../lesson.db") as conn:
    cursor = conn.cursor()
```

4. Use the **execute** method from the cursor to set **PRAGMA foreign_keys = 1**:

```
cursor.execute("PRAGMA foreign_keys = 1")
```

5. Create a **sql** variable that will contain the **SELECT** command and use the join command to join the databases:

```
sql = """
    SELECT user.email, user.first_name, user.last_name, \
    user.age, user.gender, comments.comments FROM comments \
    JOIN user ON comments.user_id = user.email \
    WHERE user.email = 'tom@web.com' \
    """
```

6. Use the execute method of **cursor** to execute the **sql** command:

```
rows = cursor.execute(sql)
```

7. Append the rows to the data list:

```
for row in rows:
    data.append(row)
```

8. Create a DataFrame using the data list and print out the result:

```
df = pd.DataFrame(data, columns=columns)
df
```

The output will be:

	Email	First Name	Last Name	Age	Gender	Comments
0	tom@web.com	Tom	Fake	39	M	This is comment 0 by Tom Fake
1	tom@web.com	Tom	Fake	39	M	This is comment 1 by Tom Fake
2	tom@web.com	Tom	Fake	39	M	This is comment 2 by Tom Fake
3	tom@web.com	Tom	Fake	39	M	This is comment 3 by Tom Fake
4	tom@web.com	Tom	Fake	39	M	This is comment 4 by Tom Fake
5	tom@web.com	Tom	Fake	39	M	This is comment 5 by Tom Fake
6	tom@web.com	Tom	Fake	39	M	This is comment 6 by Tom Fake
7	tom@web.com	Tom	Fake	39	M	This is comment 7 by Tom Fake
8	tom@web.com	Tom	Fake	39	M	This is comment 8 by Tom Fake
9	tom@web.com	Tom	Fake	39	M	This is comment 9 by Tom Fake

Figure 8.9: Output of the dataframe

NOTE

To access the source code for this specific section, please refer to https://packt.live/2YPSdZX.

You can also run this example online at https://packt.live/37HZaAi. You must execute the entire Notebook in order to get the desired result.

This ends our journey into the world of databases. It was a basic introduction. Nonetheless, we managed to cover a wide range of essential topics. DBMS and related fields are a mature stream in computer science and are still under active development and research. We strongly encourage the reader to read more about it.

ACTIVITY 8.01: RETRIEVING DATA ACCURATELY FROM DATABASES

The goal of this activity is to fetch data and retrieve information from two tables, **persons** and **pets**, which are a part of the **petsdb** database.

> **NOTE**
>
> You can find the **petsdb** database at https://packt.live/3dcH0rx.

The **persons** table is defined as follows:

	id	first_name	last_name	age	city	zip_code
0	1	Erica	None	22	south port	2345678
1	2	Jordi	None	73	east port	123456
2	3	Chasity	None	70	new port	76856785
3	4	Gregg	None	31	new port	76856785
4	5	Tony	Lindgren	7	west port	2345678

Figure 8.10: The persons table

The **persons** table has the following columns:

- **first_name**: The first name of the person

- **last_name**: The last name of the person (can be **null**)

- **age**: The age of the person

- **city**: The city where they are from

- **zip_code**: The zip code of the city

As we can see, the **id** column in the **persons** table (which is an integer) serves as the primary key for that table and as a foreign key for the **pets** table, which is linked via the **owner_id** column.

The **pets** table is defined as follows:

	owner_id	pet_name	pet_type	treatment_done
0	57	mani	1.0	0
1	80	tamari	NaN	0
2	25	raba	NaN	0
3	27	olga	NaN	0
4	60	raba	NaN	0

Figure 8.11: The pets table

The pets table has the following columns:

- **pet_name**: The name of the pet.

- **pet_type**: What type of pet it is, for example, **cat** or **dog**. Due to a lack of further information, we do not know which number represents what, but it is an integer and can be **null**.

- **treatment_done**: This is also an integer column, and **0** here represents **No**, whereas **1** represents **Yes**.

In this activity, you will first connect to the **petsdb** database and check whether the connection has been successful. You will then create and execute a few SQL commands to answer the following questions:

1. What is the count of people belonging to different age groups in the **persons** table?

2. Which age group has the maximum number of people?

3. How many people do not have a last name?

4. How many people have more than one pet?

5. How many pets have received treatment?

6. How many pets have received treatment, and the type of pet is known?

7. How many pets are from the city called east port?

8. How many pets are from the city called east port, and who received treatment?

The output should be as follows:

Answer to question 1 (the following is partial output):

```
We have 2 people aged 5
We have 1 people aged 6
We have 1 people aged 7
We have 3 people aged 8
We have 1 people aged 9
We have 2 people aged 11
We have 3 people aged 12
We have 1 people aged 13
We have 4 people aged 14
We have 2 people aged 16
We have 2 people aged 17
We have 3 people aged 18
We have 1 people aged 19
We have 3 people aged 22
We have 2 people aged 23
We have 3 people aged 24
We have 2 people aged 25
We have 1 people aged 27
We have 1 people aged 30
We have 3 people aged 31
We have 1 people aged 32
We have 1 people aged 33
We have 2 people aged 34
```

Figure 8.12: Partial output of the count of people belonging to different age groups
from the persons table

Answer to question 2:

```
Highest number of people is 5 and came from 73 age group
```

Answer to question 3:

```
(60,)
```

Answer to question 4:

```
43 people has more than one pet
```

Answer to question 5:

```
(36,)
```

Answer to question 6:

```
(16,)
```

Answer to question 7:

```
(49,)
```

Answer to question 8:

```
(11,)
```

> **NOTE**
>
> The solution to this activity and the answers can be found on page 505.

In this activity, we have applied all the skills we learned in this chapter concerning databases.

SUMMARY

We have come to the end of the database chapter. We have learned how to connect to SQLite using Python. We have brushed up on the basics of relational databases and how to open and close a database. We then learned how to export this relational database into Python DataFrames.

In the next chapter, we will be performing data wrangling on datasets that are used in business use cases. We will use different types of datasets and then clean and process the data in a meaningful way. We will be able to apply all the skills and tricks we have learned so far in this book to process data and get valuable insights from them.

9

APPLICATIONS IN BUSINESS USE CASES AND CONCLUSION OF THE COURSE

OVERVIEW

This chapter will allow you to utilize the skills you have learned throughout the course of the previous chapters. You will be able to easily handle data wrangling tasks for business use cases. Throughout the chapter, you will be testing the data wrangling skills you've acquired so far by applying them on interesting business problems. These tests, will help you shore up your data wrangling skills, thus giving you the confidence to use them to tackle interesting business problems in the real world.

INTRODUCTION

In the previous chapter, we learned about databases. It is time to combine our knowledge of data wrangling and Python with a realistic scenario. Usually, data from one source is often inadequate to perform analysis. Generally, a data wrangler has to distinguish between relevant and non-relevant data and combine data from different sources.

The primary job of a data wrangling expert is to pull data from multiple sources, format and clean it (impute the data if it is missing), and finally combine it in a coherent manner to prepare a dataset for further analysis by data scientists or machine learning engineers.

In this chapter, we will try to mimic a typical task flow by downloading and using two different datasets from reputed web portals. Each dataset contains partial data pertaining to the key question that is being asked. Let's examine this more closely.

APPLYING YOUR KNOWLEDGE TO A DATA WRANGLING TASK

Suppose you are asked the following question:

In India, did the enrollment in primary/secondary/tertiary education increase with the improvement of per capita GDP in the past 15 years? To provide an accurate and analyzed result, machine learning and data visualization techniques will be used by an expert data scientist. The actual modeling and analysis will be done by a senior data scientist, who will use machine learning and data visualization for analysis. As a data wrangling expert, *your job will be to acquire and provide a clean dataset that contains educational enrollment and GDP data side by side.*

Suppose you have a link for a dataset from the United Nations and you can download the dataset of education (for all the nations around the world). But this dataset has some missing values and, moreover, it does not have any **Gross Domestic Product** (**GDP**) information. Someone has also given you another separate CSV file (downloaded from the World Bank site) that contains GDP data but in a messy format.

In the following activity, we will examine how to handle these two separate sources and clean the data to prepare a simple final dataset with the required data and save it to the local drive as a SQL database file:

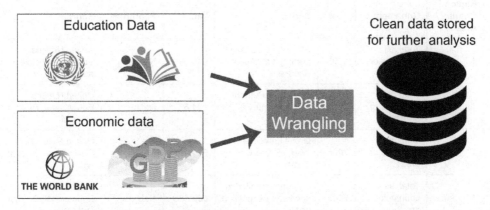

Figure 9.1: Pictorial representation of merging education and economic data

You are encouraged to follow along with the code and results in the notebook and try to understand and internalize the nature of the data wrangling flow. You are also encouraged to try extracting various data from these files and answer your own questions about a nation's socio-economic factors and their inter-relationships.

> **NOTE**
>
> Coming up with interesting questions about social, economic, technological, and geo-political topics and then answering them using freely available data and a little bit of programming knowledge is one of the most fun ways to learn about any data science topic. You will get a taste of that process in this chapter.

Let's take a look at the following table, which shows information from a dataset of education from the UN data:

	Region / Country / Area	Unnamed: 1	Year	Series	Value	Footnotes	Source
0	1	Total, all countries or areas	2005	Students enrolled in primary education (thousa...	678,990	NaN	United Nations Educational, Scientific and Cul...
1	1	Total, all countries or areas	2005	Gross enrollement ratio – Primary (male)	104.8	NaN	United Nations Educational, Scientific and Cul...
2	1	Total, all countries or areas	2005	Gross enrollment ratio – Primary (female)	99.8	NaN	United Nations Educational, Scientific and Cul...
3	1	Total, all countries or areas	2005	Students enrolled in secondary education (thou...	509,100	NaN	United Nations Educational, Scientific and Cul...
4	1	Total, all countries or areas	2005	Gross enrollment ratio – Secondary (male)	65.7	NaN	United Nations Educational, Scientific and Cul...

Figure 9.2: UN data

From the preceding table, we can observe that we are missing some data. Let's say we decide to impute these data points by performing simple linear interpolation between the available data points. We can take a calculator and compute those values and manually create a dataset. But being a data wrangler, we will, of course, take advantage of Python programming, and use **pandas** imputation methods for this task.

But to do that, we need to create a DataFrame with missing values in it; that is, we need to append another DataFrame with missing values to the current DataFrame.

ACTIVITY 9.01: DATA WRANGLING TASK – FIXING UN DATA

The goal of this activity is to perform data analysis on the UN data to find out whether the enrollment in primary, secondary, or tertiary education has increased with the improvement of per capita GDP in the past 15 years. For this task, we will need to clean or wrangle the two datasets, that is, the education enrollment and GDP data.

The UN data is available at https://packt.live/30ZIS4N.

> **NOTE**
>
> If you download the CSV file and open it using Excel, then you will see that the **Footnotes** column sometimes contains useful notes. We may not want to drop it in the beginning. If we are interested in a particular country's data (like we are in this task), then it may well turn out that **Footnotes** will be **NaN**, that is, blank. In that case, we can drop it at the end. But for some countries or regions, it may contain information.

These steps will guide you through this activity:

1. Download the dataset from the UN data from GitHub from the following link: https://packt.live/2AMoeu6.

   The UN data contains missing values. Clean the data to prepare a simple final dataset with the required data and save it to your local drive as a SQL database file.

2. Use the **pd.read_csv** method of **pandas** to create a DataFrame.

3. Since the first row does not contain useful information, skip it using the **skiprows** parameter.

4. Drop the column region/country/area and source.

5. Assign the following names as columns of the DataFrame: Region/County/Area, Year, Data, Value, and Footnotes.

6. Check how many unique values are present in the **Footnotes** column.

7. Check the type of the **value** column.

8. Create a function to convert the value column into floating-point numbers.

9. Use the **apply** method to apply this function to a value.

10. Print the unique values in the data column.

The final output should be as follows:

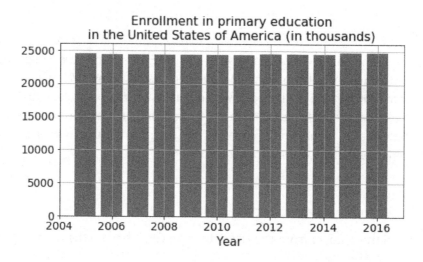

Figure 9.3: Bar plot for the enrollment in primary education in the USA

> **NOTE**
>
> The solution to this activity can be found on page 509.

With this, we've reached the end of this activity. Here, we have looked into how to examine a particular real-life dataset to see what kind of data is missing. We also used the interpolate method from our DataFrame to fill in certain missing values.

ACTIVITY 9.02: DATA WRANGLING TASK — CLEANING GDP DATA

The GDP data is available at https://data.worldbank.org/ and is available on GitHub at https://packt.live/2AMoeu6.

In this activity, we will clean the GDP data. Follow these steps to complete this activity:

1. Create three DataFrames from the original DataFrame using filtering. Create the **df_primary**, **df_secondary**, and **df_tertiary** DataFrames for students enrolled in primary education, secondary education, and tertiary education in thousands, respectively.

2. Plot bar charts of the enrollment of primary students in a low-income country such as India and a higher-income country such as the USA.

3. Since there is missing data, use **pandas** imputation methods to impute these data points by simple linear interpolation between data points. To do that, create a DataFrame with missing values inserted and append a new DataFrame with missing values to the current DataFrame.

4. (For India) Append the rows corresponding to the missing years: **2004 – 2009, 2011 – 2013**.

5. Create a dictionary of values with **np.nan**. Note that there are **9** missing data points, so we need to create a list with identical values repeated **9** times.

6. Create a DataFrame of missing values (from the preceding dictionary) that we can append.

7. Append the DataFrames together.

8. Sort by year and reset the indices using **reset_index**. Use **inplace=True** to execute the changes on the DataFrame itself.

9. Use the interpolate method for linear interpolation. It fills all the **NaN** values with linearly interpolated values. See the following link for more details about this method: http://pandas.pydata.org/pandas-docs/version/0.17/generated/pandas.DataFrame.interpolate.html.

10. Repeat the same steps for USA (or other countries).

11. If there are values that are unfilled, use the **limit** and **limit_direction** parameters with the interpolate method to fill them in.

12. Plot the final graph using the new data.

13. Read the GDP data using the **pandas read_csv** method. It will generally throw an error.

14. To avoid errors, try using the **error_bad_lines = False** option.

15. Since there is no delimiter in the file, add the **\t** delimiter.

16. Use the **skiprows** function to remove rows that are not useful.

17. Examine the dataset. Filter the dataset with information that states that it is similar to the previous education dataset.

18. Reset the index for this new dataset.

19. Drop the rows that aren't useful and re-index the dataset.

20. Rename the columns properly. This is necessary for merging the two datasets.

21. We will concentrate only on the data from **2003** to **2016**. Eliminate the remaining data.

22. Create a new DataFrame called **df_gdp** with rows **43** to **56**.

The final output should be as follows:

```
0        2003
1        2004
2        2005
3        2006
4        2007
5        2008
6        2009
7        2010
8        2011
9        2012
10       2013
11       2014
12       2015
13       2016
Name: Year, dtype: object
```

Figure 9.4: DataFrame focusing on year

Now that we've seen how to clean and format the datasets, in the following activity, we'll learn how to merge these two datasets.

> **NOTE**
>
> The solution to the activity can be found on page 524.

ACTIVITY 9.03: DATA WRANGLING TASK – MERGING UN DATA AND GDP DATA

The aim of this activity is to merge the two datasets: UN data and GDP data.

The steps to merge these two databases is as follows:

1. Reset the indexes for merging.

2. Merge the two DataFrames, **primary_enrollment_india** and **df_gdp**, on the **Year** column.

3. Drop the data, footnotes, and region/county/area.

4. Rearrange the columns for proper viewing and presentation.

The output should be as follows:

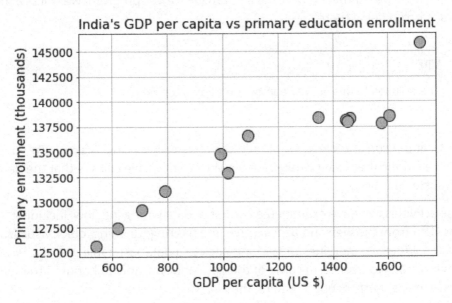

Figure 9.5: Final output

In this activity, we saw how to merge two DataFrames to create a unified view and how to examine that view a little bit. In the next activity, we will learn how to store some of that data in a database.

> **NOTE**
>
> The solution to the activity can be found on page 537.

ACTIVITY 9.04: DATA WRANGLING TASK – CONNECTING THE NEW DATA TO THE DATABASE

The steps to connect the data to the database is as follows:

1. Import the **sqlite3** module of Python and use the **connect** function to connect to the database. The main database engine is embedded. But for a different database such as **Postgresql** or **MySQL**, we will need to connect to them using those credentials. We designate **Year** as the **PRIMARY KEY** of this table.

2. Then, run a loop with the dataset rows one by one to insert them into the table.

The output: If we look at the current folder, we should see a file called **Education_ GDP.db**, and if we examine that using a database viewer program, we will see the data transferred being there.

> **NOTE**
>
> The solution to this activity can be found on page 541.

If we look at the current folder, we should see a file called **Education_GDP.db**, and if we can examine that using a database viewer program, we will see that the data has been transferred there.

In these activities, we have examined a complete data wrangling flow, including reading data from the web and a local drive and filtering, cleaning, quick visualization, imputation, indexing, merging, and writing back to a database table. We also wrote custom functions to transform some of the data and saw how to handle situations where we may get errors upon reading the file.

AN EXTENSION TO DATA WRANGLING

This is the concluding chapter of this book; we want to give you a broad overview of some of the exciting technologies and frameworks that you may need to learn about beyond data wrangling to work as a full-stack data scientist. Data wrangling is an essential part of the whole data science and analytics pipeline, but it is not the whole enterprise. You have learned invaluable skills and techniques in this book, but it is always good to broaden your horizons and look beyond to see what other tools that are out there that can give you an edge in this competitive and ever-changing world.

ADDITIONAL SKILLS REQUIRED TO BECOME A DATA SCIENTIST

To practice as a fully qualified data scientist/analyst, you should have some basic skills in your repertoire, irrespective of the particular programming language you choose to focus on. These skills and know-how are language-agnostic and can be utilized with any framework that you have to embrace, depending on your organization and business needs. We will describe them in brief here:

- **Git and version control**: Git and version control is what RDBMS is to data storage and query. It simply means that there is a huge gap between the pre and post Git era of version controlling your code. As you may have noticed, all the notebooks for this book are hosted on GitHub, and this was done to take advantage of the powerful Git **Version Control System (VCS)**. It gives you, out of the box, version control, history, branching facilities for different code, merging different code branches, and advanced operations such as cherry picking, diff, and so on. It is a very essential tool to master as you can be almost sure that you will face it at one point of time in your journey.

- **Linux command line**: People coming from a Windows background (or even MacOS, if you have not done any development before) are not very familiar, usually, with the command line. The superior UI of those OSes hides the low-level details of interaction with the OS using a command line. However, as a data professional, it is important that you know the command line well. There are so many operations that you can do by simply using the command line that it is astonishing.

- **SQL and basic relational database concepts**: We dedicated an entire chapter to SQL and RDBMS, Chapter 8, SQL and RDBMS. However, as we have already mentioned there, it was really not enough. This is a vast subject and needs years of study to be mastered. Try to read more about it (including getting theory and practical experience) from books and online sources. Don't forget that, despite all the other sources of data being used nowadays, we still have hundreds of millions of bytes of structured data stored in legacy database systems. You can be sure to come across one, sooner or later.

- **Docker and containerization**: Since its first release in 2013, Docker has changed the way we distribute and deploy software in server-based applications. It gives you a clean and lightweight abstraction over the underlying OS and lets you iterate fast on development without the headache of creating and maintaining a proper environment. It is very useful in both the development and production phases. With virtually no competitor present, they are becoming the default in the industry very fast. We strongly advise that you explore it in great detail.

BASIC FAMILIARITY WITH BIG DATA AND CLOUD TECHNOLOGIES

Big data and cloud platforms are the latest trends. We will introduce them here briefly and we encourage you to go ahead and learn about them as much as you can. If you are planning to grow as a data professional, then you can be sure that without these necessary skills, it will be hard for you to transition to the next level:

- **Fundamental characteristics of big data**: Big data is simply data that is very big in size. The term size is a bit ambiguous here. It can mean one static chunk of data (such as the detail census data of a big country such as India or the US) or data that is dynamically generated as time passes, and each time it is huge. To give an example for the second category, we can think of how much data is generated by Facebook per day. It's about 500+ TB per day. You can easily imagine that we will need specialized tools to deal with that amount of data. There are three different categories of big data, that is, structured, unstructured, and semi-structured. The main features that define big data are volume, variety, velocity, and variability.

- **Hadoop ecosystem**: Apache Hadoop (and the related ecosystem) is a software framework that aims to use the MapReduce programming model to simplify the storage and processing of big data. It has since become one of the backbones of big data processing in the industry. The modules in Hadoop are designed to keep in mind that hardware failures are common occurrences, and they should be automatically handled by the framework. The four base modules of Hadoop are common, HDFS, YARN, and MapReduce. The Hadoop ecosystem consists of Apache Pig, Apache Hive, Apache Impala, Apache Zookeeper, Apache HBase, and more. They are very important bricks in many high-demand and cutting-edge data pipelines. We encourage you to study them in more depth. They are essential in any industry that aims to leverage data.

- **Apache Spark**: Apache Spark is a general-purpose cluster computing framework that was initially developed at the University of California, Barkley, and released in 2014. It gives you an interface to program an entire cluster of computers with built-in data parallelism and fault tolerance. It contains Spark Core, Spark SQL, Spark Streaming, MLlib (for machine learning), and GraphX. It is now one of the main frameworks that's used in the industry to process a huge amount of data in real time based on streaming data. We encourage you to read about it and master it if you want to go toward real-time data engineering.

- **Amazon Web Services (AWS)**: Amazon Web Services (often abbreviated to AWS) are a bunch of managed services offered by Amazon ranging from Infrastructure-as-a-Service, Database-as-a-Service, Machine-Learning-as-a-Service, cache, load balancer, NoSQL database, to message queues and several other types. They are very useful for all sorts of applications. It can be a simple web app or a multi-cluster data pipeline. Many famous companies run their entire infrastructure on AWS (such as Netflix). They give us on-demand provisioning, easy scaling, a managed environment, a slick UI to control everything, and also a very powerful command-line client. They also expose a rich set of APIs, and we can find an AWS API client in virtually any programming language. The Python one is called Boto3. If you are planning to become a data professional, then it can be said with near certainty that you will end up using many of their services at one point or another.

WHAT GOES WITH DATA WRANGLING?

We learned in *Chapter 1*, *Introduction to Data Wrangling with Python*, that the process of data wrangling lies in-between data gathering and advanced analytics, including visualization and machine learning. However, the boundaries that exist between these processes may not always be strict and rigid. It depends largely on organizational culture and team composition.

Therefore, we need to not only be aware of data wrangling but also the other components of the data science platform to wrangle data effectively. Even if you are performing pure data wrangling tasks, having a good grasp over how data is sourced and utilized will give you an edge for coming up with unique and efficient solutions to complex data wrangling problems and enhance the value of those solutions for the machine learning scientist or the business domain expert:

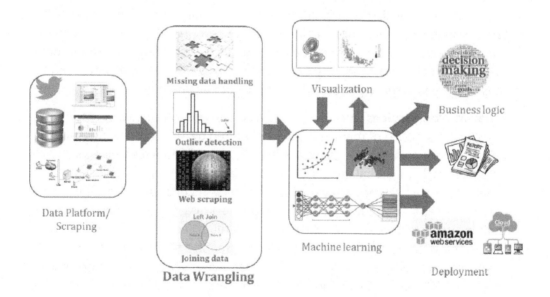

Figure 9.6: Process of data wrangling

Now, we have, in fact, already laid out a solid groundwork in this book for the data platform part, assuming that it is an integral part of data wrangling workflow. For example, we have covered web scraping, working with RESTful APIs, and database access and manipulation using Python libraries in detail.

We also touched on basic visualization techniques and plotting functions in Python using **matplotlib**. However, there are other advanced statistical plotting libraries, such as **seaborn**, that you can master for more sophisticated visualization for data science tasks.

Business logic and domain expertise is a varied topic and it can only be learned on the job; however, it will come eventually with experience. If you have an academic background and/or work experience in domains such as finance, medicine and healthcare, or engineering, that knowledge will come in handy in your data science career.

The fruit of the hard work of data wrangling is realized fully in the domain of machine learning. It is the science and engineering of making machines learn patterns and insights from data for predictive analytics and intelligent, automated decision-making with a deluge of data that cannot be analyzed efficiently by humans. Machine learning has become one of the most sought-after skills in the modern technology landscape. It has truly become one of the most exciting and promising intellectual fields, with applications ranging from e-commerce to healthcare and virtually everything in-between. Data wrangling is intrinsically linked with machine learning as it prepares the data so that it's suitable for intelligent algorithms to process. Even if you start your career in data wrangling, it could be a natural progression to move to machine learning.

Packt has published numerous books and books on this topic that you should explore. In the next section, we will touch upon some approaches to adopt and Python libraries to check out that will give you a boost in your learning.

TIPS AND TRICKS FOR MASTERING MACHINE LEARNING

Machine learning is difficult to start with. We have listed some structured MOOCs and incredible free resources that are available so that you can begin your journey:

- Understand the definition of and differentiation between the buzzwords– artificial intelligence, machine learning, deep learning, and data science. Cultivate the habit of reading great posts or listening to the expert talks on these topics and understand their true reach and applicability to some business problem.

- There are some great MOOCs that will help you understand all these and also learn advanced skills in machine learning and AI. Some of them are as follows:

  a) Machine Learning – Andrew Ng, Stanford University

  b) Machine Learning for Undergraduates – Nando de Freitas, University of British Columbia

  c) Machine Learning – Tom Mitchell, CMU

  d) Deep Learning – Nando de Freitas, University of Oxford

- Stay updated with the recent trends by watching videos, reading books such as *The Master Algorithm: How the Quest for the Ultimate Learning Machine Will Remake Our World*, as well as articles, and following influential blogs such as KDnuggets, Brandon Rohrer's blog, Open AI's blog about their research, Toward Data Science publication on Medium, and so on.

- As you learn new algorithms or concepts, pause and analyze how you can apply these machine learning concepts or algorithms in your daily work. This is the best method for learning and expanding your knowledge base.

- If you choose Python as your preferred language for machine learning tasks, then you have a great machine learning library in `scikit-learn`. It is the most widely used general machine learning package in the Python ecosystem. `scikit-learn` has a wide variety of supervised and unsupervised learning algorithms, which are exposed via a stable consistent interface. Moreover, it is specifically designed to interface seamlessly with other popular data wrangling and numerical libraries, such as NumPy and pandas.

- Another hot skill in today's job market is deep learning. Packt has many books on deep learning. For Python libraries, you can learn and practice with **TensorFlow**, **Keras**, or **PyTorch** for deep learning.

SUMMARY

Data is everywhere and it is all around us. In these nine chapters, we have learned how data from different types and sources can be cleaned, corrected, and combined. Hopefully, this chapter must have tested your skills enough to shore up the concepts you've learned so far. If you want, you can revisit some of the prior chapters to practice your data wrangling skills a bit more. Using the power of Python and the knowledge of data wrangling and applying the tricks and tips that you have studied in this book, you are ready to be a data wrangler.

APPENDIX

CHAPTER 1: INTRODUCTION TO DATA WRANGLING WITH PYTHON

ACTIVITY 1.01: HANDLING LISTS

Solution:

These are the steps to complete this activity:

1. Import the **random** library:

```
import random
```

2. Use the **randint** method from the **random** library to create **100** random numbers:

```
random_number_list = [random.randint(0, 100) \
                          for x in range(0, 100)]
```

3. Print **random_number_list**:

```
random_number_list
```

The sample output is as follows:

```
100,
46,
22,
43,
80,
45,
47,
37,
47,
61,
78,
66,
68,
4,
46,
65,
47,
20,
```

Figure 1.20: Section of output for random_number_list

> **NOTE**
>
> The output is susceptible to change since we are generating
> random numbers.

4. Create a **list_with_divisible_by_3** list from **random_number_list**, which will contain only numbers that are divisible by **3**:

```
list_with_divisible_by_3 = [a for a in \
                             random_number_list if a % 3 == 0]
list_with_divisible_by_3
```

The sample output is as follows:

```
[0,
 54,
 54,
 51,
 27,
 78,
 84,
 6,
 42,
 81,
 30,
 30,
 99,
 9,
```

Figure 1.21: Section of the output for random_number_list divisible by 3

5. Use the **len** function to measure the length of the first list and the second list, and store them in two different variables, **length_of_random_list** and **length_of_3_divisible_list**. Calculate the difference in length in a variable called **difference**:

```
length_of_random_list = len(random_number_list)
length_of_3_divisible_list = len(list_with_divisible_by_3)
difference = length_of_random_list - length_of_3_divisible_list
difference
```

The sample output is as follows:

```
71
```

6. Combine the tasks we have performed so far and add a **for** loop to it. Run the loop 10 times and add the values of the difference variables to a list:

```
NUMBER_OF_EXPERIMENTS = 10
difference_list = []
for i in range(0, NUMBER_OF_EXPERIMENTS):
    random_number_list = [random.randint(0, 100) \
                            for x in range(0, 100)]
    list_with_divisible_by_3 = [a for a in random_number_list \
                            if a % 3 == 0]

    length_of_random_list = len(random_number_list)
    length_of_3_divisible_list = len(list_with_divisible_by_3)
    difference = length_of_random_list \
                - length_of_3_divisible_list
    difference_list.append(difference)
difference_list
```

The sample output is as follows:

```
[64, 61, 67, 60, 73, 66, 66, 75, 70, 61]
```

7. Then, calculate the arithmetic mean (common average) for the differences in the lengths that you have:

```
avg_diff = sum(difference_list) / float(len(difference_list))
avg_diff
```

The sample output is as follows:

```
66.3
```

> **NOTE**
>
> The output is susceptible to change since we have used random numbers.
>
> To access the source code for this specific section, please refer to https://packt.live/30VMjt3.
>
> You can also run this example online at https://packt.live/3eh0Jlb.

With this, we have successfully completed our first activity. Let's move on to the next section, where we will discuss another type of data structure – **sets**.

ACTIVITY 1.02: ANALYZING A MULTILINE STRING AND GENERATING THE UNIQUE WORD COUNT

Solution:

These are the steps to complete this activity:

1. Open a new Jupyter Notebook, create a string called **multiline_text**, and copy the text present in the first chapter of *Pride and Prejudice*.

> **NOTE**
>
> Part of the first chapter of *Pride and Prejudice* by Jane Austen has been made available on this book's GitHub repository at https://packt. live/2N6ZGP6.

Use *Ctrl + A* to select the entire text and then *Ctrl + C* to copy it and use *Ctrl + V* to paste the text you just copied into it:

```
multiline_text= """"It is a truth universally acknowledged, that a single man in possession of a good f
However little known the feelings or views of such a man may be on his first entering a neighbourhood,
"My dear Mr. Bennet," said his lady to him one day, "have you heard that Netherfield Park is let at la
Mr. Bennet replied that he had not.
"But it is," returned she; "for Mrs. Long has just been here, and she told me all about it."
Mr. Bennet made no answer.
"Do you not want to know who has taken it?" cried his wife impatiently.
"You want to tell me, and I have no objection to hearing it."
This was invitation enough.
"Why, my dear, you must know, Mrs. Long says that Netherfield is taken by a young man of large fortune
"What is his name?"""
```

Figure 1.22: Initializing the mutliline_text string

2. Find the type of the string using the **type** function:

```
type(multiline_text)
```

The output is as follows:

```
str
```

3. Now, find the length of the string using the **len** function:

```
len(multiline_text)
```

The output is as follows:

```
1228
```

4. Use string methods to get rid of all the new lines (**\n** or **\r**) and symbols. Remove all new lines by replacing them with the following:

```
multiline_text = multiline_text.replace('\n', "")
```

5. Then, we will print and check the output:

```
multiline_text
```

The output is as follows:

```
'It is a truth universally acknowledged, that a single man in possession of a good fortune, must be i
n want of a wife.However little known the feelings or views of such a man may be on his first enterin
g a neighbourhood, this truth is so well fixed in the minds of the surrounding families, that he is c
onsidered the rightful property of some one or other of their daughters."My dear Mr. Bennet," said hi
s lady to him one day, "have you heard that Netherfield Park is let at last?"Mr. Bennet replied that
he had not."But it is," returned she; "for Mrs. Long has just been here, and she told me all about i
t."Mr. Bennet made no answer."Do you not want to know who has taken it?" cried his wife impatientl
y."You want to tell me, and I have no objection to hearing it."This was invitation enough."Why, my de
ar, you must know, Mrs. Long says that Netherfield is taken by a young man of large fortune from the
north of England; that he came down on Monday in a chaise and four to see the place, and was so much
delighted with it, that he agreed with Mr. Morris immediately; that he is to take possession before M
ichaelmas, and some of his servants are to be in the house by the end of next week.""What is his nam
e?'
```

Figure 1.23: The multiline_text string after removing the new lines

6. Remove the special characters and punctuation:

```
# remove special chars, punctuation etc.
cleaned_multiline_text = ""
for char in multiline_text:
    if char == " ":
        cleaned_multiline_text += char
    elif char.isalnum():  # using the isalnum() method of strings.
        cleaned_multiline_text += char
    else:
        cleaned_multiline_text += " "
```

7. Check the content of **cleaned_multiline_text**:

```
cleaned_multiline_text
```

The output is as follows:

```
'It is a truth universally acknowledged  that a single man in possession of a good fortune  must be i
n want of a wife However little known the feelings or views of such a man may be on his first enterin
g a neighbourhood  this truth is so well fixed in the minds of the surrounding families  that he is c
onsidered the rightful property of some one or other of their daughters  My dear Mr  Bennet    said hi
s lady to him one day   have you heard that Netherfield Park is let at last  Mr  Bennet replied that
he had not  But it is   returned she   for Mrs  Long has just been here  and she told me all about it
Mr  Bennet made no answer  Do you not want to know who has taken it   cried his wife impatiently  You
want to tell me  and I have no objection to hearing it  This was invitation enough  Why  my dear   you
must know  Mrs  Long says that Netherfield is taken by a young man of large fortune from the north of
England  that he came down on Monday in a chaise and four to see the place  and was so much delighted
with it  that he agreed with Mr  Morris immediately  that he is to take possession before Michaelmas
and some of his servants are to be in the house by the end of next week   What is his name '
```

Figure 1.24: The cleaned_multiline_text string

8. Generate a list of all the words from the cleaned string using the following command:

```
list_of_words = cleaned_multiline_text.split()
list_of_words
```

The section of the output is shown below:

```
['It',
 'is',
 'a',
 'truth',
 'universally',
 'acknowledged',
 'that',
 'a',
 'single',
 'man',
 'in',
 'possession',
 'of',
 'a',
 'good',
 'fortune',
 'must',
 'be',
 'in',
 'want',
```

Figure 1.25: The section of output displaying the list_of_words

9. Find the number of words:

```
len(list_of_words)
```

The output is **236**.

10. Create a list from the list you just created, which includes only unique words:

```
unique_words_as_dict = dict.fromkeys(list_of_words)
len(list(unique_words_as_dict.keys()))
```

The output is **135**.

11. Count the number of times each of the unique words appeared in the cleaned text:

```
for word in list_of_words:
    if unique_words_as_dict[word] is None:
        unique_words_as_dict[word] = 1
    else:
        unique_words_as_dict[word] += 1
unique_words_as_dict
```

The section of the output is shown below:

```
{'It': 1,
 'is': 8,
 'a': 8,
 'truth': 2,
 'universally': 1,
 'acknowledged': 1,
 'that': 8,
 'single': 1,
 'man': 3,
 'in': 5,
 'possession': 2,
 'of': 10,
 'good': 1,
 'fortune': 2,
 'must': 2,
 'be': 3,
 'want': 3,
 'wife': 2,
```

Figure 1.26: Section of output showing unique_words_as_dict

You just created, step by step, a unique word counter using all the neat tricks that you've learned about in this chapter.

12. Find the top 25 words from **unique_words_as_dict**:

```
top_words = sorted(unique_words_as_dict.items(), \
                   key=lambda key_val_tuple: key_val_tuple[1], \
                   reverse=True)
top_words[:25]
```

The output (partially shown) is as follows:

```
[('of', 10),
 ('is', 8),
 ('a', 8),
 ('that', 8),
 ('the', 8),
 ('to', 7),
 ('in', 5),
 ('his', 5),
 ('he', 5),
 ('it', 5),
 ('and', 5),
 ('Mr', 4),
 ('man', 3),
 ('be', 3),
```

Figure 1.27: Top 25 unique words from multiline_text

> **NOTE**
>
> To access the source code for this specific section, please refer to https://packt.live/2ASNIWL.
>
> You can also run this example online at https://packt.live/3dcIKkz.

CHAPTER 2: ADVANCED OPERATIONS ON BUILT-IN DATA STRUCTURES

ACTIVITY 2.01: PERMUTATION, ITERATOR, LAMBDA, AND LIST

Solution:

These are the detailed steps to solve this activity:

1. Look up the definition of **permutations** and **dropwhile** from **itertools**. There is a way to look up the definition of a function inside Jupyter itself. Just type the function name, followed by *?*, and press *Shift + Enter*:

```
from itertools import permutations, dropwhile
permutations?
dropwhile?
```

You will see a long list of definitions after each **?**. We will skip it here.

2. Write an expression to generate all the possible three-digit numbers using **1**, **2**, and **3**:

```
permutations(range(3))
```

The output (which will vary in your case) is as follows:

```
<itertools.permutations at 0x7f6c6c077af0>
```

3. Loop over the iterator expression you generated before. Use the **print** method to print each element returned by the iterator. Use **assert** and **isinstance** to make sure that the elements are tuples:

```
for number_tuple in permutations(range(3)):
    print(number_tuple)
    assert isinstance(number_tuple, tuple)
```

The output is as follows:

```
(0, 1, 2)
(0, 2, 1)
(1, 0, 2)
(1, 2, 0)
(2, 0, 1)
(2, 1, 0)
```

4. Write the loop again. But this time, use **dropwhile** with a lambda expression to drop any leading zeros from the tuples. As an example, **(0, 1, 2)** will become **[0, 2]**. Also, cast the output of **dropwhile** to a list.

   An extra task can be to check the actual type that **dropwhile** returns without casting:

```
for number_tuple in permutations(range(3)):
    print(list(dropwhile(lambda x: x <= 0, number_tuple)))
```

   The output is as follows:

```
[1, 2]
[2, 1]
[1, 0, 2]
[1, 2, 0]
[2, 0, 1]
[2, 1, 0]
```

5. Write all the logic you wrote before, but this time write a separate function where you will be passing the list generated from **dropwhile**; the function will return the whole number contained in the list. As an example, if you pass **[1, 2]** to the function, it will return **12**. Make sure that the return type is indeed a number and not a string. Although this task can be achieved using other tricks, we require you to treat the incoming list as a stack in the function and generate the number there:

```
import math
def convert_to_number(number_stack):
    final_number = 0
    for i in range(0, len(number_stack)):
        final_number += (number_stack.pop() \
                        * (math.pow(10, i)))
    return final_number

for number_tuple in permutations(range(3)):
    number_stack = list(dropwhile(lambda x: x <= 0, number_tuple))
    print(convert_to_number(number_stack))
```

The output is as follows:

```
12.0
21.0
102.0
120.0
201.0
210.0
```

> **NOTE**
>
> To access the source code for this specific section, please refer to https://packt.live/37Gk9DT.
>
> You can also run this example online at https://packt.live/3hEWt7f.

ACTIVITY 2.02: DESIGNING YOUR OWN CSV PARSER

Solution:

These are the detailed steps to solve this activity:

1. Import **zip_longest** from **itertools**:

```
from itertools import zip_longest
```

2. Define the **return_dict_from_csv_line** function so that it contains **header**, **line**, and **fillvalue** as **None**, and add it to a dictionary:

```
def return_dict_from_csv_line(header, line):
    # Zip them
    zipped_line = zip_longest(header, line, fillvalue=None)
    # Use dict comprehension to generate the final dict
    ret_dict = {kv[0]: kv[1] for kv in zipped_line}
    return ret_dict
```

3. Open the accompanying **sales_record.csv** file using **r** mode inside a **with** block. First, check that it is opened, read the first line, and use string methods to generate a list of all the column names as follows:

```
with open("../datasets/sales_record.csv", "r") as fd:
```

> **NOTE**
>
> Don't forget to change the path (highlighted) based on where you have stored the **csv** file.

4. When you read each line, pass that line to a function along with the list of the headers. The work of the function is to construct a dictionary out of these two and fill up the **key:values** variables. Keep in mind that a missing value should result in **None**:

```
first_line = fd.readline()
header = first_line.replace("\n", "").split(",")
for i, line in enumerate(fd):
    line = line.replace("\n", "").split(",")
    d = return_dict_from_csv_line(header, line)
    print(d)
    if i > 10:
        break
```

The output (partially shown) is as follows:

```
{'Region': 'Central America and the Caribbean', 'Country'
d', 'Sales Channel': 'Online', 'Order Priority': 'M', 'Orc
'Ship Date': '1/11/2014', 'Units Sold': '552', 'Unit Price
ue': '140914.56', 'Total Cost': '87999.84', 'Total Profit
{'Region': 'Central America and the Caribbean', 'Country'
l': 'Offline', 'Order Priority': 'C', 'Order Date': '7/5/2
6/2010', 'Units Sold': '2167', 'Unit Price': '152.58', 'Ur
'Total Cost': '211152.48', 'Total Profit': '119488.38'}
```

Figure 2.15: Section of output

> **NOTE**
>
> To access the source code for this specific section, please refer to https://packt.live/37FlVVK.
>
> You can also run this example online at https://packt.live/2YepGyb.

CHAPTER 3: INTRODUCTION TO NUMPY, PANDAS, AND MATPLOTLIB

ACTIVITY 3.01: GENERATING STATISTICS FROM A CSV FILE

Solution:

These are the steps to complete this activity:

1. Load the necessary libraries:

```
import numpy as np
import pandas as pd
import matplotlib.pyplot as plt
```

2. Read in the Boston Housing dataset (given as a **.csv** file) from the local directory:

```
df=pd.read_csv("../datasets/Boston_housing.csv")
```

> **NOTE**
>
> Don't forget to change the path of the dataset (highlighted) based on where it is saved on your system.

3. Check the first 10 records:

```
df.head(10)
```

The output is as follows:

	CRIM	ZN	INDUS	CHAS	NOX	RM	AGE	DIS	RAD	TAX	PTRATIO	B	LSTAT	PRICE
0	0.00632	18.0	2.31	0	0.538	6.575	65.2	4.0900	1	296	15.3	396.90	4.98	24.0
1	0.02731	0.0	7.07	0	0.469	6.421	78.9	4.9671	2	242	17.8	396.90	9.14	21.6
2	0.02729	0.0	7.07	0	0.469	7.185	61.1	4.9671	2	242	17.8	392.83	4.03	34.7
3	0.03237	0.0	2.18	0	0.458	6.998	45.8	6.0622	3	222	18.7	394.63	2.94	33.4
4	0.06905	0.0	2.18	0	0.458	7.147	54.2	6.0622	3	222	18.7	396.90	5.33	36.2
5	0.02985	0.0	2.18	0	0.458	6.430	58.7	6.0622	3	222	18.7	394.12	5.21	28.7
6	0.08829	12.5	7.87	0	0.524	6.012	66.6	5.5605	5	311	15.2	395.60	12.43	22.9
7	0.14455	12.5	7.87	0	0.524	6.172	96.1	5.9505	5	311	15.2	396.90	19.15	27.1
8	0.21124	12.5	7.87	0	0.524	5.631	100.0	6.0821	5	311	15.2	386.63	29.93	16.5
9	0.17004	12.5	7.87	0	0.524	6.004	85.9	6.5921	5	311	15.2	386.71	17.10	18.9

Figure 3.30: Output displaying the first 10 records

4. Find the total number of records:

```
df.shape
```

The output is as follows:

```
(506, 14)
```

5. Create a smaller DataFrame with columns that do not include **CHAS**, **NOX**, **B**, and **LSTAT**:

```
df1=df[['CRIM','ZN','INDUS',\
        'RM','AGE','DIS','RAD',\
        'TAX','PTRATIO','PRICE']]
```

6. Check the last **7** records of the new DataFrame you just created:

```
df1.tail(7)
```

The output is as follows:

	CRIM	ZN	INDUS	RM	AGE	DIS	RAD	TAX	PTRATIO	PRICE
499	0.17783	0.0	9.69	5.569	73.5	2.3999	6	391	19.2	17.5
500	0.22438	0.0	9.69	6.027	79.7	2.4982	6	391	19.2	16.8
501	0.06263	0.0	11.93	6.593	69.1	2.4786	1	273	21.0	22.4
502	0.04527	0.0	11.93	6.120	76.7	2.2875	1	273	21.0	20.6
503	0.06076	0.0	11.93	6.976	91.0	2.1675	1	273	21.0	23.9
504	0.10959	0.0	11.93	6.794	89.3	2.3889	1	273	21.0	22.0
505	0.04741	0.0	11.93	6.030	80.8	2.5050	1	273	21.0	11.9

Figure 3.31: Last seven records of the DataFrame

7. Plot histograms of all the variables (columns) in the new DataFrame by using a for loop:

```
for c in df1.columns:
    plt.title("Plot of "+c,fontsize=15)
    plt.hist(df1[c],bins=20)
    plt.show()
```

The output is as follows:

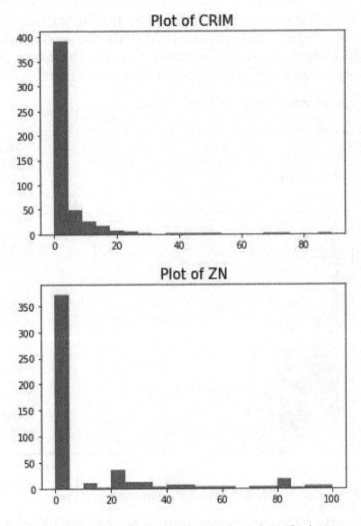

Figure 3.32: Partial plot of all variables using a for loop

> **NOTE**
>
> To take a look at all the plots, head over to the following
> link: https://packt.live/2AGb95F.

Crime rate could be an indicator of house price (people don't want to live in high-crime areas). In some cases, having multiple charts together can allow for the easy analysis of a variety of variables. In the preceding group of charts, we can see several unique spikes in the data: **INDIUS**, **TAX**, and **RAD**. With further exploratory analysis, we can find out more. We might want to plot one variable against another after looking at the preceding group of charts.

8. Create a scatter plot of crime rate versus price:

```
plt.scatter(df1['CRIM'], df1['PRICE'])
plt.show()
```

The output is as follows:

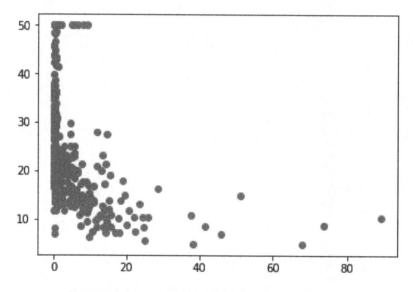

Figure 3.33: Scatter plot of crime rate versus price

We can understand this relationship better if we plot **log10(crime)** versus **price**.

9. Create a plot of **log10(crime)** versus price:

```
plt.scatter(np.log10(df1['CRIM']),df1['PRICE'], c='red')
plt.title("Crime rate (Log) vs. Price plot", fontsize=18)
plt.xlabel("Log of Crime rate",fontsize=15)
plt.ylabel("Price",fontsize=15)
plt.grid(True)
plt.show()
```

The output is as follows:

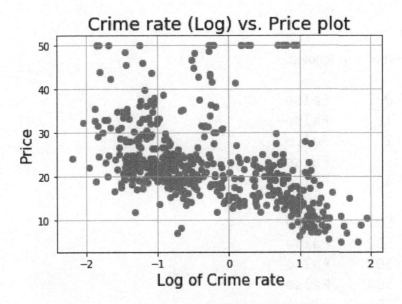

Figure 3.34: Scatter plot of crime rate (Log) versus price

10. Calculate the mean rooms per dwelling:

```
df1['RM'].mean()
```

The output is as follows:

```
6.284634387351788
```

11. Calculate the median age:

```
df1['AGE'].median()
```

The output is as follows:

```
77.5
```

12. Calculate the average (mean) distances to five Boston employment centers:

```
df1['DIS'].mean()
```

The output is as follows:

```
3.795042687747034
```

13. Calculate the price of the housing that's less than **20**:

```
low_price=df1['PRICE']<20
print(low_price)
```

The output is as follows:

```
0          False
1          False
2          False
3          False
4          False
          ...
501        False
502        False
503        False
504        False
505         True
Name: PRICE, Length: 506, dtype: bool
```

Figure 3.35: Output of low_price

This creates a Boolean array of **True, False**, **True = 1**, and **False = 0**. If you take an average of this NumPy array, you will know how many **1 (True)** values are there.

14. Calculate the mean of this array:

```
# That many houses are priced below 20,000.
# So that is the answer.
low_price.mean()
```

The output is:

```
0.4150197628458498
```

15. Calculate the percentage of houses with a low price (< **$20,000**):

```
# You can convert that into percentage
# Do this by multiplying with 100
pcnt=low_price.mean()*100
print("\nPercentage of house with <20,000 price is: ", pcnt)
```

The output is as follows:

```
Percentage of house with <20,000 price is:  41.50197628458498
```

> **NOTE**
>
> To access the source code for this specific section, please refer to https://packt.live/2AGb95F.
>
> You can also run this example online at https://packt.live/2YT3Hfg.

CHAPTER 4: A DEEP DIVE INTO DATA WRANGLING WITH PYTHON

ACTIVITY 4.01: WORKING WITH THE ADULT INCOME DATASET (UCI)

Solution:

These are the steps to complete this activity:

1. Load the necessary libraries:

```
import numpy as np
import pandas as pd
import matplotlib.pyplot as plt
```

2. Read in the Adult Income Dataset (given as a **.csv** file) from the local directory and check the first five records:

```
df = pd.read_csv("../datasets/adult_income_data.csv")
df.head()
```

> **NOTE**
>
> The highlighted path must be changed based on the location of the file on your system.

The output is as follows:

	39	State-gov	77516	Bachelors	13	Never-married	Adm-clerical	Not-in-family	Male	2174	0	40	United-States	<=50K
0	50	Self-emp-not-inc	83311	Bachelors	13	Married-civ-spouse	Exec-managerial	Husband	Male	0	0	13	United-States	<=50K
1	38	Private	215646	HS-grad	9	Divorced	Handlers-cleaners	Not-in-family	Male	0	0	40	United-States	<=50K
2	53	Private	234721	11th	7	Married-civ-spouse	Handlers-cleaners	Husband	Male	0	0	40	United-States	<=50K
3	28	Private	338409	Bachelors	13	Married-civ-spouse	Prof-specialty	Wife	Female	0	0	40	Cuba	<=50K
4	37	Private	284582	Masters	14	Married-civ-spouse	Exec-managerial	Wife	Female	0	0	40	United-States	<=50K

Figure 4.76: DataFrame displaying the first five records from the .csv file

3. Create a script that will read a text file line by line and extract the first line, which is the header of the `.csv` file:

```
names = []
with open('../datasets/adult_income_names.txt','r') as f:
    for line in f:
        f.readline()
        var=line.split(":")[0]
        names.append(var)
names
```

> **NOTE**
>
> The highlighted path must be changed based on the location of the file on your system.

The output is as follows:

```
['age',
 'workclass',
 'fnlwgt',
 'education',
 'education-num',
 'marital-status',
 'occupation',
 'relationship',
 'sex',
 'capital-gain',
 'capital-loss',
 'hours-per-week',
 'native-country']
```

Figure 4.77: Names of the columns in the database

4. Add a name of **Income** for the response variable (last column) to the dataset by using the **append** command:

```
names.append('Income')
```

5. Read the new file again using the following command:

```
df = pd.read_csv("../datasets/adult_income_data.csv", names=names)
df.head()
```

> **NOTE**
>
> The highlighted path must be changed based on the location of the file on your system.

The output is as follows:

	age	workclass	fnlwgt	education	education-num	marital-status	occupation	relationship
0	39	State-gov	77516	Bachelors	13	Never-married	Adm-clerical	Not-in-family
1	50	Self-emp-not-inc	83311	Bachelors	13	Married-civ-spouse	Exec-managerial	Husband
2	38	Private	215646	HS-grad	9	Divorced	Handlers-cleaners	Not-in-family
3	53	Private	234721	11th	7	Married-civ-spouse	Handlers-cleaners	Husband
4	28	Private	338409	Bachelors	13	Married-civ-spouse	Prof-specialty	Wife

Figure 4.78: DataFrame with the income column added

6. Use the **describe** command to get the statistical summary of the dataset:

```
df.describe()
```

The output is as follows:

	age	fnlwgt	education-num	capital-gain	capital-loss	hours-per-week
count	32561.000000	3.256100e+04	32561.000000	32561.000000	32561.000000	32561.000000
mean	38.581647	1.897784e+05	10.080679	1077.648844	87.303830	40.437456
std	13.640433	1.055500e+05	2.572720	7385.292085	402.960219	12.347429
min	17.000000	1.228500e+04	1.000000	0.000000	0.000000	1.000000
25%	28.000000	1.178270e+05	9.000000	0.000000	0.000000	40.000000
50%	37.000000	1.783560e+05	10.000000	0.000000	0.000000	40.000000
75%	48.000000	2.370510e+05	12.000000	0.000000	0.000000	45.000000
max	90.000000	1.484705e+06	16.000000	99999.000000	4356.000000	99.000000

Figure 4.79: Statistical summary of the dataset

Note that only a small number of columns are included. Many variables in the dataset have multiple factors or classes.

7. Make a list of all the variables in the classes by using the following command:

```
# Make a list of all variables with classes
vars_class = ['workclass','education','marital-status',\
              'occupation','relationship','sex','native-country']
```

8. Create a loop to count and print them by using the following command:

```
for v in vars_class:
    classes=df[v].unique()
    num_classes = df[v].nunique()
    print("There are {} classes in the \"{}\" column. "\
          "They are: {}".format(num_classes,v,classes))
    print("-"*100)
```

The output (partially shown) is as follows:

```
There are 9 classes in the "workclass" column. They are:
e' ' Federal-gov' ' Local-gov'
 ' ?' ' Self-emp-inc' ' Without-pay' ' Never-worked']
--------------------------------------------------------
There are 16 classes in the "education" column. They are
s' ' 9th' ' Some-college'
 ' Assoc-acdm' ' Assoc-voc' ' 7th-8th' ' Doctorate' ' Pr
 ' 5th-6th' ' 10th' ' 1st-4th' ' Preschool' ' 12th']
```

Figure 4.80: Output of different factors or classes

9. Find the missing values by using the following command:

```
df.isnull().sum()
```

The output is as follows:

```
age                 0
workclass           0
fnlwgt              0
education           0
education-num       0
marital-status      0
occupation          0
relationship        0
sex                 0
capital-gain        0
capital-loss        0
hours-per-week      0
native-country      0
Income              0
dtype: int64
```

Figure 4.81: Finding the missing values

10. Create a DataFrame with only **age**, **education**, and **occupation** by using subsetting:

```
df_subset = df[['age','education', 'occupation']]
df_subset.head()
```

The output is as follows:

	age	education	occupation
0	39	Bachelors	Adm-clerical
1	50	Bachelors	Exec-managerial
2	38	HS-grad	Handlers-cleaners
3	53	11th	Handlers-cleaners
4	28	Bachelors	Prof-specialty

Figure 4.82: Subset of the DataFrame

11. Plot a histogram of age with a bin size of 20.

```
df_subset['age'].hist(bins=20)
```

The output is as follows:

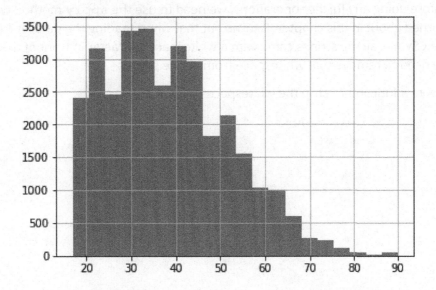

Figure 4.83: Histogram of age with a bin size of 20

12. Plot box plots for **age** grouped by **education** (use a long figure size of **25x10** and make the **x** ticks font size **15**):

```
df_subset.boxplot(column='age',by='education',figsize=(25,10))
plt.xticks(fontsize=15)
plt.xlabel("Education",fontsize=20)
plt.show()
```

The output is as follows:

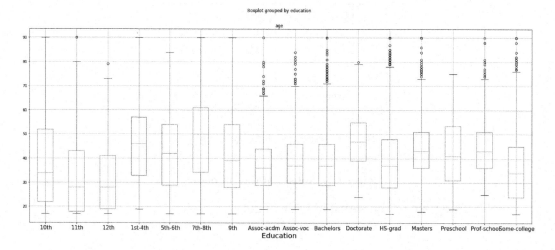

Figure 4.84: Box plot of age grouped by education

Before doing any further operations, we need to use the **apply** method we learned about in this chapter. It turns out that when reading the dataset from the CSV file, all the strings came with a whitespace character in front of them. So, we need to remove that whitespace from all the strings.

13. Create a function to strip the whitespace characters:

```
def strip_whitespace(s):
    return s.strip()
```

14. Use the **apply** method to apply this function to all the columns with string values, create a new column, copy the values from this new column to the old column, and drop the new column. This is the preferred method so that you don't accidentally delete valuable data. Most of the time, you will need to create a new column with a desired operation and then copy it back to the old column if necessary. Ignore any warning messages that are printed:

```
# Education column
df_subset['education_stripped'] = df['education']\
                                .apply(strip_whitespace)
df_subset['education'] = df_subset['education_stripped']
df_subset.drop(labels = ['education_stripped'],\
            axis=1, inplace=True)


# Occupation column
df_subset['occupation_stripped'] = df['occupation']\
                                .apply(strip_whitespace)
df_subset['occupation'] = df_subset['occupation_stripped']
df_subset.drop(labels = ['occupation_stripped'],\
            axis=1, inplace=True)
```

This is the sample warning message, which you should ignore:

```
C:\Users\ranuk\Anaconda3\lib\site-packages\ipykernel_launcher.py:2: SettingWithCopyWarning:
A value is trying to be set on a copy of a slice from a DataFrame.
Try using .loc[row_indexer,col_indexer] = value instead

See the caveats in the documentation: http://pandas.pydata.org/pandas-docs/stable/user_guide
g.html#returning-a-view-versus-a-copy

C:\Users\ranuk\Anaconda3\lib\site-packages\ipykernel_launcher.py:3: SettingWithCopyWarning:
A value is trying to be set on a copy of a slice from a DataFrame.
Try using .loc[row_indexer,col_indexer] = value instead
```

Figure 4.85: Warning message to be ignored

15. Find the number of people who are aged between **30** and **50** (inclusive) by using the following command:

```
# Conditional clauses and join them by & (AND)
df_filtered=df_subset[(df_subset['age']>=30) \
                    & (df_subset['age']<=50)]
```

16. Check the contents of the new dataset:

```
df_filtered.head()
```

The output is as follows:

	age	education	occupation
0	39	Bachelors	Adm-clerical
1	50	Bachelors	Exec-managerial
2	38	HS-grad	Handlers-cleaners
5	37	Masters	Exec-managerial
6	49	9th	Other-service

Figure 4.86: Contents of the new DataFrame

17. Find the **shape** of the filtered DataFrame and specify the index of the tuple as 0 to return the first element:

```
answer_1=df_filtered.shape[0]
answer_1
```

The output is as follows:

```
16390
```

18. Print the number of people aged between **30** and **50** using the following command:

```
print("There are {} people of age between 30 and 50 "\
      "in this dataset.".format(answer_1))
```

The output is as follows:

```
There are 16390 people of age between 30 and 50 in this dataset.
```

19. Group by **occupation** and show the summary statistics of age. Find which profession has the oldest workers on average and which profession has its largest share of the workforce above the **75th** percentile:

```
df_subset.groupby('occupation').describe()['age']
```

The output is as follows:

occupation	count	mean	std	min	25%	50%	75%	max
?	1843.0	40.882800	20.336350	17.0	21.0	35.0	61.0	90.0
Adm-clerical	3770.0	36.964456	13.362998	17.0	26.0	35.0	46.0	90.0
Armed-Forces	9.0	30.222222	8.089774	23.0	24.0	29.0	34.0	46.0
Craft-repair	4099.0	39.031471	11.606436	17.0	30.0	38.0	47.0	90.0
Exec-managerial	4066.0	42.169208	11.974548	17.0	33.0	41.0	50.0	90.0
Farming-fishing	994.0	41.211268	15.070283	17.0	29.0	39.0	52.0	90.0
Handlers-cleaners	1370.0	32.165693	12.372635	17.0	23.0	29.0	39.0	90.0
Machine-op-inspct	2002.0	37.715285	12.068266	17.0	28.0	36.0	46.0	90.0
Other-service	3295.0	34.949621	14.521508	17.0	22.0	32.0	45.0	90.0
Priv-house-serv	149.0	41.724832	18.633688	17.0	24.0	40.0	57.0	81.0
Prof-specialty	4140.0	40.517633	12.016676	17.0	31.0	40.0	48.0	90.0
Protective-serv	649.0	38.953775	12.822062	17.0	29.0	36.0	47.0	90.0
Sales	3650.0	37.353973	14.186352	17.0	25.0	35.0	47.0	90.0
Tech-support	928.0	37.022629	11.316594	17.0	28.0	36.0	44.0	73.0
Transport-moving	1597.0	40.197871	12.450792	17.0	30.0	39.0	49.0	90.0

Figure 4.87: DataFrame with data grouped by age and education

The code returns **79 rows × 1 columns**.

20. Use subset and **groupBy** to find the outliers:

```
occupation_stats=df_subset.groupby('occupation').describe()['age']
```

21. Plot the values on a bar chart:

```
plt.figure(figsize=(15,8))
plt.barh(y=occupation_stats.index, \
        width=occupation_stats['count'])
plt.yticks(fontsize=13)
plt.show()
```

The output is as follows:

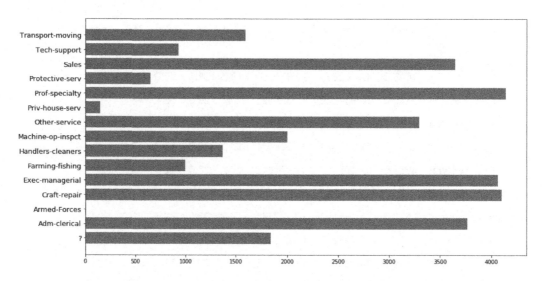

Figure 4.88: Bar chart displaying occupation statistics

Is there a particular occupation group that has very low representation? Perhaps we should remove those pieces of data because, with very low data, the group won't be useful in analysis. Just by looking at *Figure 4.89*, you should be able to see that the **Armed-Forces** group has only got a **9** count, that is, **9** data points. But how can we detect this? By plotting the count column in a bar chart. Note how the first argument to the **barh** function is the index of the DataFrame, which is the summary stats of the occupation groups. We can see that the **Armed-Forces** group has almost no data. This activity teaches you that, sometimes, the outlier is not just a value, but can be a whole group. The data of this group is fine, but it is too small to be useful for any analysis. So, it can be treated as an outlier in this case. But always use your business knowledge and engineering judgment for such outlier detection and how to process them. We will now practice merging two datasets using a common key.

22. Suppose you are given two datasets where the common key is **occupation**. First, create two such disjoint datasets by taking random samples from the full dataset and then try merging. Include at least two other columns, along with the common key column for each dataset. Notice how the resulting dataset, after merging, may have more data points than either of the two starting datasets if your common key is not unique:

```
df_1 = df[['age','workclass','occupation']]\
        .sample(5,random_state=101)
df_1.head()
```

The output is as follows:

	age	workclass	occupation
22357	51	Private	Machine-op-inspct
26009	19	Private	Sales
20734	40	Private	Exec-managerial
17695	17	Private	Handlers-cleaners
27908	61	Private	Craft-repair

Figure 4.89: Output after merging the common keys

The second dataset is as follows:

```
df_2 = df[['education','occupation']].sample(5,random_state=101)
df_2.head()
```

The output is as follows:

	education	occupation
22357	HS-grad	Machine-op-inspct
26009	11th	Sales
20734	HS-grad	Exec-managerial
17695	10th	Handlers-cleaners
27908	7th-8th	Craft-repair

Figure 4.90: Output after merging the common keys

23. Merge the two datasets together:

```
df_merged = pd.merge(df_1,df_2,on='occupation',\
                    how='inner').drop_duplicates()
df_merged
```

The output is as follows:

	age	workclass	occupation	education
0	51	Private	Machine-op-inspct	HS-grad
1	19	Private	Sales	11th
2	40	Private	Exec-managerial	HS-grad
3	17	Private	Handlers-cleaners	10th
4	61	Private	Craft-repair	7th-8th

Figure 4.91: Output of distinct occupation values

NOTE

To access the source code for this specific section, please refer to https://packt.live/37IamwR.

You can also run this example online at https://packt.live/2YhuF1j.

CHAPTER 5: GETTING COMFORTABLE WITH DIFFERENT KINDS OF DATA SOURCES

ACTIVITY 5.01: READING TABULAR DATA FROM A WEB PAGE AND CREATING DATAFRAMES

Solution:

These are the steps to complete this activity:

1. Import **BeautifulSoup** and load the data by using the following command:

```
from bs4 import BeautifulSoup
import pandas as pd
```

2. Open the Wikipedia file by using the following command:

```
fd = open("../datasets/List of countries by GDP (nominal) "\
        "- Wikipedia.htm", "r", encoding = "utf-8")
soup = BeautifulSoup(fd)
fd.close()
```

> **NOTE**
>
> Don't forget to change the path of the dataset (highlighted) based on its location on your system

3. Calculate the tables by using the following command:

```
all_tables = soup.find_all("table")
print("Total number of tables are {} ".format(len(all_tables)))
```

There are nine tables in total.

4. Find the right table using the **class** attribute by using the following command:

```
data_table = soup.find("table", {"class": '"wikitable"|}'})
print(type(data_table))
```

The output is as follows:

```
<class 'bs4.element.Tag'>
```

5. Separate the source and the actual data by using the following command:

```
sources = data_table.tbody.findAll('tr', recursive=False)[0]
sources_list = [td for td in sources.findAll('td')]
print(len(sources_list))
```

The output is as follows:

```
3
```

6. Use the **findAll** function to find the data from the **body** tag of **data_table** using the following command:

```
data = data_table.tbody.findAll('tr', recursive=False)[1]\
                        .findAll('td', recursive=False)
```

7. Use the **findAll** function to find the data from the **data_table td** tag by using the following command:

```
data_tables = []
for td in data:
    data_tables.append(td.findAll('table'))
```

8. Find the length of **data_tables** by using the following command:

```
len(data_tables)
```

The output is as follows:

```
3
```

9. Check how to get the source names by using the following command:

```
source_names = [source.findAll('a')[0].getText() \
                for source in sources_list]
print(source_names)
```

The output is as follows:

```
['International Monetary Fund', 'World Bank', 'United Nations']
```

10. Separate the header and data for the first source:

```
header1 = [th.getText().strip() for th in \
            data_tables[0][0].findAll('thead')[0].findAll('th')]
header1
```

The output is as follows:

```
['Rank', 'Country', 'GDP(US$MM)']
```

11. Find the rows from **data_tables** using **findAll**:

```
rows1 = data_tables[0][0].findAll('tbody')[0].findAll('tr')[1:]
```

12. Find the data from **rows1** using the **strip** function for each **td** tag:

```
data_rows1 = [[td.get_text().strip() for td in \
              tr.findAll('td')] for tr in rows1]
```

13. Find the DataFrame:

```
df1 = pd.DataFrame(data_rows1, columns=header1)
df1.head()
```

The output is as follows:

	Rank	Country	GDP(US$MM)
0		World[19]	79,865,481
1	1	United States	19,390,600
2	2	China[n 1]	12,014,610
3	3	Japan	4,872,135
4	4	Germany	3,684,816

Figure 5.35: DataFrame created from the web page

14. Do the same for the other two sources by using the following command:

```
header2 = [th.getText().strip() for th in data_tables[1][0]\
          .findAll('thead')[0].findAll('th')]
header2
```

The output is as follows:

```
['Rank', 'Country', 'GDP(US$MM)']
```

15. Find the rows from **data_tables** using **findAll** by using the following command:

```
rows2 = data_tables[1][0].findAll('tbody')[0].findAll('tr')
```

16. Define **find_right_text** using the **strip** function by using the following command:

```
def find_right_text(i, td):
    if i == 0:
        return td.getText().strip()
    elif i == 1:
        return td.getText().strip()
    else:
        index = td.text.find("♠")
        return td.text[index+1:].strip()
```

17. Find the rows from **data_rows** using **find_right_text** by using the following command:

```
data_rows2 = [[find_right_text(i, td) for i, td in \
                enumerate(tr.findAll('td'))] for tr in rows2]
```

18. Calculate the **df2** DataFrame by using the following command:

```
df2 = pd.DataFrame(data_rows2, columns=header2)
df2.head()
```

The output is as follows:

	Rank	Country	GDP(US$MM)
0		World	80,683,787
1	1	United States	19,390,604
2		European Union[23]	17,277,698
3	2	China[n 4]	12,237,700
4	3	Japan	4,872,137

Figure 5.36: Output of the DataFrame

19. Now, perform the same operations for the third DataFrame by using the following command:

```
header3 = [th.getText().strip() for th in data_tables[2][0]\
            .findAll('thead')[0].findAll('th')]
header3
```

The output is as follows:

```
['Rank', 'Country', 'GDP(US$MM)']
```

20. Find the rows from **data_tables** using **findAll** by using the following command:

```
rows3 = data_tables[2][0].findAll('tbody')[0].findAll('tr')
```

21. Find the rows from **data_rows3** by using **find_right_text**:

```
data_rows3 = [[find_right_text(i, td) for i, td in \
             enumerate(tr.findAll('td'))] for tr in rows2]
```

22. Calculate the **df3** DataFrame by using the following command:

```
df3 = pd.DataFrame(data_rows3, columns=header3)
df3.head()
```

The output is as follows:

	Rank	Country	GDP(US$MM)
0		World	80,683,787
1	1	United States	19,390,604
2		European Union[23]	17,277,698
3	2	China[n 4]	12,237,700
4	3	Japan	4,872,137

Figure 5.37: The third DataFrame

NOTE

To access the source code for this specific section, please refer to https://packt.live/2NaCrDB.

You can also run this example online at https://packt.live/2YRAukP.

CHAPTER 6: LEARNING THE HIDDEN SECRETS OF DATA WRANGLING

ACTIVITY 6.01: HANDLING OUTLIERS AND MISSING DATA

Solution:

The steps to completing this activity are as follows:

> **NOTE**
>
> The dataset to be used for this activity can be found at https://packt.live/2YajrLJ.

1. Load the data:

```
import pandas as pd
import numpy as np
import matplotlib.pyplot as plt
%matplotlib inline
```

2. Read the **.csv** file:

```
df = pd.read_csv("../datasets/visit_data.csv")
```

> **NOTE**
>
> Don't forget to change the path (highlighted) based on where the CSV file is saved on your system.

3. Print the data from the DataFrame:

```
df.head()
```

The output is as follows:

	id	first_name	last_name	email	gender	ip_address	visit
0	1	Sonny	Dahl	sdahl0@mysql.com	Male	135.36.96.183	1225.0
1	2	NaN	NaN	dhoovart1@hud.gov	NaN	237.165.194.143	919.0
2	3	Gar	Armal	garmal2@technorati.com	NaN	166.43.137.224	271.0
3	4	Chiarra	Nulty	cnulty3@newyorker.com	NaN	139.98.137.108	1002.0
4	5	NaN	NaN	sleaver4@elegantthemes.com	NaN	46.117.117.27	2434.0

Figure 6.11: The contents of the CSV file

As we can see, there is data where some values are missing, and if we examine this, we will see some outliers.

4. Check for duplicates by using the following command:

```
print("First name is duplicated - {}"\
      .format(any(df.first_name.duplicated())))
print("Last name is duplicated - {}"\
      .format(any(df.last_name.duplicated())))
print("Email is duplicated - {}"\
      .format(any(df.email.duplicated())))
```

The output is as follows:

```
First name is duplicated - True
Last name is duplicated - True
Email is duplicated - False
```

There are duplicates in both the first and last names, which is normal. However, as we can see, there are no duplicates in email. That's good.

5. Check whether any essential column contains **NaN**:

```
"""
Notice that we have different ways to
format boolean values for the % operator
"""
print("The column Email contains NaN - %r " % \
      df.email.isnull().values.any())
print("The column IP Address contains NaN - %s " % \
      df.ip_address.isnull().values.any())
print("The column Visit contains NaN - %s " % \
      df.visit.isnull().values.any())
```

The output is as follows:

```
The column Email contains NaN - False
The column IP Address contains NaN - False
The column Visit contains NaN - True
```

The **Visit** column contains some **NaN** values. Given that the final task at hand will probably be predicting the number of visits, we cannot do anything with rows that do not have that information. They are a type of outlier. Let's get rid of them.

6. Get rid of the outliers:

```
"""
There are various ways to do this. This is just one way. We encourage
you   to explore other ways. But before that we need to store the
previous size of the data set and we   will compare it with the new
size
"""
size_prev = df.shape
df = df[np.isfinite(df['visit'])]
#This is an inplace operation.
# After this operation the original DataFrame is lost.
size_after = df.shape
```

7. Report the size difference:

```
# Notice how parameterized format is used.
# Then, the indexing is working inside the quote marks
print("The size of previous data was - {prev[0]} rows and "\
      "the size of the new one is - {after[0]} rows"\
      .format(prev=size_prev, after=size_after))
```

The output is as follows:

```
The size of previous data was - 1000 rows and the size of the new one
is - 974 rows
```

8. Plot a box plot to find whether the data has outliers:

```
plt.boxplot(df.visit, notch=True)
```

The box plot is as follows:

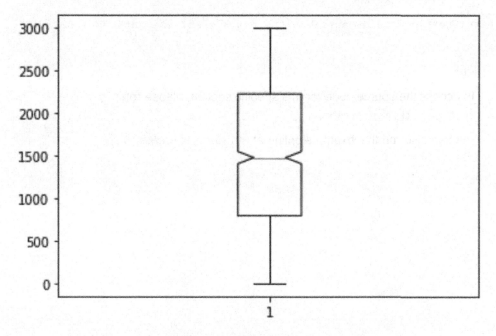

Figure 6.12: Box plot using the data

As we can see, we have data in this column in the interval (**0 , 3000**). However, the main concentration of the data is between **~700** and **~2300**.

9. Get rid of values beyond **2900** and below **100** – these are outliers for us. We need to get rid of them:

```
df1 = df[(df['visit'] <= 2900) & (df['visit'] >= 100)]
# Notice the  powerful & operator
"""
Here we abuse the fact the
number of variable can be greater
than the number of replacement targets
"""
print("After getting rid of outliers the new size of the data "\
      "is - {}".format(*df1.shape))
```

The output is as follows:

```
After getting rid of outliers the new size of the data is - 923
```

> **NOTE**
>
> To access the source code for this specific section, please refer to https://packt.live/2AFcSbn.
>
> You can also run this example online at https://packt.live/3fAL9qY

CHAPTER 7: ADVANCED WEB SCRAPING AND DATA GATHERING

ACTIVITY 7.01: EXTRACTING THE TOP 100 E-BOOKS FROM GUTENBERG

Solution:

These are the steps to complete this activity:

1. Import the necessary libraries, including regex and **BeautifulSoup**:

```
import urllib.request, urllib.parse, urllib.error
import requests
from bs4 import BeautifulSoup
import ssl
import re
```

2. Read the HTML from the URL:

```
top100url = 'https://www.gutenberg.org/browse/scores/top'
response = requests.get(top100url)
```

3. Write a small function to check the status of the web request:

```
def status_check(r):
    if r.status_code==200:
        print("Success!")
        return 1
    else:
        print("Failed!")
        return -1
```

4. Check the status of response:

```
status_check(response)
```

The output is as follows:

```
Success!
1
```

5. Decode the response and pass it on to **BeautifulSoup** for HTML parsing:

```
contents = response.content.decode(response.encoding)
soup = BeautifulSoup(contents, 'html.parser')
```

6. Find all the href tags and store them in the list of links.

```
# Empty list to hold all the http links in the HTML page
lst_links=[]
# Find all href tags and store them in the list of links
for link in soup.find_all('a'):
    #print(link.get('href'))
    lst_links.append(link.get('href'))
```

7. Check what the list looks like – print the first 30 elements:

```
lst_links[:30]
```

The output (partially shown) is as follows:

```
['/wiki/Main_Page',
 '/catalog/',
 '/ebooks/',
 '/browse/recent/last1',
 '/browse/scores/top',
 '/wiki/Gutenberg:Offline_Catalogs',
 '/catalog/world/mybookmarks',
 '/wiki/Main_Page',
'https://www.paypal.com/xclick/business=donate%40gutenberg.org&item_
name=Donation+to+Project+Gutenberg',
 '/wiki/Gutenberg:Project_Gutenberg_Needs_Your_Donation',
 'http://www.ibiblio.org',
 'http://www.pgdp.net/',
 'pretty-pictures',
 '#books-last1',
 '#authors-last1',
 '#books-last7',
 '#authors-last7',
 '#books-last30',
 '#authors-last30',
```

```
    '/ebooks/1342',
    '/ebooks/84',
    '/ebooks/1080',
    '/ebooks/46',
    '/ebooks/219',
    '/ebooks/2542',
    '/ebooks/98',
    '/ebooks/345',
    '/ebooks/2701',
    '/ebooks/844',
    '/ebooks/11']
```

8. Use a regular expression to find the numeric digits in these links. These are the file numbers for the top 100 books. Initialize the empty list to hold the file numbers:

```
booknum=[]
```

Numbers 19 to 118 in the original list of links have the top 100 eBooks' numbers.

9. Loop over the appropriate range and use a regex to find the numeric digits in the link (**href**) string. Use the **findall()** method:

```
for i in range(19,119):
    link=lst_links[i]
    link=link.strip()
    """
    Regular expression to find the numeric digits in the link (href)
string
    """
    n=re.findall('[0-9]+',link)
    if len(n)==1:
        # Append the filenumber casted as integer
        booknum.append(int(n[0]))
```

10. Print the file numbers:

```
print("\nThe file numbers for the top 100 ebooks",\
      "on Gutenberg are shown below\n"+"-"*70)
print(booknum)
```

The output is as follows:

```
The file numbers for the top 100 ebooks on Gutenberg are shown below
--------------------------------------------------------------------
--
[1342, 84, 1080, 46, 219, 2542, 98, 345, 2701, 844, 11, 5200,
43, 16328, 76, 74, 1952, 6130, 2591, 1661, 41, 174, 23, 1260,
1497, 408, 3207, 1400, 30254, 58271, 1232, 25344, 58269, 158,
44881, 1322, 205, 2554, 1184, 2600, 120, 16, 58276, 5740, 34901,
28054, 829, 33, 2814, 4300, 100, 55, 160, 1404, 786, 58267, 3600,
19942, 8800, 514, 244, 2500, 2852, 135, 768, 58263, 1251, 3825,
779, 58262, 203, 730, 20203, 35, 1250, 45, 161, 30360, 7370,
58274, 209, 27827, 58256, 33283, 4363, 375, 996, 58270, 521,
58268, 36, 815, 1934, 3296, 58279, 105, 2148, 932, 1064, 13415]
```

> **NOTE**
>
> Since the list of top 100 books is frequently updated, the output you get will vary.

What does the **soup** object's text look like?

11. Use the `.text` method and print only the first 2,000 characters (do not print the whole thing as it is too long).

You will notice a lot of empty spaces/blanks here and there. Ignore them. They are part of the HTML page's markup and its whimsical nature:

```
print(soup.text[:2000])
```

The output is as follows:

```
if (top != self) {
        top.location.replace (http://www.gutenberg.org);
        alert ('Project Gutenberg is a FREE service with NO
membership required. If you paid somebody else to get here, make them
give you your money back!');
        }
    Top 100 - Project Gutenberg
Online Book Catalog
 Book  Search
-- Recent  Books
-- Top  100
```

```
-- Offline Catalogs
-- My Bookmarks
Main Page
...
Pretty Pictures
Top 100 EBooks yesterday —
  Top 100 Authors yesterday —
  Top 100 EBooks last 7 days —
  Top 100 Authors last 7 days —
  Top 100 EBooks last 30 days —
  Top 100 Authors last 30 days
Top 100 EBooks yesterday
Pride and Prejudice by Jane Austen (1826)
Frankenstein; Or, The Modern Prometheus by Mary Wollstonecraft
Shelley (1367)
A Modest Proposal by Jonathan Swift (1020)
A Christmas Carol in Prose; Being a Ghost Story of Christmas by
Charles Dickens (953)
Heart of Darkness by Joseph Conrad (887)
Et dukkehjem. English by Henrik Ibsen (761)
A Tale of Two Cities by Charles Dickens (741)
Dracula by Bram Stoker (732)
Moby Dick; Or, The Whale by Herman Melville (651)
The Importance of Being Earnest: A Trivial Comedy for Serious People
by Oscar Wilde (646)
Alice's Adventures in Wonderland by Lewis Carrol
```

12. Search the extracted text (using regex) from the **soup** object to find the names of the top 100 eBooks (yesterday's ranking):

```
lst_titles_temp=[]
```

13. Create a starting index. It should point at the text Top 100 Ebooks yesterday. Use the **splitlines** method of **soup.text**. It splits the lines of the text of the **soup** object:

```
start_idx=soup.text.splitlines().index('Top 100 EBooks yesterday')
```

> **NOTE**
>
> Since the list of top 100 books is frequently updated, the output you get will vary.

14. Run the **for** loop from **1-100** to add the strings of the next **100** lines to this temporary list. **Hint:** use the **splitlines** method:

```
for i in range(100):
    lst_titles_temp.append(soup.text.splitlines()[start_idx+2+i])
```

15. Use regex to extract only text from the name strings and append them to an empty list. Use **match** and **span** to find the indices and use them:

```
lst_titles=[]
for i in range(100):
    id1,id2=re.match('^[a-zA-Z ]*',lst_titles_temp[i]).span()
    lst_titles.append(lst_titles_temp[i][id1:id2])
```

16. Print the list of titles:

```
for l in lst_titles:
    print(l)
```

The partial output is as follows:

```
Pride and Prejudice by Jane Austen
Frankenstein
A Modest Proposal by Jonathan Swift
A Christmas Carol in Prose
Heart of Darkness by Joseph Conrad
Et dukkehjem
A Tale of Two Cities by Charles Dickens
Dracula by Bram Stoker
Moby Dick
The Importance of Being Earnest
Alice
Metamorphosis by Franz Kafka
The Strange Case of Dr
Beowulf
...
The Russian Army and the Japanese War
Calculus Made Easy by Silvanus P
Beyond Good and Evil by Friedrich Wilhelm Nietzsche
An Occurrence at Owl Creek Bridge by Ambrose Bierce
Don Quixote by Miguel de Cervantes Saavedra
Blue Jackets by Edward Greey
The Life and Adventures of Robinson Crusoe by Daniel Defoe
```

```
The Waterloo Campaign
The War of the Worlds by H
Democracy in America
Songs of Innocence
The Confessions of St
Modern French Masters by Marie Van Vorst
Persuasion by Jane Austen
The Works of Edgar Allan Poe
The Fall of the House of Usher by Edgar Allan Poe
The Masque of the Red Death by Edgar Allan Poe
The Lady with the Dog and Other Stories by Anton Pavlovich Chekhov
```

> **NOTE**
>
> Since the list of top 100 books is frequently updated, the output you get will vary.

Here, we have seen how we can use web scraping and parsing using a mix of **BeautifulSoup** and regex to find information from very untidy and vast source data. These are some essential steps that you will have to perform on a daily basis when you are dealing with data wrangling.

> **NOTE**
>
> To access the source code for this specific section, please refer to https://packt.live/2BltmFo.
>
> You can also run this example online at https://packt.live/37FdLwD.

ACTIVITY 7.02: BUILDING YOUR OWN MOVIE DATABASE BY READING AN API

SOLUTION

> **NOTE**
>
> Before you begin, ensure that you modify the **APIkeys.json** file and add your secret API key there. Link to the file: https://packt.live/2CmIpze.

These are the steps to complete this activity:

1. Import **urllib.request**, **urllib.parse**, **urllib.error**, and **json**:

```
import urllib.request, urllib.parse, urllib.error
import json
```

2. Load the secret API key (you have to get one from the OMDb website and use that; it has a daily API key limit of 1,000) from a JSON file, stored in the same folder, into a variable, by using **json.loads()**:

> **NOTE**
>
> The following cell will not be executed in the solution notebook because the author cannot give out their private API key.

The students/users will need to obtain a key and store it in a JSON file. We are calling this file **APIkeys.json**.

3. Open the **APIkeys.json** file by using the following command:

```
with open('APIkeys.json') as f:
    keys = json.load(f)
    omdbapi = keys['OMDBapi']
```

The final URL to be passed should look like this: http://www.omdbapi.com/?t=movie_name&apikey=secretapikey.

4. Assign the OMDb portal (http://www.omdbapi.com/?) as a string to a variable called **serviceurl** by using the following command:

```
serviceurl = 'http://www.omdbapi.com/?'
```

5. Create a variable called **apikey** with the last portion of the URL (**&apikey=secretapikey**), where **secretapikey** is your own API key. The movie name portion is **t=movie_name**, and it will be addressed later:

```
apikey = '&apikey='+omdbapi
```

6. Write a utility function called **print_json** to print the movie data from a JSON file (which we will get from the portal). Here are the keys of a JSON file: **'Title', 'Year', 'Rated', 'Released', 'Runtime', 'Genre', 'Director', 'Writer', 'Actors', 'Plot', 'Language','Country', 'Awards', 'Ratings', 'Metascore', 'imdbRating', 'imdbVotes', and 'imdbID':**

```
def print_json(json_data):
    list_keys = ['Title', 'Year', 'Rated', 'Released',\
                'Runtime', 'Genre', 'Director', 'Writer', \
                'Actors', 'Plot', 'Language', 'Country', \
                'Awards', 'Ratings','Metascore', 'imdbRating', \
                'imdbVotes', 'imdbID']
    print("-"*50)
    for k in list_keys:
        if k in list(json_data.keys()):
            print(f"{k}: {json_data[k]}")
    print("-"*50)
```

7. Write a utility function to download a poster of the movie based on the information from the JSON dataset and save it in your local folder. Use the **os** module. The poster data is stored in the JSON key Poster. You may want to split the name of the Poster file and extract the file extension only. Let's say that the extension is **.jpg**. We could later join this extension to the movie name and create a filename such as **movie.jpg**. Use the **open** Python command open to open a file and write the poster data. Close the file after you're done. This function may not return anything. It just saves the poster data as an image file:

```
def save_poster(json_data):
    import os
    title = json_data['Title']
    poster_url = json_data['Poster']
    """
    Splits the poster url by '.' and
    picks up the last string as file extension
    """
    poster_file_extension=poster_url.split('.')[-1]
    # Reads the image file from web
    poster_data = urllib.request.urlopen(poster_url).read()
```

```
    savelocation=os.getcwd()+'\\'+'Posters'+'\\'

    """
    Creates new directory if the directory does not exist.
    Otherwise, just use the existing path.
    """

    if not os.path.isdir(savelocation):
        os.mkdir(savelocation)
    filename=savelocation+str(title)\
            +'.'+poster_file_extension
    f=open(filename,'wb')
    f.write(poster_data)
    f.close()
```

8. Write a utility function called **search_movie** to search a movie by its name,
   print the downloaded JSON data (use the **print_json** function for this), and
   save the movie poster in the local folder (use the **save_poster** function for
   this). Use a try-except loop for this, that is, try to connect to the web portal. If
   successful, proceed, but if not (that is, if an exception is raised), then just print
   an error message. Use the previously created variables, **serviceurl** and
   apikey. You have to pass on a dictionary with a key, t, and the movie name as
   the corresponding value to the **urllib.parse.urlencode** function and then
   add the **serviceurl** and **apikey** variables to the output of the function to
   construct the full URL. This URL will be used to access the data. The JSON data
   has a key called Response. If it is True, that means that the read was successful.
   Check this before processing the data. If it was not successful, then print the
   JSON key Error, which will contain the appropriate error message that's returned
   by the movie database:

```
def search_movie(title):
    try:
        url = serviceurl \
                + urllib.parse.urlencode({'t':str(title)})+apikey
        print(f'Retrieving the data of "{title}" now... ')
        print(url)
        uh = urllib.request.urlopen(url)
        data = uh.read()
        json_data=json.loads(data)
        if json_data['Response']=='True':
            print_json(json_data)
            """
```

```
            Asks user whether to download the poster of the movie
        """
        if json_data['Poster']!='N/A':
            save_poster(json_data)
        else:
            print("Error encountered: ", json_data['Error'])
    except urllib.error.URLError as e:
        print(f"ERROR: {e.reason}")
```

9. Test the **search_movie** function by entering **Titanic**:

```
search_movie("Titanic")
```

The following is the retrieved data for Titanic:

```
http://www.omdbapi.com/?t=Titanic&apikey=<your api key>
-------------------------------------------------------
Title: Titanic
Year: 1997
Rated: PG-13
Released: 19 Dec 1997
Runtime: 194 min
Genre: Drama, Romance
Director: James Cameron
Writer: James Cameron
Actors: Leonardo DiCaprio, Kate Winslet, Billy Zane, Kathy Bates
Plot: A seventeen-year-old aristocrat falls in love with a kind but
poor artist aboard the luxurious, ill-fated R.M.S. Titanic.
Language: English, Swedish
Country: USA
Awards: Won 11 Oscars. Another 111 wins & 77 nominations.
Ratings: [{'Source': 'Internet Movie Database', 'Value': '7.8/10'},
{'Source': 'Rotten Tomatoes', 'Value': '89%'}, {'Source':
'Metacritic', 'Value': '75/100'}]
Metascore: 75
imdbRating: 7.8
imdbVotes: 913,780
imdbID: tt0120338

-------------------------------------------------------
```

10. Test the **search_movie** function by entering **Random_error** (obviously, this will not be found, and you should be able to check whether your error-catching code is working properly):

```
search_movie("Random_error")
```

Retrieve the data of **Random_error**:

```
Retrieving the data of "Random_error" now...
http://www.omdbapi.com/?t=Random_error&apikey=<your api key>
Error encountered: Movie not found!
```

> **NOTE**
>
> In the last two steps, we've not shown the private API key (highlighted) for security reasons.
>
> To access the source code for this specific section, please refer to https://packt.live/3hLJvoy.
>
> You can also run this example online at https://packt.live/3efkDTZ.

CHAPTER 8: RDBMS AND SQL

ACTIVITY 8.01: RETRIEVING DATA ACCURATELY FROM DATABASES

Solution:

These are the steps to complete this activity:

1. Connect to the supplied **petsdb** database:

```
import sqlite3
conn = sqlite3.connect("petsdb")
```

2. Write a function to check whether the connection has been successful:

```
# a tiny function to make sure the connection is successful
def is_opened(conn):
    try:
        conn.execute("SELECT * FROM persons LIMIT 1")
        return True
    except sqlite3.ProgrammingError as e:
        print("Connection closed {}".format(e))
        return False
print(is_opened(conn))
```

The output is as follows:

```
True
```

3. Close the connection:

```
conn.close()
```

4. Check whether the connection is open or closed:

```
print(is_opened(conn))
```

The output is as follows:

```
Connection closed Cannot operate on a closed database.
False
```

5. Connect to the **petsdb** database:

```
conn = sqlite3.connect("petsdb")
c = conn.cursor()
```

6. Find out the different age groups in the persons table. Execute the following command:

```
for ppl, age in c.execute("SELECT count(*), \
                           age FROM persons GROUP BY age"):
    print("We have {} people aged {}".format(ppl, age))
```

The output is as follows:

```
We have 2 people aged 5
We have 1 people aged 6
We have 1 people aged 7
We have 3 people aged 8
We have 1 people aged 9
We have 2 people aged 11
We have 3 people aged 12
We have 1 people aged 13
We have 4 people aged 14
We have 2 people aged 16
We have 2 people aged 17
We have 3 people aged 18
We have 1 people aged 19
We have 3 people aged 22
We have 2 people aged 23
We have 3 people aged 24
We have 2 people aged 25
We have 1 people aged 27
We have 1 people aged 30
We have 3 people aged 31
We have 1 people aged 32
We have 1 people aged 33
We have 2 people aged 34
```

Figure 8.13: Section of output grouped by age

7. To find out which age group has the maximum number of people, execute the following command:

```
for ppl, age in c.execute("SELECT count(*), age FROM persons \
                           GROUP BY age ORDER BY count(*)DESC"):
    print("The highest number of people is {} and "\
          "came from {} age group".format(ppl, age))
    break
```

The output is as follows:

```
The highest number of people is 5 and came from 73 age group
```

8. To find out how many people do not have a full name (the last name is blank/null), execute the following command:

```
res = c.execute("SELECT count(*) FROM persons \
                WHERE last_name IS null")
for row in res:
    print(row)
```

The output is as follows:

```
(60,)
```

9. To find out how many people have more than one pet, execute the following command:

```
res = c.execute("SELECT count(*) FROM \
                (SELECT count(owner_id) FROM pets \
                GROUP BY owner_id HAVING count(owner_id) >1)")
for row in res:
    print("{} people have more than one pets".format(row[0]))
```

The output is as follows:

```
43 People have more than one pets
```

10. To find out how many pets have received treatment, execute the following command:

```
res = c.execute("SELECT count(*) FROM pets \
                WHERE treatment_done=1")
for row in res:
    print(row)
```

The output is as follows:

```
(36,)
```

11. To find out how many pets have received treatment and the type of pet is known, execute the following command:

```
res = c.execute("SELECT count(*) FROM pets \
                WHERE treatment_done=1 AND pet_type IS NOT null")
for row in res:
    print(row)
```

The output is as follows:

```
(16,)
```

12. To find out how many pets are from the city called **east port**, execute the following command:

```
res = c.execute("SELECT count(*) FROM pets \
                JOIN persons ON pets.owner_id = persons.id \
                WHERE persons.city='east port'")
for row in res:
    print(row)
```

The output is as follows:

```
(49,)
```

13. To find out how many pets are from the city called **east port** and who received treatment, execute the following command:

```
res = c.execute("SELECT count(*) FROM pets \
                JOIN persons ON pets.owner_id = \
                persons.id WHERE persons.city='east port' \
                AND pets.treatment_done=1")
for row in res:
    print(row)
```

The output is as follows:

```
(11,)
```

> **NOTE**
>
> To access the source code for this specific section, please refer to https://packt.live/3derN9D.
>
> You can also run this example online at https://packt.live/2ASWYKi.

CHAPTER 9: APPLICATIONS IN BUSINESS USE CASES AND CONCLUSION OF THE COURSE

ACTIVITY 9.01: DATA WRANGLING TASK — FIXING UN DATA

Solution:

These are the steps to complete this activity:

1. Import the required libraries:

```
import numpy as np
import pandas as pd
import matplotlib.pyplot as plt
import warnings
warnings.filterwarnings('ignore')
```

2. Save the URL of the dataset (highlighted) and use the pandas **read_csv** method to directly pass this link and create a DataFrame:

```
education_data_link="http://data.un.org/_Docs/SYB/CSV/"\
                    "SYB61_T07_Education.csv"
df1 = pd.read_csv(education_data_link)
```

3. Print the data in the DataFrame:

```
df1.head()
```

The output (partially shown) is as follows:

	T07	Enrolment in primary, secondary and tertiary education levels	Unnamed: 2	Unnamed: 3
0	Region/Country/Area	NaN	Year	Series
1	1	Total, all countries or areas	2005	Students enrolled in primary education (thousa...
2	1	Total, all countries or areas	2005	Gross enrollement ratio - Primary (male)

Figure 9.7: Partial DataFrame from the UN data

4. As the first row does not contain useful information, use the **skiprows** parameter to remove the first row:

```
df1 = pd.read_csv(education_data_link,skiprows=1)
```

5. Print the data in the DataFrame:

```
df1.head()
```

The output is as follows:

	Region/Country/Area	Unnamed: 1	Year	Series
0	1	Total, all countries or areas	2005	Students enrolled in primary education (thousa...
1	1	Total, all countries or areas	2005	Gross enrollement ratio - Primary (male)
2	1	Total, all countries or areas	2005	Gross enrollment ratio - Primary (female)
3	1	Total, all countries or areas	2005	Students enrolled in secondary education (thou...

Figure 9.8: Partial DataFrame after removing the first row

6. Drop the **Region/Country/Area** and **Source** columns as they will not be very helpful:

```
df2 = df1.drop(['Region/Country/Area','Source'],axis=1)
```

7. Assign the following names as the columns of the DataFrame: **['Region/Country/Area','Year','Data','Value','Footnotes']**

```
df2.columns=['Region/Country/Area','Year','Data',\
             'Enrollments (Thousands)','Footnotes']
```

8. Print the data in the DataFrame:

```
df2.head()
```

The output is as follows:

	Region/Country/Area	Year	Data	Enrollments (Thousands)	Footnotes
0	Total, all countries or areas	2005	Students enrolled in primary education (thousa...	678,990	NaN
1	Total, all countries or areas	2005	Gross enrollement ratio - Primary (male)	104.8	NaN
2	Total, all countries or areas	2005	Gross enrollment ratio - Primary (female)	99.8	NaN
3	Total, all countries or areas	2005	Students enrolled in secondary education (thou...	509,100	NaN
4	Total, all countries or areas	2005	Gross enrollment ratio - Secondary (male)	65.7	NaN

Figure 9.9: DataFrame after dropping the Region/Country/Area and Source columns

9. Check how many unique values the **Footnotes** column contains:

```
df2['Footnotes'].unique()
```

The output is as follows:

```
array([nan, 'Estimate.',
       'For statistical purposes, the data for China do not include those for the Hong Kong Special Administrative Region (Hong
Kong SAR), Macao Special Administrative Region (Macao SAR) and Taiwan Province of China.'],
      dtype=object)
```

Figure 9.10: Unique values of the Footnotes column

10. Convert the **Value** column data into a numeric one for further processing:

```
type(df2['Enrollments (Thousands)'][0])
```

The output is as follows:

```
str
```

11. Create a utility function to convert the strings in the **Value** column into floating-point numbers:

```
def to_numeric(val):
    """

    Converts a given string (with one or more commas) to a numeric
value
    """
    if ',' not in str(val):
        result = float(val)
    else:
        val=str(val)
        val=''.join(str(val).split(','))
        result=float(val)
    return result
```

12. Use the **apply** method to apply this function to the **Value** column data:

```
df2['Enrollments (Thousands)']=df2['Enrollments (Thousands)']\
                                .apply(to_numeric)
```

13. Print the unique types of data in the **Data** column:

```
df2['Data'].unique()
```

The output is as follows:

```
array(['Students enrolled in primary education (thousands)',
       'Gross enrollement ratio - Primary (male)',
       'Gross enrollment ratio - Primary (female)',
       'Students enrolled in secondary education (thousands)',
       'Gross enrollment ratio - Secondary (male)',
       'Gross enrollment ratio - Secondary (female)',
       'Students enrolled in tertiary education (thousands)',
       'Gross enrollment ratio - Tertiary (male)',
       'Gross enrollment ratio - Tertiary (female)'], dtype=object)
```

Figure 9.11: Unique values in a column

14. Create three DataFrames by filtering and selecting them from the original DataFrame:

df_primary: Only students enrolled in primary education (thousands)

df_secondary: Only students enrolled in secondary education (thousands)

df_tertiary: Only students enrolled in tertiary education (thousands):

```
df_primary = df2[df2['Data']=='Students enrolled in primary '\
                           'education (thousands)']
df_secondary = df2[df2['Data']=='Students enrolled in secondary '\
                             'education (thousands)']
df_tertiary = df2[df2['Data']=='Students enrolled in tertiary '\
                           'education (thousands)']
```

15. Compare them using bar charts of the primary students' enrollment of a low-income country and a high-income country:

```
primary_enrollment_india = df_primary[df_primary\
                        ['Region/Country/Area']=='India']
primary_enrollment_USA = df_primary[df_primary\
                      ['Region/Country/Area']\
                      =='United States of America']
```

16. Print the **primary_enrollment_india** data:

```
primary_enrollment_india
```

The output is as follows:

	Region/Country/Area	Year	Data	Enrollments (Thousands)	Footnotes
3729	India	2003	Students enrolled in primary education (thousa...	125569.0	NaN
3744	India	2010	Students enrolled in primary education (thousa...	138414.0	NaN
3753	India	2014	Students enrolled in primary education (thousa...	137809.0	NaN
3762	India	2015	Students enrolled in primary education (thousa...	138518.0	NaN
3771	India	2016	Students enrolled in primary education (thousa...	145803.0	NaN

Figure 9.12: Data for enrollment in primary education in India

17. Print the **primary_enrollment_USA** data:

```
primary_enrollment_USA
```

The output is as follows:

	Region/Country/Area	Year	Data	Enrollments (Thousands)	Footnotes
7858	United States of America	2005	Students enrolled in primary education (thousa...	24455.0	NaN
7865	United States of America	2010	Students enrolled in primary education (thousa...	24393.0	NaN
7872	United States of America	2014	Students enrolled in primary education (thousa...	24538.0	NaN
7879	United States of America	2015	Students enrolled in primary education (thousa...	24786.0	NaN

Figure 9.13: Data for enrollment in primary education in USA

18. Plot the data for India:

```python
plt.figure(figsize=(8,4))
plt.bar(primary_enrollment_india['Year'],\
primary_enrollment_india['Enrollments (Thousands)'])
plt.title("Enrollment in primary education\nin India "\
          "(in thousands)",fontsize=16)
plt.grid(True)
plt.xticks(fontsize=14)
plt.yticks(fontsize=14)
plt.xlabel("Year", fontsize=15)
plt.show()
```

The output is as follows:

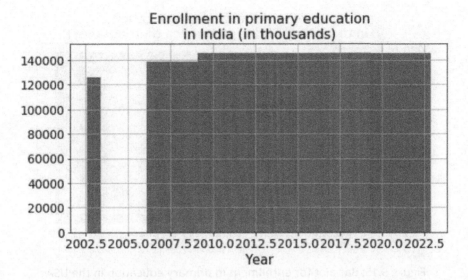

Figure 9.14: Bar plot for enrollment in primary education in India

19. Plot the data for the USA:

```
plt.figure(figsize=(8,4))
plt.bar(primary_enrollment_USA['Year'],\
primary_enrollment_USA['Enrollments (Thousands)'])
plt.title("Enrollment in primary education\nin the "\
        "United States of America (in thousands)",fontsize=16)
plt.grid(True)
plt.xticks(fontsize=14)
plt.yticks(fontsize=14)
plt.xlabel("Year", fontsize=15)
plt.show()
```

The output is as follows:

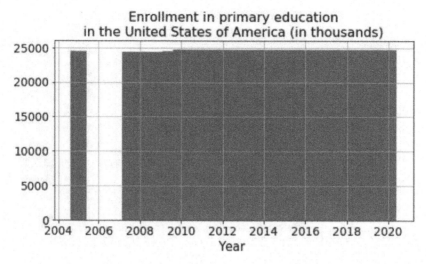

Figure 9.15: Bar plot for enrollment in primary education in the USA

As we can see, we have missing data. Now is the time to use **pandas** methods to do the data imputation. But to do that, we need to create a DataFrame with missing values inserted into it – that is, we need to append another DataFrame with missing values to the current DataFrame.

20. Find the missing years:

```
missing_years = [y for y in range(2004,2010)]\
                +[y for y in range(2011,2014)]
```

21. Print the value in the **missing_years** variable:

```
missing_years
```

The output is as follows:

```
[2004, 2005, 2006, 2007, 2008, 2009, 2011, 2012, 2013]
```

22. Create a dictionary of values with **np.nan**. Note that there are nine missing data points, so we need to create a list with identical values repeated nine times:

```
dict_missing = \
{'Region/Country/Area':['India']*9,\
 'Year':missing_years,\
 'Data':'Students enrolled in primary education(thousands)'*9,\
 'Enrollments (Thousands)':[np.nan]*9,'Footnotes':[np.nan]*9}
```

23. Create a DataFrame of missing values (from the preceding dictionary) that we can **append**:

```
df_missing = pd.DataFrame(data=dict_missing)
```

24. Append the new DataFrames to the previously existing ones:

```
primary_enrollment_india=primary_enrollment_india\
                        .append(df_missing,ignore_index=True,\
                                sort=True)
```

25. Print the data in **primary_enrollment_india**:

```
primary_enrollment_india
```

The output is as follows:

	Data	Enrollments (Thousands)	Footnotes	Region/Country/Area	Year
0	Students enrolled in primary education (thousa...	125569.0	NaN	India	2003
1	Students enrolled in primary education (thousa...	138414.0	NaN	India	2010
2	Students enrolled in primary education (thousa...	137809.0	NaN	India	2014
3	Students enrolled in primary education (thousa...	138518.0	NaN	India	2015
4	Students enrolled in primary education (thousa...	145803.0	NaN	India	2016
5	Students enrolled in primary education (thousa...	NaN	NaN	India	2004

Figure 9.16: Partial Data for enrollment in primary education
in India after appending the data

26. Sort by **year** and reset the indices using **reset_index**. Use **inplace=True** to execute the changes on the DataFrame itself:

```
primary_enrollment_india.sort_values(by='Year',inplace=True)
primary_enrollment_india.reset_index(inplace=True,drop=True)
```

27. Print the data in **primary_enrollment_india**:

```
primary_enrollment_india
```

The output is as follows:

	Data	Enrollments (Thousands)	Footnotes	Region/Country/Area
0	Students enrolled in primary education (thousa...	125569.0	NaN	India
1	Students enrolled in primary education (thousa...	NaN	NaN	India
2	Students enrolled in primary education (thousa...	NaN	NaN	India
3	Students enrolled in primary education (thousa...	NaN	NaN	India
4	Students enrolled in primary education (thousa...	NaN	NaN	India
5	Students enrolled in primary education (thousa...	NaN	NaN	India

Figure 9.17: Partial Data for enrollment in primary education in India after sorting the data

28. Use the **interpolate** method for linear interpolation. It fills all the **NaN** values with linearly interpolated values. Check out this link for more details about this method: http://pandas.pydata.org/pandas-docs/version/0.17/generated/pandas.DataFrame.interpolate.html:

```
primary_enrollment_india.interpolate(inplace=True)
```

29. Print the data in **primary_enrollment_india**:

```
primary_enrollment_india
```

The output is as follows:

	Data	Enrollments (Thousands)	Footnotes	Region/Country/Area	Year
0	Students enrolled in primary education (thousa...	125569.00	NaN	India	2003
1	Students enrolled in primary education (thousa...	127404.00	NaN	India	2004
2	Students enrolled in primary education (thousa...	129239.00	NaN	India	2005
3	Students enrolled in primary education (thousa...	131074.00	NaN	India	2006
4	Students enrolled in primary education (thousa...	132909.00	NaN	India	2007
5	Students enrolled in primary education (thousa...	134744.00	NaN	India	2008
6	Students enrolled in primary education (thousa...	136579.00	NaN	India	2009
7	Students enrolled in primary education (thousa...	138414.00	NaN	India	2010

Figure 9.18: Data for enrollment in primary education in India after interpolating the data

30. Plot the data:

```
plt.figure(figsize=(8,4))
plt.bar(primary_enrollment_india['Year'],\
        primary_enrollment_india['Enrollments (Thousands)'])
plt.title("Enrollment in primary education\nin India "\
          "(in thousands)", fontsize=16)
plt.grid(True)
plt.xticks(fontsize=14)
plt.yticks(fontsize=14)
plt.xlabel("Year", fontsize=15)
plt.show()
```

The output is as follows:

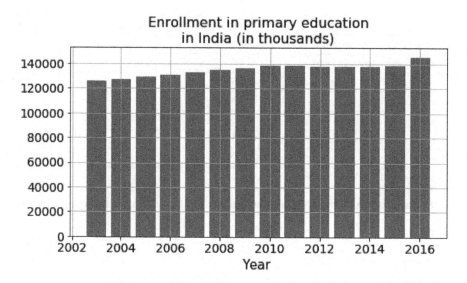

Figure 9.19: Bar plot for enrollment in primary education in India

31. Repeat the same steps for the USA:

```
missing_years = [2004]+[y for y in range(2006,2010)]\
                +[y for y in range(2011,2014)]+[2016]
```

32. Print the value in **missing_years**.

```
missing_years
```

The output is as follows:

```
[2004, 2006, 2007, 2008, 2009, 2011, 2012, 2013, 2016]
```

33. Create **dict_missing**, as follows:

```
dict_missing = \
{'Region/Country/Area':['United States of America']*9,\
 'Year':missing_years, \
 'Data':'Students enrolled in primary education (thousands)'*9, \
 'Value':[np.nan]*9,'Footnotes':[np.nan]*9}
```

34. Create the DataFrame for **df_missing**, as follows:

```
df_missing = pd.DataFrame(data=dict_missing)
```

35. Append this to the **primary_enrollment_USA** variable, as follows:

```
primary_enrollment_USA=primary_enrollment_USA\
                       .append(df_missing,\
                               ignore_index =True,sort=True)
```

36. Sort the values in the **primary_enrollment_USA** variable, as follows:

```
primary_enrollment_USA.sort_values(by='Year',inplace=True)
```

37. Reset the index of the **primary_enrollment_USA** variable, as follows:

```
primary_enrollment_USA.reset_index(inplace=True,drop=True)
```

38. Interpolate the **primary_enrollment_USA** variable, as follows:

```
primary_enrollment_USA.interpolate(inplace=True)
```

39. Print the **primary_enrollment_USA** variable:

```
primary_enrollment_USA
```

The output is as follows:

	Data	Enrollments (Thousands)	Footnotes	Region/Country/Area	Value	Year
0	Students enrolled in primary education (thousa...	NaN	NaN	United States of America	NaN	2004
1	Students enrolled in primary education (thousa...	24455.00	NaN	United States of America	NaN	2005
2	Students enrolled in primary education (thousa...	24442.60	NaN	United States of America	NaN	2006
3	Students enrolled in primary education (thousa...	24430.20	NaN	United States of America	NaN	2007
4	Students enrolled in primary education (thousa...	24417.80	NaN	United States of America	NaN	2008
5	Students enrolled in primary education (thousa...	24405.40	NaN	United States of America	NaN	2009

Figure 9.20: Data for enrollment in primary education in the USA
after all operations have been completed

40. Still, the first value is unfilled. We can use the `limit` and `limit_direction` parameters with the interpolate method to fill it in. How did we know this? By searching on Google and looking at the StackOverflow page. Always search for the solution to your problem and look for what has already been done and try to implement it:

```
primary_enrollment_USA.interpolate(method='linear',\
                                   limit_direction='backward',\
                                   limit=1)
```

The output is as follows:

	Data	Enrollments (Thousands)	Footnotes	Region/Country/Area	Value	Year
0	Students enrolled in primary education (thousa...	24455.00	NaN	United States of America	NaN	2004
1	Students enrolled in primary education (thousa...	24455.00	NaN	United States of America	NaN	2005
2	Students enrolled in primary education (thousa...	24442.60	NaN	United States of America	NaN	2006
3	Students enrolled in primary education (thousa...	24430.20	NaN	United States of America	NaN	2007
4	Students enrolled in primary education (thousa...	24417.80	NaN	United States of America	NaN	2008
5	Students enrolled in primary education (thousa...	24405.40	NaN	United States of America	NaN	2009

Figure 9.21: Data for enrollment in primary education in the USA after limiting the data

41. Print the data in **primary_enrollment_USA**:

```
primary_enrollment_USA
```

The output is as follows:

	Data	Enrollments (Thousands)	Footnotes	Region/Country/Area	Value	Year
0	Students enrolled in primary education (thousa...	NaN	NaN	United States of America	NaN	2004
1	Students enrolled in primary education (thousa...	24455.00	NaN	United States of America	NaN	2005
2	Students enrolled in primary education (thousa...	24442.60	NaN	United States of America	NaN	2006
3	Students enrolled in primary education (thousa...	24430.20	NaN	United States of America	NaN	2007
4	Students enrolled in primary education (thousa...	24417.80	NaN	United States of America	NaN	2008
5	Students enrolled in primary education (thousa...	24405.40	NaN	United States of America	NaN	2009

Figure 9.22: Data for enrollment in primary education in the USA

42. Plot the data:

```
plt.figure(figsize=(8,4))
plt.bar(primary_enrollment_USA['Year'],\
        primary_enrollment_USA['Enrollments (Thousands)'])
plt.title("Enrollment in primary education\nin the "\
        "United States of America (in thousands)",fontsize=16)
plt.grid(True)
plt.xticks(fontsize=14)
plt.yticks(fontsize=14)
plt.xlabel("Year", fontsize=15)
plt.show()
```

The output is as follows:

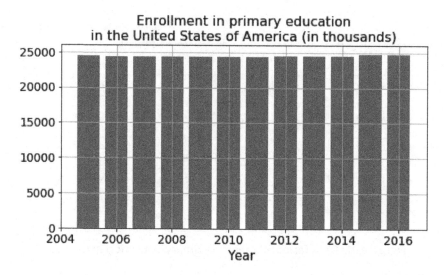

Figure 9.23: Bar plot for enrollment in primary education in the USA

> **NOTE**
>
> To access the source code for this specific section, please refer to https://packt.live/3fylqy8.
>
> You can also run this example online at https://packt.live/3fQ0PXJ.

ACTIVITY 9.02: DATA WRANGLING TASK – CLEANING GDP DATA

Solution:

These are the steps to complete this activity:

1. Import the required libraries:

```
import numpy as np
import pandas as pd
import matplotlib.pyplot as plt
import warnings
warnings.filterwarnings('ignore')
```

2. **GDP data for India**: We will try to read the GDP data for India from a CSV file that was found in a World Bank portal. It is given to you and also hosted on the Packt GitHub repository at https://packt.live/2AMoeu6. However, the **pandas read_csv** method will throw an error if we try to read it normally. Let's look at a step-by-step guide of how we can read useful information from it:

```
df3=pd.read_csv("../datasets/India_World_Bank_Info.csv")
```

> **NOTE**
>
> Throughout this activity, don't forget to change the path of the dataset (highlighted) to match its location on your system.

The output (partially shown) is as follows:

```
----------------------------------------------------------------
------
ParserError                       Traceback (most recent call last)
<ipython-input-45-9239cae67df7> in <module>()

...

ParserError: Error tokenizing data. C error: Expected 1 fields in line
6,
    saw 3
```

We can try and use the **error_bad_lines=False** option in this kind of situation.

3. Read the India World Bank Information .**csv** file.

```
df3=pd.read_csv("../datasets/India_World_Bank_Info.csv",\
                error_bad_lines=False)
```

The output (partially shown) will be:

```
b'Skipping line 6: expected 1 fields, saw 3\nSkipping line 7: expected 1 fields, saw 2\nSkipping line 8: e
xpected 1 fields, saw 3\nSkipping line 9: expected 1 fields, saw 3\nSkipping line 10: expected 1 fields, s
aw 2\nSkipping line 11: expected 1 fields, saw 2\nSkipping line 12: expected 1 fields, saw 2\nSkipping lin
e 19: expected 1 fields, saw 2\nSkipping line 23: expected 1 fields, saw 2\nSkipping line 48: expected 1 f
ields, saw 2\nSkipping line 52: expected 1 fields, saw 2\nSkipping line 53: expected 1 fields, saw 2\nSkip
ping line 54: expected 1 fields, saw 2\nSkipping line 61: expected 1 fields, saw 2\nSkipping line 62: expe
cted 1 fields, saw 2\nSkipping line 63: expected 1 fields, saw 2\nSkipping line 64: expected 1 fields, saw
2\nSkipping line 65: expected 1 fields, saw 2\nSkipping line 66: expected 1 fields, saw 2\nSkipping line 6
7: expected 1 fields, saw 2\nSkipping line 68: expected 1 fields, saw 2\nSkipping line 69: expected 1 fiel
ds, saw 2\nSkipping line 76: expected 1 fields, saw 2\nSkipping line 77: expected 1 fields, saw 2\nSkippin
g line 80: expected 1 fields, saw 2\nSkipping line 81: expected 1 fields, saw 2\nSkipping line 83: expecte
d 1 fields, saw 2\nSkipping line 84: expected 1 fields, saw 2\nSkipping line 86: expected 1 fields, saw 3
\nSkipping line 87: expected 1 fields, saw 3\nSkipping line 88: expected 1 fields, saw 4\nSkipping line 8
9: expected 1 fields, saw 4\nSkipping line 90: expected 1 fields, saw 3\nSkipping line 91: expected 1 fiel
ds, saw 2\nSkipping line 93: expected 1 fields, saw 2\nSkipping line 95: expected 1 fields, saw 2\nSkippin
```

Figure 9.24: Partial output of the warnings.

4. Then, let's take a look at the contents of the DataFrame.

```
df3.head(10)
```

The output is as follows:

Data Source World Development Indicators

0	Last Updated Date\t11/14/2018\t\t\t\t\t\t\t\...
1	Country Name\tCountry Code\tIndicator Name\t19...
2	India\tIND\tBattle-related deaths (number of p...
3	India\tIND\tTravel services (% of commercial s...
4	India\tIND\tTransport services (% of commercia...
5	India\tIND\tHigh-technology exports (% of manu...
6	India\tIND\tHigh-technology exports (current U...
7	India\tIND\tCommercial service exports (curren...
8	India\tIND\tExport value index (2000 = 100)\t\...
9	India\tIND\tMerchandise exports to low- and mi...

Figure 9.25: DataFrame from the India World Bank Information

> **NOTE**
>
> At times, the output may not be found because there are three rows instead of the expected one row.

5. Clearly, the delimiter in this file is tab (**\t**):

```
df3=pd.read_csv("../datasets/India_World_Bank_Info.csv", \
                error_bad_lines=False,delimiter='\t')
df3.head(10)
```

The output is as follows:

	Data Source	World Development Indicators	Unnamed: 2	Unnamed: 3	Unnamed: 4	Unnamed: 5
0	NaN	NaN	NaN	NaN	NaN	NaN
1	Last Updated Date	11/14/2018	NaN	NaN	NaN	NaN
2	NaN	NaN	NaN	NaN	NaN	NaN
3	Country Name	Country Code	Indicator Name	1960.0	1961.0	1962.0
4	India	IND	Presence of peace keepers (number of troops, p...	NaN	NaN	NaN

Figure 9.26: Partial output of the DataFrame from the India World Bank Information after using a delimiter

6. Use the **skiprows** parameter to skip the first four rows:

```
df3=pd.read_csv("../datasets/India_World_Bank_Info.csv",\
                error_bad_lines=False,delimiter='\t',\
                skiprows=4)
df3.head(10)
```

The output is as follows:

	Country Name	Country Code	Indicator Name	1960	1961	1962	1963	1964	1965	1966
0	India	IND	Presence of peace keepers (number of troops, p...	NaN	NaN	NaN	NaN	NaN	NaN	NaN
1	India	IND	Intentional homicides (per 100,000 people)	NaN	NaN	NaN	NaN	NaN	NaN	NaN
2	India	IND	Intentional homicides, male (per 100,000 male)	NaN	NaN	NaN	NaN	NaN	NaN	NaN

Figure 9.27: Partial output of DataFrame from the India World Bank Information after using skiprows

Closely examine the dataset. In this file, the columns are the yearly data and the rows are the various types of information. Upon examining the file with Excel, we find that the **Indicator Name** column is the one with the name of a particular data type, which is GDP per capita. We filter the dataset with the information we are interested in and also transpose (the rows and columns are interchanged) it to put it in a similar format to what our previous education dataset was in:

```
df4=df3[df3['Indicator Name']=='GDP per capita (current US$)'].T
df4.head(10)
```

The output is as follows:

	981
Country Name	India
Country Code	IND
Indicator Name	GDP per capita (current US$)
1960	81.2848
1961	84.4264
1962	88.9149
1963	100.049
1964	114.315
1965	118.063
1966	89.0536

Figure 9.28: DataFrame focusing on GDP per capita

7. There is no index, so let's use **reset_index** again:

```
df4.reset_index(inplace=True)
df4.head(10)
```

The output is as follows:

	index	981
0	Country Name	India
1	Country Code	IND
2	Indicator Name	GDP per capita (current US$)
3	1960	81.2848
4	1961	84.4264
5	1962	88.9149
6	1963	100.049
7	1964	114.315
8	1965	118.063
9	1966	89.0536

Figure 9.29: DataFrame from the India World Bank Information using reset_index

8. The first three rows aren't useful. We can redefine the DataFrame without them. Then, we re-index again:

```
df4.drop([0,1,2],inplace=True)
df4.reset_index(inplace=True,drop=True)
df4.head(10)
```

The output is as follows:

index	981
0	1960	81.2848
1	1961	84.4264
2	1962	88.9149
3	1963	100.049
4	1964	114.315
5	1965	118.063
6	1966	89.0536
7	1967	95.3308
8	1968	98.8312
9	1969	106.496

Figure 9.30: DataFrame from the India World Bank Information
after dropping and resetting the index

9. Let's rename the columns properly (this is necessary for merging, which we will look at shortly):

```
df4.columns=['Year','GDP']
df4.head(10)
```

The output is as follows:

	Year	GDP
0	1960	81.2848
1	1961	84.4264
2	1962	88.9149
3	1963	100.049
4	1964	114.315
5	1965	118.063
6	1966	89.0536
7	1967	95.3308
8	1968	98.8312
9	1969	106.496

Figure 9.31: DataFrame focusing on Year and GDP

10. It looks like we have GDP data from 1960 onward. However, we are only interested in **2003 – 2016**. Let's examine the last 20 rows:

```
df4.tail(20)
```

The output is as follows:

	Year	GDP
38	1998	409.194
39	1999	437.586
40	2000	438.865
41	2001	447.014
42	2002	466.201
43	2003	541.135
44	2004	621.318
45	2005	707.008
46	2006	792.026
47	2007	1018.17
48	2008	991.485
49	2009	1090.32

Figure 9.32: DataFrame from the India World Bank Information

11. So, we should be good with rows **43-56**. Let's create a DataFrame called **df_gdp**:

```
df_gdp=df4.iloc[[i for i in range(43,57)]]
df_gdp
```

The output is as follows:

	Year	GDP
43	2003	541.135
44	2004	621.318
45	2005	707.008
46	2006	792.026
47	2007	1018.17
48	2008	991.485
49	2009	1090.32
50	2010	1345.77
51	2011	1461.67

Figure 9.33: DataFrame from the India World Bank Information

12. We need to reset the index again (for merging):

```
df_gdp.reset_index(inplace=True,drop=True)
df_gdp
```

The output is as follows:

	Year	GDP
0	2003	541.135
1	2004	621.318
2	2005	707.008
3	2006	792.026
4	2007	1018.17
5	2008	991.485
6	2009	1090.32
7	2010	1345.77
8	2011	1461.67

Figure 9.34: DataFrame from the India World Bank Information

13. The year in this DataFrame is not of the **int** type. So, it will have problems merging with the education DataFrame:

```
df_gdp['Year']
```

The output is as follows:

```
0       2003
1       2004
2       2005
3       2006
4       2007
5       2008
6       2009
7       2010
8       2011
9       2012
10      2013
11      2014
12      2015
13      2016
Name: Year, dtype: object
```

Figure 9.35: DataFrame focusing on year

14. Use the **apply** method with Python's built-in **int** function. Ignore any warnings that are thrown:

```
df_gdp['Year']=df_gdp['Year'].apply(int)
```

> **NOTE**
>
> To access the source code for this specific section, please refer to https://packt.live/3fyIqy8.
>
> You can also run this example online at https://packt.live/3fQ0PXJ.

ACTIVITY 9.03: DATA WRANGLING TASK – MERGING UN DATA AND GDP DATA

Solution:

These are the steps to complete this activity:

1. Now, merge the two DataFrames, that is, **primary_enrollment_india** and **df_gdp**, on the **Year** column:

```
primary_enrollment_with_gdp=\
primary_enrollment_india.merge(df_gdp,on='Year')
primary_enrollment_with_gdp
```

The output is as follows:

	Data	Enrollments (Thousands)	Footnotes	Region/Country/Area	Year	GDP
0	Students enrolled in primary education (thousa...	125569.00	NaN	India	2003	541.135
1	Students enrolled in primary education (thousa...	127404.00	NaN	India	2004	621.318
2	Students enrolled in primary education (thousa...	129239.00	NaN	India	2005	707.008
3	Students enrolled in primary education (thousa...	131074.00	NaN	India	2006	792.020
4	Students enrolled in primary education (thousa...	132909.00	NaN	India	2007	1018.17

Figure 9.36: Merged data

2. Now, we can drop the **Data**, **Footnotes**, and **Region/Country/Area** columns:

```
primary_enrollment_with_gdp.drop(['Data','Footnotes',\
                                  'Region/Country/Area'],\
                                  axis=1,inplace=True)
primary_enrollment_with_gdp
```

The output is as follows:

	Enrollments (Thousands)	Year	GDP
0	125569.00	2003	541.135
1	127404.00	2004	621.318
2	129239.00	2005	707.008
3	131074.00	2006	792.026
4	132909.00	2007	1018.17
5	134744.00	2008	991.485
6	136579.00	2009	1090.32
7	138414.00	2010	1345.77
8	138262.75	2011	1461.67
9	138111.50	2012	1446.99
10	137960.25	2013	1452.2
11	137809.00	2014	1576
12	138518.00	2015	1606.04
13	145803.00	2016	1717.47

Figure 9.37: Merged data after dropping the Data, Footnotes, and Region/Country/Area columns

3. Rearrange the columns for proper viewing and presentation to a data scientist:

```
primary_enrollment_with_gdp = \
primary_enrollment_with_gdp[['Year',\
                        'Enrollments (Thousands)','GDP']]
primary_enrollment_with_gdp
```

The output is as follows:

	Year	Enrollments (Thousands)	GDP
0	2003	125569.00	541.135
1	2004	127404.00	621.318
2	2005	129239.00	707.008
3	2006	131074.00	792.026
4	2007	132909.00	1018.17
5	2008	134744.00	991.485
6	2009	136579.00	1090.32
7	2010	138414.00	1345.77
8	2011	138262.75	1461.67
9	2012	138111.50	1446.99
10	2013	137960.25	1452.2
11	2014	137809.00	1576
12	2015	138518.00	1606.04
13	2016	145803.00	1717.47

Figure 9.38: Merged data after rearranging the columns

4. Plot the data:

```
plt.figure(figsize=(8,5))
plt.title("India's GDP per capita vs primary education "\
        "enrollment",fontsize=16)
plt.scatter(primary_enrollment_with_gdp['GDP'],\
        primary_enrollment_with_gdp['Enrollments (Thousands)'],\
        edgecolor='k',color='orange',s=200)
plt.xlabel("GDP per capita (US $)",fontsize=15)
plt.ylabel("Primary enrollment (thousands)", fontsize=15)
plt.xticks(fontsize=14)
plt.yticks(fontsize=14)
plt.grid(True)
plt.show()
```

The output is as follows:

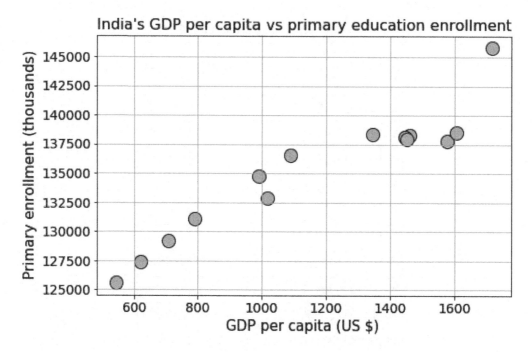

Figure 9.39: Scatter plot of merged data

ACTIVITY 9.04: DATA WRANGLING TASK – CONNECTING THE NEW DATA TO THE DATABASE

Solution:

These are the steps to complete this activity:

1. Connect to a database and start writing values in it. We start by importing the **sqlite3** module of Python and then use the **connect** function to connect to a database. Designate **Year** as the **PRIMARY KEY** of this table:

```
import sqlite3
with sqlite3.connect("Education_GDP.db") as conn:
    cursor = conn.cursor()
    cursor.execute("CREATE TABLE IF NOT EXISTS \
                education_gdp(Year INT, Enrollment \
                FLOAT, GDP FLOAT, PRIMARY KEY (Year))")
```

2. Run a loop with the dataset rows one by one to insert them into the table:

```
with sqlite3.connect("Education_GDP.db") as conn:
    cursor = conn.cursor()
    for i in range(14):
        year = int(primary_enrollment_with_gdp.iloc[i]['Year'])
        enrollment = \
        primary_enrollment_with_gdp.iloc[i]\
        ['Enrollments (Thousands)']
        gdp = primary_enrollment_with_gdp.iloc[i]['GDP']
        #print(year,enrollment,gdp)
        cursor.execute("INSERT INTO \
                    education_gdp (Year,Enrollment,GDP) \
                    VALUES (?,?,?)",(year,enrollment,gdp))
```

If we look at the current folder, we should see a file called **Education_GDP.db**, and if we can examine that using a database viewer program, we will see that the data has been transferred there.

> **NOTE**
>
> To access the source code for this specific section, please refer to https://packt.live/3fylqy8.
>
> You can also run this example online at https://packt.live/3fQ0PXJ.

INDEX

Made in United States
Orlando, FL
01 June 2024

47397238R00317